Advances in Cyberology and the Advent of the Next–Gen Information Revolution

Mohd Shahid Husain
College of Applied Sciences, University of Technology and Applied Sciences, Oman

Mohammad Faisal
Integral University, Lucknow, India

Halima Sadia
Integral University, Lucknow, India

Tasneem Ahmad
Advanced Computing Research Lab, Integral University, Lucknow, India

Saurabh Shukla
Data Science Institute, National University of Ireland, Galway, Ireland

A volume in the Advances in Human and Social Aspects of Technology (AHSAT) Book Series

Published in the United States of America by
    IGI Global
    Information Science Reference (an imprint of IGI Global)
    701 E. Chocolate Avenue
    Hershey PA, USA 17033
    Tel: 717-533-8845
    Fax: 717-533-8661
    E-mail: cust@igi-global.com
    Web site: http://www.igi-global.com

Library of Congress Cataloging-in-Publication Data

Names: Husain, Muḥammad Shāhid, editor. | Faisal, Mohammad (Professor of
    computer application), editor. | Sadia, Halima, 1984- editor. | Ahmed,
    Tasneem, 1985- editor. | Shukla, Saurabh, 1985- editor.
Title: Advances in cyberology and the advent of the next-gen information
    revolution / edited by Mohd Shahid Husain, Mohammad Faisal, Halima
    Sadia, Tasneem Ahmad and Saurabh Shukla.
Description: Hershey, PA : Information Science Reference, [2023] | Includes
    bibliographical references and index. | Summary: "Advances in Cyberology
    and the Advent of the Next-Gen Information Revolution creates awareness
    of the information threats that these technologies play on personal,
    societal, business, and governmental levels. It discusses the
    development of information and communication technologies (ICT), their
    connection with the cyber revolution, and the impact that they have on
    every facet of human life. Covering topics such as cloud computing,
    deepfake technology, and social networking, this premier reference
    source is an ideal resource for security professionals, IT managers,
    administrators, students and educators of higher education, librarians,
    researchers, and academicians"-- Provided by publisher.
Identifiers: LCCN 2023002099 (print) | LCCN 2023002100 (ebook) | ISBN
    9781668481332 (hardcover) | ISBN 9781668481349 (paperback) | ISBN
    9781668481356 (ebook)
Subjects: LCSH: Computer networks--Security measures. | Computer security.
    | Information storage and retrieval systems--Security measures. |
    Cyberspace.
Classification: LCC TK5105.59 .A3823 2023 (print) | LCC TK5105.59 (ebook)
    | DDC 658.4/78--dc23/eng/20230210
LC record available at https://lccn.loc.gov/2023002099
LC ebook record available at https://lccn.loc.gov/2023002100

This book is published in the IGI Global book series Advances in Human and Social Aspects of Technology (AHSAT) (ISSN: 2328-1316; eISSN: 2328-1324)

British Cataloguing in Publication Data
A Cataloguing in Publication record for this book is available from the British Library.

For electronic access to this publication, please contact: eresources@igi-global.com.

Advances in Human and Social Aspects of Technology (AHSAT) Book Series

Mehdi Khosrow-Pour, D.B.A.
Information Resources Management Association, USA

ISSN:2328-1316
EISSN:2328-1324

MISSION

In recent years, the societal impact of technology has been noted as we become increasingly more connected and are presented with more digital tools and devices. With the popularity of digital devices such as cell phones and tablets, it is crucial to consider the implications of our digital dependence and the presence of technology in our everyday lives.

The **Advances in Human and Social Aspects of Technology (AHSAT) Book Series** seeks to explore the ways in which society and human beings have been affected by technology and how the technological revolution has changed the way we conduct our lives as well as our behavior. The AHSAT book series aims to publish the most cutting-edge research on human behavior and interaction with technology and the ways in which the digital age is changing society.

COVERAGE

- ICTs and human empowerment
- Human Development and Technology
- Technology Adoption
- Technology and Social Change
- Computer-Mediated Communication
- Digital Identity
- Human Rights and Digitization
- Public Access to ICTs
- Activism and ICTs
- Technoself

IGI Global is currently accepting manuscripts for publication within this series. To submit a proposal for a volume in this series, please contact our Acquisition Editors at Acquisitions@igi-global.com or visit: http://www.igi-global.com/publish/.

Titles in this Series

For a list of additional titles in this series, please visit: www.igi-global.com/book-series

Impact of Disruptive Technologies on the Socio-Economic Development of Emerging Countries
Fredrick Japhet Mtenzi (Institute for Educational Development, The Aga Khan University, Tanzania) George S. Oreku (The Open University of Tanzania, Tanzania) and Dennis M. Lupiana (Institute of Finance Management, Tanania)
Information Science Reference • © 2023 • 279pp • H/C (ISBN: 9781668468739) • US $225.00

Analyzing New Forms of Social Disorders in Modern Virtual Environments
Milica Boskovic (Faculty for Diplomacy and Security, University Union Nikola Tesla, Serbia) Gordana Misev (Ministry of Mining and Energy Republic of Serbia, Serbia) and Nenad Putnik (Faculty of Security Studies, University of Belgrade, Srbia)
Information Science Reference • © 2023 • 320pp • H/C (ISBN: 9781668457603) • US $225.00

Exergaming Intervention for Children, Adolescents, and Elderly People
Shahnawaz Khan (Bahrain Polytechnic, Bahrain) Thirunavukkarasu Kannapiran (S2 Integrators, USA) Arunachalam Muthiah (Karnavati University, India) and Sharad Shetty (Karnavati University, India)
Information Science Reference • © 2023 • 278pp • H/C (ISBN: 9781668463208) • US $215.00

Handbook of Research on Andragogical Leadership and Technology in a Modern World
Viktor Wang (California State University, San Bernardino, USA)
Information Science Reference • © 2023 • 474pp • H/C (ISBN: 9781668478325) • US $270.00

ICT as a Driver of Women's Social and Economic Empowerment
Pankaj Dhaundiyal (CHRIST University (Deemed), India) and Sana Moid (Amity University, India)
Information Science Reference • © 2023 • 306pp • H/C (ISBN: 9781668461181) • US $215.00

Handbook of Research on Digitalization Solutions for Social and Economic Needs
Richard Pettinger (University College London, UK) Brij B. Gupta (Asia University, Taiwan) Alexandru Roja (West University of Timisoara, Romania) and Diana Cozmiuc (West University of Timisoara, Romania)
Engineering Science Reference • © 2023 • 387pp • H/C (ISBN: 9781668441022) • US $380.00

Digital Psychology's Impact on Business and Society
Muhammad Anshari (Universiti Brunei Darussalam, Brunei) Abdur Razzaq (Universitas Islam Negeri Raden Fatah Palembang, Indonesia) Mia Fithriyah (Indonesia Open University, Indonesia) and Akmal Nasri Kamal (Universiti Brunei Darussalam, Brunei)
Information Science Reference • © 2023 • 330pp • H/C (ISBN: 9781668461082) • US $270.00

701 East Chocolate Avenue, Hershey, PA 17033, USA
Tel: 717-533-8845 x100 • Fax: 717-533-8661
E-Mail: cust@igi-global.com • www.igi-global.com

Table of Contents

Preface..xiii

Acknowledgment.. xx

Chapter 1
Cloud Computing Cyber Threats and Vulnerabilities... 1
    Sami Ouali, University of Technology and Applied Sciences, Oman

Chapter 2
The Critical Analysis of E-Commerce Web Application Vulnerabilities............................ 22
    Gausiya Yasmeen, Integral University, India
    Syed Adnan Afaq, Integral University, India

Chapter 3
The Link Between Privacy and Disclosure Behavior in Social Networks........................... 38
    Mohammad Daradkeh, University of Dubai, UAE & Yarmouk University, Jordan

Chapter 4
Cyber Threat Migration: Perpetuating in the Healthcare Sector and Agriculture and Food
Industries.. 62
    Minhaj Akhtar Usmani, Era University, India
    Kainat Akhtar Usmani, Integral University, India
    Adil Kaleem, NCS Group, Australia
    Mohammad Samiuddin, University of Technology and Applied Sciences, Oman

Chapter 5
The Critical Impact of Cyber Threats on Digital Economy.. 86
    Syed Adnan Afaq, Integral University, India
    Saman Uzma, Cubeight Solutions, Australia
    Gausiya Yasmeen, Integral University, India

Chapter 6
Cyber Threats in Agriculture and the Food Industry: An Indian Perspective 109
    Harish Chandra Verma, ICAR-Central Institute for Subtropical Horticulture, India
    Saurabh Srivastava, Integral University, India
    Tasneem Ahmed, Integral University, India
    Nayyar Ali Usmani, PUMA SE, Germany

Chapter 7
Security Issues in the Internet of Things for the Development of Smart Cities 123
    Mohammad Haroon, Integral University, India
    Dinesh Kumar Misra, Indian Space Research Organization, India
    Mohammad Husain, Islamic University of Madinah, Saudi Arabia
    Manish Madhav Tripathi, Integral University, India
    Afsaruddin Khan, Dr. A.P.J. Abdul Kalam Technical University, India

Chapter 8
Forensics Analysis of NTFS File Systems 138
    Kumarbhai Shamjibhai Sondarva, Sardar Vallabhbhai National Institute of Technology, India
    Adarsh Kumar, Sardar Vallabhbhai National Institute of Technology, India
    Bhavesh N. Gohil, Sardar Vallabhbhai National Institute of Technology, India
    Sankita J. Patel, Sardar Vallabhbhai National Institute of Technology, India
    Sarang Rajvansh, National Forensics Sciences University, India
    Ramya T. Shah, National Forensic Sciences University, India

Chapter 9
Workplace Cyberbullying in the Remote-Work Era: A New Dimension of Cyberology 166
    Nashra Javed, Integral University, India
    Tasneem Ahmed, Integral University, India
    Mohammad Faisal, Integral University, India
    Halima Sadia, Integral University, India
    Emilly Zoë Jeanne Sidaine-Daumiller, Osnabrück Universität, Germany

Chapter 10
The Rise of Deepfake Technology: Issues, Challenges, and Countermeasures 178
    Mohd Akbar, Integral University, India
    Mohd Suaib, Integral University, India
    Mohd Shahid Hussain, College of Applied Sciences, University of Technology and Applied
        Sciences, Oman

Chapter 11
An Extensive Study and Review on Dark Web Threats and Detection Techniques 202
    Wasim Khan, Koneru Lakshmaiah Education Foundation, India
    Mohammad Ishrat, Koneru Lakshmaiah Education Foundation, India
    Mohd Haleem, Era University, India
    Ahmad Neyaz Khan, Integral University, India
    Mohammad Kamrul Hasan, Universiti Kebangsaan Malaysia, Malaysia
    Nafees Akhter Farooqui, Babu Banarsi Das University, India

Chapter 12
Recent Advances in Cyber Security Laws and Practices in India: Implementation and

Awareness 220
Neyha Malik, Integral University, India
Firoz Husain, Integral University, India
Anis Ali, Prince Sattam Bin Abdulaziz University, Saudi Arabia
Yasir Arafat Elahi, Integral University, India

Compilation of References 242

About the Contributors 264

Index 270

Detailed Table of Contents

Preface... xiii

Acknowledgment xx

Chapter 1
Cloud Computing Cyber Threats and Vulnerabilities.. 1
    Sami Ouali, University of Technology and Applied Sciences, Oman

Cloud computing has become an integral part of modern business operations, with organizations of all sizes and in all industries turning to the cloud to improve efficiency, reduce costs, and increase flexibility. However, the adoption of cloud computing has also introduced a range of new security challenges, as sensitive data and critical systems are moved to cloud-based infrastructure that may be managed by third parties. This chapter discusses the various types of cyber threats that can occur in the cloud, including data breaches, malware, and cloud-based attacks, as well as the measures that organizations can take to protect themselves against these threats on their data, infrastructure, and applications. This chapter examines also the role of cloud providers in securing data in the cloud, and the importance of implementing strong security measures to protect against these threats. By understanding the nature of these threats and the steps that can be taken to mitigate them, organizations and individuals can more effectively protect themselves and their sensitive data in the cloud.

Chapter 2
The Critical Analysis of E-Commerce Web Application Vulnerabilities 22
    Gausiya Yasmeen, Integral University, India
    Syed Adnan Afaq, Integral University, India

Large-scale deployments of web applications occur continuously. The failure to validate or sanitize form inputs, improperly configured web servers, and application design flaws are the main causes of security vulnerabilities that continue to infect web applications, allowing hackers to access sensitive data and using legitimate websites as a breeding ground for malware. These vulnerabilities can be used to compromise the security of the application. The largest problem that enterprises face is how to create a web application that satisfies their needs for safe processes, E-Commerce, and the transmission of sensitive data. OWASP updates and releases a list of the top 10 web application vulnerabilities every few years. Along with the OWASP Top 10 Threats, this chapter also discusses each vulnerability's possible effects and how to avoid them. According to the OWSP (Open Online Application Security Project) Top Ten, this document analyses the most serious web vulnerabilities, their causes, and their impacts.

Chapter 3

The Link Between Privacy and Disclosure Behavior in Social Networks.. 38
Mohammad Daradkeh, University of Dubai, UAE & Yarmouk University, Jordan

Based on the antecedent-privacy concern-outcome (APCO) model of privacy concerns, this study developed a moderated mediation model to investigate the mechanisms by which social media privacy policies (including both privacy policy understanding and perceived effectiveness dimensions) influence self-disclosure. The model was tested in this study using a deductive approach and a quantitative research strategy. In this study, a self-reported questionnaire was used to collect information from social media users. To test the research model and hypotheses, we used multiple regression analysis. According to the results of this study, trust in social media mediated the relationship between privacy policy and self-disclosure, while privacy costs moderated the relationship between privacy policy and trust in social media. Furthermore, the link between privacy policy and self-disclosure is a complex multicollinear model with mediating effects rather than a simple linear model.

Chapter 4

Cyber Threat Migration: Perpetuating in the Healthcare Sector and Agriculture and Food
Industries... 62
Minhaj Akhtar Usmani, Era University, India
Kainat Akhtar Usmani, Integral University, India
Adil Kaleem, NCS Group, Australia
Mohammad Samiuddin, University of Technology and Applied Sciences, Oman

'Globalization,' 'industrialization,' 'cyber connectivity,' 'digitalization,' and 'e-commerce' are not fantasy words in today's era. They all amalgamated towards the growth and development of every sector in the country. But as on other side of the coin, cyber security is on the verge of serious threats in digital world. The danger posed by cyber security threats in today's world cannot be understated. The health sector, agriculture, and food and beverage industries are no exemptions. As they all are inter-related, they manage an array of assets, including infrastructure, applications, managed and unmanaged endpoints, mobile devices, and cloud services, all of which can be attacked. Information and cyber security are trending topics. As the security risk is scooping high, different organizations should take steps forward to protect themselves. This chapter focuses on the frightening hikes in incidences of cyber-attacks, and also focuses on major cyber security approaches to minimize the risk of cyber breaches and making these industries flourish like never before.

Chapter 5

The Critical Impact of Cyber Threats on Digital Economy.. 86
Syed Adnan Afaq, Integral University, India
Saman Uzma, Cubeight Solutions, Australia
Gausiya Yasmeen, Integral University, India

Internet users need to know that there are many different kinds of threats in the online world. Improving cyber security and keeping private information safe is important for a country's safety and economy. For a country's safety and economy, it's important to improve cyber security and keep private information safe. The term "digital economy" refers to a business for digitally delivered goods and services that are created using electronic business models and linked to a global system of economic and social networks. Cyber risk is the most complex issue of the twenty-first century, arising from a wide diversity of causes such as a hacker, terrorists, criminals, insider groups, foreign states, etc. This study includes cyber threats in the digital world. It emphasizes challenges in the healthcare sector, agriculture and food industries.

Chapter 6

Cyber Threats in Agriculture and the Food Industry: An Indian Perspective 109

Harish Chandra Verma, ICAR-Central Institute for Subtropical Horticulture, India
Saurabh Srivastava, Integral University, India
Tasneem Ahmed, Integral University, India
Nayyar Ali Usmani, PUMA SE, Germany

A cyber threat is a harmful act meant to steal, corrupt, or undermine an organization's digital stability. At present cyber threats in agriculture and food industry is a rising concern because farming is becoming more dependent on computers and Internet access. The attacks that fall under this category include denial of service attacks, computer viruses. Growing food demand and shortage of skilled labours have necessitated for the adoption of digital agriculture. The major challenge is to prevent it from cyber threats for successful implementation. As ransomware hackers are increasingly likely to target food supply chain, the food industry is experiencing an increase in cyber-security threats, which might result in business interruptions. Due to the fragile nature of the food supply, the entire food sector needs to be protected . In this chapter, major issue on cyber threats, challenges of cyber-security, some notable cyber-attacks, and cyber-security solutions for the food/agriculture industry are discussed in detail.

Chapter 7

Security Issues in the Internet of Things for the Development of Smart Cities 123

Mohammad Haroon, Integral University, India
Dinesh Kumar Misra, Indian Space Research Organization, India
Mohammad Husain, Islamic University of Madinah, Saudi Arabia
Manish Madhav Tripathi, Integral University, India
Afsaruddin Khan, Dr. A.P.J. Abdul Kalam Technical University, India

A city is defined as a group of living and nonliving objects; cities generally have good systems for housing, transportation, hygiene, services, among other things. In prior years, a larger amount of the population was rural, whereas in modern times, the concept of urbanization and a mass exodus to cities has had a profound impact of sustainability on a global scale. A smart city is a concept that participates in information and communication technology with the use of various physical devices to help reduce and optimize the city's daily routine. When thinking of a smart city, one can imagine a layered architecture with infrastructure at the bottom; and connectivity accessibility in security systems in the middle; and at the top are different services that are gearted towards various consumers of the city.

Chapter 8

Forensics Analysis of NTFS File Systems... 138

Kumarbhai Shamjibhai Sondarva, Sardar Vallabhbhai National Institute of Technology, India
Adarsh Kumar, Sardar Vallabhbhai National Institute of Technology, India
Bhavesh N. Gohil, Sardar Vallabhbhai National Institute of Technology, India
Sankita J. Patel, Sardar Vallabhbhai National Institute of Technology, India
Sarang Rajvansh, National Forensics Sciences University, India
Ramya T. Shah, National Forensic Sciences University, India

The internet and computers are reaching everywhere, and all are getting connected through it. Users are utilizing computers to make life easier and work faster. At the same time, many attacks and instances of cybercrime have happened. Therefore, digital forensics is necessary and plays a crucial role. NTFS is one of the most popular file systems used by the Windows operating system, and this chapter provides information for forensic analysis of NTFS file system. This chapter describes digital forensics, stages of digital forensics, and types of digital forensics. NTFS is discussed in brief along with the master file table (MFT). In the same section, it also discusses the method to detect the hidden data in the boot sector, analysis of registry, prefetch, shellbags, and web browsers. They have discussed the collection of volatile and non-volatile data. It also provides the artifacts which an investigator must be seeking, along with the tools used to collect and analyze them and strategies used for investigation and analysis. Data recovery and file carving are also discussed.

Chapter 9

Workplace Cyberbullying in the Remote-Work Era: A New Dimension of Cyberology 166
    Nashra Javed, Integral University, India
    Tasneem Ahmed, Integral University, India
    Mohammad Faisal, Integral University, India
    Halima Sadia, Integral University, India
    Emilly Zoë Jeanne Sidaine-Daumiller, Osnabrück Universität, Germany

Information and communication technologies are being used as weapons in a combat zone created by the norm that forces individuals to work from home during this pandemic. The upsurge in workplace cyberbullying is visible in various reports. Workplace cyberbullying may appear to be a less severe form of harassment, but the shift to a more dispersed workforce has made it worse. It is the intimidation experienced by a remote or hybrid employee which results in a breakdown in communication with or mistreatment from leaders. While it makes sense to believe that because we are not at the office, occurrences of antagonism and harassment are drastically reduced, that's not the reality. Spiteful employers and demeaning coworkers might pose a virtual threat. Remote work settings are becoming toxic due to harmful, unkind workplace behavior, including derogatory language, social exclusion, and threats via phone, email, or social media. This chapter unveils a new dimension of cyberology.

Chapter 10

The Rise of Deepfake Technology: Issues, Challenges, and Countermeasures................................ 178
    Mohd Akbar, Integral University, India
    Mohd Suaib, Integral University, India
    Mohd Shahid Hussain, College of Applied Sciences, University of Technology and Applied
        Sciences, Oman

Deepfake technology is an emerging technology prevailing in today's digital world. It is used to create fake videos by exploiting some of the artificial intelligence (AI) based techniques and deep learning methodology. The facial expressions and motion effects are primarily used to train and manipulate the seed frame of someone to generate the desired morphed video frames that mimic as if they are real. Deepfake technology is used to make a highly realistic fake video that can be widely used to spread the wrong information or fake news by regarding any celebrity or political leader which is not created by them. Due to the high impact of social media, these fake videos can reach millions of views within an hour and create a negative impact on our society. This chapter includes the crucial points on methodology, approach, and counter applications pertinent to deep-fake technology highlighting the issues, challenges, and counter measures to be adopted. Through observations and analysis, the chapter will conclude with profound findings and establishes the future directions of this technology.

Chapter 11
An Extensive Study and Review on Dark Web Threats and Detection Techniques 202
    Wasim Khan, Koneru Lakshmaiah Education Foundation, India
    Mohammad Ishrat, Koneru Lakshmaiah Education Foundation, India
    Mohd Haleem, Era University, India
    Ahmad Neyaz Khan, Integral University, India
    Mohammad Kamrul Hasan, Universiti Kebangsaan Malaysia, Malaysia
    Nafees Akhter Farooqui, Babu Banarsi Das University, India

The Dark Web is a difficult and anonymous network used by cybercriminals, terrorists, and state-sponsored agents to carry out their illicit goals. Dark web cybercrime is very similar to offline crime. However, the vastness of the Dark Web, its unpredictable ecology, and the anonymity it provides are all obstacles that must be overcome in order to track down criminals. To reach the dark web, which is not indexed by search engines, you must use the anonymous Tor browser. The anonymity and covert nature of the network make it ideal for criminal activity and the launch of carefully orchestrated, malicious assaults. Online criminal activity is rampant and getting more intense, according to specialists in cyber security. This chapter has provided a thorough analysis of the various attacks and attack strategies utilized on the dark web. In addition, the authors examine the strengths and weaknesses of the various methods currently in use for threat detection, and how they apply to anonymity networks such as Tor, I2P, and Freenet.

Chapter 12
Recent Advances in Cyber Security Laws and Practices in India: Implementation and
Awareness 220
    Neyha Malik, Integral University, India
    Firoz Husain, Integral University, India
    Anis Ali, Prince Sattam Bin Abdulaziz University, Saudi Arabia
    Yasir Arafat Elahi, Integral University, India

The growth of the internet and proliferation of applications, products, and services has given rise to cyber threats which require far more stringent security measures than ever before. Some common types of cybercrimes are job fraud, phishing, baiting, vishing, smishing, credit and debit card fraud, child pornography, cyberbullying, etc. Cyber laws need constant upgrading and refinement to keep pace with the increasing technology. In India, various statutes and initiatives have been launched to ensure its cyber security such as Information Technology Act, 2000 (IT Act), Indian Penal Code, 1860 (IPC), National Cybersecurity Framework (NCFS), financial assistance, Cyber Crime Prevention against Women & Children (CCPWC), Indian Cyber Crime Coordination Centre (I4C), National Cyber Crime Reporting Portal, Citizen Financial Cyber Fraud Reporting and Management System, Indian Computer Emergency Response Team (CERT-In), and Ministry of Electronics & Information Technology (MeitY).

Compilation of References 242

About the Contributors 264

Index 270

Preface

In the ever-evolving landscape of the digital age, human-technology interaction has become increasingly complex and an integral part of our daily lives. The world has witnessed an unprecedented expansion of interconnected systems that have profoundly changed societies, economies and even our own identities. The need for a comprehensive understanding of the complex relationship between humans and technology is becoming increasingly important as we navigate this dynamic and rapidly changing environment.

Entitled *Advances in Cyberology and the Advent of the Next-Gen Information Revolution: Exploring the relationship between Humans and Technology,* this book explores the fascinating intersection of human psychology and technology, revealing the multidimensional dimensions of this complex relationship. Experts in the field of cyber science, have had the privilege of observing the development of technology and its impact on human life for many years. From the dawn of the internet to the rise of artificial intelligence, we have witnessed how these advances have shaped the behavior, perceptions and interactions of people.

Covering a wide range of topics, from the issues and challenges in the cyber world to the legal/ethical considerations arising from new technologies, this book aims to provide readers with a holistic understanding of cyberlogy.

The first few chapters lay the groundwork by examining the vulnerabilities and threats in cyber world. We explore the impact of privacy disclosure behavior in social media on identity and relationships, and the psychological impact of virtual environments. Building on this foundation, the next chapters deal with the ethical, legal and social aspects of cyberlogy in various domains like economy, agriculture, food industry and healthcare. It explores the ethical challenges posed by artificial intelligence, the impact of automation on employees, and cybersecurity threats and opportunities. Additionally, the book explores the latest trends of cyberlogy and envisions the opportunities and challenges that lie ahead. We look at emerging areas such as Workplace Cyberbullying, Deep fake Technology, and dark web. It also addresses the importance of digital literacy and responsible use of technology in an increasingly connected world by providing insight about cyber security laws and practices. We hope this book will be a valuable resource for researchers, scientists, students, and anyone seeking a deeper understanding of the complex relationship between humans and technology. By focusing on different aspects of cyberlogy, we aim to stimulate further exploration and discussion in this rapidly evolving field.

EMERGING NEED

As we enter the twenty-first century, the world is rapidly becoming dependent on technology. With this increasing dependence, the need for those who understand the complexities of the digital world grows ever more pressing. Cyberology is the field that seeks to bridge the gap between the physical world and the virtual world, exploring the potential of the digital age while also understanding the risks associated with this new and ever-expanding frontier.

This book is an exploration of the discipline of cyberology, offering an accessible and comprehensive guide to the field. Written by experts in the field, it provides readers with an understanding of the key concepts, theories, and applications of cyberology. It covers topics such as cybersecurity, artificial intelligence, data management, and digital ethics. It also examines the broader implications of this interdisciplinary field on society, and explores the challenges it poses as we continue to progress into the digital age.

PURPOSE

The purpose of this book is to provide readers with a comprehensive exploration of cyber science, providing insight, analysis, and a practical perspective on the profound impact of technology on humanity. Each chapter of the book takes an interdisciplinary approach, drawing on knowledge and research from various fields such as business, agriculture, healthcare, psychology, sociology, computer science, and economy. Each chapter looks at different aspects of the human-technology relationship, revealing its complexities and examining its implications.

AUDIENCE

This book is essential reading for anyone interested in the possibilities of the digital future, and for those who want to gain a better understanding of the complexities of the cyber world. It is a valuable resource for students, professionals, and anyone interested in the rapidly expanding field of cyberology.

We hope that this book will prove to be an illuminating and thought-provoking guide to the field for all readers.

EMPHASIS

This book is a comprehensive exploration of the fascinating and ever-evolving field of cyberology. In this book, readers will learn the basics of cyberology and its implications, as well as its applications in the real world. Cyberology's applications in various fields, such as business, government, and education, will be explored in detail.

The book will also discuss the ethical and legal considerations of cyberology, and how cyberology can be used responsibly and ethically. Additionally, readers will be provided with the latest research and data in the field, as well as tips and strategies for succeeding in the world of cyberology.

This book is an essential resource for anyone interested in cyberology, providing both an introduction and a comprehensive guide to this rapidly-growing field. It is sure to be an invaluable asset for students, professionals, and researchers alike.

WHAT YOU WILL LEARN

In addition to exploring the core aspects of cyberology, this book also offers valuable insights into the various applications of the field. It provides readers with practical examples of how the principles of cyberology can be applied in everyday life, offering a thorough understanding of the potential of the digital age.

BOOK ORGANIZATION

The book discusses how technology is increasingly mediating our relationships with one another, from communication to learning and working. This book has 12 chapters which deals with different aspects of cyberology.

Chapter 01 deals with "Cloud Computing Cyber Threats and Vulnerabilities." Cloud computing has become an integral part of modern business operations, with organizations of all sizes and in all industries turning to the cloud to improve efficiency, reduce costs, and increase flexibility. However, the adoption of cloud computing has also introduced a range of new security challenges, as sensitive data and critical systems are moved to cloud-based infrastructure that may be managed by third parties. This chapter discusses the various types of cyber threats that can occur in the cloud, including data breaches, malware, and cloud-based attacks, as well as the measures that organizations can take to protect themselves against these threats on their data, infrastructure, and applications. This chapter also examines the role of cloud providers in securing data in the cloud, and the importance of implementing strong security measures to protect against these threats. By understanding the nature of these threats and the steps that can be taken to mitigate them, organizations and individuals can more effectively protect themselves and their sensitive data in the cloud.

Chapter 02 deals with "The Critical Analysis of E-Commerce Web Application Vulnerabilities." Large-scale deployments of web applications occur continuously. The failure to validate or sanitize form inputs, improperly configured web servers, and application design flaws are the main causes of security vulnerabilities that continue to infect web applications, allowing hackers to access sensitive data and using legitimate websites as a breeding ground for malware. These vulnerabilities can be used to compromise the security of the application. The largest problem that enterprises face is how to create a web application that satisfies their needs for safe processes, E-Commerce, and the transmission of sensitive data. OWASP updates and releases a list of the top 10 web application vulnerabilities every few years. Along with the OWASP Top 10 Threats, this chapter also discusses each vulnerability's possible effects and how to avoid them. According to the OWSP (Open Online Application Security Project) Top Ten, this document analyses the most serious web vulnerabilities, their causes, and their impacts.

Chapter 03 deals with "The Link between Privacy and Disclosure Behavior in Social Networks." With the increased use of social media platforms, privacy concerns and self-disclosure habits have received much attention in both the academic and business communities. Based on the antecedent-privacy concern-outcome (APCO) model of privacy concerns, this study developed a moderated mediation model to investigate the mechanisms by which social media privacy policies (including both privacy policy understanding and perceived effectiveness dimensions) influence self-disclosure. The model was tested in this study using a deductive approach and a quantitative research strategy. In this study, a self-reported questionnaire was used to collect information from social media users. To test the research model and hypotheses, we used multiple regression analysis. According to the results of this study, trust in social media mediated the relationship between privacy policy and self-disclosure, while privacy costs moderated the relationship between privacy policy and trust in social media. Furthermore, the link between privacy policy and self-disclosure is a complex multicollinear model with mediating effects rather than a simple linear model. This study presents empirical data to understand the impact of social media privacy regulations on self-disclosure and the variables that influence users' decisions to disclose on social media platforms.

Chapter 04 deals with the "Cyber Threats Mitigation- Perpetuating in Healthcare Sector, Agriculture and Food Industry." The Globalization, industrialization, cyber connectivity, digitalization, and e-commerce are not the fantasy words in today's era. They all are amalgamated towards the growth and development of every sector in the country. But as on other side of the coin, cyber security is on the verge for the threats in digital world. The danger posed by cyber security threats in today's world cannot be understated. Attacks and data leaks are already affecting many industries/organizations, hampering operations and halting production, also services. The Health sector, Agriculture and Food & Beverage Industry are no exemptions. As they all are inter-related, they manage an array of assets, including infrastructure, applications, managed and unmanaged endpoints, mobile devices, and cloud services, all of which can be attacked. Information and cyber security are trending topics for concern on corporate agendas, becoming a core governance issue for everyone from boards to management.

As the security risk is scooping high, different organizations should take steps forward to protect themselves. A proper management system based on international standards should be developed with a robust and structured approach to manage risks and safeguard valuable assets of companies.

This chapter focuses on the frightening hikes in incidences of cyber-attacks on the food, agriculture and health-care industries in recent past. It emphasizes on the major cyber security risk factors and loopholes of the system. It also focuses on major cyber security approaches to minimize the risk of cyber breaches and making these industries flourish like never before.

Chapter 05 deals with the "Critical Impact of Cyber Threats on Digital Economy." Users of the Internet need to know that there are many different kinds of threats in the online world. Improving cyber security and keeping private information safe is important for a country's safety and economy. It is a set of procedures and technological security measures that are used to protect data resources (computer systems, machines, records, and numerous applications). People who use the Internet need to know that there are many different kinds of dangers out there. For a country's safety and economy, it's important to improve cyber security and keep private information safe.

Today, data and information security are one of the most important things to worry about. Several companies and management groups are taking different steps to stop and control these cybercrimes. Even though there are many precautions and strategies, cyber security is still a big worry for many people.

Cyber society has evolved into a common and unavoidable foundation of information exchange and different proficient activities such as commercial, shopping, bank transactions, agriculture, healthcare sectors, food industries, etc. This rapid growth in cyberspace use has resulted in an enormous rise in cybercriminal behavior. This is mostly due to the growing use of Web apps. Cyber risk is the most complex issue of the twenty-first century, arising from a wide diversity of causes such as a hacker, terrorists, criminals, insider groups, foreign states, etc. This presents a challenge to governments, businesses, and individuals all across the world. Furthermore, while the expense of security standards is rising, it is becoming increasingly cheaper to launch cyber-attacks. Healthcare is increasingly becoming digitalized because of the advent of smart technologies and online capability which allows for the generalization of user survives. On the one hand, this offers excellent potential, and that also brings healthcare organizations at risk from a variety of non-digital and digital risks, which might allow attackers could compromise the security of medical operations. This paper includes the cyber threats in the digital world. It emphasizes on challenges in the healthcare sector, agriculture and food industries.

Chapter 06 deals with the "Cyber Threats in Agriculture and Food Industry- an Indian Perspective." A cyber threat is a harmful act meant to steal, corrupt, or undermine an organization's digital stability. At present cyber threats in agriculture and food industry is a rising concern because farming is becoming more dependent on computers and Internet access. The attacks that fall under this category include denial of service attacks, computer viruses. Growing food demand and shortage of skilled labours have necessitated for the adoption of digital agriculture. The major challenge is to prevent it from cyber threats for successful implementation. As ransomware hackers are increasingly likely to target food supply chain, the food industry is experiencing an increase in cyber-security threats, which might result in business interruptions. Due to the fragile nature of the food supply, the entire food sec-tor needs to be protected. In this chapter major, issue on cyber threats, challenges of cyber-security, some notable cyber-attacks and cyber-security solutions for the food/agriculture industry are discussed in detail.

Chapter 07 deals with the "Security Issues in the Internet of Things for the Development of Smart Cities." A city is defined as several living and non-living things, a group of objects. Cities have generally good systems for housing, transportation, hygiene, services, and other things. Earlier we used to have small cities with sparse population and a huge number of populations were rural. Whereas if you look at the modern trend, what we have is the concept of urbanization where people are moving to cities and that has a profound impact on sustainability on a global scale. A smart city is a concept that facilitates huge population with the help of Information and Communication Technology and various physical devices to optimize our daily routine. Smart City is built entirely on technology and focuses on outcomes. There are a lot of factors that have controlled the development of smart cities. A smart City consist basically a layered architecture where we have the infrastructure at the bottom, your connectivity accessibility in security systems that Make place various policies, and at the top, we have different services that are geared towards various consumers of the city.

Chapter 08 deals with the "Forensics Analysis of NTFS File System." The Internet and computers are reaching everywhere and all are getting connected through it. Users are utilizing the computers to make life easier and work faster. At the same time many attacks and cybercrime have happened. Therefore, digital forensics is necessary and plays a crucial role. NTFS is one of the most popular file systems used by Windows operating system and this chapter provides information for forensic analysis of NTFS file system. This chapter describes the digital forensics, stages of digital forensics, and types of digital forensics. NTFS is discussed in brief along with the MFT (Master File Table). In the same section it also discusses the method to detect the hidden data in the boot sector, analysis of registry, prefetch, shellbags and web browsers. They have discussed the collection of volatile and non-volatile data. It also provides the artifacts which an investigator must be seeking along with the tools used to collect and analyze them and strategies used for investigation and analysis. Data recovery and File Carving is also discussed.

Chapter 09 deals with the "Workplace Cyberbullying in Remote-Work Era: A New Dimension of Cyberology." Information and communication technologies are being used as weapons in a combat zone created by the norm that forces individuals to work from home during this pandemic. The upsurge in workplace cyberbullying is visible in various reports. Workplace cyberbullying may appear to be a less severe form of harassment, but the shift to a more dispersed workforce has made it worse. It is the intimidation experienced by a remote or hybrid employee which results in a breakdown in communication with or mistreatment from leaders. While it makes sense to believe that because we are not at the office, occurrences of antagonism and harassment are drastically reduced, that's not the reality. Spiteful employers and demeaning coworkers might pose a virtual threat. Remote work settings are becoming toxic due to harmful, unkind workplace behavior, including derogatory language, social exclusion, and threats via phone, email, or social media. It harms both the work efficiency and mental health of an individual who has been the victim of cyberbullying. This chapter will unveil the perpetrator traits from an organizational aspect, and discuss how to prevent it.

Chapter 10 deals with "The Rise of Deepfake Technology: Issues, Challenges and Counter Measures." Deepfake is a sophisticated application of artificial intelligence where machine learning techniques especially deep learning is used to synthesize media to widely publicized falsehood through social media which impact the thinking and mindset of wide audience globally. Manipulating audios, images or videos to create fake media content is not new but earlier it needs lot of time and efforts from skilled professionals to create these fake media. With the advancement of technologies now there ae many applications available which anyone can use it to create fake media. Although most of these applications are used for fun however there are some serious issues associated with this technology. In this chapter will discuss the basic concept, issues and challenges of deepfake. This chapter also discusses a case study to show how deepfake content can be identified using machine learning techniques.

Chapter 11 deals with "An Extensive Study and Review on DarkWeb Threats and Detection Techniques." The Dark Web is a difficult and anonymous network used by cybercriminals, terrorists, and state-sponsored agents to carry out their illicit goals. Dark web cybercrime is very similar to offline crime. However, the vastness of the Dark Web, its unpredictable ecology, and the anonymity it provides are all obstacles that must be overcome in order to track down criminals. To reach the dark web, which is not indexed by search engines, you must use the anonymous Tor browser. The anonymity and covert nature of the network make it ideal for criminal activity and the launch of carefully orchestrated, malicious assaults. Online criminal activity is rampant and getting more intense, according to specialists in cyber security. This paper has provided a thorough analysis of the various attacks and attack strategies utilized on the dark web. In addition, we examine the strengths and weaknesses of the various methods currently in use for threat detection, and how they apply to anonymity networks such as Tor, I2P, and Freenet.

Chapter 12 deals with "Recent Advances in Cyber Security Laws and Practices in India-Implementation and Awareness." The growth of internet and proliferation of applications, products & services has given rise to cyber threats which requires far stringent security measures than ever before. Some common types of cybercrimes are job fraud, phishing, baiting, vishing, smishing, credit and debit card fraud, child pornography, cyberbullying etc. Cyber laws need constant up-gradation and refinement to keep pace with the increasing technology. In India, various statutes and initiatives have been launched to ensure its cyber security such as Information Technology Act, 2000 (IT Act), Indian Penal Code, 1860 (IPC), National Cybersecurity Framework (NCFS), Financial Assistance, Cyber Crime Prevention against Women & Children (CCPWC), Indian Cyber Crime Coordination Centre (I4C), National Cyber Crime

Reporting Portal, Citizen Financial Cyber Fraud Reporting and Management System, Indian Computer Emergency Response Team (CERT-In), Ministry of Electronics & Information Technology (MeitY).

In conclusion, *Advances in Cyberology and the Advent of the Next-Gen Information Revolution* invites you to embark on a captivating journey through the realm of cyberology, where the boundaries between humans and technology blur, and new possibilities emerge. Together, let us explore the intricate tapestry of the human-technology relationship and embrace the challenges and opportunities it presents.

Mohd Shahid Husain
College of Applied Sciences, University of Technology and Applied Sciences, Oman

Mohammad Faisal
Integral University, Lucknow, India

Halima Sadia
Integral University, Lucknow, India

Tasneem Ahmad
Advanced Computing Research Lab, Integral University, Lucknow, India

Saurabh Shukla
Data Science Institute, National University of Ireland, Galway, Ireland

Acknowledgment

This work was a great experience for us into the domain of cyberology. There are lots of people who helped us directly and indirectly to make this book a reality. We would like to acknowledge the contribution of each individual who helped us in the conception and completion of this book.

We want to take this opportunity to offer our sincere gratitude to them. A very special thanks to IGI publication team, particularly Jan Travers, Mikaela Felty, Elizabeth Barrantes, Lindsay Wertman and Jocelynn Hessler without their continuous encouragement and support this book would not have been possible. We also thank esteemed technical experts Dr. T J Siddiqui (Prof. University of Allahabad), Dr. Rashid Ali (Prof. AMU Aligarh), Dr. M Z Khan (Asst. Prof. Bisha University, KSA), and Dr. Nawazish Naveed (Asst. Prof, UTAS, Oman) for their efforts in time constrained impartial and critical review, proof reading and providing constructive feedbacks.

Thanks to our friends and colleagues for providing help wherever and whenever necessary.

This acknowledgement will not be complete until we pay our gratitude and regards to our parents and family members for their unflinching and encouragement to us in all our pursuits. It's the confidence of our family members in us that has made us the person that we are today. We dedicate this book to them.

I would like to express my gratitude to the contributors of this book, whose expertise and insights have greatly enriched its content. I would also like to extend my appreciation to the readers, whose curiosity and thirst for knowledge inspire the pursuit of understanding.

Finally, we wish to thank the organizations and individuals who granted me permission to use the research material and information necessary for the completion of this book.

Last but not the least we are heartily thankful to almighty God for showering His blessings forever during our entire life.

Chapter 1
Cloud Computing Cyber Threats and Vulnerabilities

Sami Ouali

University of Technology and Applied Sciences, Oman

ABSTRACT

Cloud computing has become an integral part of modern business operations, with organizations of all sizes and in all industries turning to the cloud to improve efficiency, reduce costs, and increase flexibility. However, the adoption of cloud computing has also introduced a range of new security challenges, as sensitive data and critical systems are moved to cloud-based infrastructure that may be managed by third parties. This chapter discusses the various types of cyber threats that can occur in the cloud, including data breaches, malware, and cloud-based attacks, as well as the measures that organizations can take to protect themselves against these threats on their data, infrastructure, and applications. This chapter examines also the role of cloud providers in securing data in the cloud, and the importance of implementing strong security measures to protect against these threats. By understanding the nature of these threats and the steps that can be taken to mitigate them, organizations and individuals can more effectively protect themselves and their sensitive data in the cloud.

INTRODUCTION

A standalone computing device is a computer that is designed to operate independently, without the need for connection to other devices or a network. Standalone computers can be used for a variety of purposes, such as desktop or laptop computers, servers, and embedded systems (Kahanwal and Singh, 2012). They typically have their own storage, processing power, and operating system, and can be used to perform a wide range of tasks, including running software applications, storing and accessing data, and connecting to the internet. Standalone computers can be connected to other devices or networks, but they are able to operate independently if necessary. Standalone computers are often used in situations where it is important to ensure the security and integrity of the data being processed, such as in financial institutions or government agencies. Standalone computers are typically more secure than computers

DOI: 10.4018/978-1-6684-8133-2.ch001

that are connected to networks, as they are less vulnerable to cyber threats such as malware and data breaches. However, they may not be as efficient or convenient to use as computers that are connected to networks, as they are not able to share resources or access information from other systems.

Distributed computing involves a network of computers that work together to solve a problem or perform a task (Kahanwal and Singh, 2012). Distributed computing is a field of computer science that focuses on the design and development of systems that involve the distribution of computing tasks across multiple computers, often connected over a network. These computers can be located in the same physical location or dispersed across different locations, and they communicate with each other over a network to share resources and information. Distributed computing allows for the distribution of work among multiple computers, which can increase efficiency and speed up the processing of large amounts of data. There are many different approaches to distributed computing, and the choice of which one to use depends on the specific needs and constraints of the system being developed. Some common types of distributed systems include: Client-server systems, Peer-to-peer systems, Grid computing, Cloud computing...

Cloud computing is a type of distributed computing that involves delivering computing resources, such as storage, processing power, and software, over the internet. Instead of storing and processing data on a standalone computer or a local network, users can access these resources through the cloud (Mell and Grance, 2011). This allows them to scale up or down as needed, pay only for the resources they use, and access their data and applications from any device with an internet connection. Cloud computing relies on a network of servers that are owned and operated by a third-party provider, and users access these resources remotely through the internet.

Cloud computing has become increasingly popular in recent years, with organizations of all sizes and in all industries turning to the cloud to improve efficiency, reduce costs, and increase flexibility (Marinescu, 2013). However, the adoption of cloud computing has also introduced a range of new security challenges, as sensitive data and critical systems are moved to cloud-based infrastructure that may be managed by third parties. In this chapter, we will discuss the various types of cyber threats that can occur in the cloud, as well as the measures that organizations can take to protect themselves against these threats.

One of the key challenges of securing data in the cloud is that it is often stored and processed by third parties, who may have different security practices and policies (Alouffi et al., 2021). This can make it difficult for organizations to ensure that their data is being properly protected, and to respond quickly to any security breaches that do occur. In addition, the use of shared infrastructure in the cloud means that a single security breach can potentially affect multiple organizations.

One common type of cyber threat in the cloud is data breaches, in which unauthorized parties gain access to sensitive data. These breaches can be caused by a variety of factors, including weak passwords, unpatched vulnerabilities, and malicious insiders. To protect against data breaches, organizations should implement strong password policies, regularly patch and update their systems, and carefully monitor access to their data. They should also consider using encryption to protect sensitive data, and implement access controls to limit who can access certain data.

Another common threat in the cloud is malware, which is software designed to disrupt, damage, or gain unauthorized access to a computer system. Malware can be delivered through a variety of means, including email attachments, malicious websites, and infected software. To protect against malware, organizations should implement strong anti-malware measures, such as firewalls and antivirus software, and educate their employees on how to recognize and avoid suspicious emails and websites.

In addition to these threats, organizations should also be aware of the risks posed by cloud-based attacks, in which attackers target the infrastructure of a cloud provider rather than a specific organization (Chitturi and Swarnalatha, 2020). These attacks can be particularly difficult to detect and mitigate, as they may not be immediately apparent to the affected organizations. To protect against cloud-based attacks, organizations should ensure that their cloud providers have robust security measures in place, and should consider implementing additional security measures at their own end.

Overall, the adoption of cloud computing brings a range of security challenges that organizations must be prepared to address. By implementing strong security measures and staying vigilant, organizations can protect themselves against the various types of cyber threats that can occur in the cloud.

The remainder of this paper is organized as follows: In the next section, we will present the relevant concepts related to the cloud computing, including the deployment models, infrastructure, and cloud services. Following this, we will describe how the security is a key concern in cloud computing and how cloud providers implement security measures at various levels. The cyber-threats and vulnerabilities for cloud computing will be presented in the following section. We will then discuss the best practices against cloud-based cyber-threats and vulnerabilities. Then, the main research areas will be discussed. Finally, we will summarize the main points of the chapter and highlight the significance of our study in the conclusion.

CLOUD COMPUTING

Cloud computing is a model for delivering computing resources, including data storage, processing power, and software applications, over the Internet (the cloud). Instead of using local servers or personal devices to store and process data, organizations and individuals can access these resources remotely from a cloud provider (Mell and Grance, 2011). According to the Cloud Security Alliance (Cloud Security Alliance, 2017), cloud computing is "a model for enabling ubiquitous, convenient, on-demand network access to a shared pool of configurable computing resources (e.g., networks, servers, storage, applications, and services) that can be rapidly provisioned and released with minimal management effort or service provider interaction". Cloud computing allows users to access and use resources on demand, rather than having to purchase and maintain expensive hardware and software infrastructure. It also enables users to scale up or down their usage as needed, paying only for the resources they consume. The cloud computing allows organizations and individuals to take advantage of the economies of scale and efficiency of shared resources, while also providing flexibility and scalability.

Cloud Computing Deployment Model

A cloud computing deployment model refers to the way in which a cloud computing service is deployed and made available to users. There are five main deployment models: public cloud, private cloud, hybrid cloud, community cloud, and multi-cloud (Fife, Kraus, & Lewis, 2021).

1. Public cloud: In a public cloud deployment model, cloud services are made available to the general public over the internet. Public clouds are owned and operated by third-party service providers, who provide access to a shared pool of computing resources on a pay-as-you-go basis.

2. Private cloud: In a private cloud deployment model, cloud services are provided for the exclusive use of a single organization. Private clouds can be owned and operated by the organization itself, or by a third-party service provider on behalf of the organization.
3. Hybrid cloud: A hybrid cloud deployment model combines elements of both public and private clouds. An organization can use a hybrid cloud to run certain workloads on a private cloud and others on a public cloud, depending on the specific needs and requirements of each workload.
4. Community cloud: A community cloud is a cloud infrastructure that is shared by several organizations within a specific community with common interests or goals. This deployment model is often used by government agencies, educational institutions, or nonprofit organizations.
5. Multi-cloud: A multi-cloud deployment model involves the use of multiple cloud services from different cloud providers. An organization might use a multi-cloud deployment model to take advantage of the different capabilities and pricing models offered by different cloud providers.

When choosing a cloud computing deployment model, organizations should consider factors such as cost, control, security, and compliance requirements.

Public Cloud

A public cloud deployment model refers to cloud computing services that are made available to the general public over the Internet. In a public cloud, the infrastructure, platform, or software is owned and operated by a third-party cloud service provider, and the resources are made available to the public on a pay-as-you-go basis. Public cloud services are typically provided on a self-service basis, where users can sign up for an account, choose the resources they need, and start using them without the need for any upfront infrastructure investment. Public clouds are highly scalable, and users can easily add or remove resources as needed. Public cloud services are a popular choice for many organizations because they offer a flexible, scalable, and cost-effective way to access computing resources. Some examples of public cloud providers include Amazon Web Services (AWS), Microsoft Azure, and Google Cloud Platform.

Private Cloud

A private cloud deployment model refers to cloud computing services that are implemented within an organization's own IT infrastructure, either on-premises or at a third-party data center that is used exclusively by that organization. In a private cloud, the infrastructure, platform, or software is owned and operated by the organization itself, or by a third party on behalf of the organization. Private clouds offer many of the same benefits as public clouds, such as scalability, flexibility, and cost-effectiveness, but they offer additional security and control since the resources are not shared with other organizations. Private clouds are often used by organizations that have strict compliance requirements or that need to keep their data and applications behind their own firewall. Private clouds can be implemented in a number of ways, including through the use of virtualization technologies, through the use of cloud management platforms, or through the use of cloud-based infrastructure as a service (IaaS) offerings. Some organizations choose to build their own private clouds from scratch, while others choose to outsource the implementation and management of their private clouds to third-party service providers.

Hybrid Cloud

A hybrid cloud deployment model refers to a cloud computing environment that combines both public cloud services and private cloud resources. In a hybrid cloud, an organization can choose to keep some of its workloads and data in-house, on its own private cloud infrastructure, while using public cloud services to handle peaks in demand or to provide additional capacity on an as-needed basis. Hybrid clouds offer organizations the ability to take advantage of the benefits of both public and private clouds, depending on their needs. They can use the public cloud for flexibility and scalability, and the private cloud for security and control. Hybrid clouds also allow organizations to move workloads between the two environments as needed, providing additional flexibility and agility. To implement a hybrid cloud, an organization can use a variety of tools and technologies, including cloud management platforms, hybrid cloud management software, and APIs (application programming interfaces) that allow communication between the two environments. Some organizations choose to use a single cloud provider for both their public and private cloud resources, while others choose to use multiple providers.

Community Cloud

The community cloud deployment model involves a cloud computing infrastructure that is shared by several organizations within a specific community with common interests or goals (Dubey et al., 2019). This type of cloud deployment is often used to share resources and services among government agencies, educational institutions, or nonprofit organizations. The community cloud can be owned, managed, and operated by one of the participating organizations, a third-party service provider, or a combination of both. The main advantage of the community cloud is that it allows organizations to share the cost and resources of a cloud infrastructure while still maintaining control over their data and applications. This deployment model can be more secure and cost-effective compared to using a public cloud or building a private cloud, especially for organizations that have unique compliance or security requirements.

Multi-Cloud

A multi-cloud deployment model refers to a cloud computing environment that uses resources from multiple cloud service providers. In a multi-cloud setup, an organization can choose to use different cloud services from different providers for different purposes, or to achieve certain goals such as increased reliability, flexibility, or cost-effectiveness (Ardagna, 2015). Multi-cloud environments can be created in a number of ways, depending on the needs of the organization. Some organizations choose to use different cloud providers for different types of workloads, such as using one provider for development and testing and another for production. Others use multiple cloud providers to achieve geographical diversity, or to avoid vendor lock-in. To implement a multi-cloud environment, an organization can use a variety of tools and technologies, including cloud management platforms, hybrid cloud management software, and APIs (application programming interfaces) that allow communication between the different cloud environments. Some organizations choose to use a single cloud management platform to manage resources across multiple cloud providers, while others choose to use separate tools for each provider.

Cloud Computing Infrastructure

Cloud computing infrastructure refers to the hardware, software, and networking resources that are used to deliver cloud services. It includes the data centers, servers, storage systems, and networking equipment that make up the underlying infrastructure of a cloud computing platform. A cloud computing infrastructure is designed to be scalable, flexible, and highly available, allowing it to meet the demands of a large and diverse user base (Marinescu, 2013). It typically includes multiple layers, including:

1. Hardware layer: This includes the physical servers, storage systems, and networking equipment that make up the infrastructure.
2. Virtualization layer: This layer abstracts the hardware resources and creates a virtual environment in which multiple virtual machines (VMs) can be run.
3. Cloud management layer: This layer manages and monitors the infrastructure, including tasks such as provisioning, allocating, and scaling resources.
4. Cloud services layer: This is the layer at which cloud services are delivered to users. It includes the platforms and APIs that allow users to access and use the services.

Hardware Layer

The hardware layer in cloud computing refers to the physical infrastructure that is used to provide cloud computing services. This includes the servers, storage systems, networking equipment, and other hardware components that make up the cloud infrastructure. In a public cloud deployment model, the hardware layer is owned and operated by the cloud service provider, and the resources are made available to the public over the Internet. In a private cloud deployment model, the hardware layer is owned and operated by the organization itself, or by a third party on behalf of the organization. The hardware layer is one of the three main layers of a cloud computing infrastructure, along with the virtualization layer and the application layer. The hardware layer is responsible for providing the physical resources that are used to host and run the virtualized computing resources and applications that make up the cloud.

Virtualization Layer

The virtualization layer in cloud computing refers to the software and technologies that are used to create and manage virtualized computing resources (Marinescu, 2013). These resources can include virtual machines, virtual networks, and virtual storage systems, among others. In a cloud computing environment, the virtualization layer sits on top of the hardware layer and provides the abstraction and isolation of resources that are needed to enable the creation of a cloud infrastructure. It allows multiple virtualized resources to be created and run on a single physical hardware infrastructure, enabling efficient utilization of resources and rapid scaling of computing capacity. The virtualization layer is one of the three main layers of a cloud computing infrastructure, along with the hardware layer and the application layer. It is responsible for creating and managing the virtualized resources that make up the cloud, and for providing the APIs and interfaces that enable users and applications to access and use those resources.

Cloud Management Layer

The cloud management layer refers to the software and technologies that are used to manage and operate a cloud computing infrastructure. This includes tasks such as provisioning and de-provisioning of resources, monitoring and management of resources, security and compliance, and billing and metering. The cloud management layer sits on top of the virtualization layer and is responsible for providing the tools and capabilities needed to manage and operate a cloud infrastructure. It can include both software that is provided by the cloud service provider, as well as tools and technologies that are used by the organization to manage its own cloud resources. The cloud management layer is an important part of a cloud computing infrastructure, as it enables organizations to effectively and efficiently manage their cloud resources and ensure that they are meeting the needs of their users and applications. It also plays a critical role in enabling the scalability, reliability, and security of a cloud environment.

Cloud Services Layer

The cloud services layer in cloud computing refers to the various types of services that are provided by a cloud service provider. These services can be grouped into three main categories: infrastructure as a service (IaaS), platform as a service (PaaS), and software as a service (SaaS). The cloud services layer is the top layer of a cloud computing infrastructure, and it is responsible for providing the various types of services that are consumed by users and applications. It sits on top of the cloud management layer and the virtualization layer, and is the interface through which users and applications access and use the resources and capabilities of the cloud.

Cloud Computing Services

Cloud computing services are a type of Internet-based computing that provides shared processing resources and data to computers and other devices on demand. They are designed to provide users with scalable, on-demand access to computing resources, including applications, data storage, and networking, without the need for upfront infrastructure investment. Cloud computing services can be classified into three main categories as shown in Figure 1: infrastructure as a service (IaaS), platform as a service (PaaS), and software as a service (SaaS) (Fife, Kraus, & Lewis, 2021).

1. Infrastructure as a Service (IaaS): This type of cloud computing provides access to virtualized computing resources, such as virtual machines, storage, and networking.
2. Platform as a Service (PaaS): This type of cloud computing provides access to a platform for developing, testing, and deploying software applications.
3. Software as a Service (SaaS): This type of cloud computing provides access to software applications that are hosted and managed by the provider.

Figure 1. Cloud computing services
(Salas-Zárate and Colombo-Mendoza, 2012)

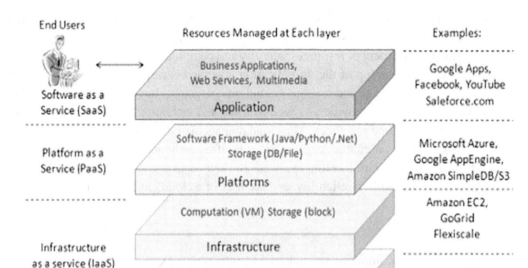

Infrastructure as a Service (IaaS)

Infrastructure as a Service (IaaS) is a cloud computing delivery model in which a provider makes infrastructure resources, such as servers, storage, and networking equipment, available to customers over the internet (Fife, Kraus, & Lewis, 2021). Customers can access these resources on a pay-per-use basis and can use them to build and run their own applications and services. IaaS offers a number of benefits to businesses. It can be a cost-effective way to obtain and scale infrastructure resources, as businesses only pay for the resources they use and can easily increase or decrease their usage as needed. Additionally, because the provider is responsible for the maintenance and management of the infrastructure, businesses don't have to worry about these tasks, which can be time-consuming and resource-intensive. IaaS can also be a flexible solution for businesses, as it allows them to customize their infrastructure to meet their specific needs. For example, they can choose the types and numbers of servers and storage devices they need, and they can select the operating systems and software they want to use. This can be especially useful for businesses that have unique or complex infrastructure requirements.

Platform as a Service (PaaS)

Platform as a Service (PaaS) is a cloud computing model in which an organization outsources the development and deployment of its applications to a third-party provider (Fife, Kraus, & Lewis, 2021). With PaaS, the provider offers a development platform and tools that allow organizations to build and deploy their applications without the need to maintain their own infrastructure. One of the main benefits of PaaS is that it allows organizations to focus on developing and deploying their applications, rather than worrying about the underlying infrastructure. This can help to reduce costs and improve efficiency, as organizations do not need to invest in and maintain their own servers, storage, and networking resources. PaaS providers typically offer a range of tools and services that can be used to build and deploy applications, including development environments, database services, and integration tools. This allows organizations to take advantage of pre-built components and services, rather than having to build everything from scratch. PaaS provides a flexible and cost-effective way to build and deploy their applications, without the need to maintain their own infrastructure or development tools.

Software as a Service (SaaS)

Software as a Service (SaaS) is a software delivery model in which a software application is hosted by a third-party provider and made available to customers over the internet (Fife, Kraus, & Lewis, 2021). Customers can access the software through a web browser or a program interface, and they pay for use of the software on a subscription basis or on a pay-per-use basis. SaaS offers a number of benefits to both customers and businesses. For customers, the main advantage is that they can access the software from anywhere with an internet connection, without having to install it on their own devices. This can be especially useful for small businesses or organizations that don't have the resources or technical expertise to set up and maintain software on their own. Additionally, SaaS providers typically handle all maintenance, updates, and support for the software, so customers don't have to worry about these tasks. For businesses, the main benefit of SaaS is that it can be a cost-effective way to deliver software to customers. Because the software is hosted by the provider, businesses don't have to invest in the infrastructure and resources needed to run the software in-house. This can make it easier for businesses to scale up or down as needed, and it can also reduce their overall operating costs.

SECURITY IN CLOUD COMPUTING

Cloud computing is a model for delivering computing resources, including storage, networking, processing, and software, over the internet. It enables organizations to access and use these resources on a pay-as-you-go basis, without the need to invest in and maintain their own in-house infrastructure. Security is a key concern in cloud computing, as it involves the handling of sensitive data and the potential for unauthorized access to systems and resources. To address these concerns, cloud providers implement a variety of security measures at various levels, including:

1. Physical security: Cloud providers typically maintain secure data centers with measures such as biometric access control, video surveillance, and physical security personnel.
2. Network security: Cloud providers implement network security measures such as firewalls, intrusion detection and prevention systems, and virtual private networks (VPNs) to protect against cyber threats.
3. Access control: Cloud providers use identity and access management (IAM) systems to control and monitor access to resources. This includes authentication and authorization processes to ensure that only authorized users can access specific resources.
4. Data protection: Cloud providers implement measures to protect data at rest and in transit, such as encryption, data backup and recovery, and data loss prevention (DLP).

5. Compliance: Cloud providers often need to meet various compliance requirements related to data protection and privacy, such as the General Data Protection Regulation (GDPR) in the European Union and the Health Insurance Portability and Accountability Act (HIPAA) in the United States.

It is important for organizations using cloud services to carefully evaluate the security measures in place and ensure that they meet their own security and compliance needs. This may involve implementing additional security measures, such as encryption and secure access controls, and working with the cloud provider to ensure that these measures are properly implemented.

Physical Security

Physical security refers to the protection of the hardware that is used to run cloud computing services. This includes the servers, storage devices, and networking equipment that make up the infrastructure of a cloud computing system. It also includes the facilities in which this hardware is housed, such as data centers. There are several measures that can be taken to ensure the physical security of a cloud computing system. These include:

1. Secure data centers: Data centers should be located in secure facilities that are protected by physical security measures such as fencing, guards, and surveillance cameras.
2. Controlled access: Access to data centers should be restricted to authorized personnel only, and should be monitored and logged.
3. Environmental controls: Data centers should have measures in place to protect against environmental hazards such as fires, floods, and extreme temperatures.
4. Physical security of hardware: The servers and other hardware in a data center should be securely housed and protected from tampering or theft.
5. Regular security audits: Regular security audits can help identify and address any vulnerabilities in the physical security of a cloud computing system.

Network Security

Network security in cloud computing refers to the measures that are taken to protect the networks that support cloud-based systems and data. This includes both the networks within a cloud provider's infrastructure, as well as the networks that connect an organization's systems to the cloud. Ensuring the security of cloud-based networks is important, as it helps to prevent unauthorized access to data and systems, and to ensure the integrity and availability of these resources. Network security measures can include a range of techniques, such as:

1. Firewalls: Firewalls can be used to control incoming and outgoing network traffic and to block unauthorized access to the network.
2. Encryption: Encrypting data that is transmitted over the network can help protect it from being intercepted and accessed by unauthorized parties.
3. Virtual private networks (VPNs): VPNs can be used to create secure, encrypted connections between devices and the cloud computing system, protecting data as it is transmitted over the internet.

4. Security protocols: Implementing security protocols such as HTTPS (Hypertext Transfer Protocol Secure) can help protect against man-in-the-middle attacks and other types of cyber threats.
5. Regular security audits: Regular security audits can help identify and address any vulnerabilities in the network security of a cloud computing system.

Access Control

Access control in cloud computing refers to the measures that are taken to ensure that only authorized users are able to access cloud-based systems and data. This includes the implementation of user authentication and authorization systems, as well as the establishment of policies and procedures to govern access to these resources. Ensuring the security of cloud-based systems through access control is important, as it helps to prevent unauthorized access to data and systems, and to ensure the integrity and confidentiality of these resources. Access control measures can include a range of techniques, such as password-based authentication, two-factor authentication, and biometric authentication to verify the identity of users. In addition to these measures, cloud providers may also implement a range of technical controls to further restrict access to their systems, such as access controls lists and role-based access controls, as well as monitoring and alerting systems to detect and respond to potential threats.

Data Protection

Data protection in cloud computing refers to the measures that are taken to ensure the confidentiality, integrity, and availability of cloud-based data. This includes the implementation of controls to prevent unauthorized access to data, as well as measures to ensure the integrity and availability of these resources. To prevent unauthorized access to sensitive information and ensure the availability and integrity of cloud-based resources, it is important to guarantee the security of the data. Data protection measures can include a range of techniques, such as:

1. Encryption: Encrypting data that is stored in the cloud can help protect it from being accessed by unauthorized parties.
2. Access controls: Implementing access controls such as authentication and authorization protocols can help ensure that only authorized users can access data in the cloud.
3. Data backup and recovery: Having a robust data backup and recovery plan in place can help ensure that data can be recovered in the event of a data loss or breach.
4. Regular security audits: Regular security audits can help identify and address any vulnerabilities in the data protection of a cloud computing system.

In addition to these measures, cloud providers may also implement a range of technical controls to further protect data, such as access controls and data masking, as well as monitoring and alerting systems to detect and respond to potential threats.

Compliance

Compliance in cloud computing refers to the process of ensuring that an organization's use of cloud services meets all relevant regulations, laws, and industry standards. This can include a wide range of considerations, such as data privacy, data security, data residency, data retention, and data access. Ensuring compliance in the cloud can be complex and challenging, as it requires a thorough understanding of the specific regulations and standards that apply to the organization's industry, as well as a clear understanding of the capabilities and limitations of the cloud services being used. To help ensure compliance, it is important for organizations to carefully review and understand the terms of service for their cloud services, as well as to implement appropriate security controls and monitoring processes.

CYBER-THREATS AND VULNERABILITIES FOR CLOUD COMPUTING

A vulnerability is a weakness in a system or its design that can be exploited by an attacker to gain unauthorized access to, or disrupt the normal functioning of, the system. Vulnerabilities can exist in a variety of systems, including computer systems, networks, software applications, and physical infrastructure. According to (Johnson et al., 2016), a vulnerability is "a weakness in an information system, system security procedures, internal controls, or implementation that could be exploited by a threat source". Vulnerabilities can be exploited by attackers using a variety of tactics, such as malware, phishing attacks, or physical access to systems. They can also result from human error, such as failure to follow security procedures or use of weak passwords. Identifying and addressing vulnerabilities is an important part of maintaining the security and integrity of systems and networks.

A cyber threat is a type of threat that is carried out using the Internet or other types of digital communication networks. It can take a variety of forms, including malware, phishing attacks, denial of service attacks, and data breaches, and can be aimed at individuals, organizations, or entire countries. According to (Johnson et al., 2016), a cyber-threat is "a potential for unauthorized access, use, disclosure, disruption, modification, or destruction of information systems and the information contained therein that could compromise the confidentiality, integrity, or availability of the systems and the information they contain". Cyber threats can have a range of impacts, including financial losses, reputational damage, and loss of sensitive or confidential information. They are a growing concern for individuals, organizations, and governments around the world, as the reliance on digital communication networks continues to increase. A cyber threat is a potential danger that can exploit vulnerabilities in a computer system or network to cause harm or steal sensitive information (Chitturi and Swarnalatha, 2020). A vulnerability, on the other hand, is a weakness in a computer system or network that can be exploited by a cyber-threat. In other words, a vulnerability is a gap in the system's defenses that a cyber-threat can potentially exploit. It is important to identify and address vulnerabilities in order to prevent or mitigate the effects of cyber threats.

Cloud's Vulnerabilities

Cloud computing can introduce a number of vulnerabilities that can potentially compromise the security, integrity, and availability of an organization's data and systems (Subramanian and Jeyaraj, 2018). Some of the main vulnerabilities associated with cloud computing include:

1. Data breaches: Data stored in the cloud can be vulnerable to breaches, either through cyber-attacks or through unauthorized access by malicious insiders.

2. Inadequate security controls: If the cloud provider does not have adequate security controls in place, it is possible for cybercriminals to gain access to the data stored on the cloud.
3. Lack of visibility and control: In a cloud computing environment, users may not have full visibility and control over the security measures that are in place to protect their data. This can make it difficult to identify and address potential vulnerabilities.
4. Misconfigured cloud storage: It refers to cloud storage that has been set up in an insecure or improper manner, potentially exposing data to unauthorized access. This can occur when the user fails to properly configure the security settings for their cloud storage, or when the cloud provider has not implemented sufficient security measures.
5. Data loss: Data stored in the cloud can be lost due to a variety of factors such as hardware failures, software bugs, or natural disasters.
6. Account hijacking: Cloud accounts can be hijacked by attackers, who can then access and manipulate data stored in the cloud.
7. Insecure APIs: APIs (application programming interfaces) used to access cloud resources can be vulnerable to attacks if they are not properly secured.
8. Shared resources: In a cloud computing environment, multiple users may share the same physical resources, such as servers and storage devices. This can create the potential for one user's actions to affect the security of other users.
9. Shared technology vulnerabilities: Cloud environments often rely on shared technology infrastructure, which can introduce vulnerabilities if the technology is not properly secured or maintained.
10. Dependency on the cloud provider: In a cloud computing environment, users are dependent on the cloud provider to properly secure their data and maintain the availability of services. If the cloud provider fails to do so, it can create vulnerabilities for the users.
11. Compliance issues: Organizations may be subject to compliance requirements for data storage and handling, and failure to comply with these requirements can introduce vulnerabilities.
12. Complexity: The complexity of a cloud computing environment can make it difficult to properly secure and maintain the system. This can create opportunities for vulnerabilities to go unnoticed.

Cloud's Threats

Cloud computing can be vulnerable to a variety of threats (Alwaheidi and Islam, 2022), including:

1. Data breaches: unauthorized access to data stored in the cloud can compromise sensitive information.
2. Denial of service (DoS) attacks: these attacks can disrupt the availability of cloud-based services.
3. Malware: malware can be introduced to the cloud through infected devices or through the internet, potentially compromising data or causing service disruptions.
4. Insider threats: employees or contractors with access to the cloud infrastructure may intentionally or unintentionally compromise data security.
5. Account hijacking: attackers may gain access to a user's cloud account through phishing or other methods, allowing them to access sensitive data.
6. Inadequate security controls: if a cloud provider does not have sufficient security controls in place, it can leave data and systems vulnerable to attack.

Data Breaches

A data breach occurs when unauthorized individuals gain access to sensitive data (Alwaheidi and Islam, 2022). In a cloud computing environment, data is stored on servers that are managed by the cloud provider. If these servers are not properly secured, it is possible for cybercriminals to gain access to the data stored on them. A data breach is a security incident in which sensitive, protected, or confidential data is accessed, used, or disclosed without authorization. Data breaches can occur through a variety of means, including hacking, malware attacks, social engineering, and insider threats. Data breaches can have serious consequences for businesses and organizations, including financial losses, reputational damage, and legal penalties. They can also have serious consequences for individuals whose personal information is exposed in a breach, including identity theft and financial fraud.

Denial of Service Attacks

A denial of service (DoS) attack is a type of cyberattack that is designed to disrupt the normal functioning of a network, server, or website by overwhelming it with traffic or requests (Alwaheidi and Islam, 2022). DoS attacks can be launched using a single device or a network of compromised computers known as a botnet. The goal of a DoS attack is to make a website or network resource unavailable to users, often by flooding it with so much traffic that it becomes impossible for the server or network to handle the request and respond in a timely manner. There are several types of DoS attacks that can occur in a cloud environment, including:

1. Flooding attacks: These attacks involve sending a large volume of traffic or requests to a targeted server or network in an attempt to overwhelm it and prevent it from responding to legitimate requests.
2. Protocol attacks: These attacks involve exploiting vulnerabilities in a network's protocols or systems to prevent them from functioning correctly.
3. Application layer attacks: These attacks involve targeting a specific application or service running on a server or network, such as a website or email server.

DoS attacks can have serious consequences for businesses and organizations, including lost revenue, damage to reputation, and the cost of recovering from the attack. It is important for businesses and organizations to implement measures to prevent and mitigate DoS attacks, such as firewalls, intrusion detection systems, and load balancers.

Malware

Malware is a type of malicious software that can infect a computer system and cause harm. In a cloud computing environment, malware can spread rapidly between virtual machines and cause widespread damage. One of the main risks of malware in a cloud computing environment is that it can potentially infect multiple systems at once, as multiple users may be sharing the same physical resources. This can make it more difficult to contain and remove the malware, and can cause significant disruptions to the availability of cloud-based services. There are several types of malware that can potentially infect a cloud computing environment, including:

1. Viruses: A virus is a type of malware that replicates itself and spreads to other systems. In a cloud computing environment, a virus can potentially spread rapidly between virtual machines.
2. Worms: A worm is a type of malware that replicates itself and spreads to other systems, but unlike a virus, it does not require a host program to execute. In a cloud computing environment, worms can potentially spread rapidly between virtual machines.
3. Trojans: A Trojan is a type of malware that disguises itself as a legitimate program, but is actually designed to cause harm. In a cloud computing environment, Trojans can potentially gain access to sensitive data or disrupt services.
4. Ransomware: Ransomware is a type of malware that encrypts a victim's files and demands a ransom from the victim to restore access. In a cloud computing environment, ransomware can potentially cause widespread disruptions to the availability of cloud-based services.
5. Adware: Adware is a type of malware that displays unwanted advertisements on a victim's computer. In a cloud computing environment, adware can potentially disrupt the user experience and consume resources.

Insider Threats

Insider threats in cloud computing refer to situations where a malicious or compromised insider, such as a disgruntled employee or contractors, intentionally or unintentionally causes harm to an organization's data or systems. In a cloud computing environment, insider threats may include individuals with access to sensitive data who misuse their privileges. Insider threats can be particularly difficult to detect and prevent, as the insider typically has legitimate access to the organization's systems and data. Some specific examples of insider threats in the cloud include:

1. Intellectual property theft: An insider may try to steal sensitive data, such as trade secrets or confidential business information, and use it for personal gain or to benefit a competitor.
2. Data sabotage: An insider may intentionally delete or modify data stored in the cloud, potentially causing significant disruption to an organization's operations.
3. Unauthorized access: An insider may try to access data or systems that they do not have permission to access, potentially leading to a data breach.
4. Unauthorized data sharing: An insider may share sensitive data with unauthorized individuals, potentially violating privacy laws or industry regulations.

Account Hijacking

Account hijacking in cloud computing refers to the unauthorized takeover of a user's cloud account by an attacker (Alwaheidi and Islam, 2022). This can occur through a variety of means, including:

1. Stolen login credentials: If an attacker is able to obtain a user's login credentials, such as their username and password, they can use them to gain unauthorized access to the user's cloud account.
2. Phishing attacks: Attackers may use phishing tactics, such as sending fake login prompts or creating fake websites, to trick users into providing their login credentials.
3. Vulnerabilities in security: If an attacker is able to exploit vulnerabilities in the security of a user's cloud account, they may be able to gain unauthorized access to the account.

Once an attacker has gained access to a user's cloud account, they can potentially access and manipulate sensitive data stored in the account, disrupt the user's operations, and incur charges on the user's account.

Inadequate Security Controls

Inadequate security controls in cloud computing refer to a lack of sufficient measures to protect data and systems in the cloud from unauthorized access, misuse, or other threats. These measures may include things like encryption, access controls, and security policies. If these controls are not implemented or are not effective, it can lead to a variety of problems such as data breaches, data loss, compliance issues, and loss of control. To ensure that data and systems in the cloud are adequately protected, it is important for organizations to implement and maintain appropriate security controls.

MEASURES TO PREVENT CYBER-THREATS

Measures to prevent cyber-threats in cloud computing refer to the various steps that organizations can take to protect their data and systems in the cloud from cyber-attacks and other threats. These measures may include using strong, unique passwords, implementing multi-factor authentication, using encryption, implementing access controls, regularly updating systems and software, conducting regular security assessments, and training employees on cyber-security best practices (Alwaheidi and Islam, 2022). By implementing these measures, organizations can significantly reduce their risk of falling victim to cyber-threats in the cloud. These measures depend from the threat's nature.

Data Breaches

To protect against data breaches, it is important for businesses and organizations to implement robust security measures (Alwaheidi and Islam, 2022), including:

1. Strong passwords: Use complex passwords that are hard to guess and change them regularly.
2. Two-factor authentication: Use two-factor authentication (2FA) to provide an extra layer of security.
3. Firewalls: Use firewalls to block unauthorized access to your network.
4. Encryption: Use encryption to protect data in transit and at rest.
5. Security awareness training: Provide security awareness training to employees to help them recognize and avoid common security threats.
6. Regular updates: Keep all software and systems up to date to ensure that any known vulnerabilities are patched.
7. Backup and recovery: Implement a backup and recovery plan to ensure that you can recover from a data breach or other security incident.

By implementing these measures, businesses and organizations can reduce the risk of data breaches and protect their sensitive information.

Denial of Service (DoS)

There are several measures that organizations can take to prevent Denial of Service (DoS) attacks in cloud computing (Alwaheidi and Islam, 2022):

1. Use a cloud-based DoS protection service: Many cloud providers offer DoS protection services that can help mitigate the effects of a DoS attack. These services use various techniques such as rate limiting, traffic shaping, and filtering to block or mitigate malicious traffic.
2. Use a content delivery network (CDN): A CDN is a network of servers that are distributed across the globe, and it can help absorb the traffic from a DoS attack by routing traffic through the closest server.
3. Implement rate limiting: Rate limiting is a technique that is used to restrict the number of requests that a server can receive from a single IP address within a specific time period. This can help prevent a DoS attack by limiting the amount of traffic that a server has to handle.
4. Use a firewall: A firewall is a security system that controls incoming and outgoing network traffic based on predetermined security rules. By using a firewall, organizations can block traffic from known malicious sources and limit the amount of traffic that can reach their servers.
5. Monitor traffic patterns: Regularly monitoring traffic patterns can help organizations identify unusual spikes in traffic, which may indicate a DoS attack. By monitoring traffic patterns, organizations can take action to mitigate the effects of an attack.
6. Use load balancing: Load balancing is a technique that is used to distribute incoming traffic across multiple servers. This can help prevent a DoS attack from overloading a single server and causing it to become unavailable.

Malware

To prevent malware in a cloud computing environment, it is important to implement robust security measures, such as antivirus software and firewalls. It is also a good idea to regularly update and patch systems to address any known vulnerabilities that could be exploited by malware. Users should also be cautious when opening emails or downloading files from untrusted sources, as these can be common vectors for malware attacks.

Insider Threats

To help mitigate the risk of insider threats in the cloud, organizations can take several steps, such as:

1. Implementing strict access controls: Limiting access to sensitive data and systems to only those who need it can help prevent unauthorized access.
2. Conducting background checks on employees and contractors who will have access to sensitive data and systems can help identify potential security risks.
3. Implementing monitoring and detection systems can help identify unusual activity that may be indicative of an insider threat.
4. Providing employee training on security best practices can help reduce the risk of unintentional insider threats.

5.   Establishing an incident response plan: Having an incident response plan in place can help an organization quickly and effectively respond to an insider threat.

Account Hijacking

To help prevent account hijacking in the cloud, it is important for users to implement strong passwords and enable multifactor authentication whenever possible. Additionally, users should be vigilant about protecting their login credentials and be cautious about providing them to others. If a user suspects that their account has been compromised, they should contact their cloud service provider immediately to report the issue and request assistance in securing their account.

Inadequate Security Controls

To address these issues, it is important for organizations to implement appropriate security controls in the cloud. This can include measures such as encryption, strong passwords, and access controls to ensure that data is protected against unauthorized access. It is also important to regularly review and update security controls to ensure that they remain effective.

RESEARCH AREAS IN CLOUD COMPUTING'S CYBER THREATS

Cloud computing has completely transformed the way businesses operate, providing unparalleled flexibility and scalability. However, this technology is not without its own set of challenges, especially when it comes to cybersecurity. Unfortunately, as the popularity of cloud computing continues to grow, so does the number of cyber threats that specifically target cloud-based systems. To combat these threats, researchers are constantly working on new frameworks and technologies that will improve the security of cloud computing environments. Some of the most recent research areas in this field include cloud security frameworks, threat detection and intelligence, cloud data privacy and protection, cloud forensics, malware analysis for cloud systems, cloud access control, and cloud-based threat hunting. By tackling these challenges head-on, organizations can continue to reap the benefits of cloud computing while minimizing their vulnerability to cyber threats. In order to achieve this, it's important for organizations to have a deep understanding of cyber threats, even if gaining this comprehension presents some challenges. Efforts have been made to predict cyber threats before they even occur, and these efforts continue to evolve.

In their recent work, (Gayathri and Gowri, 2023) suggest a solution to tackle the growing challenge of cloud data privacy and protection. They address the storage complexity and cloud security concerns that arise due to the increasing use of Internet of Things (IoT) applications, which has led to a rise in the generation of images and other data over the cloud platform. They proposed a lightweight dynamic processing of data approach instead of storing large amounts of data in the cloud, specifically in the context of privacy preserving medical data communication. A cryptographic technique is used to encode and decode medical data, while a proposed image denoising scheme with a hybrid classification model is used to ensure secure and reliable communication. This approach involves using deep learning algorithms and enables dynamic data processing at the edge devices, reducing storage complexity.

(Yesmin et al., 2023) tackle the challenges posed by crimes and the potential harm they can cause to individuals' safety. Their focus is on comprehending the essential measures and procedures required to prevent crimes. This involves examining the various factors, variables, and relationships between different types of crimes, and identifying effective techniques to control and reduce criminal activity. The authors explore the use of the SRNN algorithm classification techniques to predict crime data and analyze them to identify high-risk regions and crime-prone areas. Additionally, they emphasize the significance of fortifying the security system by leveraging advanced algorithms, cloud computing capabilities, and IoT to enhance security measures.

(Otta et al., 2023) focus more on the importance security of cloud computing and unauthorized access prevention to its services and resources. The authors suggested various approaches to improve cloud authentication robustness. The authors recognized that single-factor authentication, which has been commonly used for a long time, is prone to attacks. To address this issue, they investigated the more secure alternative of multi-factor authentication, which involves multiple levels of authentication checks, including biometric characteristics. In this paper, the authors conducted a thorough survey of various authentication factors and assessed their appropriateness for multi-factor authentication mechanisms.

CONCLUSION

In summary, cloud computing is a type of distributed computing that delivers resources over the internet, allowing users to access and use them on demand. Cloud computing has revolutionized the way businesses operate and has brought numerous benefits including cost savings, scalability, and flexibility. However, it has also introduced new cyber threats that must be addressed to ensure the security and integrity of sensitive data.

Cyber threats in cloud computing are a major concern for businesses and individuals alike. These threats can take many forms, including malware, data breaches, and ransomware attacks. To mitigate these risks, it is important for organizations to implement robust security measures, such as encryption, access controls, and regular security assessments. Additionally, it is critical for individuals to practice good cyber hygiene, such as using strong passwords and being cautious when clicking on links or downloading files. As the use of cloud computing continues to grow, so too will the need for effective cybersecurity measures. It is essential for businesses and individuals to stay informed about the latest threats and to take proactive steps to protect themselves.

In conclusion, researchers are continuously working on improving the security of cloud-based systems, through various research areas such as cloud security frameworks, threat detection and intelligence, cloud data privacy and protection, cloud forensics, malware analysis for cloud systems, cloud access control, and cloud-based threat hunting. Organizations can minimize their vulnerability to cyber threats by gaining a deep understanding of the potential risks and implementing the necessary measures to prevent them. As the threat landscape continues to evolve, it is crucial for organizations to stay up-to-date with the latest cybersecurity developments and to proactively predict and prevent cyber threats.

REFERENCES

Alouffi, B., Hasnain, M., Alharbi, A., Alosaimi, W., Alyami, H., & Ayaz, M. (2021). *A Systematic Literature Review on Cloud Computing Security: Threats and Mitigation Strategies* (Vol. 9). IEEE Access., doi:10.1109/ACCESS.2021.3073203

Alwaheidi, M. K. S., & Islam, S. (2022). Data-Driven Threat Analysis for Ensuring Security in Cloud Enabled Systems. *Sensors (Basel)*, *22*(15), 5726. doi:10.339022155726 PMID:35957281

Ardagna, D. (2015). Cloud and Multi-cloud Computing: Current Challenges and Future Applications. *IEEE/ACM 7th International Workshop on Principles of Engineering Service-Oriented and Cloud Systems*, pp. 1-2. 10.1109/PESOS.2015.8

Chitturi, A. K., & Swarnalatha, P. (2020). *Exploration of Various Cloud Security Challenges and Threats. Soft Computing for Problem Solving*. Springer., doi:10.1007/978-981-15-0184-5_76

Cloud Security Alliance. (2017). *Security Guidance for Critical Areas of Focus in Cloud Computing v4.0*. Cloud Security Alliance. https://cloudsecurityalliance.org/artifacts/security-guidance-v4/

Dubey, K., Shams, M. Y., Sharma, S. C., Alarifi, A., Amoon, M., & Nasr, A. A. (2019). A Management System for Servicing Multi-Organizations on Community Cloud Model in Secure Cloud Environment. *IEEE Access: Practical Innovations, Open Solutions*, *7*, 159535–159546. doi:10.1109/ACCESS.2019.2950110

Fife, L., Kraus, A., & Lewis, B. (2021). *Cloud Concepts, Architecture, and Design. The Official (ISC)2 CCSP CBK Reference*. Wiley., doi:10.1002/9781119603399.ch1

Gayathri, S., & Gowri, S. (2023). Securing medical image privacy in cloud using deep learning network. *Journal of Cloud Computing (Heidelberg, Germany)*, *12*(1), 40. doi:10.118613677-023-00422-w

Hogan, M., Liu, F., Sokol, A., & Jin, T. (2011). *NIST-SP 500-291, NIST Cloud Computing Standards Roadmap. Special Publication (NIST SP)*. National Institute of Standards and Technology. https://tsapps.nist.gov/publication/get_pdf.cfm?pub_id=909024 doi:10.6028/NIST.SP.500-291v1

Johnson, C., Badger, M., Waltermire, D., Snyder, J., & Skorupka, C. (2016). *Guide to Cyber Threat Information Sharing. Special Publication (NIST SP)*. National Institute of Standards and Technology. doi:10.6028/NIST.SP.800-150

Kahanwal, B., & Singh, T. P. (2012). The Distributed Computing Paradigms: P2P, Grid, Cluster, Cloud, and Jungle. *International Journal of Latest Research in Science and Technology*, *1*(2), 183–187. doi:10.48550/arXiv.1311.3070

Marinescu, D. C. (2013). *Cloud Computing Theory and Practice*. Elsevier.

Mell, P., & Grance, T. (2011). *The NIST Definition of Cloud Computing. Special Publication (NIST SP)*. National Institute of Standards and Technology. doi:10.6028/NIST.SP.800-145

Otta, S. P., Panda, S., Gupta, M., & Hota, C. (2023). A Systematic Survey of Multi-Factor Authentication for Cloud Infrastructure. *Future Internet*, *15*(4), 146. doi:10.3390/fi15040146

Salas-Zárate, M., & Colombo-Mendoza, L. (2012). Cloud Computing: A Review of Paas, Iaas, Saas Services and Providers. *Lámpsakos*, 7(7), 47–57. doi:10.21501/21454086.844

Subramanian, N., & Jeyaraj, A. (2018). Recent security challenges in cloud computing. *Computers & Electrical Engineering*, 7(1), 28–42. doi:10.1016/j.compeleceng.2018.06.006

Yesmin, T., Agasti, S., Pandit, J. K., & Mondal, B. (2023). Cyber Security and Its Prediction with Cloud Data Computing and IoT. In J. Choudrie, P. Mahalle, T. Perumal, & A. Joshi (Eds.), *ICT with Intelligent Applications. Smart Innovation, Systems and Technologies* (Vol. 311). Springer. doi:10.1007/978-981-19-3571-8_6

Chapter 2
The Critical Analysis of E-Commerce Web Application Vulnerabilities

Gausiya Yasmeen
Integral University, India

Syed Adnan Afaq
Integral University, India

ABSTRACT

Large-scale deployments of web applications occur continuously. The failure to validate or sanitize form inputs, improperly configured web servers, and application design flaws are the main causes of security vulnerabilities that continue to infect web applications, allowing hackers to access sensitive data and using legitimate websites as a breeding ground for malware. These vulnerabilities can be used to compromise the security of the application. The largest problem that enterprises face is how to create a web application that satisfies their needs for safe processes, E-Commerce, and the transmission of sensitive data. OWASP updates and releases a list of the top 10 web application vulnerabilities every few years. Along with the OWASP Top 10 Threats, this chapter also discusses each vulnerability's possible effects and how to avoid them. According to the OWSP (Open Online Application Security Project) Top Ten, this document analyses the most serious web vulnerabilities, their causes, and their impacts.

INTRODUCTION

Online forms, shopping carts, word processors, spreadsheets, video and photo editors, file conversion, file scanning, and email clients like Gmail, Hotmail, and AOL are illustrations of web apps out of which Google Apps and Microsoft 365 are two common programmes. In simple words, web applications are remote software application hosted on internet and accessed through web browsers. We can also define as, web services are web applications, and not all of them but most of the websites have web applications. For the purpose of shielding web applications, web servers, and online services like APIs from assault by Internet-based risks, web application security refers to a range of procedures, technologies, or techniques.

DOI: 10.4018/978-1-6684-8133-2.ch002

Figure 1. Web application architecture

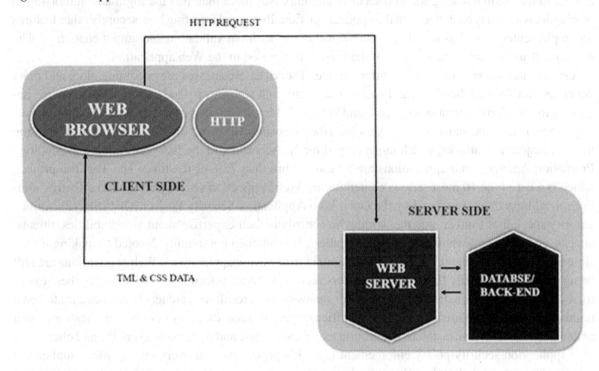

As we know, online applications include users' private and personal information, protecting them against data theft, disruptions in business continuity, and other harmful repercussions of cybercrime is of utmost importance. The concept of designing websites to work as expected even when they are attacked is known as web application security. The idea entails a set of security measures built together into web application to safeguard its resources from potentially harmful agents. Like any software, web applications inherently have flaws. Some of these flaws represent genuine vulnerabilities that can be used against businesses. Security for web applications guards against these flaws. It entails utilising secure development methodologies and putting security controls in place at every stage of the software development life cycle (SDLC), making sure that both implementation- and design-level defects are fixed(1). Protecting websites, programmes, and APIs from assaults is the practise of web application security. Although it is a diverse field, its ultimate goals are to maintain web applications operating efficiently and safeguard businesses against cyber vandalism, data theft, unethical competition, and other unfavourable effects. Web applications and APIs are vulnerable to assaults of varying sizes and sophistication due to the Internet's worldwide reach. Web application security hence comprises of various areas of the software supply chain and a wide range of tactics. Today's world is driven by apps, from e-commerce and personal entertainment delivery to online banking and remote employment. It should come as no surprise that applications are a top target for attackers that take advantage of faults in design as well as in APIs, open-source code, third-party widgets, and access control. Finding security flaws in Web applications and their settings is the goal of web security testing. The application layer is the main target (i.e., what is running on the HTTP protocol). Sending various inputs to a Web application to elicit errors and cause the system to react unexpectedly is a common practise for testing its security(1) These so-called "negative tests" check to see if the system is performing tasks that it wasn't intended to. It's also critical to realise that testing for web security encompasses more than just the login and authorisation mechanisms that may be included in the application. Equally crucial is testing how securely other features are implemented (e.g., business logic and the use of proper input validation and output encoding). The objective is to guarantee the security of the functions exposed in the Web application.

On the Internet, various websites offer a range of services. Businesses are becoming more and more dependent on Web applications, and social contact through websites is likely to continue growing, according to the "Communications Usage Trend Survey"1. Most businesses install firewalls, Secure Sockets Layer (SSL), network, and host security tools on their websites. However, these systems are unable to stop the vast majority of attacks, which target apps directly. According to the IPA (Information-Technology Promotion Agency), web applications are attacked more than 75% of the time. The Top Ten project, which is a list of the 10 most serious contemporary Web application security issues and effective solutions to address them, is offered by the Open Web Application Security Project (OWASP) (2). Various security specialists from around the world who contribute their expertise about vulnerabilities, threats, attacks, and countermeasures are project members. It is an open community devoted to making it possible for businesses to create, acquire, and maintain trustworthy applications. Web applications are still being infected by security flaws, giving hackers access to private information and allowing them to use trustworthy websites as a distribution point for malware. As a result, researchers have concentrated on a number of strategies to identify and stop significant types of security flaws in online applications, such as anomaly-based and misuse-based detection techniques, static and dynamic server-side and client-side web application security policy enforcement (3). This paper gives an overview of online application security features, including key flaws, hacking tools, and methods for raising the level of security for websites and web applications.

Figure 2. Various cyber outbreaks
(Zhang, Zhibo et.al. (2022))

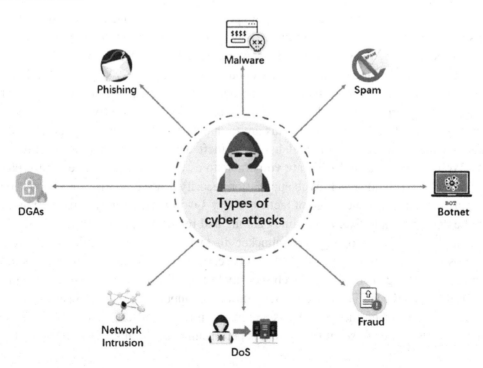

Figure 3. OWSP top 10 vulnerabilities
(https://www.indusface.com/learning/what-are-the-owasp-top-10
-risks-2021)

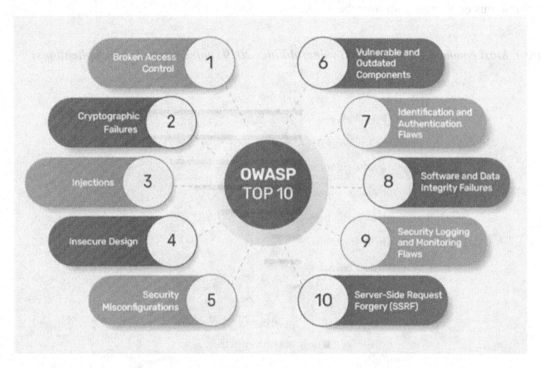

OWSP- OPEN WEB APPLICATION SECURITY PROJECT

The illustration above Fig 1 shows several of the most common attacks employed by attackers, which can seriously harm a specific application or the entire corporation. Your company will be able to accurately test for vulnerabilities and pre-emptively address them if you are aware of the many attacks that can weaken an application as well as the possible results of an assault. OWASP is a company that offers objective, useful, and reasonably priced information about computer and Internet applications (2). A multinational non-profit group devoted to online application security is called OWASP, or the Open Web Application Security Project. One of OWASP's guiding principles is that all of their resources should be publicly available and simple to find on their website, enabling anybody to increase the security of their own online applications. They provide forums, tools, videos, and documentation among other things. The OWASP Top 10 is a project that they may be most recognised for (4). The OWASP Top 10 is a regularly updated report that lists the top 10 threats to the security of online applications. The research was created by a team of international security experts from several nations. In order to reduce and/or mitigate security threats, OWASP refers to the Top 10 as an "awareness document" and advises that all businesses include the report into their procedures. OWASP comprises of (3) (4):

- Complete books on application security testing, secure code development, and code review
- Application security standards and tools
- Standard security controls and libraries
- Local chapters all over the world

- Cutting-edge research
- Mailing lists
- Numerous conferences all over the world

Figure 4. Most common OWASP top 10 vulnerabilities 2019 (percentage of web applications)

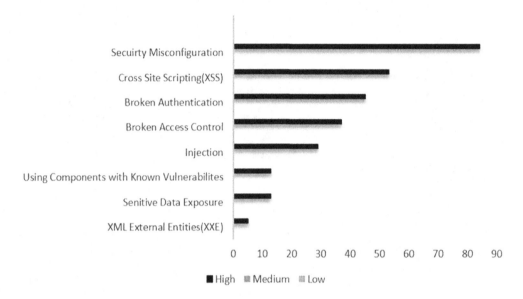

The above chart 1 shows the top vulnerabilities of the year 2019 as per the reports of OWSP. According to a poll done by "owasp.org," broken access control, cryptographic failures, and injections were among the top web applications security dangers of 2021. The categories of possible targets for each of these threats include client, server, and data transfer.

WEB APPLICATION AND VULNERABILITIES

The vulnerabilities impact web servers, application servers, and web applications. Such flaws are also known as application security hazards. There are often three main types of security flaws in web applications, each at a different level: an input validation flaw at the request level, a session management flaw somewhere at session level, and an application logic flaw at the programme as a whole. The three types of vulnerabilities mentioned above are described in the paragraphs that follow, along with typical attacks that take advantage of them (5). Application security risks involve attackers who may use numerous illegal methods to hurt the company and inflict significant damages on the organisations. Through your application, attackers may employ a variety of techniques to harm your company or organisation. Web applications often have three different types of security flaws at distinct levels: an input validation flaw at the request level, a session management flaw at the session level, and an application logic flaw at the scope of the entire programme (5). The three types of vulnerabilities mentioned above are described in the paragraphs that follow, along with typical attacks that take advantage of them.

Vulnerabilities in Input Validation

Considering input from the user data cannot be trusted, input data validation is a typical security observation. Data validation is a technique for ensuring that a programme runs on clean, accurate, and beneficial input data. Attackers are prepared to create distorted inputs whenever inputs don't appear to be adequately or correctly genuine. These inputs might change how programmes execute and provide them unauthorised access to resources. The input validation vulnerability in software system security may be a long-lasting flaw. A variety of attacks, including buffer overflow threats and code injection attacks, may be enabled by inadequate or incorrect input validation (6). Web applications may be vulnerable to a wide range of input validation flaws. A web application must ensure that user inputs are handled and used in a very safe manner throughout the execution because the entire web request, including request headers and payload data, is under the full supervision of users. A web application works on two side basis: Client-Side and Server Side, each side is equally vulnerable to cyber threats.

Threats to Client-Side- In cyber security, the words "client-side security," "client-side vulnerabilities," and "client-side attacks" are used to characterise security events and breaches that take place on the computer system of the customer (or user), as opposed to the business (on the server side), or anyplace in between. There are several techniques to target people using the client side. Client-Side threats can be Cross-Site Scripting, Magecart Attack, Broken Link Hijacking, and SQL Injection Attack.

Threats to Server-Side- An intruder (the customer) targets a listening service directly using a server-side assault. Assaults against a server's data and programmes are known as "server-side attacks.". Server-Side threats can be Denial of Service (DoS), Botnet, Unpatched Software, Data Transmission Threats, Broken Authentication.

i.   **Injection-SQL -** Injection issues happen when untrusted data is provided to an interpreter as part of a command or query. Examples include SQL, OS, and LDAP injection. The interpreter may be tricked by the attacker's hostile data into issuing unlawful instructions or accessing unauthorised data. When using the code injection technique known as SQL Injection, an attacker inserts erroneous code into strings that are then sent to a SQL server for execution. Once harmful content enters SQL queries that aren't completely sanitised, putting a web application at risk for SQL injection attacks, the offender is able to start malicious SQL operations by inserting SQL keywords or operators (7). As an instance, the offender may attach a different SQL query to the current one, forcing the application to drop the entire table or alter the return result. In addition to user inputs, cookies, and server variables, malicious SQL queries may also be inserted into a weak programme. Utilizing web sites that allow users to enter data into form fields for database queries is known as a SQL injection attack. Unintentional commands are conveyed to an interpreter as injection. The modified SQL query can be entered by attackers to obtain user information. For actions on data such data deletion, creation, and alteration, the queries speak directly with the database. For illustration, an intruder may input SQL database code into a form that asks for a plaintext username. If the form input is not sufficiently secured, SQL code will be executed. What this is is a SQL injection attack. After filling out and submitting online forms, user-provided data must be deleted or verified to prevent injection attacks. Sanitization refers to clearing out the suspicious-looking portions of the data, whereas validation refers to rejecting suspicious-looking data (7). A database administrator can also implement restrictions to limit the data that an injection attack can reveal.

ii. **Cross-Site Scripting -** Cross-site scripting vulnerabilities emerge anytime online programmes allow users to add custom code to a URL route or onto a website that is accessible to other users. It is possible to inject malicious JavaScript code on a victim's browser by taking advantage of this vulnerability (8). An attacker may, for instance, send a victim an email that looks to originate from a reputable bank and contains a link to the bank's website. There may be harmful JavaScript code attached to the end of this link. If the bank's website is not adequately safeguarded from cross-site scripting, the victim's web browser will execute the malicious code once users follow the link (8). Possible methods for preventing cross-site scripting include escaping untrusted HTTP requests, as well as validating and/or sanitising user-generated information. Cross-site scripting prevention is also embedded into recent website design platforms like ReactJS and Ruby on Rails. When an application delivers unverified data to a web browser without properly validating and escaping it, an XSS vulnerability results. XSS enables attackers to run script in the victim's browser that can manipulate user sessions, attack websites, or lead users to harmful websites. Obtaining client-side code in a web - based application to run in the attacker's desired manner is the aim of XSS (9). In order to intercept data traffic, deface domains, or drive users to malicious websites, attackers can employ XSS to execute code in the victim's browser.

iii. **Broken Authentication -** Despite weaknesses in authentication (logging) systems, hackers could get user account access, and by using an admin account, they may even be able to take control of the entire system. An attacker, for instance, may use a script to try each combination on a login system to determine if among the thousands of known username/password combinations work. on the list work. Requiring two-factor authentication (2FA) and restricting or delaying frequent login attempts via rate limitation are some mitigation techniques for authentication issues (10). The implementation of application functionalities relating to authentication and session management is frequently flawed, exposing attackers to acquire credentials, keys, authentication information, or exploit implementation vulnerabilities to assume the identities of other users. Securing the user's private information is the developer's top priority while creating any programme. The likelihood of exposing the Broken Authentication and Session Management risk is increasing due to the attackers' ingenuity, the system's bad architecture, and the improper usage of web applications. As a result of the exploitation described above, it's possible for sensitive information to be removed or altered in addition to identity theft (10).

iv. **Security Misconfiguration –**One of the most frequent threat on the index is security misconfiguration, whose key reason is the default setups or too verbose error messages. For instance, if a user encounters overly specific problems in a software, it may be a sign that the application is flawed. This may be avoided by deleting any unnecessary code features and making sure that glitches are more inclusive (11). A secure setup for the application, framework, web server, application server, and platform is necessary for security. Many of these settings are not supplied with secure defaults, thus they must all be specified, implemented, and maintained.

v. **XML External Entities (XEE) -**This is an offensive on a web application which reads input from XML* files. Such inputs may involve an outside source making an effort to weaken the parser. An "external entity" in this sense refers to a storage device, such as a hard disc. An XML parser could be misled into sending data to an unauthorised external entity, which might subsequently divulge sensitive information to an intrusive party. The greatest defence against XEE assaults is to have web applications accept a less sophisticated format of data, like JSON, or, at the absolute least, to patch XML parsers and limit the use of external entities in an XML application (12). Extensible

Markup Language is a type of markup language that can be read by computers and people. Despite to its complexity and security problems, it is presently being phased out of many web applications. A sort of straightforward, legible notation that is frequently used to communicate data over the internet is called JSON- JavaScript Object Notation (13). JSON was primarily designed for JavaScript, although it is language-independent and is compatible with many other programming languages.

LEADING CYBER OUTBREAK AREAS OF 2023

The development of technology has also changed how crimes are committed. Criminal activity gets increasingly deadly and undetectable. Cybersecurity professionals issue a warning about the evolving type and scope of cybercrime in 2023. Figure 4 presents a glimpse of top 5 cybercrimes occurred in the year 2023.

Figure 5. Top 5 cyber outbreak areas of 2023

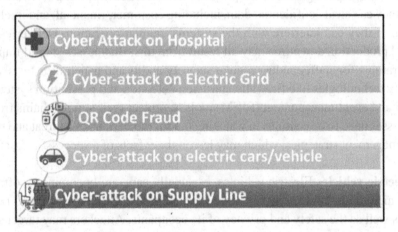

a.   **Field of Medical** – Cyberattacks in the medical field, like in hospitals, can have huge repercussions because they can compromise patient safety and impede healthcare delivery. Cybercriminals frequently target hospitals because they may have important patient financial and personal information on hand and because a successful assault might have disastrous results (14). In a cyberattack against a hospital system, the attacker may attempt to obtain unauthorized access to the facility's computer networks to steal or alter data, interfere with the functionality of medical equipment, or impair the provision of treatment. Ransomware, in which the attacker holds the hospital's data hostage and requests payment in exchange for access, may also be used in the assault (14). To defend against cyberattacks, hospitals must have robust cybersecurity procedures in place. The use of safeguards like firewalls, antivirus software, and secure passwords may be part of this, along with regular training for staff members on how to identify and stop cyberattacks.

b. **Digital Payment using QR** — If the QR code is connected to a malicious website or is being used to steal your personal information, scanning it might jeopardise your personal data. When reading QR codes, you should use caution, especially if they come from unreliable sources. It's also a good idea to verify the website's URL to make sure the QR code connects to a real page and not a phishing or other scam website (14). Using QR code scanner software that performs safety and building security checks is also a smart option. Updating your device and QR scanner app on a regular basis will ensure that you have the most recent security updates. Avoiding scanning QR codes from unauthorised sources and only doing so from reliable sites is a smart idea.

c. **Field of Logistics Network** – A cyberattack on the logistics network or supply chain might have serious repercussions for the impacted businesses and their clients. Attacks of this nature can obstruct the delivery of products and services, causing delays, lost money, and sometimes even harm to a company's image. In a supply chain cyberattack, attackers often target the networks and systems that businesses use to control and monitor their inventories, orders, and shipments. A transportation management system (TMS), which is used to track shipments and deliveries, or an enterprise resource planning (ERP) system, which is used to manage inventories and production, can be the targets of an attacker (14). The attacker can access these systems using a number of techniques, including social engineering techniques, phishing schemes, and exploiting software flaws. Once they get access, they can steal confidential data, including customer, financial, and intellectual property information, or they can interfere with the systems' regular operation. Deliveries, stakeouts, and unscheduled production downtime may all result from this. Businesses should implement security awareness training for staff, conduct regular security audits and penetration tests, and use cutting-edge security technologies like firewalls, intrusion detection and prevention systems, and security information and event management (SIEM) tools to protect their supply chains from cyberattacks (15). Businesses need to be cautious in watching out for indications of a threat and be prepared with incident management strategies, which may lessen the effects of a successful assault and speed up recovery.

d. **Field of electric vehicles** Electric vehicles, especially cars, are becoming a soft target for cyber attackers, which might have major repercussions, jeopardising the systems and network integrity of the EV as well as the safety and privacy of its occupants. Attackers may target an EV by taking advantage of flaws in the electronic control units (ECUs) of the vehicle, which are the computer systems in charge of things like the steering, brakes, and engine. Attackers may take over these systems and alter the way the car behaves, which might lead to crashes or other harmful circumstances. Attackers may also target EVs by taking advantage of holes in the onboard diagnostics (OBD) port or other communication or wireless connectivity technologies, such as Bluetooth or cellular networks (15). As a result, attackers may be able to access the vehicle's systems and data and perhaps steal private information, including location information, driving records, and occupant information. Manufacturers must create cars with security in mind while designing and manufacturing them in order to reduce the possibility of cyberattacks on EVs. This entails the adoption of secure coding techniques, frequent software updates to fix known flaws, and the implementation of strong security protocols to safeguard the communication systems of the vehicle.

Additionally, it's critical for EV owners to be aware of the dangers and take precautions to safeguard their vehicles. This might involve updating the software in their cars, exercising caution when connecting them to new networks or gadgets, and not storing sensitive data like personal information in their cars.

Cybersecurity in electric cars will be a vital area to maintain the safety and security of both vehicles and their occupants as the trend towards electric cars becomes more widespread and technological innovation increases.

e. **Threats to Electric Grid** – Power generators, transmission and distribution networks, and control systems are only a few of the many interrelated parts that make up the complicated systems that make up an electric grid. Attackers may target an electric grid by taking advantage of flaws in the industrial control systems (ICS) and supervisory control and data acquisition (SCADA) systems that are used to monitor and manage the grid (14). Attackers may obtain access to these systems and alter the behaviour of the grid via malware, phishing schemes, or other methods, which may result in power outages or other interruptions to the delivery of electricity. Attackers may also target an electric grid by taking advantage of flaws in the communication networks that are used to transport data and control signals among various grid components.

This may entail attacking the systems in use to control the transmission and distribution systems of the grid or exploiting weaknesses in the networks connecting power plants, substations, and other grid components. It's critical for utilities and grid operators to adopt a proactive strategy for cybersecurity in order to reduce the dangers of cyberattacks on electric systems. As part of this, effective security mechanisms like firewalls, intrusion detection and prevention systems, and security information and event management (SIEM) technologies must be put in place. Additionally, it's crucial to do frequent security audits, penetration tests, and personnel cybersecurity training. Additionally, it's critical that government organizations, utilities, and grid operators collaborate in order to exchange threat intelligence and plan incident response actions. Additionally, recommendations for safeguarding industrial control systems, such as those used in the electric grid, are provided by industry standards and regulations like NIST-CIP, IEC62443, and others.

Given the significant role that electric grids play in our everyday lives, maintaining their cybersecurity is a crucial first step in shielding our infrastructure and communities from possible online attacks.

CASE STUDIES

• **Social Media Business (Snapchat Jan'14/Facebook Aug'15)** - Gibson Security described flaws in the Snapchat service, but they were brushed off as simply theoretical threats. After a week, 4.6 million usernames and phone numbers had been discovered by brute-force enumeration. The claim made by Snapchat that the attack was hypothetical and that they had not taken any action appears to have played a role in the attack, at least in part. This led to a data breach of user information, including phone numbers that might be used for a number of purposes (15). Laxman Muthiyah discovered that a malicious person might make use of a request to give oneself admin rights for a certain Facebook page. You may see an example of a request below:

```
Request:-
POST /<page_id>/userpermissions HTTP/1.1
Host: graph.facebook.com
Content-Length: 245
```

```
role=MANAGER&user=<target_user_id>&business=<associated_business_id>&access_
token=<application_access_token>
Response:- true
```

- A rogue user might add himself as an administrator and prevent the genuine manager or administrator from accessing the feature of business pages, which is commonly used. Both problems were brought on by the absence of access control procedures that served a particular purpose (16).

- **Cloudbleed (2017) – A**n issue with Cloudflare's edge servers, some of which were cached by search engines, allowed memory to be dumped, possibly carrying sensitive data, according to Google's Project Zero. The name of this security flaw was Cloudbleed (14). Cloudflare stated that a private key between Cloudflare machines had leaked and that the incident may have started as early as September 22nd, 2016. The impact might be significant given that Cloudflare's services are used by almost 6 million websites and that many web application defences are constructed under the premise of a secure TLS communication channel. According to Cloudflare estimates, the bug was activated 1,242,071 times between September 22, 2016, and February 18, 2017 (16). This ought to be plainly obvious. The initial weakness was caused by the way broken HTML tags were processed, which resulted in information being returned from a random area of the server's memory.

- **Insecure Design –** One recent instance of unsafe design stopped PC users and gamers from getting new Nvidia GPUs at suggested retail pricing (17). Many e-commerce sites lacked security against the bots that scalpers exploited to purchase up their initial, small supply levels. Scalpers then resold the cards on auction platforms at exorbitant markups, forcing individuals who actually required a new GPU to pay sums that were several times greater than the suggested retail price.

- **Incident of Panama Papers(April'16) –** The 11.5 million records from Mossack Fonseca that make up the Panama Papers were first disclosed to German journalist Bastian Obermyer in 2015. The International Consortium of Investigative Journalists was contacted because of the magnitude of the data (15). Many well-known people, both past and current, have had their financial dealings made public, connecting them to terrorist organisations, drug cartels, and tax havens. Other famous personalities' careers were impacted, and in other cases, the revelations directly sparked an uproar in the public. This is particularly noteworthy from the perspective of cybersecurity since it highlighted the potential weakness and simplicity with which law firms may be attacked given the importance of the information they hold.

- **Mirai(未来) –** After being discovered, the IoT-based botnet Mirai managed to carry out a number of high-profile assaults until its developer (Anna-senpai) was forced to flee after publishing the source code (15). To avoid the routers, DVRs, and CCTV cameras, Mirai ran. In essence, tried using widely used passwords, which is something that is readily avoidable. Below is a list of every password that was used: With such a straightforward technique, the Mirai botnet was able to assault DNS provider Dyn, producing 280 Gbps and 130 Mpps in DDOS capacity, rendering websites like GitHub, Twitter, Reddit, Netflix, and Airbnb inaccessible. Security setup errors may be as basic as giving a user account too many rights or as complex as not limiting access to resources to external addresses (18).

- **Amazon S3 –** Notably, several businesses recently have neglected to secure their Amazon S3 storage case in point:

- ○ Australian Broadcasting Corporation leakage of internal resources, including keys and hashed passwords. Files from the United States Army Intelligence and Security Command, including Oracle Virtual Appliance (.ova), were uploaded in November 2017. volumes containing top-secret parts.
- ○ Accenture (Sept. 2017) – Sensitive client data as well as authentication data, including certificates, keys, and plaintext passwords.

Governmental and military organisations, among many others, rely on Amazon's S3 data storage service (15). According to earlier instances discovered, this is a widespread issue and the information released frequently has a significant influence on the organisation in question. When you have cloud infrastructure, a CSPM solution can help you keep an eye on typical cloud misconfigurations.

- **Vulnerability in Log4j2 (Dec'21)** – On December 9, 2021, it was discovered that the Apache logging package Log4j2 versions 2.14.1 and below have a Remote Code Execution (RCE) vulnerability (15).

What made this important?

The Apache Software Foundation offers the open-source Log4j2 library, which is frequently used in web applications and services to collect logs for development, operational, and security purposes. The open-source library is used by dozens of large internet service providers, including Amazon, Microsoft, IBM, and Google. As there is no need to reinvent the wheel, modern software development methodologies push the usage of such software libraries, resulting in a speedier go-to-market (18). As a result, the library might occasionally be found at many levels within programmes. To exploit the vulnerability, relatively little technical knowledge was needed. Threat actors simply need to know how to convert a string into a URL to take control of servers, steal data and passwords, put malware and crypto-mining software on them, and even sell access to other people like Ransomware-as-a-Service (RaaS) providers. According to Microsoft, hackers and state-sponsored RaaS are taking advantage of the Log4j2 vulnerability.

What does this have to do with outdated and vulnerable components?

On December 27, 2021, the Apache Software Foundation published an upgrade for Log4j, version 2.17.1, to fix all previously identified vulnerabilities in Log4j2. The updates' release history is provided below:

- 6 December 2021, 2.15.0
- 13 December 2021, year 2.16.0
- 17 December 2021, 2.17.0
- 27 December 2021 (2.17.1)

Version 2.17.0 of Log4j was released to fix the new vulnerability when it was discovered that version 2.16.0 was susceptible to DoS attacks. As the Log4j2 library is so widely used, it will take time to completely eliminate the threat (19). You may run a compromise assessment to make sure you are not already penetrated and perform penetration testing to test your network and endpoints in addition to implementing vendor updates and updating your Log4j2 versions. By deploying a CSPM like Warden, which can assist in identifying susceptible workloads and serve as defense-in-depth to break a chain of attacks in the case that a vulnerable Log4j2 instance exists, you may even take it a step further to reduce the likelihood of exploitation while you are upgrading Log4j2 (15).

DISCUSSION AND FUTURE SCOPE

Although significant efforts are made to address user input vulnerabilities and assaults, many outstanding issues remain unresolved, and XSS continues to be the most prevalent internet attack today. A recent research demonstrates that although web application development frequently includes auto sanitization solutions, they nevertheless fall short of the demands made by modern online services (20). Context-sensitive sanitization routine design and reasoning still require a lot of work. It is still difficult to identify input validation flaws in older internet apps. This essay discusses the issue that both consumers and programmers alike are facing in the current world and seeks to offer a solution to efficiently address any potential dangers.

We have spoken about the main issues on both the client and server sides as well as the dangers related to data transfer following Table 1 depicts the vulnerabilities discussed in the paper. We have also suggested remedies for the aforementioned concerns that we have discovered in practise to assist deal with the challenges.

Table 1. Shows various vulnerabilities discussed in the paper

Vulnerability	Affects
Cross-Site Scripting	Client Side
Sql Injection Attack	Client Side
Reflected XSS	Client Side
Magecart Attack	Client Side
Broken Link Hijacking	Client Side
Broken Authentication	Server Side
Security Misconfiguration	Server Side
Denial Of Service	Server Side
Botnet	Server Side
Unpatched Software	Server Side
Sensitive Data Exposure	Server Side

Strong session management methods need developers to consistently adhere to secure coding techniques, even for the construction of modern secure online apps. Internet application security against logical errors and assaults is still a relatively unexplored area. Only a small number of different approaches are envisaged (21). The majority of them only deal with a certain type of application logic vulnerability, such as access and authorization management flaws or discrepancies in client and server validations. The lack of application logic definition is the primary problem with Endeavour's general logic defects. One of the intrinsic causes for the inadequacy of the majority of app scanners and firewalls to handle logic faults and assaults is the absence of a generic and automated system for describing the application logic (21). Several scholars said that the government should prioritise developing rigorous laws and regulations to guard against harmful attacks and scams in addition to encouraging digitalization. There must be appropriate penalties for those who violate these laws in order to enforce them (22). By updating massive datasets online and creating web and mobile applications that allow users to access these data and submit sensitive data, huge corporations have aided in the cause of digitalization.

Therefore, it is the obligation of the businesses to maintain online security by using hackers to find flaws in web applications and offer solutions to fix them. Web security is a crucial component that, if effectively supplied, will increase consumers' trust in online web applications and encourage more people to use them (20). Finding flaws is like looking for a needle in a haystack, therefore total online security is impossible to achieve. However, we can try our best to assure web security and earn the confidence of consumers. Web security is the most important prerequisite to accomplish digitalization since it is a very major step towards a bright, better, and faster-paced future (22). Therefore, JAVA rather than less secure platforms should be used to construct online applications that primarily deal with sensitive user credentials including personal information, user ids, and passwords.

CONCLUSION

Web application attacks have the ability to execute arbitrary system instructions, grant unauthorised access to databases, and even change the content of websites. Due to the significance of web security, this paper reviewed the most serious vulnerabilities in web applications, their essential fixes, and mitigation measures. It also provided an overview of the most popular website and web application hacking tools. Servers might protect themselves against attackers and harmful activity by understanding web application vulnerabilities and remedies. Hackers are actually incredibly inventive, and as time goes on, more cyber-attacks are initiated that seek out novel approaches to the problems our current solutions can solve. Security is still a major concern even if various methods and frameworks are well-known and widely used in interactive online applications. To maintain optimal application safety, all applications must be regularly monitored and reviewed at regular intervals.

REFERENCES

OWASP. (n.d.). *OWASP Top Ten*. OWASP. https://www.owasp.org/index.php/Category:OWASP_Top_Ten_Project

Cloudflare. (n.d.). *What is OWASP? What is the OWASP Top Ten?* Cloudflare. https://www.cloudflare.com/learning/security/threats/owasp-top-10/

Akram, M. S. (2023). Top Five Cyber Crimes in 2023. *Modern Diplomacy*. https://moderndiplomacy.eu/2023/01/12/top-five-cyber-crimes-in-2023/

Al Ameen, A. (2015). Building a Robust Client-Side Protection Against Cross Site Request Forgery. *International Journal of Advanced Computer Science and Applications*, 6(6). doi:10.14569/IJACSA.2015.060610

Atashzar, H., Torkaman, A., Bahrololum, M., & Tadayon, M. (2011). *A survey on web application vulnerabilities and countermeasures,* 647-652. Research Gate.

Azfar, A., Choo, K. K. R., & Liu, L. (2013). A Study of Ten Popular Android Mobile Voip Applications: Are the Communications Encrypted? SSRN *Electronic Journal.* doi:10.2139/ssrn.2340228

Bashah Mat Ali, A., Yaseen Ibrahim Shakhatreh, A., Syazwan Abdullah, M., & Alostad, J. (2011). SQL-injection vulnerability scanning tool for automatic creation of SQL-injection attacks. *Procedia Computer Science*, *3*, 453–458. doi:10.1016/j.procs.2010.12.076

Bhanwarlal & Khan, I. (2022). XSS and SQL Injection Detection and Prevention Techniques (A Review). *International Journal of Scientific Research in Computer Science, Engineering and Information Technology*, 53–60. . doi:10.32628/CSEIT22816

Chua, I. (2022). Real Life Examples of Web Vulnerabilities. *Horangi.* https://www.horangi.com/blog/real-life-examples-of-web-vulnerabilities

Network Security. (2002). Cross-site scripting closed E-commerce site. (2002, February). *Network Security*, *4*(2), 4. doi:10.1016/S1353-4858(02)00209-X

Dwivedi, V., Yadav, H., & Jain, A. (2014). Web Application Vulnerabilities: A Survey. *International Journal of Computer Applications*, *108*(1), 25–31. doi:10.5120/18877-0144

Jaiswal, A., Raj, G., & Singh, D. (n.d.). Security Testing of web applications. Triaxiom Security.

Jovanovic, N., Kruegel, C., & Kirda, E. (2010, August 16). Static analysis for detecting taint-style vulnerabilities in web applications. *Journal of Computer Security*, *18*(5), 861–907. doi:10.3233/JCS-2009-0385

Kumar, S., Mahajan, R., Kumar, N., & Khatri, S. (2017). *A study on web application security and detecting security vulnerabilities*, 451-455. IEEE. . doi:10.1109/ICRITO.2017.8342469

Lawton, G. (2007, October). Web 2.0 Creates Security Challenges. *Computer*, *40*(10), 13–16. doi:10.1109/MC.2007.367

Nagpal, B., Chauhan, N., & Singh, N. (2014, May 15). Cross-Site Request Forgery: Vulnerabilities and Defenses. *I-Manager's. Journal of Information Technology*, *3*(2), 13–21. doi:10.26634/jit.3.2.2778

Durai, K. & Priyadharsini, K. (2014). A Survey on Security Properties and Web Application Scanner. *International Journal of Computer Science and Mobile Computing.*

Sukhanand & Sharma. (2017, December 4). A Review Paper on SQL Injection and Cross Site Scripting Vulnerabilities. *IJCRT, 4*(5). https://ijcrt.org/papers/IJCRT1704497.pdf

Swarup, S., & Kapoor, D. R. (2014, February 1). Web Vulnerability Scanner (WVS): A Tool for detecting Web Application Vulnerabilities. *International Journal of Engine Research*, *3*(2), 126–131. doi:10.17950/ijer/v3s2/219

Tajpour, A., & Masrom, M. (2010). SQL injection detection and prevention tools assessment. *In Computer Science and Information Technology (ICCSIT), 3rd IEEE International Conference on, (vol. 9, pp. 518-522). IEEE.*

Wang, X., Wu, R., Ma, J., Long, G., & Han, J. (2018). Research on Vulnerability Detection Technology for WEB Mail System. *Procedia Computer Science*, *131*, 124–130. doi:10.1016/j.procs.2018.04.194

Wassermann, G., & Su, Z. (2007, June 10). Sound and precise analysis of web applications for injection vulnerabilities. *SIGPLAN Notices*, *42*(6), 32–41. doi:10.1145/1273442.1250739

Yadav, D., Gupta, D., Singh, D., Kumar, D., & Sharma, U. (2018). *Vulnerabilities and Security of Web Applications.*, *1-5*, 1–5. doi:10.1109/CCAA.2018.8777558

Zhang, Z., Al Hamadi, H., Damiani, E., Yeun, C., & Taher, F. (2022). *Explainable Artificial Intelligence Applications in Cyber Security: State-of-the-Art Research.* 10.48550/arXiv.2208.14937.

Chapter 3
The Link Between Privacy and Disclosure Behavior in Social Networks

Mohammad Daradkeh

ⓘ https://orcid.org/0000-0003-2693-7363

University of Dubai, UAE & Yarmouk University, Jordan

ABSTRACT

Based on the antecedent-privacy concern-outcome (APCO) model of privacy concerns, this study developed a moderated mediation model to investigate the mechanisms by which social media privacy policies (including both privacy policy understanding and perceived effectiveness dimensions) influence self-disclosure. The model was tested in this study using a deductive approach and a quantitative research strategy. In this study, a self-reported questionnaire was used to collect information from social media users. To test the research model and hypotheses, we used multiple regression analysis. According to the results of this study, trust in social media mediated the relationship between privacy policy and self-disclosure, while privacy costs moderated the relationship between privacy policy and trust in social media. Furthermore, the link between privacy policy and self-disclosure is a complex multicollinear model with mediating effects rather than a simple linear model.

INTRODUCTION

The growing popularity of social media as an important communication and information dissemination channels has attracted much attention from both academia and business in recent years. Taddei and Contena (2013) describes social media as interconnected communication platforms where users: (1) publish their personal profiles that include user-supplied media, other user-supplied content, and system-supplied data; (2) interact and connect with other users; and (3) interact with or access user-generated content provided by user associations in social media networks (Ahmed, 2015; Lyngdoh, El-Manstrly, & Jeesha, 2023; McCarthy, Rowan, Mahony, & Vergne, 2023; Smith, Dinev, & Xu, 2011). Social media platforms and other Web 2.0 technologies provide users with convenient and easily accessible ways to interact

DOI: 10.4018/978-1-6684-8133-2.ch003

and disclose personal information not only with their friends and acquaintances, but also with complete and relative strangers with unprecedented openness. This, in turn, has increased people's longevity and ability to share more information about themselves and their relationships with their families and friends through a variety of media, including video, photo, and text, enabling them to build and maintain social and business relationships. However, when using social networks, users often face privacy disclosure risks, leading to increasingly serious privacy threats, including privacy disclosure and privacy sharing without the user's consent; as a result, users are becoming more cautious about disclosing private information (Ampong et al., 2018; Arpaci, 2020; Bandara, Fernando, & Akter, 2020; Klostermann, Meißner, Max, & Decker, 2023; Lane, Ramirez, & Patton, 2023). According to Brown (2020), nearly half of Internet users were affected by cybersecurity incidents in the first half of 2020, of which 23.3% were due to personal data disclosure (Cottrill, Jacobs, Markovic, & Edwards, 2020; Hong, Hu, & Zhao, 2023; Khan, Ikram, Murtaza, & Asadi, 2023). To address this issue, social media platforms often protect users' privacy and related rights by publishing privacy policies. Privacy policies include a set of procedures for managing and protecting users' personal data, as well as establishing basic rights and obligations, with the aim of reducing perceived risks arising from users' transactions with the platform (Amon et al., 2023; Choi, 2023; Dhir, Talwar, Kaur, Budhiraja, & Islam, 2021).

Previous research on social media has examined various features and capabilities that promote self-disclosure (Cain & Imre, 2022; Cerruto, Cirillo, Desiato, Gambardella, & Polese, 2022; Dhir et al., 2021; Dienlin & Trepte, 2015; Gioia & Boursier, 2021; Taddei & Contena, 2013), weighed the costs and benefits of privacy measures, and highlighted concerns about privacy and the extent of control over information collected from users (Gupta & Dhami, 2015; Ireland, 2020). Nevertheless, there is a paucity of research that addresses the determinants and motivators of self-disclosure behavior from a privacy and information flow perspective. Previous studies (Ahmed, 2015; Alkis & Kose, 2022; Arica et al., 2022; Guo, Wang, & Wang, 2021; Gupta & Dhami, 2015; Ireland, 2020) have examined only a few variables limited to a specific social network such as Facebook. In their theoretical Antecedent-Privacy Concern-Outcome (APCO) model, Smith et al. (2011) propose that privacy policies are positively associated with self-disclosure. Although the APCO model provides a systematic explanation of the influence mechanism of privacy policies and self-disclosure, it is limited to the unidirectional path "privacy policies → trust → self-disclosure" and lacks an explanation of the influence mechanism of privacy policies (Chan, 2021; Dienlin & Trepte, 2015; Gruzd & Hernández-García, 2018; Venkatesh, Hoehle, Aloysius, & Nikkhah, 2021; Zhen, Nan, & Pham, 2021). Therefore, to understand the influence mechanism of privacy policies and self-disclosure in the context of social media use, it is necessary to further elaborate the mechanism, including the policies and practices related to the collection, use, processing, storage, transfer and disclosure of personal data. To explore this mechanism in depth, this study divides privacy policy into two dimensions: privacy policy understanding and perceived effectiveness, conceptualizes a research framework based on privacy theory, incorporates the moderating variable of privacy cost, and examines the interaction mechanism with self-disclosure.

The purpose of this study is to empirically examine the relationship between social media privacy policies and user self-disclosure and determine whether this relationship is mediated by trust in social media, taking into account the moderating effect of privacy costs. To this end, this study used a deductive approach and quantitative research design by developing a moderated meditation model and empirically testing hypotheses that establish a relationship between social media policies and user self-disclosure. Data were collected from 212 social media users using a self-administered questionnaire. Stepwise multiple regression and regression-based path analysis were used to test the research model and hypotheses. The results of the study show that trust in social media has a mediating effect between privacy policies and self-disclosure. Privacy costs play a moderating role between perceived understanding and effectiveness of privacy policies and trust in social media. When users' perceived privacy costs are low, the understanding and effectiveness of privacy policies promotes self-disclosure through trust in social media. Based on these findings, this study shows that the influence path of privacy policies and self-disclosure is not a simple linear model, but a complex multi-linear model with mediated effects. This study fills the gaps in the literature by providing empirical evidence of the influence of privacy policies on self-disclosure and examines the factors that influence self-disclosure decisions on social media platforms. It also provides practical guidance for network and online service providers to predict factors that encourage users to disclose more about themselves and share information on their social media profiles.

The remainder of this study is organized as follows. The next section provides a brief literature review of social media privacy policies and their impact on user self-disclosure, followed by a detailed discussion of the research model and hypothesis development. Then, the methodology, results, and discussions of the study are presented. Finally, the study concludes with the results of the study, implications for research and practice, and suggestions for future research.

LITERATURE REVIEW

Cybersecurity and IT Security

Cybersecurity is the practice used to protect critical systems and sensitive information from digital attacks. Also known as information technology (IT) security, cybersecurity measures are designed to combat threats to networked systems and applications, whether they originate inside or outside the enterprise. In 2020, the average cost of a data breach globally was $3.86 million, compared with $8.64 million in the United States. These costs include the cost of detecting and responding to data breaches, downtime costs and lost revenue, and long-term damage to the reputation of the business and its brand. Cybercriminals target customers' personally identifiable information (PII), including names, addresses, ID numbers (eg, Social Security numbers in the U.S., fiscal codes in Italy), and credit card information, and then sell these records on underground digital marketplaces . A breach of PII often results in a loss of customer trust, regulatory fines, and even legal action. Complex security systems created by disparate technologies and a lack of in-house expertise can amplify these costs. And businesses with a comprehensive cybersecurity strategy, managed through best practices and automated using advanced analytics, artificial intelligence (AI), and machine learning, can more effectively combat cyberthreats and can shorten their lifecycle in the event of a data breach and reduce impact.

A robust cybersecurity strategy provides multiple layers of protection against cybercrime, including cyberattacks that attempt to access, alter or destroy data; extort money from users or businesses; or aim to disrupt normal business operations. The countermeasures taken should address the following aspects:

- **Critical Infrastructure Security** - These practices are used to protect computer systems, networks, and other assets that society relies on for national security, economic health, and/or public safety. The National Institute of Standards and Technology (NIST) created a cybersecurity framework to assist organizations in the field, while the U.S. Department of Homeland Security (DHS) provided additional guidance.

- **Network Security** - Security measures used to protect computer networks from intruders, including wired and wireless (Wi-Fi) connections.
- **Application Security** - Processes that help protect applications running on-premises and in the cloud. Security should be built into the application at the design stage, considering how data is handled, user authentication, etc.
- **Cloud security** - specifically refers to true confidential computing for encryption of cloud data at rest (in storage), in motion (in transit to, from and in the cloud) and in use (while processing), This safeguards customer privacy and meets business requirements and compliance standards.
- **Information Security** - Data protection measures, such as the General Data Protection Regulation (GDPR), protect your most sensitive data from unauthorized access, exposure or theft.

End User Education - Build security awareness across the enterprise and strengthen endpoint security. For example, users can be trained to delete suspicious email attachments, avoid unknown USB devices, etc.

- **Disaster Recovery/Business Continuity Planning** - Tools and procedures for responding to unplanned events (such as natural disasters, power outages, or cybersecurity incidents) with minimal disruption to critical operations.

Social Media Privacy Law and Internet Literacy

With the popularity of smartphones, advances in media technology and social life, social media is playing an increasingly important role in people's lives. As recording and sharing become the norm, so do issues of personal information security. In 2018, the Facebook data breach erupted when London-based political consultancy Cambridge Analytica was accused of using the personal information of 50 million users obtained from it to influence the UK's EU referendum and the US election. In the same year, the China Consumers Association conducted an assessment of personal information collection and privacy policies of 100 APPs and found that all communication and social networking software allegedly collected or used personal information excessively, especially location information, Internet access records and other information most prominently.

Faced with the changing status of personal information in social life, many legal scholars believe that the concept of privacy is no longer sufficient to cover the protection of personal information, and the status of the right to personal information needs to be clarified in the legal system. Under the imperfection of existing laws and regulations, the user service agreements formulated by social media service providers have become an important basis for the protection of personal information rights and have great value for textual analysis.

The traditional right to privacy is the result of balancing the conflict between individual interests and public interests. With the advent of the information age, the economic value of personal information has become an integral part of the public interest, and the concept of privacy is no longer sufficient to cover the protection of personal information. This paper analyzes the user service agreements of six domestic and foreign social media, including WeChat, Facebook, Weibo, Twitter, Douban and Instagram, from the perspective of the "right to personal information" advocated by the legal profession to ensure the protection of their personal information rights. The situation was studied. Different social media are found to have different tendencies and problems in protecting users' personal information rights, and suggestions are made for future legislative directions.

In the United States, the right to privacy is guaranteed by both constitutional and civil law, showing the dual attributes of a constitutional right and a civil right (Lee, Hsiao, Weng, & Chen, 2021). In the field of civil law, Richards and Solove (2010) analyzed a large number of precedents and summarized four types of violations of the right to privacy that should be recognized in the law of tort liability. The constitutional guarantee of citizens' right to privacy is determined by a number of well-known precedents. The Supreme Court has successively banned contraception for couples on the grounds of invasion of citizens' privacy and restricted abortion, banned consensual sex between adults and other state laws have been ruled unconstitutional, and the right to privacy has been considered as "the right to be free from right from government intrusion" (protection from Government intrusion, 1965) (Gruzd & Hernández-García, 2018). In English law, which is also part of the Anglo-American legal system, there is no cause of action for infringement of privacy and the privacy regime is extremely underdeveloped (Y. Li, Guo, & Chen, 2021; Zhou & Liu, 2023; Zulfahmi et al., 2023). The outcome of the Human Rights Convention. The Convention entered into force in 1953 and its ratification was also a necessary condition for accession to the Council of Europe. Article 8 of it is "the right to respect for private and family life" and emphasizes that the intervention of public institutions in this right must be within a legal framework and within the constraints of the public interest. Major European countries such as Germany and France have also made relatively more explicit provisions for the right to privacy in their domestic laws (Liang, Shen, & Fu, 2017; Wei, Gong, Xu, Eeza Zainal Abidin, & Destiny Apuke, 2023; Yi et al., 2023).

Compared with the United States and Europe, the protection of privacy rights in China started late. after the late 1980s, the Supreme People's Court began to make sporadic provisions on privacy protection in the form of various judicial interpretations; since the 1990s, some special legislation in the field of administrative law and social law has also appeared (Graf & Antoni, 2021; Tang & Ning, 2023; van der Schyff & Flowerday, 2023). In 2017, as a milestone in the history of China's legal development event, the General Principles of the Civil Law was promulgated and implemented. Among them, Article 110 formally establishes the right to privacy as a civil right of natural persons, achieving a major breakthrough in the protection of privacy in China.

Various countries, including India, China, and the Middle East, have enacted laws and regulations to address privacy issues on social media. Alongside, internet literacy has also become an important factor in ensuring the safe usage of social media platforms. India has enacted the Personal Data Protection Bill, 2019, which aims to protect the personal data of individuals and establish a regulatory framework for data processing. The bill mandates social media platforms to obtain user consent before collecting and processing their personal data (McCarthy et al., 2023; Nabity-Grover, Cheung, & Bennett Thatcher, 2023). Additionally, the bill also provides individuals with the right to access and control their personal data and allows them to request the deletion of their data from social media platforms. In China, the Cybersecurity Law, 2017, regulates data privacy on social media platforms. The law requires social media platforms to obtain user consent before collecting their personal data and mandates the protection of personal data during its transmission and storage (Sheng, Yang, Han, & Jou, 2023; Tang & Ning, 2023; Wei et al., 2023). Additionally, the law also empowers the government to investigate and penalize social media platforms that violate data privacy regulations. In the Middle East, several countries have enacted laws to regulate data privacy on social media platforms. For example, in Saudi Arabia, the Electronic Transactions and National Address Law, 2007, regulates the collection, processing, and storage of personal data by social media platforms (Khan et al., 2023; Klostermann et al., 2023; Lane et al., 2023). Similarly, in the United Arab Emirates, the Federal Law on Data Protection, 2019, mandates social media platforms to obtain user consent before processing their personal data.

Additionally, Internet literacy has become an essential factor in ensuring the safe usage of social media platforms in India, China, and the Middle East. In India, the government has launched several initiatives to promote internet literacy, including the Digital India campaign, which aims to make India a digitally empowered society (Choi, 2023; Hong et al., 2023). Similarly, in China, the government has implemented the National Cybersecurity Awareness Month campaign to promote internet literacy and cybersecurity (Alkis & Kose, 2022; Amon et al., 2023). In the Middle East, several countries have also launched initiatives to promote internet literacy, including the UAE's National Cybersecurity Strategy, which aims to raise awareness about cybersecurity threats and promote safe internet usage (Amon et al., 2023; Zulfahmi et al., 2023).

Whether it is a privacy regime under the conflict between citizens and government in the United States or a universal model of citizen privacy beyond national borders under the constraints of public interest in Europe (Cerruto et al., 2022; Tang & Ning, 2023; Xie & Kang, 2015), there is clearly an important question of weighing privacy interests. The question is: what is only a matter of individual freedom that does not have to be interfered with by governmental power or disclosed by the mass media. That is, how to adjust the conflict between the individual's privacy interests and the interests of others in freedom of expression and the right to know. In the relationship between the two conflicting rights, the law uses the principle of "public interest" to determine the boundary of the right: any personal privacy that does not involve public interest is protected by law; any privacy that involves public interest is not protected or restricted by law, and it cannot be used as a defense against government power or mass media (Taddei & Contena, 2013).

However, in the information age, this pattern of a dual system of interests has been broken. Although there is still academic debate on whether humanity has entered the information society (Omrani & Soulié, 2020), whether there has been an essential shift from capitalist society to information society (Matthes, Koban, Neureiter, & Stevic, 2021; Mutimukwe, Kolkowska, & Grönlund, 2020), and whether information has been in a productive position for knowledge products in today's socio-economic activities controversial (Arica et al., 2022; Kim, Nan, & Kim, 2021; Lee et al., 2021), but there is no doubt that the value of information is becoming increasingly important in today's society and that personal information is becoming increasingly important. As people become more involved in economic life, the relationship between how to measure the use of personal information and the protection of personal information has become a new legal issue (Alkis & Kose, 2022; Wei et al., 2023).

The pattern of interests has evolved from a dichotomy to a tripartite check and balance. Individuals need to protect information from being used by others, while gaining benefits through independent disclosure and use of their own information; information providers gain economic benefits by collecting personal information, and economic development promotes overall social progress and translates into social public however, excessive collection of personal benefits may also cause damage to individual and national interests; the government collects personal information for social management and improves governance efficiency, a process that also However, excessive collection of personal information may also be detrimental to individual and national interests. Based on this, scholars also advocate distinguishing the concept of "personal sensitive information" from "personal general information. The former focuses on protection and safeguarding the core interests of individuals in personal information protection; the legitimate and reasonable needs of the information industry and the state for the use of personal information (Dhir et al., 2021; Klostermann et al., 2023; Lane et al., 2023).

Social Network Privacy Policies

Privacy policies succinctly explain how the social media platform collects, stores, and shares the personal data it collects. According to Ahmed (2015), privacy policies are an important trust-building resource during the initial interactions between social media platforms and their users. Privacy policies serve as a guide for users, businesses, and government agencies to promote privacy and information security; therefore, improving their quality is a worthwhile effort that can lead to resilient and trustworthy relationships. Current academic discussion of privacy policies relies primarily on textual analysis and speculative, descriptive formulations of privacy concerns. Researchers have found that the privacy policies of various social media platforms still face various problems, such as unclear application and incomplete content (Adu, Mills, & Todorova, 2021; Cain & Imre, 2022; Hong et al., 2023); yet studies on social media privacy practices lack rigorous conclusions about the causal relationship among various factors. Similarly, there are few studies that use quantitative analysis methods to investigate privacy policies and focus on the impact of privacy policies on users. For example, Ahmed (2015) and others applied grounded theory methods and found that the characteristics of privacy policies and the content of privacy policies have a direct influence on the expressions of users of medical advice apps (Alemany, Del Val, & García-Fornes, 2021); however, the framework derived from grounded theory needs further verification.

Early research on social media privacy has emphasized the impact of privacy policies on user behavior, privacy concerns, and self-disclosure (Ampong et al., 2018; Arpaci, 2020; Bandara et al., 2020). Self-disclosure refers to the behavior of users who openly share their personal, intimate information and feelings with others (Baruh, Secinti, & Cemalcilar, 2017). Numerous studies have shown that privacy policies can influence self-disclosure, but scholarly opinion on the relationship between these two aspects is mixed. Current research on users' self-disclosure behavior mainly focuses on personal characteristics and social factors such as psychological needs (Blackhart, Hernandez, Wilson, & Hance, 2021), privacy knowledge and willingness to actively protect (Liang et al., 2017; Masur, 2021; Nemec Zlatolas, Welzer, Heričko, & Hölbl, 2015; Smith et al., 2011; Zulfahmi et al., 2023), subjective well-being (Brown, 2020; Schwartz-Chassidim, Oshrat, Tamir, Ron, & Eran, 2020), and attachment relationships with adults (Chan, 2021; Sharif, Soroya, Ahmad, & Mahmood, 2021). Previous studies have also shown that users who have a positive attitude towards privacy policies are more likely to advocate for themselves (Cottrill et al., 2020). However, some researchers take the opposite view and argue that users who have negative attitudes toward privacy policies still self-disclose (Dhir et al., 2021; Yi et al., 2023). Other researchers argue that privacy policies and self-disclosure intentions are not only correlated, but may also have a mediation effect (Dienlin & Trepte, 2015; McCarthy et al., 2023), such that privacy policies may positively influence users' self-disclosure intentions by increasing their trust (Gioia & Boursier, 2021). Gioia and Boursier (2021) argue that privacy is context-dependent, and we can only answer privacy questions with greater explanatory power if we consider users' online and psychological context. Therefore, an in-depth study of the relationship between privacy policies and self-disclosure can help improve the quality of social media privacy policies and users' online privacy literacy.

Previous studies have examined the relationship between privacy policies and self-disclosure in a simplistic manner, ignoring the context in which privacy policies are adopted. In reviewing the existing literature, it was found that few studies have addressed the broad dimensions of privacy policies. In light of this, this study examines the micro-mechanisms of the relationship between privacy policies and self-disclosure in the context of social media based on the APCO model (Smith et al., 2011) and privacy computing theory (Dienlin & Trepte, 2015) to understand whether the understandability and effectiveness of privacy policies affect users' trust in social media and thus self-disclosure behavior, and whether the mechanisms of privacy policies and self-disclosure operate differently under different privacy costs. By adopting privacy policies and self-disclosure as key factors to explore the mediating role of trust in social media and privacy costs, we attempt to frame privacy costs in a prescriptive mode, which is an original contribution of this study as it relates to the APOC model (Smith et al., 2011) and privacy computing theory (Dienlin & Trepte, 2015).

RESEARCH MODEL AND HYPOTHESIS DEVELOPMENT

In this study, a moderated mediation model is developed to investigate the influence mechanisms between privacy policies and self-disclosure behaviors in the context of social media (see Figure 1).

Figure 1. Research model

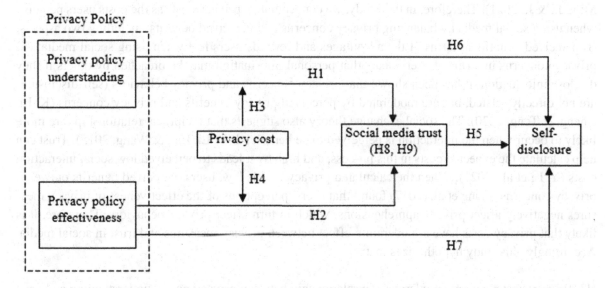

Privacy Policy and Social Media Trust

Trust in social media is one of the outcome indicators for users' evaluation of social media. Empirical studies have shown that the quality of privacy policies can form the basis of users' trust in the platform (Gioia & Boursier, 2021). In addition, researchers have examined the perceived effectiveness (Graf & Antoni, 2021), perceived clarity (Gruzd & Hernández-García, 2018), degree of permission (Gruzd & Hernández-García, 2018), degree of protection (Daradkeh, 2021), perceived authenticity, and understanding of notification (Guo et al., 2021) of privacy policies. Gupta and Dhami (2015) argued that social media operators should consider both user understanding and perceived effectiveness of privacy policies when developing high-quality privacy policies and practices. In this study, we aim to measure the holistic perception of privacy policies by examining users' understanding and perceived effectiveness of privacy policies. Understanding of privacy policies refers to users' understanding of the literal expression of the policy's content. Privacy policy perceived effectiveness refers to the extent to which users trust that privacy policies posted online by social media platforms accurately and effectively reflect their privacy practices (Ireland, 2020). The more understandable a privacy policy is, the more positive the prediction of users' trust in the platform (Kim et al., 2021). It has also been found that users' understanding of privacy policies is positively related to the perceived effectiveness of privacy policies (Lee et al., 2021). Therefore, this study hypothesizes that:

H1: The better users understand the privacy policy, the more they trust social media.
H2: The more users perceive the privacy policy to be effective, the more they trust social media.

Moderating Effect of Privacy Cost

According to privacy computing theory, users' privacy and self-disclosure behavior is a decision made after weighing perceived benefits and privacy concerns. In previous studies, privacy concerns and perceived benefits are important cost factors in measuring social media usage (J. Li, Zhao H., Hussain S., Ming J., & J., 2021). Therefore, in this study, we conceptualize privacy costs as the costs users perceive when using social media by balancing privacy concerns and perceived benefits, including two aspects: (i) perceived benefits in terms of the advantages and rewards users feel when using social media; (ii) privacy concerns in terms of users' fears that personal information may be breached by others if they disclose information. It has been shown that privacy concerns and privacy behaviors (self-disclosure) are not directly related, but are moderated by perceived privacy benefits and privacy concerns (K. Li, Cheng, & Teng, 2020). The social exchange theory also suggests that reciprocal relationships are more likely to occur when the interaction is perceived to be beneficial (K. Li, Lin, & Wang, 2015). Trust can help calculate the expected costs in this process, and high trust leads to perceived low social interaction costs (Y. Li et al., 2021). When the calculated privacy cost is low, users' perceived benefits outweigh privacy concerns. Liang et al. (2017) found that users' perceptions of the effectiveness of privacy measures negatively affect privacy apprehensions, which in turn affect privacy behaviors. Therefore, it is likely that privacy costs have a moderating effect between privacy measures and trust in social media. Accordingly, this study hypothesizes that:

H3: Privacy cost positively moderates the relationship between privacy policy understanding and trust in social media.
H4: Privacy cost positively moderates the relationship between perceived effectiveness of privacy policies and trust in social media.

Mediating Effect of Social Network Trust

Previous research on social media has found that the willingness, extent, and volume of self-disclosure increase when users have higher levels of trust in social media (Lin, Chou, & Huang, 2021). This influence relationship can be direct (Masur, 2021) or indirect (Masinde, Khitman, Dlikman, & Graffi, 2020). To increase user activity, social media must first gain users' trust, and an easily understood privacy policy can positively predict users' trust in a social media platform (Matthes et al., 2021). Studies have also shown that social media platforms can effectively reduce users' perceived privacy risks by developing reliable privacy policies that encourage self-disclosure (Mutimukwe et al., 2020). Moreover, trust in social media has been found to be significantly related to privacy risk perception (Nemec Zlatolas et al., 2015; Spiliotopoulos & Oakley, 2021; Thompson & Brindley, 2021), and the trajectory between privacy policy, trust, and self-disclosure in Smith's theoretical APCO model (Smith et al., 2011) is shown to be "privacy policy → trust → self-disclosure". Therefore, this study hypothesizes that:

H5: The greater users' trust in social media, the higher the level of self-disclosure.
H6: Trust in social media mediates the relationship between understanding of privacy policies and self-disclosure.
H7: Trust in social media mediates the relationship between perceived effectiveness of privacy policies and self-disclosure.

Based on the previous discussion of moderating and mediating effects, the analysis and hypotheses suggest that users' understanding and perceived effectiveness of privacy policies positively predict users' trust in social media, and trust in social media positively influences self-disclosure when privacy processing costs are low. Moreover, privacy processing costs further attenuate the effect of trust in social media between privacy policy understanding and self-disclosure or perceived privacy policy effectiveness and self-disclosure, i.e., there is a moderated mediation effect. The strength of this mediation effect may be influenced by the cost of privacy, as users' understanding of the content and perceived effectiveness of privacy policies may increase self-disclosure by increasing trust in social media. In particular, when the computational cost of privacy is low, users believe that the benefits of the privacy transaction outweigh the drawbacks and are therefore more likely to accept the privacy policies provided by social media (Omrani & Soulié, 2020; Pizzi & Scarpi, 2020), understand the content of the privacy policies, and acknowledge the effectiveness of the privacy policies. At this point, the social media platform is perceived as a worthwhile transaction, so trust in it increases and the end user's level of self-disclosure increases. Therefore, this study hypothesizes the following:

H8: When privacy costs are low, perceived understanding of privacy policies may promote self-disclosure by increasing trust in social media.
H9: When privacy costs are low, perceived effectiveness of privacy policies may promote self-disclosure by increasing trust in social media.

RESEARCH METHODOLOGY

Questionnaire Design

Data were collected using a questionnaire survey conducted between April and August 2021. The questionnaire survey included five main constructs and a separate section on demographics and social media use. To improve content validity, the current study adopted measurement items from previous studies. However, the items were reworded to fit the context of the current study. Privacy policy understanding (PPU) was measured with four items adapted from Sharif et al. (2021), and privacy policy effectiveness (PPE) items were derived from Sindermann, Schmitt, Kargl, Herbert, and Montag (2021). Social media trust (SMT) was measured with five items derived from Smith et al. (2011) and Taddei and Contena (2013). Privacy cost (PC) was measured using eight items derived from Spence, Lin, Lachlan, and Hutter

(2020). Finally, self-disclosure (SD) was measured using five items derived from Taddei and Contena (2013). The constructs and corresponding items used in this study are listed in Table 1. All measures were presented in English and rated on a five-point Likert scale ranging from "strongly disagree" (1) to "strongly agree" (5). The questionnaire was collected online from various social media users using a snowball sampling method. The total sample size was 298, and after excluding incomplete or incorrect surveys, 212 valid samples remained for analysis.

Table 1. Constructs and associated measures

Construct		Measurement item	Source
Privacy Policy Understanding (PPU)	PPU1	I can understand the content of the privacy policy relatively well	(Sharif et al., 2021)
	PPU2	There is nothing in the privacy policy that confuses me	
	PPU3	I do not think there is anything in the privacy policy that I do not understand	
	PPU4	I do not think the privacy policy uses language that is difficult or confusing to understand	
Privacy Policy Effectiveness (PPE)	PPE 1	I think the privacy policy focuses on protecting the privacy of users	(Sindermann et al., 2021)
	PPE 2	I believe the privacy policy is effective	
	PPE 3	Through the privacy policy, I trust social media to keep my personal information confidential	
	PPE 4	I think the privacy policy is sound and needs no improvement	
Social Media Trust (SMT)	SMT1	I think social media is trustworthy	(Smith et al., 2011)
	SMT2	I think social media will protect my private information	
	SMT3	I believe that social media will not misuse my personal information	
	SMT4	I believe that social media will be truthful and responsible in accordance with the content of the privacy policy	
	SMT5	I believe that the private information I share on social media is safe	
Privacy cost (PC)	PC1	I think posting personal information on social media is useful for my life	(Spence et al., 2020)
	PC2	I think that posting personal information on social media helps to create a good personal image for me	
	PC3	I think posting personal information on social media helps me to improve my relationship with my friends	
	PC4	I think posting personal information on social media is useful to help others get to know me better	
	PC5	I believe that submitting personal information on social media is dangerous	
	PC6	There is a risk that personal information submitted on social media will be leaked	
	PC7	Social media asks for too much of my personal information	
	PC8	I think there is a risk that personal information submitted on social media will be used inappropriately	
Self-disclosure (SD)	SD1	I usually reveal my personal information in social media	(Taddei & Contena, 2013)
	SD2	I leave my personal information in social media such as my friends' circle and family	
	SD3	I share a variety of personal topics on social media	
	SD4	I share information such as personal photos, address location, etc. on social media	
	SD5	I don't mind putting my personal information on social media	

Descriptive Statistics

Table 2 shows the demographic data of the respondents. The sample in this study has a relatively balanced proportion of both genders, 57% men and 43% women. The age group is predominantly young, with 58% of respondents aged 16-24 and 42% aged 25-40, which is consistent with the findings of Gioia and Boursier (2021) sample that found 61% of social media users are aged 16-34 and that those under 34 remain the most important market segment. In addition, 74.1% of study participants have been using social media for more than a year. This indicates that the majority of study participants in this study have been using social media for a relatively long time and are able to better understand the context of this study and complete the questionnaire based on their personal experiences of using social media in their daily lives.

Table 2. Demographic data of respondents

Profile	Measurements	Frequency	Percent
Gender	Male	121	57%
	Female	91	43%
Age range	<18	46	22%
	18-24	76	36%
	25-30	53	25%
	31-40	37	17%
Level of Study	High School graduates	33	16%
	Undergraduate	124	58%
	Postgraduate	55	26%
Privacy settings for sharing my private information in social media	Friends only	62	29%
	Friends and their friends	47	22%
	Public	74	35%
	Don't know	29	14%
Frequency of self-disclosure	Several times a day	78	37%
	Once a day	53	25%
	Once a week	36	17%
	Bi-weekly	23	11%
	Once a month	22	10%

MODEL VALIDATION

Model Path Analysis

In this study, data were analyzed using SPSS software, and Cronbach's alpha, composite reliability (CR), and average variance extracted (AVE) were used to test the reliability and validity of the constructs and their associated measures (Fornell & Larcker, 1981; Hair, Hult, Ringle, & Sarstedt, 2017; Hair, Risher,

Sarstedt, & Ringle, 2019). As shown in Table 3, the Kaiser-Meyer-Olkin (KMO) measure for each construct was greater than 0.7, the α-value was greater than 0.5, the AVE value was greater than 0.5, and the CR value was greater than 0.6. In addition, the results in Table 4 show that the square root of the AVE for each construct is greater than the cross-correlation with other constructs, indicating good reliability, convergent validity, and discriminant validity of the study constructs.

Table 3. Construct reliability, convergent validity, and discriminant validity

Construct	Item	Item loading	KMO	CR	Cronbach's α
Privacy Policy Understanding (PPU)	PPU1	0.907	0.71	0.74	0.72
	PPU2	0.923			
	PPU3	0.894			
	PPU4	0.760			
Privacy Policy Effectiveness (PPE)	PPE 1	0.758	0.74	0.81	0.77
	PPE 2	0.814			
	PPE 3	0.883			
	PPE 4	0.877			
Social Network Trust (SNT)	SNT1	0.936	0.78	0.82	0.74
	SNT2	0.763			
	SNT3	0.727			
	SNT4	0.813			
	SNT5	0.894			
Self-disclosure (SD)	SD1	0.799	0.84	0.86	0.68
	SD2	0.794			
	SD3	0.873			
	SD4	0.883			
	SD5	0.891			
Privacy cost (PC)	PC1	0.759	0.81	0.83	0.72
	PC2	0.806			
	PC3	0.786			
	PC4	0.729			
	PC5	0.659			
	PC6	0.727			
	PC7	0.802			
	PC8	0.841			

The Enter method of multiple regression in IBM SPSS was used in this study to investigate the causal relationship between the constructs of the study, estimate the path coefficients, and test their significance. As shown in Figure 2, hypotheses H1, H2, and H5 were supported, i.e., understanding privacy policies positively affects trust in social media, perceived effectiveness of privacy policies positively affects trust in social media, and trust in social media positively affects self-disclosure.

Table 4. Square root of the average variance extracted (AVE) and correlations matrix

Construct	AVE	1	2	3	4	5
1. Privacy Policy Understanding	0.66	**0.812***				
2. Privacy Policy Effectiveness	0.76	0.512	**0.872****			
3. Social Network Trust	0.62	0.411	0.511	**0.787****		
4. Self-disclosure	0.63	0.345	0.502	0.389	**0.794****	
5. Privacy cost	0.59	0.452	0.413	0.334	0.566	**0.768****
*p <0.05,**p <0.01,***p <0.001						

Figure 2. Path coefficients

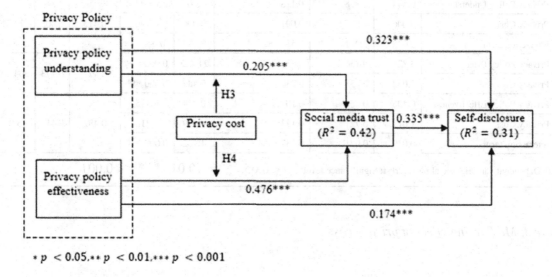

$*p < 0.05,**p < 0.01,***p < 0.001$

Moderated Mediation Effect

As shown in Table 5, the interaction term between privacy policy understanding and privacy cost is significant ($t = 2.894$, $p = 0.003 < 0.01$). The interaction term between perceived effectiveness of privacy policy and privacy cost is significant ($t = 4.803$, $p = 0.000 < 0.01$); therefore, there is a moderating effect of privacy cost in the model; accordingly, hypotheses H3 and H4 are supported. Figure 3 shows that the moderating effect of privacy cost is positive in all scenarios.

As shown in Table 6, the mediation effect of social media trust was significant, with a mediation effect of 80.776% for social media trust between privacy policy understanding and self-disclosure. The mediation effect between perceived effectiveness of privacy policies and self-disclosure was 78.2%; thereby H6 and H7 were supported.

In this study, we used the bootstrapping method to test for a moderated mediation effect. As shown in Table 7, the interaction term between privacy policy understanding and privacy cost has a significant effect on social media trust, while the effect of social media trust on self-disclosure remains significant, with a nonzero confidence interval. The moderated mediation effect of privacy costs is significant; therefore, H8 was supported. The interaction term between perceived effectiveness of privacy policies and privacy costs had a significant effect on trust in social media, while the effect of trust in social media on self-disclosure remained significant, with a nonzero confidence interval. The mediating effect of privacy costs on self-disclosure was significant, supporting H9.

Table 5. Moderating effect of privacy cost

	Model	Unstandardized coefficients		Standardized coefficients	t	Sig.	Adjusted R²	ΔR²	ΔF
		β	Std Dev	Beta					
1	Privacy Policy Understanding	3.037	0.148	0.463	18.156	0.000 ***	0.408	0.410	288.914
	Privacy Cost	2.522	0.249	0.315	11.192	0.000 ***			
2	Privacy Policy Understanding	0.544	0.838	0.118	0.705	0.423	0.415	0.408	7.921
	Privacy Cost	0.006	0.827	0.001	0.006	0.996			
	Interaction term	0.038	0.021	0.511	2.894	0.003 **			
3	Privacy Policy Effectiveness	3.32	0.136	0.633	21.442	0.000 ***	0.471	0.473	364.808
	Privacy Cost	2.082	0.233	0.236	9.487	0.000 ***			
4	Privacy Policy Effectiveness	0.406	0.680	0.101	0.714	0.475	0.482	0.412	15.015
	Privacy Cost	1.013	0.721	0.123	1.169	0.216			
	Interaction term	0.039	0.021	0.637	4.702	0.000 ***			

Note: Dependent variable: social media trust; Significance level: $*p < 0.05$, $**p < 0.01$, $***p < 0.001$

Figure 3. Moderating effect of privacy cost

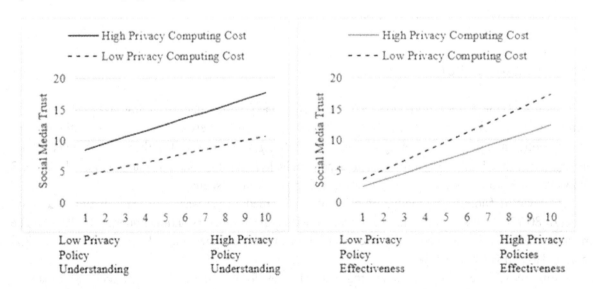

Note: The high privacy cost value is 1 and the low privacy cost value is -1.

Table 6. Mediating effect of social media trust

Outcome	Predictor	Significance of coefficients		Goodness-of-Fit indicators	
		t	p	R^2	F
Self-disclosure	Social Media Trust	7.032	0.000	0.352	61.431
	Privacy Policy Understanding	2.465	0.131		
Self-disclosure	Social Media Trust			0.238	61.047
	Privacy Policy Understanding	6.869	0.000		
Social Media Trust	Social Media Trust			0.322	342.15
	Privacy Policy Understanding	18.342	0.000		
Self-disclosure	Social Media Trust	7.348	0.000	0.351	95.489
	Privacy Policy Effectiveness	2.525	0.094		
Self-disclosure	Social Media Trust			0.403	110.162
	Privacy Policy Effectiveness	11.476	0.000		
Social Media Trust	Social Media Trust			0.419	512.614
Self-disclosure	Social Media Trust	7.356	0.000	0.351	86.598

Table 7. Moderated mediating effect

Regression model				Significance		Mediation Test		Goodness-of-Fit	
Outcome	Predictor	Coeff	SE	t	p	LLCI	ULCI	R	R^2
Social Network Trust	Privacy policy understanding	0.514	0.035	17.428	0.000	0.435	0.583	0.520	0.518
	Privacy cost	0.442	0.037	8.501	0.000	0.320	0.554		
	Interaction item	0.151	0.042	2.677	0.005	0.044	0.182		
Self-disclosure	Social Network Trust	0.355	0.047	8.032	0.000	0.355	0.466	0.402	0.382
	Privacy Policy Understanding	0.192	0.053	1.364	0.131	-0.021	0.115		
Social Network Trust	Privacy policy effectiveness	0.522	0.024	18.661	0.000	0.405	0.628	0.554	0.524
	Privacy cost	0.335	0.048	8.737	0.000	0.335	0.433		
	Interaction item	0.103	0.045	3.585	0.000	0.094	0.208		
Self-disclosure	Social network trust	0.336	0.046	7.752	0.000	0.335	0.448	0.451	0.408
	Privacy policy effectiveness	0.082	0.054	1.349	0.134	-0.023	0.241		

RESEARCH FINDINGS AND IMPLICATIONS

Based on the theoretical foundation of the APCO model, this study integrates privacy costs into the context of "privacy policy → trust → self-disclosure" and validates the mediating role of trust in social media and the moderating role of privacy costs by dividing and operationalizing the dimensions of privacy policy into privacy policy understanding and privacy policy effectiveness. In this way, a moderated mediation model is constructed that makes a valuable contribution to the study of privacy policies and practices in social media. Two variables, privacy policy understanding and perceived privacy policy effectiveness, extend privacy policy and allow the impact of privacy policy on user self-disclosure to be measured at a finer scale.

The results of this study and their implications for research and practice are discussed below:

First, the results of this study show that a better understanding of privacy policies and a better perception of their effectiveness positively influence trust in social media, with the latter having a greater impact. Privacy policies often demonstrate social media's ability and commitment to privacy, and when users' understanding of privacy policies is deepened and their perceived effectiveness is improved, users' trust in social media increases. Therefore, social media companies can adopt various methods to improve users' understanding and perception of the effectiveness of privacy policies, such as bold key content and interactive reading sessions to improve privacy policies to increase users' trust (Xie & Kang, 2015; Zhen et al., 2021).

Second, the moderating effect of privacy cost on the relationship between privacy policy and trust in social media is significant. This study confirms the moderating role of privacy costs, which compensates for the neglect of this aspect in the APCO model and fully reflects the contextualization of social media use. The direct predictive influence of privacy policy understanding and perceived effectiveness on trust in social media is more significant when privacy costs are low, i.e., perceived benefits outweigh privacy concerns, which have a stronger moderating effect. The vast majority of consumers are pragmatic about privacy and maximize their personal interests by making rational choices (Varnali & Toker, 2015; Venkatesh et al., 2021). Rational choices motivate users to evaluate the reliability of online service providers based on market logic. Based on rationality, privacy computing theory interprets privacy issues as individuals achieving a certain utility exchange by allocating private information (Thompson & Brindley, 2021; Toader et al., 2020; Trepte et al., 2015), and privacy costs can play a moderating role between privacy issues and behavioral responses to privacy (Xiao, Lu, & Guo, 2020; Xie & Kang, 2015; Zhen et al., 2021). In this study, we consider privacy policies as a concrete manifestation of the privacy issue and social media trust as a behavioral response. Engagement with a privacy policy is the first step in a user's interaction with social media when the privacy policy is given as a transactional policy for both. If the privacy policy matches the user's interests and security needs, social media can be initially trusted and the transaction will occur. This result helps to strengthen the theoretical link between the APCO model and self-disclosure, and enriches and extends the research on social media privacy (Thompson & Brindley, 2021; Trepte et al., 2015).

Third, unlike previous studies, this study examines not only the direct relationship between users' perception of privacy policies and trust, but also the mediating effect of trust in social media between privacy policies and self-disclosure. The mediating effect suggests that users who understand social media's privacy policy description and structural risk assessment promises are more likely to trust social media's competence and contract fidelity, and thus perceive the strength of social media's privacy protection through privacy policies to build trust in social media and eventually self-disclose. The mediation effect of trust in social media is more significant than the mediation effect of perceived privacy policy effectiveness between privacy policy understanding and self-disclosure. By informing users about the use and processing protocols of private information through privacy policies, users' privacy concerns are reduced and trust in social media gradually increases, which in turn influences self-disclosure. This shows that in the APCO model, not only privacy concerns but also trust in social media can play a mediating role. This highlights the need to further expand the APCO model to include privacy and trust in social media (Toader et al., 2020; Varnali & Toker, 2015; Venkatesh et al., 2021; Xiao et al., 2020).

LIMITATIONS

While the current study has produced some interesting results that support previous studies, there are a number of limitations that must be considered when interpreting and generalizing the results. First, the influence of public perception on privacy policy attitudes and self-disclosure is considered, but the question of whether social norms, culture, and other extrinsic environmental factors also influence public evaluation of privacy policies is ignored; therefore, the inclusion of extrinsic environmental factors in the study is a possible direction for future research. Second, the effectiveness of users' understanding and perceptions of privacy policies was hypothesized to have a positive impact on trust in social media, and the study data support this hypothesis. However, the question of whether trust in social media affects privacy policies has been missing, so the interaction between other variables is also a possible direction for future research. Third, the data were collected from social media users in Jordan. Although this sample represents a fairly typical group of social media users, it is still not representative of all social media users. Fourth, our study used a cross-sectional design. Therefore, as user behavior changes over time, it would be interesting to consider a longitudinal design in future studies. In further studies, researchers could also investigate the interrelationships between factors identified in the current study, such as the impact of privacy breach awareness on privacy issues. Finally, researchers could also examine the moderating effects of gender and age.

CONCLUSION

Based on the APCO theoretical model of privacy concerns, this study examines the mechanism of the impact of social media users' privacy policies (including understanding of privacy policies and perceptions of their effectiveness) on self-disclosure. The results suggest that trust in social media is mediated not only by individual paths but also by the overall model. Trust in social media is positively influenced by the understanding and effectiveness of privacy policies and positively affects self-disclosure behavior. When users feel they know more about privacy policies and understand the value of privacy policies, they are more likely to trust social media's ability to protect privacy, and greater trust in social media in turn promotes self-disclosure behavior. By integrating the APCO model route and privacy computing theory, this study constructs a mediation model that explains how the overall relationship of "privacy policy → trust in social media → self-disclosure" changes depending on users' privacy costs from the perspective of privacy computing theory. This study reveals the influence mechanism of privacy policy and self-disclosure and the context in which they occur, and confirms that social media trust has a catalytic effect, making the relationship between privacy policy and self-disclosure broader and more comprehensive.

REFERENCES

Adu, E., Mills, A., & Todorova, N. (2021). Factors influencing individuals' personal health information privacy concerns. A study in Ghana. *Information Technology for Development*, 27(2), 208–234. doi:1 0.1080/02681102.2020.1806018

Ahmed, A. (2015). Sharing is Caring: Online Self-disclosure, Offline Social Support, and Social Network Site Usage in the UAE. *Contemporary Review of the Middle East*, 2(3), 192–219. doi:10.1177/2347798915601574

Alemany, J., Del Val, E., & García-Fornes, A. (2021). Who should I grant access to my post? Identifying the most suitable privacy decisions on online social networks. *Internet Research*, 31(4), 1290–1317. doi:10.1108/INTR-03-2020-0128

Alkis, A., & Kose, T. (2022). Privacy concerns in consumer E-commerce activities and response to social media advertising: Empirical evidence from Europe. *Computers in Human Behavior*, 137, 107412. doi:10.1016/j.chb.2022.107412

Amon, M., Necaise, A., Kartvelishvili, N., Williams, A., Solihin, Y., & Kapadia, A. (2023). Modeling User Characteristics Associated with Interdependent Privacy Perceptions on Social Media. *ACM Transactions on Computer-Human Interaction*, 30(3), 1–15. doi:10.1145/3577014

Ampong, G., Mensah, A., Adu, A., Addae, J., Omoregie, O., & Ofori, K. (2018). Examining Self-Disclosure on Social Networking Sites: A Flow Theory and Privacy Perspective. *Behavioral Sciences (Basel, Switzerland)*, 8(6), 58–66. doi:10.3390/bs8060058 PMID:29882801

Arica, R., Cobanoglu, C., Cakir, O., Corbaci, A., Hsu, M., & Della Corte, V. (2022). Travel experience sharing on social media: Effects of the importance attached to content sharing and what factors inhibit and facilitate it. *International Journal of Contemporary Hospitality Management*, 34(4), 1566–1586. doi:10.1108/IJCHM-01-2021-0046

Arpaci, I. (2020). What drives students' online self-disclosure behaviour on social media? A hybrid SEM and artificial intelligence approach. *International Journal of Mobile Communications*, 18(2), 229–241. doi:10.1504/IJMC.2020.105847

Bandara, R., Fernando, M., & Akter, S. (2020). Explicating the privacy paradox: A qualitative inquiry of online shopping consumers. *Journal of Retailing and Consumer Services*, 52(1), 101947. doi:10.1016/j.jretconser.2019.101947

Baruh, L., Secinti, E., & Cemalcilar, Z. (2017). Online Privacy Concerns and Privacy Management: A Meta-Analytical Review. *Journal of Communication*, 67(1), 26–53. doi:10.1111/jcom.12276

Blackhart, G., Hernandez, D., Wilson, E., & Hance, M. (2021). The Impact of Rejection Sensitivity on Self-Disclosure Within the Context of Online Dating. *Cyberpsychology, Behavior, and Social Networking*, 24(10), 690–694. Advance online publication. doi:10.1089/cyber.2020.0257 PMID:33606556

Brown, A. (2020). "Should I Stay or Should I Leave?": Exploring (Dis)continued Facebook Use After the Cambridge Analytica Scandal. *Social Media + Society*, 6(1), 2056305120913884. doi:10.1177/2056305120913884

Cain, J., & Imre, I. (2022). Everybody wants some: Collection and control of personal information, privacy concerns, and social media use. *New Media & Society*, 24(12), 2705–2724. doi:10.1177/14614448211000327

Cerruto, F., Cirillo, S., Desiato, D., Gambardella, S., & Polese, G. (2022). Social network data analysis to highlight privacy threats in sharing data. *Journal of Big Data*, *9*(1), 19. doi:10.118640537-022-00566-7

Chan, T. (2021). Does Self-Disclosure on Social Networking Sites Enhance Well-Being? The Role of Social Anxiety, Online Disinhibition, and Psychological Stress. In Z. W. Y. Lee, T. K. H. Chan, & C. M. K. Cheung (Eds.), *Information Technology in Organisations and Societies: Multidisciplinary Perspectives from AI to Technostress* (pp. 175–202). Emerald Publishing Limited. doi:10.1108/978-1-83909-812-320211007

Choi, S. (2023). Privacy Literacy on Social Media: Its Predictors and Outcomes. *International Journal of Human-Computer Interaction*, *39*(1), 217–232. doi:10.1080/10447318.2022.2041892

Cottrill, C., Jacobs, N., Markovic, M., & Edwards, P. (2020). Sensing the City: Designing for Privacy and Trust in the Internet of Things. *Sustainable Cities and Society*, *63*(1), 102453. doi:10.1016/j.scs.2020.102453

Daradkeh, M. (2021). Analyzing Sentiments and Diffusion Characteristics of COVID-19 Vaccine Misinformation Topics in Social Media: A Data Analytics Framework. *International Journal of Business Analytics*, *9*(3), 55–88. doi:10.4018/IJBAN.292056

Dhir, A., Talwar, S., Kaur, P., Budhiraja, S., & Islam, N. (2021). The dark side of social media: Stalking, online self-disclosure and problematic sleep. *International Journal of Consumer Studies*. doi:10.1111/ijcs.12659

Dienlin, T., & Trepte, S. (2015). Is the privacy paradox a relic of the past? An in-depth analysis of privacy attitudes and privacy behaviors. *European Journal of Social Psychology*, *45*(3), 285–297. doi:10.1002/ejsp.2049

Fornell, C., & Larcker, D. (1981). Evaluating structural equation models with unobservable and measurement error. *JMR, Journal of Marketing Research*, *18*(1), 39–50. doi:10.1177/002224378101800104

Gioia, F., & Boursier, V. (2021). Young adults' attitudes toward online self-disclosure and social connection as predictors of a preference for online social interactions: The mediating effect of relational closeness. *Atlantic Journal of Communication*, 1–17. doi:10.1080/15456870.2021.1952205

Graf, B., & Antoni, C. (2021). The relationship between information characteristics and information overload at the workplace - a meta-analysis. *European Journal of Work and Organizational Psychology*, *30*(1), 143–158. doi:10.1080/1359432X.2020.1813111

Gruzd, A., & Hernández-García, Á. (2018). Privacy Concerns and Self-Disclosure in Private and Public Uses of Social Media. *Cyberpsychology, Behavior, and Social Networking*, *21*(7), 418–428. doi:10.1089/cyber.2017.0709 PMID:29995525

Guo, Y., Wang, X., & Wang, C. (2021). Impact of privacy policy content on perceived effectiveness of privacy policy: the role of vulnerability, benevolence and privacy concern. *Journal of Enterprise Information Management*. doi:10.1108/JEIM-12-2020-0481

Gupta, A., & Dhami, A. (2015). Measuring the impact of security, trust and privacy in information sharing: A study on social networking sites. *Journal of Direct, Data and Digital Marketing Practice, 17*(1), 43–53. doi:10.1057/dddmp.2015.32

Hair, J., Hult, G., Ringle, C., & Sarstedt, M. (2017). *A Primer on Partial Least Squares Structural Equation Modeling (PLS-SEM)* (2nd ed.). Sage.

Hair, J., Risher, J., Sarstedt, M., & Ringle, C. (2019). When to use and how to report the results of PLS-SEM. *European Business Review, 31*(1), 2–24. doi:10.1108/EBR-11-2018-0203

Hong, Y., Hu, J., & Zhao, Y. (2023). Would you go invisible on social media? An empirical study on the antecedents of users' lurking behavior. *Technological Forecasting and Social Change, 187*, 122237. doi:10.1016/j.techfore.2022.122237

Ireland, L. (2020). Predicting Online Target Hardening Behaviors: An Extension of Routine Activity Theory for Privacy-Enhancing Technologies and Techniques. *Deviant Behavior*, 1–17. doi:10.1080/01 639625.2020.1760418

Khan, N., Ikram, N., Murtaza, H., & Asadi, M. (2023). Social media users and cybersecurity awareness: Predicting self-disclosure using a hybrid artificial intelligence approach. *Kybernetes, 52*(1), 401–421. doi:10.1108/K-05-2021-0377

Kim, Y., Nan, D., & Kim, J. (2021). Exploration of the Relationships Among Narcissism, Life Satisfaction, and Loneliness of Instagram Users and the High- and Low-Level Features of Their Photographs. *Frontiers in Psychology, 12*(1), 707074–707074. doi:10.3389/fpsyg.2021.707074 PMID:34512463

Klostermann, J., Meißner, M., Max, A., & Decker, R. (2023). Presentation of celebrities' private life through visual social media. *Journal of Business Research, 156*, 113524. doi:10.1016/j.jbusres.2022.113524

Lane, J., Ramirez, F., & Patton, D. (2023). Defending against social media: Structural disadvantages of social media in criminal court for public defenders and defendants of low socioeconomic status. *Information Communication and Society*, 1–16. doi:10.1080/1369118X.2023.2166795

Lee, Y., Hsiao, C., Weng, J., & Chen, Y.-H. (2021). The impacts of relational capital on self-disclosure in virtual communities. *Information Technology & People, 34*(1), 228–249. doi:10.1108/ITP-11-2018-0541

Li, J., Zhao H., Hussain S., Ming J., & J., W. (2021). The Dark Side of Personalization Recommendation in Short-Form Video Applications: An Integrated Model from Information Perspective Diversity, Divergence, Dialogue. iConference 2021., vol In K. Toeppe, H. Yan, & S. Chu (Eds.), *Lecture Notes in Computer Science*. Springer, Cham.

Li, K., Cheng, L., & Teng, C. (2020). Voluntary sharing and mandatory provision: Private information disclosure on social networking sites. *Information Processing & Management, 57*(1), 102128. doi:10.1016/j.ipm.2019.102128

Li, K., Lin, Z., & Wang, X. (2015). An empirical analysis of users' privacy disclosure behaviors on social network sites. *Information & Management, 52*(7), 882–891. doi:10.1016/j.im.2015.07.006

Li, Y., Guo, Y., & Chen, L. (2021). Predicting Social Support Exchanging among Male Homosexuals Who are HIV-Positive in Social Media Context: The Role of Online Self-Disclosure. *Journal of Homosexuality*, 1–17. doi:10.1080/00918369.2021.1935623 PMID:34110274

Liang, H., Shen, F., & Fu, K. (2017). Privacy protection and self-disclosure across societies: A study of global Twitter users. *New Media & Society*, *19*(9), 1476–1497. doi:10.1177/1461444816642210

Lin, C., Chou, E., & Huang, H. (2021). They support, so we talk: The effects of other users on self-disclosure on social networking sites. *Information Technology & People*, *34*(3), 1039–1064. doi:10.1108/ITP-10-2018-0463

Lyngdoh, T., El-Manstrly, D., & Jeesha, K. (2023). Social isolation and social anxiety as drivers of generation Z's willingness to share personal information on social media. *Psychology and Marketing*, *40*(1), 5–26. doi:10.1002/mar.21744

Masinde, N., Khitman, L., Dlikman, I., & Graffi, K. (2020). Systematic Evaluation of LibreSocial—A Peer-to-Peer Framework for Online Social Networks. *Future Internet*, *12*(9), 140. doi:10.3390/fi12090140

Masur, P. (2021). Understanding the effects of conceptual and analytical choices on 'finding' the privacy paradox: A specification curve analysis of large-scale survey data. *Information Communication and Society*, 1–19. doi:10.1080/1369118X.2021.1963460

Matthes, J., Koban, K., Neureiter, A., & Stevic, A. (2021). Longitudinal Relationships Among Fear of COVID-19, Smartphone Online Self-Disclosure, Happiness, and Psychological Well-being: Survey Study. *Journal of Medical Internet Research*, *23*(9), e28700. doi:10.2196/28700 PMID:34519657

McCarthy, S., Rowan, W., Mahony, C., & Vergne, A. (2023). The dark side of digitalization and social media platform governance: a citizen engagement study. *Internet Research*. doi:10.1108/INTR-03-2022-0142

Mutimukwe, C., Kolkowska, E., & Grönlund, Å. (2020). Information privacy in e-service: Effect of organizational privacy assurances on individual privacy concerns, perceptions, trust and self-disclosure behavior. *Government Information Quarterly*, *37*(1), 101413. doi:10.1016/j.giq.2019.101413

Nabity-Grover, T., Cheung, C., & Bennett Thatcher, J. (2023). How COVID-19 stole Christmas: How the pandemic shifted the calculus around social media Self-Disclosures. *Journal of Business Research*, *154*, 113310. doi:10.1016/j.jbusres.2022.113310 PMID:36188113

Nemec Zlatolas, L., Welzer, T., Heričko, M., & Hölbl, M. (2015). Privacy antecedents for SNS self-disclosure: The case of Facebook. *Computers in Human Behavior*, *45*(1), 158–167. doi:10.1016/j.chb.2014.12.012

Omrani, N., & Soulié, N. (2020). Privacy Experience, Privacy Perception, Political Ideology and Online Privacy Concern: The Case of Data Collection in Europe. [Privacy Experience, Privacy Perception, Political Ideology and Online Privacy Concern: The Case of Data Collection in Europe]. *Revue d'Economie Industrielle*, *172*(4), 217–255. doi:10.4000/rei.9706

Pizzi, G., & Scarpi, D. (2020). Privacy threats with retail technologies: A consumer perspective. *Journal of Retailing and Consumer Services*, *56*(1), 102160. doi:10.1016/j.jretconser.2020.102160

Richards, N., & Solove, D. (2010). Prosser's Privacy Law: A Mixed Legacy. *California Law Review*, *98*(6), 1887–1924.

Schwartz-Chassidim, H., Oshrat, A., Tamir, M., Ron, H., & Eran, T. (2020). Selectivity in posting on social networks: The role of privacy concerns, social capital, and technical literacy. *Heliyon*, *6*(2), e03298. doi:10.1016/j.heliyon.2020.e03298 PMID:32055733

Sharif, A., Soroya, S., Ahmad, S., & Mahmood, K. (2021). Antecedents of Self-Disclosure on Social Networking Sites (SNSs): A Study of Facebook Users. *Sustainability (Basel)*, *13*(3), 1220. doi:10.3390u13031220

Sheng, N., Yang, C., Han, L., & Jou, M. (2023). Too much overload and concerns: Antecedents of social media fatigue and the mediating role of emotional exhaustion. *Computers in Human Behavior*, *139*, 107500. doi:10.1016/j.chb.2022.107500

Sindermann, C., Schmitt, H., Kargl, F., Herbert, C., & Montag, C. (2021). Online Privacy Literacy and Online Privacy Behavior – The Role of Crystallized Intelligence and Personality. *International Journal of Human-Computer Interaction*, *37*(15), 1455–1466. doi:10.1080/10447318.2021.1894799

Smith, H., Dinev, T., & Xu, H. (2011). Information Privacy Research: An Interdisciplinary Review. *Management Information Systems Quarterly*, *35*(4), 989–1015. doi:10.2307/41409970

Spence, P., Lin, X., Lachlan, K., & Hutter, E. (2020). Listen up, I've done this before: The impact of self-disclosure on source credibility and risk message responses. *Progress in Disaster Science*, *7*, 100108. doi:10.1016/j.pdisas.2020.100108

Spiliotopoulos, T., & Oakley, I. (2021). Altruistic and selfish communication on social media: The moderating effects of tie strength and interpersonal trust. *Behaviour & Information Technology*, *40*(3), 320–336. doi:10.1080/0144929X.2019.1688392

Taddei, S., & Contena, B. (2013). Privacy, trust and control: Which relationships with online self-disclosure? *Computers in Human Behavior*, *29*(3), 821–826. doi:10.1016/j.chb.2012.11.022

Tang, Y., & Ning, X. (2023). Understanding user misrepresentation behavior on social apps: The perspective of privacy calculus theory. *Decision Support Systems*, *165*, 113881. doi:10.1016/j.dss.2022.113881

Thompson, N., & Brindley, J. (2021). Who are you talking about? Contrasting determinants of online disclosure about self or others. *Information Technology & People*, *34*(3), 999–1017. doi:10.1108/ITP-04-2019-0197

Toader, D., Boca, G., Toader, R., Măcelaru, M., Toader, C., Ighian, D., & Rădulescu, A. (2020). The Effect of Social Presence and Chatbot Errors on Trust. *Sustainability (Basel)*, *12*(1), 256. doi:10.3390u12010256

Trepte, S., Teutsch, D., Masur, P., Eicher, C., Fischer, M., Hennhöfer, A., & Lind, F. (2015). Do People Know About Privacy and Data Protection Strategies? Towards the "Online Privacy Literacy Scale" (OPLIS). In: Gutwirth S., Leenes R., de Hert P. (eds) Reforming European Data Protection Law. Law, Governance and Technology Series, vol 20. Springer, Dordrecht. . In. doi:10.1007/978-94-017-9385-8_1 van der Schyff, K., & Flowerday, S. (2023). The mediating role of perceived risks and benefits when self-disclosing: A study of social media trust and FoMO. *Computers & Security, 126*, 103071. doi:10.1016/j.cose.2022.103071

Varnali, K., & Toker, A. (2015). Self-Disclosure on Social Networking Sites. *Social Behavior and Personality, 43*(1), 1–13. doi:10.2224bp.2015.43.1.1

Venkatesh, V., Hoehle, H., Aloysius, J., & Nikkhah, H. (2021). Being at the cutting edge of online shopping: Role of recommendations and discounts on privacy perceptions. *Computers in Human Behavior, 121*(1), 106785. doi:10.1016/j.chb.2021.106785

Wei, L., Gong, J., Xu, J., Eeza Zainal Abidin, N., & Destiny Apuke, O. (2023). Do social media literacy skills help in combating fake news spread? Modelling the moderating role of social media literacy skills in the relationship between rational choice factors and fake news sharing behaviour. *Telematics and Informatics, 76*, 101910. doi:10.1016/j.tele.2022.101910

Xiao, L., Lu, Q., & Guo, F. (2020). Mobile Personalized Recommendation Model based on Privacy Concerns and Context Analysis for the Sustainable Development of M-commerce. *Sustainability (Basel), 12*(7), 3036. doi:10.3390u12073036

Xie, W., & Kang, C. (2015). See you, see me: Teenagers' self-disclosure and regret of posting on social network site. *Computers in Human Behavior, 52*(1), 398–407. doi:10.1016/j.chb.2015.05.059

Yi, Y., Zhu, N., He, J., Jurcut, A., Ma, X., & Luo, Y. (2023). A privacy-dependent condition-based privacy-preserving information sharing scheme in online social networks. *Computer Communications, 200*, 149–160. doi:10.1016/j.comcom.2023.01.010

Zhen, L., Nan, Y., & Pham, B. (2021). College students coping with COVID-19: Stress-buffering effects of self-disclosure on social media and parental support. *Communication Research Reports, 38*(1), 23–31. doi:10.1080/08824096.2020.1870445

Zhou, S., & Liu, Y. (2023). Effects of Perceived Privacy Risk and Disclosure Benefits on the Online Privacy Protection Behaviors among Chinese Teens. *Sustainability (Basel), 15*(2), 1657. doi:10.3390u15021657

Zulfahmi, M., Elsandi, A., Apriliansyah, A., Anggreainy, M., Iskandar, K., & Karim, S. (2023). Privacy protection strategies on social media. *Procedia Computer Science, 216*, 471–478. doi:10.1016/j.procs.2022.12.159

Chapter 4
Cyber Threat Migration:
Perpetuating in the Healthcare Sector and Agriculture and Food Industries

Minhaj Akhtar Usmani
Era University, India

Kainat Akhtar Usmani
Integral University, India

Adil Kaleem
NCS Group, Australia

Mohammad Samiuddin
University of Technology and Applied Sciences, Oman

ABSTRACT

'Globalization,' 'industrialization,' 'cyber connectivity,' 'digitalization,' and 'e-commerce' are not fantasy words in today's era. They all amalgamated towards the growth and development of every sector in the country. But as on other side of the coin, cyber security is on the verge of serious threats in digital world. The danger posed by cyber security threats in today's world cannot be understated. The health sector, agriculture, and food and beverage industries are no exemptions. As they all are inter-related, they manage an array of assets, including infrastructure, applications, managed and unmanaged endpoints, mobile devices, and cloud services, all of which can be attacked. Information and cyber security are trending topics. As the security risk is scooping high, different organizations should take steps forward to protect themselves. This chapter focuses on the frightening hikes in incidences of cyber-attacks, and also focuses on major cyber security approaches to minimize the risk of cyber breaches and making these industries flourish like never before.

DOI: 10.4018/978-1-6684-8133-2.ch004

BACKGROUND

In the quest for digitalization, India has become an easy target for cyber-attacks due to poor cyber security. Today, numerous organizations are plagued by cyber-attacks that are advanced, persistent, and which can wreck both operations and reputation of companies, including food companies, agriculture sector and healthcare sector. Companies manage an array of assets, including infrastructure, applications, managed and unmanaged endpoints, mobile devices, and cloud services, all of which can be attacked. Just Food cyber security dashboard tracks data and information on cyber security in the food industry.

In many ways, the risks from cyber threats are no different than the safety risks that food companies mitigate every day. The same practices used to identify and address food-processing risks, such as foreign materials and pathogens, can apply to protecting data essential for processing. These practices call for evaluating the threats, assessing the likelihood of occurrences, and establishing programs for mitigation.

The security risks to food data fall into a few categories: theft, public exposure, data corruption or loss, and data manipulation or falsification. Assessing the likelihood of attack in each category requires identifying malicious actors and how each might benefit from an attack. Is the actor a foreign agent, cyber-criminal, disgruntled employee, a competitive spy, or extremist food activist? How would a bad actor benefit from stealing, exposing, manipulating, or corrupting data? **(Woehl, 2022)**

BASIC TERMS AND DEFINITIONS

Before analyzing deep into the facts and findings related to cyber threats and cyber security it is mandatory to get acquainted with some basic terminology and definitions associated to them.

Cyber Security

Computer security, cyber security, or information technology security (IT security) is the protection of computer systems and networks from attack by malicious actors that may result in unauthorized information disclosure, theft of, or damage to hardware, software, or data, as well as from the disruption or misdirection of the services they provide. **(Schatz *et al.*, 2017)**

Security is of especially high importance for systems that govern large-scale systems with far-reaching physical effects, such as power distribution, elections, and finance. **(Kianpour *et al.*, 2021) (Stevens, 2018)**

Categories of Cyber Security

The 3 major types of cyber security are network security, cloud security, and physical security. The operating systems and network architecture make up the network security. It can include network protocols, firewalls, wireless access points, hosts, and servers.

Cyber security can be further categorized into five distinct types:

1. **Critical infrastructure security.** Critical infrastructure protection is a concept that relates to the preparedness and response to serious incidents that involve the critical infrastructure of a region or nation.

2. **Application security.** Web applications, like anything else directly connected to the Internet, are targets for threat actors. Since 2007, OWASP has tracked the top 10 threats to critical web application security flaws such as injection, broken authentication, misconfiguration, and cross-site scripting to name a few.

3. **Network security.** Network security solutions are designed to identify and block attacks on networks. Solutions include data and access controls such as Data Loss Prevention (DLP), IAM (Identity Access Management), NAC (Network Access Control), NGFW (Next-Generation Firewall), IPS (Intrusion Prevention System), NGAV (Next-Gen Antivirus), Sandboxing, and CDR (Content Disarm and Reconstruction) application controls to enforce safe web use policies.

4. **Cloud security.** A cloud security strategy includes cyber security solutions, controls, policies, and services that help to protect an organization's entire cloud deployment (applications, data, infrastructure, etc.) against attack.

5. **Internet of Things (IoT) security.** IoT security protects Internet of Things (IoT) devices with discovery and classification of the connected devices, auto-segmentation to control network activities, and using IPS as a virtual patch to prevent exploits against vulnerable IoT devices. In some cases, the firmware of the device can also be augmented with small agents to prevent exploits and runtime attacks.

6. **Endpoint Security.** With endpoint security, companies can secure end-user devices such as desktops and laptops with data and network security controls, advanced threat prevention such as anti-phishing and anti-ransomware, and technologies that provide forensics such as endpoint detection and response (EDR) solutions.

7. **Zero-Trust.** The traditional security model is perimeter-focused, building walls around an organization's valuable assets like a castle. Zero trust takes a more granular approach to security, protecting individual resources through a combination of micro-segmentation, monitoring, and enforcement of role-based access controls.

Cyber Threats/Attacks

The threats countered by cyber-security are three-fold:

1. Cybercrime includes single actors or groups targeting systems for financial gain or to cause disruption.
2. Cyber-attack often involves politically motivated information gathering.
3. Cyberterrorism is intended to undermine electronic systems to cause panic or fear.

A **cyberattack** is any offensive operation that targets computer information systems, computer networks, infrastructures, or personal computer devices employed by sovereign states, individuals, groups, societies or organizations and it may originate from an anonymous source. Cyber-attacks can range from installing spyware on a personal computer to attempting to destroy the infrastructure of entire nations.

An **attacker** is a person or process that attempts to access data, functions, or other restricted areas of the system without authorization, potentially with malicious intent.

A **cyber-weapon** is a product that facilitates a cyberattack.

Generations vs Attacks

The cyber threats of today are not the same as even a few years ago. As the cyber threat landscape changes, organizations need protection against cybercriminals' current and future tools and techniques.

The cyber security threat landscape is continually evolving, and, occasionally, these advancements represent a new generation of cyber threats. To date, we have experienced five generations of cyber threats and solutions designed to mitigate them, including:

a) **Gen I (Virus):** In the late 1980s, virus attacks against standalone computers inspired the creation of the first antivirus solutions.

b) **Gen II (Network):** As cyber-attacks began to come over the Internet, the firewall was developed to identify and block them.

c) **Gen III (Applications):** Exploitation of vulnerabilities within applications caused the mass adoption of intrusion prevention systems (IPS)

d) **Gen IV (Payload):** As malware became more targeted and able to evade signature-based defenses, anti-bot and sandboxing solutions were necessary to detect novel threats.

e) **Gen V (Mega):** The latest generation of cyber threats uses large-scale, multi-vectors attacks, making advanced threat prevention solutions a priority.

Each generation of cyber threats made previous cyber security solutions less effective or essentially obsolete. Protecting against the modern cyber threat landscape requires Gen V cyber security solutions.

Types of Cyber Threats/Attacks

Vulnerability is a weakness in design, implementation, operation, information system, system processes, or internal control of an organization. Vulnerabilities can be researched, reverse-engineered, hunted, or exploited using automated tools or customized scripts. The hackers are able to gain illegal access to the systems and cause severe damage to data privacy.

Therefore, cyber security vulnerabilities are extremely important to monitor for the overall security posture as gaps in a network can result in a full-scale breach of systems in an organization.

Below are some of the most common **types of cyber-attacks or vulnerabilities**:

1. **Malware.** Malicious software (malware) installed on a computer can leak any information, such as personal information, business information and passwords, can give control of the system to the attacker, and can corrupt or delete data permanently. **(Bendovschi, 2015)**

2. **Phishing.** Phishing is the attempt of acquiring sensitive information such as usernames, passwords, and credit card details directly from users by deceiving the users by emailing spoofing or instant messaging, and it often directs users to enter details at a fake website whose look and feel are almost identical to the legitimate one asking for personal information, such as login details and passwords which can be used to gain access to the individual's real account on the real website. Phishing attacks can lead to severe losses for their victims including sensitive information, identity theft, companies, and government secrets. **(Alkhalil *et al.*, 2021)**

3. **Man-in-the-middle attack (MITM).** A man in the middle (MITM) attack is a general term for when a perpetrator positions himself in a conversation between a user and an application—either

to eavesdrop or to impersonate one of the parties, making it appear as if a normal exchange of information is underway.

The goal of an attack is to steal personal information, such as login credentials, account details and credit card numbers. Targets are typically the users of financial applications, SaaS businesses, e-commerce sites and other websites where logging in is required.

4. **Distributed Denial-of-Service (DDoS) attack.** Denial of service attacks (DoS) are designed to make a machine or network resource unavailable to its intended users. A distributed denial-of-service (DDoS) attack is a malicious attempt to disrupt the normal traffic of a targeted server, service or network by overwhelming the target or its surrounding infrastructure with a flood of Internet traffic. DDoS attacks achieve effectiveness by utilizing multiple compromised computer systems as sources of attack traffic. Exploited machines can include computers and other networked resources such as IoT devices.

5. **SQL injection.** SQL injection is a code injection technique that might destroy one's database. It is one of the most common web hacking techniques in which there is the placement of malicious code in SQL statements, via web page input. SQL injection usually occurs when one ask a user for input, like their username/userid, and instead of a name/id, the user gives an individual an SQL statement that they will unknowingly run on their database.

6. **Zero-day exploit.** A zero-day (also known as a 0-day) is a computer-software vulnerability that describes recently discovered security vulnerabilities that hackers can use to attack systems. The term "zero-day" refers to the fact that the vendor or developer has only just learned of the flaw – which means they have "zero days" to fix it. A zero-day attack takes place when hackers exploit the flaw before developers have a chance to address it. An exploit taking advantage of a zero-day is called a zero-day exploit, or zero-day attack. **(Guo, *et al.,* 2021).**

7. **DNS Tunnelling.** DNS tunneling involves abuse of the underlying DNS protocol. Instead of using DNS requests and replies to perform legitimate IP address lookups, malware uses it to implement a command and control channel with its handler. DNS's flexibility makes it a good choice for data exfiltration; however, it has its limits.

8. **Business Email Compromise (BEC).** Business email compromise (BEC) is a type of cybercrime where the scammer uses email to trick someone into sending money or divulging confidential company info. The culprit poses as a trusted figure, then asks for a fake bill to be paid or for sensitive data they can use in another scam.

9. **Tampering.** Tampering describes a malicious modification or alteration of data. An intentional but unauthorized act resulting in the modification of a system, components of systems, its intended behavior, or data. So-called Evil Maid attacks and security services planting of surveillance capability into routers are examples. **(Gallagher, 2014)**

10. **Spoofing.** Spoofing is an act of masquerading as a valid entity through the falsification of data (such as an IP address or username), in order to gain access to information or resources that one is otherwise unauthorized to obtain **(Butterfield, 2016).** There are several types of spoofing, including:
    a) **Email spoofing,** is where an attacker forges the sending (From, or source) address of an email.
    b) **IP address spoofing,** where an attacker alters the source IP address in a network packet to hide their identity or impersonate another computing system.

c) **MAC spoofing,** where an attacker modifies the Media Access Control (MAC) address of their network interface controller to obscure their identity, or to pose as another.

d) **Biometric spoofing,** where an attacker produces a fake biometric sample to pose as another user. **(Marcel *et al.,* 2014)**

11. <u>Social engineering.</u> Social engineering, in the context of computer security, aims to convince a user to disclose secrets such as passwords, card numbers, etc. or grant physical access by, for example, impersonating a senior executive, bank, a contractor, or a customer. **(Arcos, 2013)** This generally involves exploiting peoples trust, and relying on their cognitive biases by sending emails to accounting and finance department personnel, impersonating their CEO and urgently requesting some action.

12. <u>Backdoor.</u> A backdoor in a computer system, a cryptosystem or an algorithm, is any secret method of bypassing normal authentication or security controls. They are the flaws in original design or poor configuration, or may be added by an authorized party to allow some legitimate access, or by an attacker for malicious reasons. They are usually discovered by someone who has access to application source code or intimate knowledge of the operating system of the computer.

13. <u>Direct-access attacks.</u> An unauthorized user gaining physical access to a computer is most likely able to directly copy data from it. They may also compromise security by making operating system modifications, installing software worms, keyloggers, covert listening devices or using wireless microphones. Disk encryption and Trusted Platform Module are designed to prevent these attacks.

14. <u>Eavesdropping.</u> Eavesdropping is the act of surreptitiously listening to a private computer conversation (communication), typically between hosts on a network. For instance, programs such as Carnivore and NarusInSight have been used by the Federal Bureau of Investigation (FBI) and NSA to eavesdrop on the systems of internet service providers. TEMPEST is a specification by the NSA referring to these attacks.

15. <u>Multi-vector, polymorphic attacks.</u> Surfacing in 2017, a new class of multi-vector, **(Webroot, 2018)** polymorphic **(Millman, 2017)** cyber threats combined several types of attacks and changed form to avoid cybersecurity controls as they spread.

16. <u>Privilege escalation.</u> Privilege escalation describes a situation where an attacker with some level of restricted access is able to, without authorization, elevate their privileges or access level. For example, a standard computer user may be able to exploit vulnerability in the system to gain access to restricted data; or even become root and have full unrestricted access to a system.

17. <u>Reverse engineering.</u> Reverse engineering is the process by which a man-made object is deconstructed to reveal its designs, code, and architecture, or to extract knowledge from the object; similar to scientific research, the only difference being that scientific research is about a natural phenomenon. **(Eilam, 2005)**

18. <u>Side-channel attack.</u> In Side-channel attack scenarios, the attacker would gather information about a system or network to guess its internal state and as a result access the information which is assumed by the victim to be secure.

MAJOR CYBER SECURITY RISK FACTORS AND LOOPHOLES

There is a need to identify multiple future research directions for cyber security/resilience in supply chains. A conceptual model is developed, which indicates a strong link between information technology, organizational and supply chain security systems. The human/behavioral elements within cyber security risk are found to be critical; however, behavioral risks have attracted less attention because of a perceived bias towards technical (data, application and network) risks. There is a need for raising risk awareness, standardized policies, collaborative strategies and empirical models for creating supply chain cyber-resilience.

Different types of cyber risks and their points of penetration, propagation levels, consequences and mitigation measures are identified. The conceptual model is required to be developed to drive an agenda for future research on supply chain cyber security/resilience.

A multi-perspective, systematic study provides a holistic guide for practitioners in understanding cyber-physical systems. The cyber risk challenges and the mitigation strategies identified support supply chain managers in making informed decisions. **(Ghadge** *et al.***, 2020)**

MAJOR AT-RISK ORGANIZATIONS AND AREAS

The main issue with cyber-attacks is that users and organizations are poorly trained to identify them. Even with the latest security protocols and software in place, it's impossible to fully protect against cyber threats without proper security awareness training.

Financial, health, intellectual, and government information are the most likely to be stolen. This determines which industries are most vulnerable to data breaches. There's an ongoing argument about the ranking, but the five industries at risk of cyber-attacks among them are: Public administration.

1. **FOOD-**Food safety, information and cyber security may not seem to be related topics, nevertheless cyber threats are risks within the value chain. Information and cyber security are trending topics for concern on corporate agendas, becoming a core governance issue for everyone from boards to management.

Food and beverage companies are seen as prime targets, with some notable cases including food companies have the worlds' largest meat producer JBS which underwent a cyber-attack.

Outside of the food industry, cyber-attacks are reported frequently and those that hit the headlines invariably involve corporate giants. Of course, the larger players in the food sector, companies such as the Unilever the Kraft and McDonald's – all have protective systems in place such as reliable security information management systems.

Smaller companies who are suppliers may believe this won't affect them, yet they would be mistaken as a 2022 statistic notes that 99% of cyber-attack claims were from small to medium enterprises. **(Beaty, 2022)**

Food safety, information and cyber security may not seem to be related topics, but some companies have already suffered from attacks. As the risk remains high, companies should take steps to protect themselves. A management system based on international standards such as ISO/IEC 27001 helps companies develop a robust and structured approach to manage risks and protect your company.

The advances in agriculture-related technology have brought along with them an increase in cyber threats. Before the rise of multinational consolidated agribusinesses, much of the world's food was produced by small farmers and ranchers serving a local community. Today the same economies of scale that have fueled the rise of large corporations in other sectors are applied to food production and distribution. These economies of scale are dependent on automation.

Historically the food/ag sector has not been a notable target for cybercriminals. Today, however, threat actors see the world's dependence on a well-established food supply chain as an opportunity to use malware, such as ransomware, as leverage to achieve their nefarious aims.

These aims are commonly financial gain but also include acts of political terrorism and social hacktivism. There is still work to be done in areas where the food/ag sector has been lax in its cyber warehouses.

The world's food supply chain is fragile and dominated by a relatively small number of large food companies. Because cyber threat actors aim to shut down production, thereby threatening people's lives, food production networks and food company business networks are at risk.

Shutting down any massive food production or distribution business creates an intolerable condition that provides the cybercriminal with an insurmountable advantage. Companies and authorities know that they must resolve the situation quickly to avoid societal turmoil. The need for the victim to act soon works to the criminal's advantage. Criminals think that larger businesses have the resources to pay the demands without a second thought, and smaller businesses often lack the necessary updates that are needed to fend off cybercriminals.

Cyber Attacks in Food Sector

The FBI began its notification by listing the dire ramifications of ransomware attacks:

- Financial loss
- Disruption of operations
- Negative effects on the supply chain

Cyber attacks in the food industry can be targeted at anyone in the agriculture sector, including restaurants, large producers, and tiny farms alike. No one is immune from network vulnerabilities that can be used to steal data or render networks unusable. Whether the attacked party chooses to pay or not, these businesses suffer major losses trying to deal with the aftermath.

Some incidences of ransomware attacks in food sector are following:

Loaves & Fishes: Nonprofit food provider Loaves & Fishes offers nutritionally balanced groceries to individuals and families experiencing a short-term crisis through a network of mobile "drive-through" style food distribution sites. In August 2020, they announced that sensitive customer information was exfiltrated during the more widespread Blackbaud attack.

Home Chef: Owned by Kroger Foods, Home Chef is a startup that provides food ingredients, meal kits, and recipes to its customers. Security researchers said in May 2020 that they found usernames and passwords belonging to Home Chef users for sale on the dark web.

Meatpacker, JBS: Over the Memorial Day weekend 2021, the world's largest meat company, JBS, was the victim of a ransomware attack that originated from a criminal group based in Russia. The attack crippled a large portion of the meat supply chain, sending shock waves across the entire food industry. The FBI confirmed that the REvil ransomware was used in the cyberattack. The attack stopped operations at thirteen meat plants, including JBS facilities in Colorado, Iowa, Minnesota, Pennsylvania, Nebraska, and Texas.

Other common incidences are-

A bakery lost access to their services, apps, and files, which halted production and caused a shutdown for about a week.

The network of a global meat processing company was compromised, resulting in the shutdown of some US plants and potential data loss. This ultimately caused a shortage in the meat supply and drove up wholesale prices by 25%.

A farm lost $9 million in lost productivity after being forced to shut down after a ransomware attack.

AGRICULTURE

Experts warn that as an industry, agriculture has a very soft digital underbelly that's easily breached due to very limited investment in cyber security to date.

According to the Harvard Business Review, the amount that companies paid to hackers grew by 300% in 2020. In the first 10 months of 2021, just six ransom ware groups were responsible for breaching the cyber security defenses of 292 organizations. From those attacks, these criminal organizations had tallied up more than $45 million in ransom money.

A malicious cyber-attack in late May 2021 forced the shutdown of all of JBS' beef plants and many of its pork and poultry plants. This attack on the world's largest meat processor spotlighted the vulnerability of another critical American industry. This time, agriculture was the target.

According to Vantage Market Research, the size of the global agricultural robot market is expected to reach $15.93 billion by 2028. That's up from $3.63 billion in 2020 and represents a compound annual growth rate of 20.31% during the forecast period—2021 to 2028.

A private industry notification issued by the FBI's cyber division on Sept. 1 listed five major attacks that occurred in the food sector since November 2020. **(Cubbage, 2022).** The list included everything from a bakery company to well-known beverage company to a large farming operation. Two more attacks—on grain co-ops, Iowa's NEW Cooperative and Minnesota's Crystal Valley—came less than a month after the FBI's warning.

In the last few years, smart farming has become popular and widely adopted. This transition has been accelerated further because of crop productivity and quality benefits while lowering the overall cost. However, this shift towards a connected ecosystem, exposes new attack surfaces, and provides opportunities for attackers to exploit vulnerabilities.

Smart farming also known as precision agriculture is gaining more traction for its promising potential to fulfill increasing global food demand and supply. In a smart farm, technologies and connected devices are used in a variety of ways, from finding the real-time status of crops and soil moisture content to deploying drones to assist with tasks such as applying pesticide spray. However, the use of heterogeneous internet connected devices has introduced numerous vulnerabilities within the smart farm ecosystem. Attackers can exploit these vulnerabilities to remotely control and disrupt data flowing from/to on-field sensors and autonomous vehicles like smart tractors and drones. This can cause devastating consequences especially during a high risk time, such as harvesting, where live-monitoring is critical.

Cyber-attacks on the smart farming infrastructure enables an attacker to remotely control and exploit on-field sensors and autonomous vehicles (tractors, autonomous vehicles, drones, etc.) **(Fig.1(a) & (b))**. Potential agricultural attacks can create an unsafe and unproductive farming environment. For example, exploits that have the ability to destroy an entire field of crops, flood the farmlands, over spray pesticides using smart drones, etc. can cause unsafe consumption as well as economic deterioration. Such attacks in a large coordinated manner, also referred to as **Cyber Agroterrorism (Barreto and Amaral, 2018) (Cupp *et al.*, 2004)**, also have the potential for disrupting the economy of an agriculture-dependent nation.

Sontowski *et al.*, 2020 have demonstrated a Denial of Service (DoS) attack on a smart farm ecosystem. We implemented a Wi-Fi deauthentication attack on the smart farm Wi-Fi network with a Maker Focus ESP8266 Development Board WiFi Deauther Monster, which obstructed a deployed sensor from connecting to the network. In addition, the attack was expanded to the entire network which prevented any smart device from connecting to a central cloud.

This inability to not receive real-time sensor updates can negatively impact the data driven applications and overall functionality of a farm. The demonstration of the Wi-Fi deauthentication attack exposes a weakness of the IEEE 802.11 protocol (2.4 GHz). The ability and ease of carrying out a DoS attack in the precision agriculture ecosystem can have serious implications and a large scale coordinated attack can disrupt national economies.

Figure 1. a) Smart farming conceptual architecture, b) System architecture and attack surface
(Sontowski, et al., 2020)

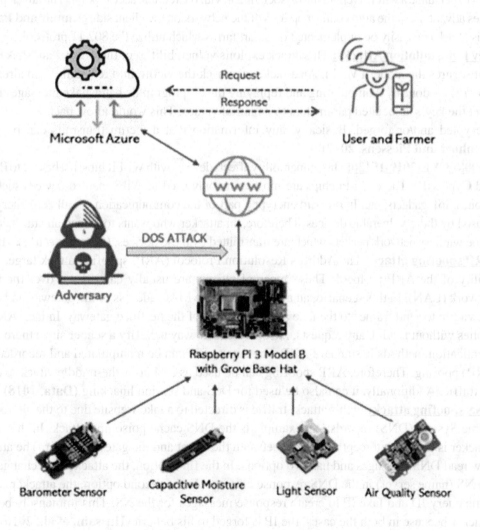

Types of Network Attacks on Smart Farms

In recent years, several security threats (**Wallgren, et al.,** 2013; **Safkhani and Bagheri, 2017; Perazzo et al., 2018; Zhang et al., 2014 and Gautam et al., 2016**) have been observed in IoT domain. Similar attacks can happen on smart farming ecosystem. It is predicted that the attacks on smart farming ecosystem are heavily dependent on the architecture and protocols used in deploying the connected environment. For example, an architecture that uses sensors that work with the Zigbee5 protocol can have additional attacks such as a replay attack that might be difficult to implement on other protocols. The following network attacks listed below can be orchestrated in smart farms that use IEEE 802.116 protocol:

a) **Password Cracking:** Hacking the Wi-Fi encrypted protocols is never a complicated task. One of the most popular ways to do that is by cracking the Wi-Fi password that would exploit the user's network. (**Pimple, 2020**)

b) **Evil Twin Access Point:** The Evil Twin access point allows an attacker to get credentials by creating a rogue access point. The rogue access point is set up on a reliable network without any permission and tries to persuade a wireless client into associating it with the reliable access point. The attack particularly takes advantage of the auto connect options of the network on the client side (**Kumar and Paul, 2016**). This attack can easily be implemented on smart farms which utilize the 802.11 protocol.

c) **Key Reinstallation Attacks:** This attack exploits vulnerabilities of the 4-way handshake in WPA2 that secures the modern Wi-Fi. An attacker can trick the victim into reinstalling an already in use key. This is done by manipulating and replaying the cryptographic handshake messages in order to reset the key's associated parameters to its initial values. This would allow packets to be replayed, decrypted and/or forged. Basically, any information that a victim transmits can be decrypted (**Vanhoef and Piessens, 2017**)

d) **Kr00k - CVE-2019-15126:** This vulnerability affects devices with Wi-Fi chips that belong to Broadcom9 and Cypress10. These Wi-Fi chips are most commonly used in WiFi enabled devices such as smart phones, IoT gadgets, etc. In order to encrypt a part of the communication, an all zero encryption key is used by these vulnerable devices. Therefore, an attacker who wants to launch an attack can decrypt some wireless network packets which are transmitted by these devices. (**Cermak *et al.*, 2019**)

e) **ARP spoofing attack:** The Address Resolution Protocol (ARP) spoofing attack targets a vulnerability of the ARP protocol. These types of attacks are usually carried out over the local area network (LAN). In this scenario, an attacker fakes the MAC address of the gateway and convinces the victim to send frames to the fake address instead of the destined gateway. In fact, ARP accepts replies without issuing any requests. Also, there is no way to verify a sender since there are no authentication methods in standard ARP. The data traffic can be manipulated and recorded by using ARP spoofing. Therefore, ARP spoofing can be used as a Man-in-the-middle attack to eavesdrop on traffic. Additionally, it can also be used for DoS and session hijacking (**Data, 2018**).

f) **DNS spoofing attack:** In this attack, traffic is directed to a fake website due to the altered Domain Name System (DNS) records. An example is the DNS cache poisoning attack. In this attack, the attacker is used to intercept the traffic between the client and the gateway router. The attacker can now read DNS messages and has two options. In the first option, the attacker can change the IP of the NS (name server) in the DNS response message. In the second option, the attacker can use the same query ID and fake IP to create response messages for the NS. This immensely benefits the attacker because in both the cases, the IP is forged to his benefit (**Hussain, et al., 2016**)

HEALTH-CARE INDUSTRIES

The combination of poor cyber security practices, sensitive data storage, and desperation to preserve business continuity at all costs, makes the healthcare industry a prime target for cybercriminals - an inevitability that was further exacerbated by the pandemic.

Phishing is the most prevalent cyber security threat in healthcare. Phishing is the practice of infecting a seemingly innocuous email with malicious links. The most common type of phishing is email phishing.

Cyber-attacks on healthcare have grown across the world as more hospitals and healthcare services providers are moving their operations and databases online. According to cyber security firm Check Point Research, healthcare suffered the highest number of ransomware attacks globally during the September quarter of 2022.

Phishing is one of the most common cyber-threats across the board, with 81% of organizations affected by phishing last year. Healthcare is no exception, and phishing attacks are one of the most common attacks in the healthcare sector.

The healthcare industry is plagued by a myriad of cybersecurity-related issues. These issues range from **malware that compromises the integrity of systems and privacy of patients, to distributed denial of service (DDoS) attacks that disrupt facilities' ability to provide patient care**.

MAIN TYPES OF VULNERABILITY IN HEALTHCARE

Vulnerability in the dictionary: physical, emotional, cognitive. Healthcare is an attractive target for cyber criminals because medical data is between ten and twenty times more lucrative than credit card or banking details. Stolen health records can be sold to fund criminal activity and facilitate identity theft, blackmail or extortion.

Overstretched Staff – The majority of breaches related to data privacy in healthcare are the result of employee error and unauthorized disclosure. In the already overstretched world of hospitals, it is no wonder that cyber security is not top of mind for most workers.

"The biggest security threat in healthcare is mobile health (mHealth) mobile applications..." Hospitals and clinical practices must be aware of the threat of security breaches and health data theft as more health and wellness programs and procedures become available on mobile devices.

Since healthcare is a valuable and vulnerable target. Hackers go after healthcare because patient data and hospital systems are lucrative prey. Hackers know they can demand a high ransom if they compromise patient data or healthcare systems.

In 2021, 45 million individuals were affected by healthcare attacks, up from 34 million in 2020.

Impact of Cyber-Attacks

The FBI's warning began with a summary of the severe consequences of ransomware attacks, which includes- Financial setback, Operation disruption and Ramifications for the supply chain.

Anyone in the agriculture sector, including restaurants, major producers, and small farms, is vulnerable to cyberattacks in the food industry. Network flaws that can be exploited to steal data or make networks unusable affect everyone. These companies experience significant costs while dealing with the aftermath, regardless of whether the attacked party decides to pay or not.

According to the FBI, this industry's infrastructure is becoming a safer bet for cybercriminals in part due to the adoption of more sophisticated technologies that provide access to the network.

Smaller firms frequently lack the necessary improvements required to fend off cybercriminals, and thieves assume that larger businesses have the financial wherewithal to fulfil the demands without a second thought.

The FBI provided numerous particular instances of ransomware that targets agriculture and food:

- A bakery's production was stopped and there was a shutdown for almost a week as a result of losing access to its services, apps, and files.
- A multinational meat processing company's network was broken into, forcing the closure of a few US factories and perhaps causing data loss. In the end, this led to a shortage of beef and a 25% increase in wholesale prices.
- A farm's lost production of $9 million came from having to shut down as a result of a ransomware attack.

According to research cited by the FBI, up to 80% of ransomware victims who paid the demanded ransom faced a further attack, either by the same culprits or by a different gang.

Additionally, it's possible that business owners will be asked to pay twice: once for the right to decrypt the data and once again to guarantee that the hackers won't release the stolen data to the public. Whatever the owner decides, cybercriminals have the ability to harass staff, inform vendors of data theft, or interrupt operations through coordinated attacks. These grave repercussions could be the reason why, between 2019 and 2020, the average payout from cyber insurance climbed by 65%.

RECENT INCIDENCES OF CYBER-ATTACKS

1. **FOOD AND AGRICULTURE**: The advances in agriculture-related technology have brought along with them an increase in cyber threats. Before the rise of multinational consolidated agribusinesses, much of the world's food was produced by small farmers and ranchers serving a local community. Today the same economies of scale that have fueled the rise of large corporations in other sectors are applied to food production and distribution. These economies of scale are dependent on automation. Today, however, threat actors see the world's dependence on a well-established food supply chain as an opportunity to use malware, such as ransomware, as leverage to achieve their nefarious aims. These aims are commonly financial gain but also include acts of political terrorism and social hacktivism. There is still work to be done in areas where the food/ag sector has been lax in its cyber warehouses. Shutting down any massive food production or distribution business creates an intolerable condition that provides the cybercriminal with an insurmountable advantage. Companies and authorities know that they must resolve the situation quickly to avoid societal turmoil. The need for the victim to act soon works to the criminal's advantage. The world's food supply chain is fragile and dominated by a relatively small number of large food companies. Because cyber threat actors aim to shut down production, thereby threatening people's lives, food production networks and food company business networks are at risk.

FC International: In March 2021, JFC International revealed that it had been hit by a ransomware attack that disrupted several of its IT systems. JFC is a major distributor and wholesaler of Asian food products and serves the European and US markets. The company said the attacks impacted JFC International's Europe Group. They were able to resume normal operations soon after notifying law enforcement, employees, and business partners about the incident.

Loaves & Fishes: Nonprofit food provider Loaves & Fishes offers nutritionally balanced groceries to individuals and families experiencing a short-term crisis through a network of mobile "drive-through" style food distribution sites. In August 2020, they announced that sensitive customer information was exfiltrated during the more widespread Blackbaud attack. Blackbaud, a provider of software and cloud hosting solutions, stopped a ransomware attack from encrypting files but still paid a ransom demand to keep the hackers from publishing protected information about their clients – one of whom was Loaves & Fishes. Blackbaud said they have no evidence that the data was sold online, but the potential exists for that to happen at any time.

Home Chef: Owned by Kroger Foods, Home Chef is a startup that provides food ingredients, meal kits, and recipes to its customers. Security researchers said in May 2020 that they found usernames and passwords belonging to Home Chef users for sale on the dark web. Soon after, the Chicago-based company said a security incident had resulted in the compromise of information about an undisclosed number of its customers. This type of security event poses no danger to the food supply but is a risk to consumers of these services.

Harvest Sherwood Food Distributors: In May 2020, data that surfaced on a Tor hidden service called the Happy Blog indicated that hackers deploying REvil ransomware attacked Harvest Sherwood Food Distributors. The attackers stole critical data from the company and threatened to disclose it publicly. REvil is the same ransomware that is later used against JBS Meats. The attackers managed to steal around 2,600 files from the food distributor. The stolen data included cash-flow analysis, distributor data, business insurance content, and vendor information. There were also scanned images of driver's licenses of people in the Harvest Sherwood distribution network.

2. **HEALTHCARE:** Cyberattacks on healthcare have grown across the world as more hospitals and healthcare services providers are moving their operations and databases online. According to cybersecurity firm CheckPoint Research, healthcare suffered the highest number of ransomware attacks globally during the September quarter of 2022.

In 2022, itself India's top government-run hospital All India Institute of Medical Sciences (AIIMS) New Delhi, was hit by a massive cyber-attack, forcing it to shut down many of its servers and switch to manual operations. AIIMS, which had earlier announced plans to digitize all services by April 2023, refuted claims that hackers asked for a ransom of ₹200 core.

India's healthcare industry faced the highest number of cyber attacks after the United States in 2021, ironically due to technological advancement.

"India recorded the second highest number of attacks, with a total of 7.7 per cent of the total attacks on the healthcare industry in 2021," according to cyber security intelligence firm CloudSEK's report seen by PTI. US healthcare industry faced 28 per cent of the total global attacks, the report titled Increased cyber attacks on the global.

RECENT STRATEGIES DEPLOYED IN HEALTHCARE CYBER SECURITY MARKET

Partnerships, Collaborations and Agreements:

Jul-2021: Fortified Health Security formed a partnership with Armis, the leading unified asset visibility, and security platform vendor. The partnership aimed to improve the overall risk posture of healthcare companies. Following the partnership, Fortified is expected to use the Armis Agentless Device Security Platform to accelerate Fortified's Managed Connected Medical Device Security Program across their joint network and is expected to work together to safeguard healthcare companies from cyber threats.

Mar-2021: FireEye formed a partnership with Norm Cyber, a leading provider of managed cyber security and data protection services. The partnership aimed to provide sophisticated threat detection and response services under its Cyber Security as a Service offering.

Mar-2021: Sensato formed a partnership with Lyniate, a company that delivers secure, proven, and flexible interoperability solutions. The partnership aimed to improve collaboration between interoperability & cybersecurity, which is expected to make healthcare companies more effective and safe.

Feb-2021: IBM partnered with Palantir Technologies, a public American software company. The partnership aimed to leverage the capabilities of IBM's hybrid cloud data platform for offering AI for business, and Palantir's advanced operations platform for developing applications. Through this partnership, the two companies is expected to support enterprises that are willing to optimize the value of massive amounts of data including in retail, manufacturing, financial services, healthcare, and telecommunications.

Dec-2020: IBM formed a partnership with Siemens Healthineers, a leading global healthcare company. Through this partnership, the two companies launched an open digital platform that is expected to enhance the networking of the German healthcare system and expand the infrastructure for the provision of digital services. The partnership aimed to leverage the capabilities of two companies in digital networking, process optimization in healthcare, and the secure operation of data centers.

MAJOR CYBER SECURITY APPROACHES TO MINIMIZE THE RISK OF CYBER BREACHES

The number of cyber security breaches is increasing; by 2023, it was predicted that there would be 15.4 million. Cyber attackers are now deploying sophisticated tools, despite the fact that technology improvements have made it possible for enterprises to strengthen their security protocols. This indicates that in order to lower their cyber security risks, one has to adopt proactive measures in addition to strong cyber security rules.

Users as a company cannot afford to rely on chance to protect their data. The financial impact might be enormous; it could lead to missed sales, system downtime, and consumer data theft. Additionally, data breaches harm their reputation, which could sometimes push them out of business.

TEN PRACTICAL STRATEGIES THAT CAN BE IMPLEMENTED TO LOWER CYBER SECURITY RISK IN THEIR FIRM ARE FOLLOWING

Data Encryption and Backups Maintenance

It should be ensured that every piece of sensitive data is encrypted. Normal-text file formats are simple and easy targets for criminals to access data. On the other side, data encryption restricts access to data to those who possess the encryption key. Additionally, it makes sure that even if unauthorized individuals access the data, they are unable to read it. Some data encryption tools even alerts the owners when someone tries to change or tamper with the data.

Furthermore, one really have to consistently backup their vital data. Data loss may occur occasionally as a result of cyber security breaches. If this happens and they don't have a trusted and secure backup, it could lead to operational disruptions and significant financial loss for their company. The 3-2-1 rule is one of the best data backup techniques. One should store at least three copies of the data using this technique. Two of them ought to be kept on various forms of media, and one ought to be kept offshore.

Organize Frequent Employee Training

Phishing emails sent to employees are most frequently opted method by cyber hackers to gain access to database. In fact, statistics show that over 3.4 billion phishing emails are sent globally. These emails contain malicious malware in the form of links that give hackers access to user data, including login credentials.

The fact that phishing emails appear real makes them difficult to spot. For instance, a hacker may send an email posing as an organization head and requesting personal information. The worker can probably end up disclosing this information if they aren't given the required training. Companies must conduct cybersecurity awareness training owing to this and educate staff on the main types of cybersecurity assaults and the effective defenses against them.

The significance of double-checking email addresses before responding to them and links before clicking on them should also be emphasized. The company policy about sharing sensitive information, including on social media, should also be highlighted.

Updated Systems and Software

Software and system updates have a significant impact on an user's digital safety and cyber security. This is because they don't just bring new features; they also correct bugs and aid in patching exploitable security breaches and vulnerabilities.

Cybercriminals create code that they employ to take advantage of the flaws. The majority of the time, this code comes bundled as malware that can harm the entire system. Therefore, businesses must utilize a patch management system to manage all updates automatically and maintain information security.

Framing Strong Passwords

An interesting statistic is that weak passwords are to blame for almost 80% of organizational data breaches. It doesn't take much for hackers to access company systems. They simply need a minor flaw, and they'll take full advantage of it.

Simple passwords are no longer sufficient due to the advancement of password cracking technology. To deter hacking in the firm, one should instead implement multi-factor authentication techniques and employ complicated passwords. Additionally, management should forbid password sharing among staff members so that the rest of the computers are safe even if one is compromised.

When it comes to passwords, some of the security risk mitigation techniques that should be used include:

- At least 8 characters should be included in every password.
- Alphanumeric characters are necessary.
- They shouldn't include any personal data.
- They ought to be original and never before utilized.
- They should ideally not contain any words that are spelled correctly.
- Password should be kept securely and in an encrypted manner.

Bring-your-own-device (BYOD) is becoming more popular as more workers choose to work from home. iOS Users should be encouraged to activate the Security Recommendations feature so they can keep an eye on the security of the passwords they've saved.

Vendors Should be Assessed and Monitored

In some companies the cyber security is highly dependent on third-party a vendor, that's why one can't afford to ignore vendor risk management. This requires the mitigation of third-party risk instead of solely relying on incident response.

One should focus on:

- **Cybersecurity risk:** onboard vendors using the right strategies and monitoring them throughout the relationship.
- **Legal, regulatory, and compliance risk:** one should confirm that the vendor won't affect the adherence to agreements, laws, and local ordinances.
- **Operational risk:** if the vendor is a critical aspect of the organization, it should be ensured that they won't disrupt the operations.
- **Strategic risk:** it should be ensured that the vendor will not impact users' ability to meet the organizational objectives.

Reducing Attack Surface

Attack surfaces are the gaps or vulnerabilities that nefarious hackers can utilize to get access to confidential information. They may include IoT devices, software, online application systems, or even workers who are frequently the targets of social engineering assaults like phishing and whaling. There are 3 main types of attack surfaces:

a) **Physical attack surface:** this includes organizational assets that a hacker can get if they have physical access to company's premises.
b) **Digital attack surface:** these are assets that are accessible through the internet and live outside a firewall. Digital attack surfaces include known assets such as corporate servers/ operating system, unknown assets such as a forgotten website, and rogue assets such as apps that impersonate the company.
c) **Social engineering attack surface:** this is one of the most critical yet often overlooked attack surfaces. In this case, the hackers exploit human psychology and manipulate your employees into divulging sensitive information.

Close Attention to Physical Security

The majority of organizational cyber risk management policies completely ignore their physical premises in favor of the digital aspect of cyber threats. They should determine whether the critical infrastructure of the company is protected from security breaches by conducting a security assessment. Additionally, owners should evaluate their data protection strategy and decide if it includes data disposal procedures.

Imagine that if company's internet systems are secure from hackers, but they nevertheless experience a breach as a result of someone breaking into the offices and searching through their file cabinets. That'd be terrible! There are also additional occasions where janitors rummage through the trash and gather private information about clients and staff.

The restricted areas should be protected using high-value systems. Companies and institutions should also use 2-factor authentication such as keycards and biometrics. This way, even if the keycard is lost or stolen, no one will be able to access the area.

Killswitch Should Be in Place

Having a killswitch protects the firm from large-scale attacks. It is a form of reactive cybersecurity protection strategy where institution's information technology department shuts down all systems as soon as they detect anything suspicious until they resolve the issues.

Most of the time, cybercriminals don't cover their tracks, especially when they don't expect to be caught. So, if an IT security team analyzes all server logs frequently and conducts cybersecurity framework audits, they can make sure their integrity is intact. Business people can invest in network forensic analysis tools that analyze information flow through their network.

Most malicious firewall and ransomware attacks are a result of human error. Some of them are even caused by the employees. In fact, statistics show that around 94% of organizations have suffered cyber security threats due to insider breaches. All new hires should be regularly scanned to ascertain that they aren't a cyber risk to the organization. Authorities should also put measures to discourage employee negligence, which is a major contributor to cyber risks.

Install Firewalls

Hackers constantly develop new techniques for gaining access to data, and cyber security dangers are evolving. Therefore, implementing firewalls is a good way to protect business networks from online threats. A trustworthy system will successfully defend them from brute force attacks or stop security mishaps from causing irreparable harm.

Additionally, firewalls keep an eye on network traffic for any unusual activity that can jeopardize the security of the data. Additionally, they protect computers against sophisticated spyware and support data privacy.

When selecting the ideal firewall for the firm, one should exercise extreme caution. Consider a system that provides owners with complete security control and visibility over their networks and applications. Additionally, it should be equipped with defense and prevention features and a simplified security system.

Creation of Secured Cybersecurity Policy

Organization's cybersecurity is highly influenced by the policies that have been placed. One should have guidelines for data breach prevention and detection. Institute's IT teams often should conduct risk assessments or penetration testing.

Management should go through their existing policies regularly and identify loopholes they may have. Some of the guidelines that should be in place include;

a) **Disaster recovery:** If a breach occurs, a disaster recovery plan ensures that the employee and IT teams know the next course of action. It's aimed at reducing the amount of time that they are offline, thereby ensuring that their operations resume as soon as possible.

b) **Access control/management:** This policy highlights the parties that can access sensitive information, reducing the risk of unauthorized access. Data mishandling has both financial and legal consequences, so it should be made sure that the access management policy specifies which stakeholders are allowed access to what and under which circumstances they can share this information.

c) **Security testing:** The policy should state the frequency of the cybersecurity tests. This allows users to uncover vulnerabilities before it's too late. Some of the security tests that one should conduct include; vulnerability scanning, security posture assessment, penetration testing, ethical hacking, cybersecurity assessments, etc.

d) **Incident response plan:** This is documentation of the steps and procedures that should be implemented in case of a breach. It also highlights the responsibility of key information security players and reduces the organization's response time.

The plan should have a clause that highlights the consequences of data mishandling as well as the legal steps that will be taken on employees that are the cause of a breach. This will discourage insider attacks.

TIPS TO DEVELOP CYBER RISK MANAGEMENT STRATEGY

During the first half of 2021 alone, over 118 million people were impacted by data breaches. In fact, statistics of this year's data breaches were significantly higher than those of the past year. The best way to ensure that the organization is safe is by taking proactive measures. This includes;

i. Creating data backups and encrypting sensitive information.
ii. Updating all security systems and software.
iii. Conducting regular employee cybersecurity training.
iv. Using strong and complex passwords.
v. Installing firewalls.
vi. Reducing your attack surfaces.
vii. Assessing your vendors.
viii. Having a kills witch in place.
ix. Creating solid cyber risk policies and strategies.
x. Protecting your physical premises.

(Sukianto, 2022)

Healthcare organizations can improve their security posture **by addressing the following 4 tenants of a resilient cybersecurity program:**

i. **Increase Visibility-** One cannot address security risks if they neglect them. An attack surface monitoring solution will instantly display all vulnerabilities associated with cloud solutions within a private network.

ii. **Improve Third-Party Security-**Almost 60% of data breaches occur via a compromised third-party vendor. In other words, if the incident response efforts are only focused on internal cyber threats, the security teams have only addressed less than half of the risks that facilitate breaches. Improving the security postures of all third-party vendors involves an orchestrated effort between risk assessments, security ratings, and Vendor Tiering.

iii. **Expand Cyber Threat Awareness-**To prevent staff from falling victim to phishing attacks and other clever social engineering attempts, they should be educated about how to identify common cyber threats and previous malicious attack behaviors. Cyber awareness training can be facilitated through webinars or by referencing free cybersecurity resources.

iv. **Implement Multi-Factor Authentication-** Multi-Factor Authentication (MFA) is one of the simplest security controls to implement, and in many cases, it could be enough of an obstacle to thwart an attack attempt. It's estimated that up to 90% of cyber-attacks could be prevented with MFA enabled on endpoints and mobile devices. Every healthcare entity should be implementing MFA as a minimum security measure.

CONCLUSION

Like energy, transportation, and financial services, millions of people depend on the food, agriculture and healthcare industry for their lives and livelihoods. As these critical sectors rely more and more on digital systems to conduct business, the threat of a significant cyber-attack carries more weight.

Deploying modern cyber defenses to protect the world's food supply chain is essential. Additionally, as new automation systems are designed, it must be done with cyber protection at the forefront. Cyber vulnerabilities in national food systems may potentially have global scale impacts in a host of different dimensions.

By engaging with relational data and forward-looking risk assessment frameworks, food system actors will be better-equipped to manage and mitigate future risks before they occur. Such advancements are necessary to move beyond reactive risk management strategies to ensure a more stable food supply nationally and globally.

Healthcare institutions need robust and reliable authentication capabilities to ensure that only real workers access internal networks or particular applications. Companies are aggressively shifting to multi-factor authentication to prevent the threats of password-based authentication. Multi-factor authentication is majorly carried out by including another component to the conventional user-name and password. This may be the hardware and software token, a biometric check, or a device authentication step.

The fragile and interdependent nature of the food supply requires that the entire industry be protected with the most advanced and effective tools and policies. Because, in the end, we all need to eat first and foremost.

REFERENCES

Ahmad, F., & Khan, M. Z. (2020). Forensic Case Studies. In Critical Concepts, Standards, and Techniques in Cyber Forensics (pp. 248-264). IGI Global. doi:10.4018/978-1-7998-1558-7.ch015

Alkhalil, Z., Hewage, C., Nawaf, L., & Khan, I. (2021). Phishing Attacks: A Recent Comprehensive Study and a New Anatomy. *Frontiers of Computer Science*, *3*, 563060. doi:10.3389/fcomp.2021.563060

Alnahari, W., & Quasim, M. T. (2021, July). Privacy concerns, IoT devices and attacks in smart cities. In *2021 International Congress of Advanced Technology and Engineering (ICOTEN)* (pp. 1-5). IEEE. 10.1109/ICOTEN52080.2021.9493559

AlShahrani, B. M. M. (2021). Classification of cyber-attack using Adaboost regression classifier and securing the network. [TURCOMAT]. *Turkish Journal of Computer and Mathematics Education*, *12*(10), 1215–1223.

Barreto, L., & Amaral, A. (2018). Smart farming: Cyber security challenges. In *2018 International Conference on Intelligent Systems (IS),* (pp. 870–876). IEEE. 10.1109/IS.2018.8710531

Bendovschi, A. (2015). Cyber-Attacks – Trends, Patterns and Security Countermeasures. *Procedia Economics and Finance*, *28*, 24–31. doi:10.1016/S2212-5671(15)01077-1

Butterfield, A., & Ngondi, G. E. (Eds.). (21 January 2016). spoofing. Oxford Reference. Oxford University Press. . doi:10.1093/acref/9780199688975.001.0001

Cupp, O. S., Walker, D. E. II, & Hillison, J. (2004). Agroterrorism in the us: Key security challenge for the 21st century. *Biosecurity and Bioterrorism*, 2(2), 97–105. doi:10.1089/153871304323146397 PMID:15225403

Cybersecurity in Food Industry. (n.d.). *Just Food*. https://www.just-food.com/cybersecurity-in-food-industry/

Data, M. (2018). The defense against arp spoofing attack using semistatic arp cache table. In *2018 International Conference on Sustainable Information Engineering and Technology (SIET)*, (pp. 206–210). 10.1109/SIET.2018.8693155

Eldad, E. (2005). *Reversing: secrets of reverseengineering*. John Wiley & Sons.

Faith, B. (2022). *Take Steps Now to Protect Your Company from a Cybersecurity Attack*. Global Food Safety Resource. https://globalfoodsafetyresource.com/take-steps-now-protect-company-cybersecurity-attack/

Gallagher, S. (2014). Photos of an NSA "upgrade" factory show Cisco router getting implant. *Ars Technica*.

Gautam, B. P., Wasaki, K., Batajoo, A., Shrestha, S., & Kazuhiko, S. (2016). Multi-master replication of enhanced learning assistant system in iot cluster. In *IEEE 30th International Conference on Advanced Information Networking and Applications (AINA)*, (pp. 1006–1012). IEEE. 10.1109/AINA.2016.110

Ghadge, A., Weib, M., Caldwell, N. D., & Wilding, R. (2020). Managing cyber risk in supply chains: A review and research agenda. *Supply Chain Management*, 25(2), 223–240. doi:10.1108/SCM-10-2018-0357

GOsafeonline. (12 November 2014). Distributed Denial of Service Attack. CSA. https://www.csa.gov.sg/gosafeonline/go-safe-for-business/smes/distributed-denial-of-service-attack#:~:text=A%20DDoS%20attack%20is%20a,sending%20it%20specially%20crafted%20requests

Guo, M., Wang, G., Hata, H., & Babar, M. A. (2021). Revenue maximizing markets for zero-day exploits. *Autonomous Agents and Multi-Agent Systems*, 35(2), 36. arXiv:2006.14184. . doi:10.1007/s10458-021-09522-w

Husain, M. S., & Khan, M. Z. (Eds.). (2019). *Critical Concepts, Standards, and Techniques in Cyber Forensics*. IGI Global.

Hussain, M. A., Jin, H., Hussien, Z. A., Abduljabbar, Z. A., Abbdal, S. H., & Ibrahim, A. (2016). Dns protection against spoofing and poisoning attacks. In *2016 3rd International Conference on Information Science and Control Engineering (ICISCE)*, (pp. 1308–1312). IEEE. 10.1109/ICISCE.2016.279

Lin, T. C. W. (2016). Financial Weapons of War. *Wikipedia*. https://en.wikipedia.org/wiki/Cyberattack#cite_ref-ssrn.com_3-0

Khan, M. Z., Husain, M. S., & Shoaib, M. (2020). Introduction to email, web, and message forensics. In *Critical concepts, standards, and techniques in cyber forensics* (pp. 174–186). IGI Global. doi:10.4018/978-1-7998-1558-7.ch010

Khan, M. Z., Mishra, A., & Khan, M. H. (2020). Cyber Forensics Evolution and Its Goals. In Critical Concepts, Standards, and Techniques in Cyber Forensics (pp. 16-30). IGI Global. doi:10.4018/978-1-7998-1558-7.ch002

Khan, M. Z., Shoaib, M., & Ahmad, F. (2020). Cyber Forensic Lab Setup and Its Requirement. In Critical Concepts, Standards, and Techniques in Cyber Forensics (pp. 103-115). IGI Global. doi:10.4018/978-1-7998-1558-7.ch007

Kianpour, M., Kowalski, S., & Øverby, H. (2021). Systematically Understanding Cybersecurity Economics: A Survey. *Sustainability (Basel), 13*(24), 13677. doi:10.3390u132413677

Kumar, A., & Paul, P. (2016). *Security analysis and implementation of a simple method for prevention and detection against evil twin attack in ieee 802.11 wireless lan. In 2016 international conference on computational techniques in information and communication technologies.* ICCTICT.

Lipovsky, R., Cermak, M., Svorencık, S., & Kubovic, O. (n.d.). KR00K - CVE-2019-15126. *We Live Security.* https://www.welivesecurity.com/wpcontent/uploads/2020/02/ESET Kr00k.pdf. [Online].

Marcel, S., Nixon, M., & Li, S. (2014). *Handbook of Biometric Anti-Spoofing: Trusted Biometrics under Spoofing Attacks. Advances in Computer Vision and Pattern Recognition.* London: Springer. . doi:10.1007/978-1-4471-6524-8

Marcella, A. J. (Ed.). (2021). *Cyber Forensics: Examining Emerging and Hybrid Technologies.* CRC Press. doi:10.1201/9781003057888

Millman, R. (2017). *New polymorphic malware evades three-quarters of AV scanners.* SC Magazine UK.

Perazzo, P., Vallati, C., Varano, D., Anastasi, G., & Dini, G. (2018). Implementation of a wormhole attack against a rpl network: Challenges and effects. In *2018 14th Annual Conference on Wireless On-demand Network Systems and Services (WONS),* (pp. 95– 102). IEEE.

Pimple, N., Salunke, T., Pawar, U., & Sangoi, J. (2020).Wireless security — an approach towards secured wi-fi connectivity. In *2020 6th International Conference on Advanced Computing and Communication Systems (ICACCS),* (pp. 872–876). IEEE.

Quasim, M. T., & Al Hawi, A. N. (2022). *Mechanisms of System Penetration: Concepts, Attack Methods, and Defense Strategies (No. 9197).* EasyChair.

Safkhani, M., & Bagheri, N. (2017). Passive secret disclosure attack on an ultralightweight authentication protocol for internet of things. *The Journal of Supercomputing, 73*(8), 3579–3585. doi:10.100711227-017-1959-0

Satter, R. (2017). What makes a cyberattack? Experts lobby to restrict the term. *Wikipedia.* https://en.wikipedia.org/wiki/Cyberattack#cite_ref-4)

Schatz, D., Bashroush, R., & Wall, J. (2017). Towards a More Representative Definition of Cyber Security. *Journal of Digital Forensics, Security and Law, 12* (2).

Sergio, A. (2013). "Social Engineering" (PDF). upc.edu. Archived (PDF) from the original on 3 December 2013. Retrieved 5 January 2023.

Sontowski, S. (2020). Cyber Attacks on Smart Farming Infrastructure. *2020 IEEE 6th International Conference on Collaboration and Internet Computing (CIC),* (pp. 135-143). IEEE. 10.1109/CIC50333.2020.00025

Sontowski, S., Gupta, M., Chukkapalli, S. S. L., Abdelsalam, M., Mittal, S., Joshik, A., & Sandhu, R. (2020). Cyber Attacks on Smart Farming Infrastructure. *Profs and Hu.* https://profsandhu.com/confrnc/misconf/smart-farm-cic-20.pdf

Steve, C. (2022). Cyber threats are a real threat to modern agriculture's expanding digital infrastructure. *AgWeb.* https://www.agweb.com/news/business/technology/cyber-threats-are-real-threat-modern-agricultures-expanding-digital

Stevens, T. (2018). "Global Cybersecurity: New Directions in Theory and Methods" (PDF). *Politics and Governance, 6*(2), 1–4. doi:10.17645/pag.v6i2.1569

Sukianto, A. (2022), UpGuard,Third-Party Risk Management,10 Ways to Reduce Cybersecurity Risk for Your Organization. *Upguard.* https://www.upguard.com/blog/reduce-cybersecurity-risk

Tripathi, M. M., Haroon, M., Khan, Z., & Husain, M. S. (2022). *Security in Digital Healthcare System. Pervasive Healthcare: A Compendium of Critical Factors for Success*, 217-231. Research Gate.

Vanhoef, M., & Piessens, F. (2017). Key reinstallation attacks: Forcing nonce reuse in wpa2. In *Proceedings of the 2017 ACM SIGSAC Conference on Computer and Communications Security*, (pp. 1313–1328). ACM. 10.1145/3133956.3134027

Wallgren, L., Raza, S., & Voigt, T. (2013). Routing attacks and countermeasures in the rpl-based internet of things. *International Journal of Distributed Sensor Networks, 9*(8), 794326. doi:10.1155/2013/794326

Webroot. (2018). *Multi-Vector Attacks Demand Multi-Vector Protection.* MSSP Alert.

Technopedia. (n.d.). *What is Spoofing?* Techopedia.

https://en.wikipedia.org/wiki/Cyberattack

Woehl, R. (2022). *Cyber Security Threats to the Food Industry: Consider the Cloud.* Global Food Safety Resource. https://globalfoodsafetyresource.com/cyber-security-threats-food industry-consider-cloud/)

Zhang, K., Liang, X., Lu, R., & Shen, X. (2014). Sybil attacks and their defenses in the internet of things. *IEEE Internet of Things Journal, 1*(5), 372–383. doi:10.1109/JIOT.2014.2344013

ADDITIONAL READING

Computer Security Resource Center. (n.d.). *Cyber Attack - Glossary.* NIST. https://csrc.nist.gov/glossary/term/cyber_attack

Chapter 5
The Critical Impact of Cyber Threats on Digital Economy

Syed Adnan Afaq
Integral University, India

Saman Uzma
Cubeight Solutions, Australia

Gausiya Yasmeen
(iD) https://orcid.org/0000-0002-7853-1376
Integral University, India

ABSTRACT

Internet users need to know that there are many different kinds of threats in the online world. Improving cyber security and keeping private information safe is important for a country's safety and economy. For a country's safety and economy, it's important to improve cyber security and keep private information safe. The term "digital economy" refers to a business for digitally delivered goods and services that are created using electronic business models and linked to a global system of economic and social networks. Cyber risk is the most complex issue of the twenty-first century, arising from a wide diversity of causes such as a hacker, terrorists, criminals, insider groups, foreign states, etc. This study includes cyber threats in the digital world. It emphasizes challenges in the healthcare sector, agriculture and food industries.

INTRODUCTION

The number of people using the internet worldwide is increasing and with it the frequency and variety of cyber threats. Cyber risks include things like cybercrime, cyber-terrorism, data theft, and cyberwarfare. These risks include identity theft, financial hardships, network infrastructure damage, and data leak, and they all cause severe risks to businesses and economies(Afaq et al., n.d.).

DOI: 10.4018/978-1-6684-8133-2.ch005

The most perplexing threat of the 21st century is the cyber threat, which may originate from anyone from hackers and terrorists to criminals and insiders to whole nations. It's a problem that affects governments, businesses, and people everywhere. It's also getting easier and cheaper to launch cyber operations, while security infrastructure is becoming more expensive. In other words, this growing imbalance is a decisive factor(Sharma & Dhote, 2021).

With the advent of digitization, the likelihood of cyber espionage attacks targeting intellectual property has dramatically increased, resulting in significant financial and reputational damage to both private and public organizations. The effects of this trend are not limited to tangible harm, as there has also been a surge in the use of deepfakes and "disinformation-for-hire," which can deepen societal mistrust. For example, deepfakes can manipulate political outcomes and influence election results. In a recent incident, cybercriminals imitated a company director's voice to transfer $35 million to fraudulent accounts. There is also a growing market for services aimed at manipulating public opinion to benefit clients or harm their competitors. As banking, health, and civic processes move online, fraud will become more prevalent and easier to commit, even with robust digital threat defenses. This may be particularly challenging for smaller businesses that dedicate a greater percentage of their operational budget to security than larger organizations. The increase in ransomware claims has led to a 96% rise in cyber insurance pricing in the United States in the third quarter of 2021, the largest increase since 2015 and a 204% year-over-year increase. Respondents to the GRPS express long-term concerns about these trends, with "adverse tech advances" listed as a top-10 risk over a 5-to-10-year horizon. (WEF, 2022).

As we progress farther into the age of digitization, the digital economy grows in importance and influence. As the global society becomes more interconnected in cyberspace, its economic opportunities and progress are more dependent on the internet. The growth of the digital economy is accompanied by cyber threats and hazards to governments. Since cybersecurity is necessary to facilitate and defend the digital economy, the national cybersecurity strategy (NCSS) is a crucial component(Qaiser, 2020).

In terms of cyber security, India is a relatively late adopter. India's cyber security effort is currently moving extremely slowly. Additionally, India does not have specific cyber security legislation that may be used in situations of cybercrimes, cyberattacks, and cyber infractions. The Information Technology Act of 2000 is inadequate to address India's cybersecurity-related problems.

Technology and the economy came together to change how businesses operate so they may reach new markets and create revenue. In the corporate world, information plays a dual role as a unifying force and a motivator for problem-solving. It is necessary to accept innovation and technological advancements since they are unheard of in business(Ramadan et al., 2021). The digital world is causing changes in the political, economic, scientific, and cultural basis of our society, and these changes are present in the process of causing the social transition. The world is being affected by the digital revolution in many ways, including the e-economy, social movements, elections for public office, and the rapid understanding of international concerns.

The technological frontier of the digital economy is constantly being pushed in the expanding internet. Bitcoin is one of the most revolutionary innovations because it dismantles conventions and establishes new ones. The first digital currency in the world is defined by this open network banking based on peer-to-peer agreement. It began as a mentoring currency in 2010, when 10,000 bitcoins were exchanged for a pizza at a price of US$0.0025 per bitcoin. The price of bitcoin reached USD 1,350 on March 10, 2017(Teoh & Mahmood, 2017).

One definition of the digital economy is "an economy based on electronic goods and services, produced by electronic business models, connected with a worldwide network of economic and social networks, and made possible by information and communication technologies (ICT) such as internet technology.".

The development and fulfillment of the digital economy's potential are tied to people's faith in the internet and cyberspace. The potential of the digital economy, which is now projected to account for 22.5% of the global economy, has not been completely realized. The United States, the world leader in the digital economy, accumulated USD 5.9 trillion, or 33 percent of its GDP, online (GDP). Investments in digital infrastructure have a multiplier effect on national GDP, increasing economic production across the board.

'The goal of the initiative known as "Digital India" is to make India a "digitally empowered society and information economy." The nation of India is working hard to bring its Digital India initiative to completion to the best of its abilities. The success of the Digital India initiative is dependent on achieving the highest possible level of the connection while simultaneously reducing the number of potential cybersecurity vulnerabilities. The objective of the Digital India programme is to change the economy of the country into a linked one; however, this goal cannot be accomplished unless the safety of the many connected devices is ensured. The idea of Digital India calls for the integration of a huge variety of technologies that must communicate with one another in a variety of different ways. Incorporating security into the development and real adoption of digital technologies, in addition to maintaining strict adherence with the regulation, is the only method to accurately anticipate and eradicate any and all potential security problems. This involves the security of individuals' privacy and data as well as adherence to applicable cyber laws. Because of the Digital India programme, a significant amount of data will be gathered by a variety of entities, and this data must be secured(Shivani, 2015).

The nations of the globe are in the early stages of the Fourth Industrial Revolution, which marks the beginning of a new era characterized by the convergence of the digital, biological, and physical worlds. In this advent of the internet revolution, the potential for development and expansion is contingent on an infrastructure and legal environment that is conducive to growth, an information and communications technology (ICT) infrastructure that is ready to support emerging technologies, and the adoption and utilization of ICT across society. For a country to survive and grow in this century, digital interference is unavoidable and cannot be avoided. The Networked Readiness Index (NRI) was developed by the World Economic Forum to evaluate and quantify the degree to which nations are prepared to seize and profit from the opportunities presented by developing technologies in the digital economy.

The most significant risks that a country faces are hacktivism, cyber terrorism, cyber espionage, and organized crime that takes place online. Threats come from a wide variety of origins, including the more obvious ones like criminals and malware, as well as more specific ones like targeted cyberattacks. On the other hand, policies pose a risk to the development of cyberspace in the future. Threats originate from a wide variety of origins, including the more obvious ones like criminals and malware, as well as more specific ones like targeted cyberattacks. On the other hand, policies present a risk to the development of cyberspace in the future. A well-balanced policy environment will encourage the growth of innovative technologies and the furtherance of cybersecurity(Manning, 2019).

As of April 2022, there were over four and a half billion individuals all over the world who were connected to the internet. This figure represents approximately 63.1 percent of the entire population of the world. In this sum, there were 4.7 billion people who used social media, which represents 59 percent of the worldwide people(Jana et al., n.d.).

Figure 1. Number of Internet users worldwide

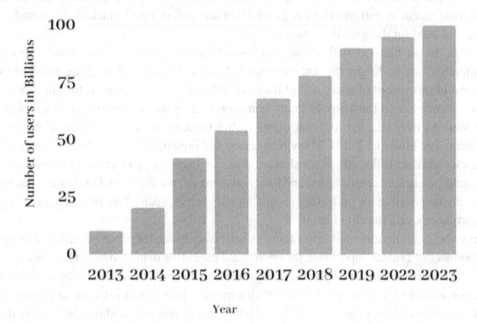

Degree of Threat

Maneuverable attacks have been used to attack enterprises, to gain consumer credentials and criminal customer details. It is quite evident that conventional methods will not be able to protect against all possible risks. There is a requirement for additional layers of protection as well as specialized visibility into these threats. In the realm of security, organizations are up against several obstacles at present. The overwhelming majority of companies do not have the personnel or the capabilities necessary to appropriately detect and protect themselves against growing cyber threats. The reason for this is that the majority of firms are not conscious of a compromise until it was far too late to do something about it. The data that is collected for cyber intelligence frequently lacks the essential enrichment to make it relevant and actionable. There is an immediate and pressing need to adapt to a posture of threat aware-ness that is more pre-emptive and "beyond the horizon."

Cyber-Physical Systems have recently been one of the prime objectives of hackers, and any dis-ruption to these systems can result in significant financial losses for a whole country. The idea that Cyber-Physical Systems (CPSs) are networks that link computers, communication systems, sensors, and controllers of the physical substratum has been widely acknowledged around the world. These networks can be heterogeneous, open, systems-of-systems, or hybrid. As more and more connections are made between different systems, complexity increases. In today's world, computer networks have entered the ranks of water, food, mobility, and electricity as one of the most important resources necessary for the functioning of an economy. CPS has a wide range of potential applications across a variety of business sectors. The development of the common sector, which includes oil and gas as well as the manufacture of electricity grids, defense, and public infrastructures, is entirely dependent on the progress of CPS. As a result of the enormous number of electronic devices that are connected to one another through various communication networks, the security of cyber-physical systems has emerged as an issue that is relevant to the societal, infrastructure, and economic concerns of each and every nation in the world(Moran, 2020). The most recent investigations have proven that the goal of cyberattacks is to damage a nation's systems that are used for the growth of the country.

These days, terms like "globalization," "industrialization," "cyber connection," "digitalization," and "e-commerce" are no longer the stuff of science fiction. They are all working together toward the expansion and improvement of every one of the country's industries. However, the flip side of the coin is that cyber security is on the brink of being compromised by the threats posed by the digital world. It is impossible to overstate the risk that exists in the modern world as a result of threats to cyber security(Spremić & Šimunic, 2018). Many businesses and organizations are already feeling the effects of cyberattacks and data leaks, which are slowing down or stopping production and services altogether. Industries including healthcare, farming, and food and drink are not immune. Due to their interconnected nature, they are responsible for protecting several attack vectors, such as servers, programs, computers, tablets, smartphones, and the cloud itself.

Concerns about information and cyber security are rising to the forefront of business agendas, making them a subject of central importance for boards and executive management. There is a serious need for proactive measures to be taken by various organizations in response to the rising security threat. To effectively control risks and protect crucial assets, businesses should establish a management system that conforms to internationally accepted standards and is based on a rigorous, methodical framework(Barefoot et al., 2018).

LITERATURE REVIEW

Today's society has become significantly more dependent on the digital economy, which makes it possible for quick and seamless communication, business, and innovation. The frequency and seriousness of cyber attacks have increased along with the usage of digital technology. Hacking, data breaches, phishing, and ransomware assaults are just a few of the many potential cyberthreats. These vulnerabilities can have a considerable effect, with possible repercussions ranging from challenges to national security to monetary loss and reputational harm.

The effects of cyber risks can be better understood by looking at real-world case studies of cyber attacks and their effects on the digital economy. For instance, the 2017 Equifax data breach cost the corporation over $1.4 billion in legal settlements, fines, and other fees, as well as causing serious reputational harm. The breach resulted in the theft of sensitive personal information from 143 million individuals. Multiple government organisations and companies were the targets of the 2020 SolarWinds supply chain attack, which brought attention to the complex nature of cyber-attacks and the requirement for strong supply chain security measures.

These case studies demonstrate the compensatory damages, legal liabilities, reputational harm, and loss of customer trust that can result from cyberattacks. In reducing the negative effects of cyber attacks on the digital economy, they also emphasise the significance of proactive cybersecurity measures including ongoing monitoring, advanced threat, and incident management preparation.

Supply chain strike on SolarWinds (2020): SolarWinds, a well-known supplier of IT management software, was the subject of an effective supply chain attack in 2020. As a result of the attack, SolarWinds' software updates were compromised, resulting in the inclusion of a gateway that gave the attackers access to various organisations, including Fortune 500 firms and government agencies, without authorization.

The attack had a huge impact on the digital economy, resulting in losses in money and reputation as well as a greater emphasis on supply chain security.

There have been numerous studies done to look at the serious effects of cyber threats on the digital economy. According to one research by the Center for Strategic and International Studies (CSIS), cybercrime hurts the world economy to the tune of about $600 billion every year. This value includes both direct and indirect costs, such as the decline in customer confidence in digital technology as well as lost revenue and recovery costs.

Other studies have emphasised the precise effects of cyberthreats on different facets of the digital economy. According to a report by Accenture, for instance, cyberattacks on the financial services industry rose by 75% in 2019 and the average cost of a data breach in the industry was $5.86 million. According to a different Verizon research, the healthcare industry is particularly vulnerable to cyberattacks, accounting for more than half of all data breaches.

2021's ransomware attack on the Colonial Pipeline, a significant US oil pipeline operator, affected business activities and forced a temporary suspension of the pipeline infrastructure. The attack's wide-ranging effects, including fuel shortages, higher petrol prices, and major economic effects, highlighted how susceptible key infrastructure is to cyberattacks.

Additionally, studies have concentrated on the numerous cyberthreats that can affect the digital economy. One research by the World Economic Forum, for instance, listed the top 10 cyber dangers to the world economy, including cloud vulnerabilities, phishing attacks, and data breaches. Over half of data breaches were caused by insider threats, such as employee irresponsibility and malicious insiders, according to another report by the Ponemon Institute.

Cyber Attack on JBS Foods (2021) In the year 2021, JBS Foods, one of the largest meat production firms in the world, was the victim of a cyber attack that caused its operations in numerous nations to be disrupted. This attack also had an effect on the company's supply chain and resulted in temporary plant closures. The attack had severe repercussions for the food industry, including delays in production and financial losses. It also caused interruptions in the supply networks for beef.

Rapid technological development in the modern period has allowed companies to digitise their processes and reap the benefits of the online economy. Unfortunately, cyber risks against organisations and individuals have also increased along with the rise of digitalization. The purpose of this literature review is to offer a snapshot of current understanding of the severe consequences cyber attacks pose to the online economy.

Businesses have been profoundly influenced by the widespread adoption of digital technologies. However, cyber attacks have become a major concern for enterprises around the world as the digital economy has grown in importance. In this literature study, we'll take a look at how cyber dangers are affecting the modern economy and the steps that can be taken to protect sensitive data and keep networks secure.

Cyber risks and their influence on the digital economy are a growing concern for both private and public sector businesses. Companies and institutions are becoming more vulnerable to cyber espionage operations, which can target intellectual property and result in considerable costs in terms of development and reputation (Campbell & Horowitz, 2018). However, the harmful implications of this tendency are not restricted to these obvious outcomes. Deepfakes and "disinformation-for-hire" are expected to worsen current mistrust among various society players such as enterprises, governments, and communities (Stamos, 2019). Deepfakes, for example, can be used to manipulate political outcomes or affect election outcomes, whilst disinformation-for-hire services can be used to impact public opinion in favour of a client or harm competitors (Sanger & Perlroth, 2019).

As organisations do more to protect themselves from cyberthreats, the cost of doing business is likely to go up for everyone.

Small and medium-sized businesses have their own range of difficulties, especially when it comes to having to spend on security, where they may spend a higher percentage of their financial plan than larger organisations (Bischof et al., 2021).

Additionally, the escalating number and severity of ransomware attacks have resulted in a significant rise in cyber insurance pricing in the United States (PwC, 2021).

The literature on cyber threats and their impact on the digital economy is extensive and multifaceted. Researchers have studied the economic, social, and political impacts of cyber threats, as well as their technical and operational aspects. For example, studies have examined the impact of cyber threats on supply chains (Economist Intelligence Unit, 2020), the challenges of managing cyber risk (Bischof et al., 2021), and the use of artificial intelligence in cybersecurity (Kshetri, 2018).

In the modern era, data breaches have become a significant obstacle for businesses to overcome. With the advent of big data in the rapidly expanding digital economy, it has become crucial to safeguard critical organizational information. The absence of awareness regarding cybersecurity can make organizations vulnerable to potential cyber threats. Hence, this study seeks to explore the diverse aspects of cybersecurity awareness capabilities. Employing the dynamic capabilities framework, the research identifies personnel-related factors (knowledge, attitude, and learning), management-related factors (training, culture, and strategic orientation), and infrastructure-related capabilities (technology and data governance) as key thematic dimensions that can address the challenges of cybersecurity awareness.

Organizations face a significant risk when employees lack security awareness, leaving sensitive assets vulnerable to potential cyber threats. Financial institutions, healthcare services, and manufacturing companies are particularly susceptible to attacks by hackers targeting their vulnerable employees. The difficulty in detecting and preventing attacks has been further amplified by the prevalence of remote or partially remote working environments. This situation is especially true for the healthcare and financial sectors, which have become increasingly attractive targets for malicious or criminal attacks. To deal with these changing threats effectively, organisations need to have ongoing information security awareness programs (Akter et al., 2022).

INTRODUCTION OF CYBEROLOGY

The study of cybernetic systems, which can encompass electronic, mechanical, and biological systems as well as those that interact with information and communication technologies, is the primary emphasis of the relatively new discipline of cyberology, which is a developing field. Because of developments in areas such as computer science, data analytics, artificial intelligence, and machine learning, the discipline of cyberology has seen a period of rapid development during the past several years.

The growing adoption of data analytics as a method for gleaning insights from huge and complicated datasets is one of the most important developments in the field of cyberology. Data analytics has emerged as an essential tool in a variety of domains, including the business world, the marketing industry, healthcare, and scientific research. It has the ability to revolutionise the ways in which we come to decisions, recognise trends, and find solutions to issues.

The development of machine learning is another significant development in the field of cyberology. These technologies provide computers the ability to learn from data and make predictions, and they are being utilised in a wide variety of applications, such as processing natural language, picture recognition, and autonomous cars. The continued development of these technologies has the potential to bring about a revolution in a variety of different industries as well as a change in the way that we work and live our lives.

However, despite its many benefits, cyberology is not without its share of severe difficulties and problems. One of the primary problems is cybersecurity, which can be defined as the safeguarding of information systems and networks against unauthorised access, theft, or damage. This is one of the most important issues. Cybersecurity is becoming increasingly critical as more information is stored and processed online and as the level of sophistication of assaults increases.

A further concern is the possible effect that technological advancements could have on individuals' privacy and personal data. There is a danger, as more information is gathered and processed, that personal data on individuals could be used in ways that those individuals did not anticipate or consent to. This risk increases as more information is collected and analysed. Because of this, concerns have been raised concerning data protection, and it has become clear that stringent rules are required to ensure that personal data is handled in an appropriate manner.

Cyberology is an area of study that is undergoing rapid development and has the potential to affect many facets of our life. Although there have been a lot of exciting breakthroughs in the sector recently, there are also a lot of critical concerns that need to be addressed in order to make sure that these technologies are used in an ethical and responsible manner. It will be important to strike a balance between the advantages and the risks of cybertechnology and to build suitable safeguards to protect both individuals and society as a whole in order to fully achieve the promise of cybertechnology.

Current State of the Field of Cybersecurity

a.   *Emerging Risk Environment:* New and sophisticated cyber threats are always emerging, changing the cyber risk landscape. Cybersecurity experts need to keep up with the most recent cyberattack types, strategies, and methods employed by cybercriminals, as well as any new trends or technology that can create vulnerabilities.

b.   *Developing Financial and Supervisory Frameworks:* To preserve private information, crucial infrastructure, and sensitive data, governments and regulatory bodies around the world are creating and enforcing stronger cybersecurity legislation. Organizations are placing a lot of emphasis on complying with these requirements, so cybersecurity professionals need to be informed of how the legal and regulatory environment is changing.

c.   *Growing Focus on Risk Management:* Cybersecurity now includes good risk management as well as attack prevention. Organizations are embracing risk-based cybersecurity strategies that put an emphasis on proactively identifying, evaluating, and reducing risks. This entails assessing the possible effect of cybersecurity risks, prioritising security investments, and putting in place the necessary risk management procedures.

d.   *Technology development:* As technology continues to grow quickly, cybersecurity must also do the same. The cybersecurity landscape is changing as a result of technologies like artificial intelligence (AI), machine learning, big data analytics, and quantum computing. These innovations offer new opportunities for threat detection, prevention, and response, but they also introduce new difficulties and vulnerabilities.

e. *Growing Cybersecurity Skills Gap:* As a result of the ongoing shortage of qualified cybersecurity workers, there is a skills gap. Because the cybersecurity field is continuously changing and needing continuing training and upskilling for workers to stay relevant, organisations struggle to acquire and keep qualified cybersecurity talent.

f. *Growing Importance of Cybersecurity in the Digital Economy*: As the digital economy develops, cybersecurity's significance is likewise rising. Cybersecurity is widely acknowledged as a crucial component of corporate operations that requires attention from top management since cyberattacks can have a substantial financial, reputational, and operational impact on firms.

IMPACT OF CYBER THREATS IN VARIOUS SECTORS

Security breaches are becoming more widespread, and they can have major ramifications for both individuals and corporations. According to a report issued in 2021 by the Identity Theft Resource Center, there were 1,108 security breaches in the U. S. in 2020. More than 300 million private details were exposed as a result of these attacks. Identity theft, financial loss, reputational damage, and legal liability are all possible outcomes of these security lapses, which can affect both individuals and businesses. Equifax's data breach in 2017 is one issue of high data breach in recent years. Other examples include the Capital One data breach in 2019 and the SolarWinds data leak in 2020.

Another significant risk to confidentiality is posed by outside organisations that improperly utilise individuals' private data. Many companies collect and utilise customers' personal data for marketing purposes, however some of these companies may sell customers' data to third parties or use it in methods that customers aren't likely to approve of. In 2018, Facebook, in particular, was at the centre of a scandal involving the political consulting firm Cambridge Analytica. Millions of Facebook users' personal information was obtained through a breach of Facebook's terms of service and then used to influence political activities.

To address these threats to privacy, there is a growing need for increased protection and regulation of personal information. The General Data Protection Regulation (GDPR) of the European Union and the California Consumer Privacy Act are two examples of laws and regulations that are now undergoing efforts to be made more stringent in order to better protect individuals' personal information (CCPA). The purpose of these regulations is to gives everyone the opportunity more control over the data that pertains to them, as well as to impose more stringent standards on businesses that collects and processes personal information.

Healthcare Sectors

Prevention Efforts to Take Into Account The Internet of Medical Things is an essential part of this shift to digital, and it will lay the groundwork for future research on cyber-physical intelligent pervasive platforms for healthcare services.. Patients might be harmed by compromised medical devices due to inadequate cyber security. IoMT devices are a tempting target for hackers because to factors like constrained versions of general working systems, operation in insecure contexts, design flaws that influence all equipment from a single supplier, etc(Ekshmi, 2022).

The goal of healthcare technology is to save lives, improve quality of life, and increase longevity. The accuracy of medical treatment has improved thanks to the introduction of cutting-edge technology, which has also led to a rise in the need for top-notch safety measures. Due to its richness of sensitive data and inadequate security posture, the healthcare industry is Considering Security One important aspect of this digital transformation is the Internet of Healthcare Devices, which will lay the groundwork for upcoming work on cyber-physical smart pervasive platforms in healthcare. One of the most targeted by attackers who constantly encounter emerging cyber threats. About 94% of healthcare organizations reported cyber-attacks, according to the SANS cyber threat report; however, only a fraction of the real number were revealed in the public domain(BRIS & ASRI, 2016).

The healthcare business has been utilising digital developments to enhance healthcare experiences. This began with using digital patient data and it has continued with the rising usage of medical applications, patient registries, portal-linked medical equipment, and wearables. Personal data is any data that may be used to determine who an individual is. In the context of medical, "sensitive medical record" refers to demographic traits, health records, test and lab results, mental problems, insurance cards, as well as other information that a medical specialist collects to determine who a person is and what type of treatment they require. As the use of technology in healthcare expands, so does the potential of cyberattacks(Nifakos et al., 2021).

With the rise of new technologies and digital tools that make people's lives easier, healthcare is moving more and more toward digitalization. On the one hand, this is a great chance, However, it exposes healthcare organisations to plenty of risks, both digital and otherwise, that might cause an attacker to endanger the privacy of clinical systems and, potentially, patient safety. Today, technical cybersecurity countermeasures are used to protect the privacy, integrity, and availability of data and information systems, especially in the healthcare field.

The insecurity of health or eHealth devices, such as those found in the Internet of Medical Things, can have a negative effect on patient treatment (IoMT). In order to build a successful digital security for individuals and the health sector, it is vital to make use of the relevant skills of the scientific community and the general public from the industry and government(Ekshmi, 2022).

Figure 2. Data breach (2019-2020)

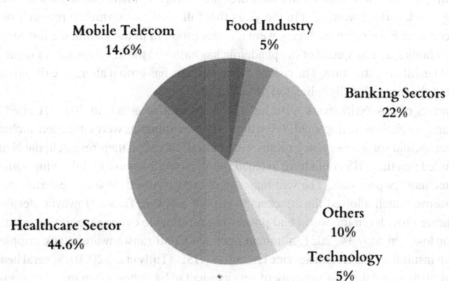

Cybersecurity and healthcare system vulnerabilities Information security is defined by ISO/IEC 27000:2018 as the maintenance of privacy, authenticity, and integrity of data, however in a complex organization like a hospital, or the health ecosystem as a whole, additional security measures are necessary. Dangers were categorized by Rainer et al. as physical, electronic, unauthorized, and authorized. Physical threats included fire and power outages. According to the findings of a case study, power outages are the greatest risk to a hospital information system, caused by staff mistake (for instance, incorrect removal or change of patient records by staff)(IEEE Engineering in Medicine and Biology Society. Annual International Conference (42nd : 2020 : Online) et al., 2020).

Vulnerabilities within a healthcare institution that might have an immediate and significant impact on a patient are the major attack surfaces (i.e. active medical). Unlike major targets, secondary attack surfaces provide no direct risk to the patient but might (inadvertently) aid in the success of attacks elsewhere. Last but not least, the tertiary attack surface comprises the hospital's or organization's financial and administrative systems, inventory systems, power infrastructure, etc., all of which might have far-reaching consequences. New attack surfaces are also available because to developments in biotechnology. This may be accomplished, for instance, if a writer were able to synthesise DNA strands that, after being sequenced and post-processed, formed a file that, when fed into a susceptible application, would result in an open channel for remote control. At the confluence of cybersecurity, cyber-physical protection, and biosecurity, the word "cyber biosecurity" is developed to encompass a wide variety of new forms of cyber-attack in the health and medical professions(Drape et al., 2021).

There was always worry about privacy leaks in the healthcare sector before the advent of digital technology, but the increased interconnection has created many new doors for access. Attacks against the healthcare business via cyberspace can be multinational or state-sponsored and motivated by socioeconomic and economic gain. Medical records of prominent athletes were leaked in a recent attack on the World Anti-Doping Agency, but the perpetrators' motivations are still unknown(Ekshmi, 2022)(Ervural & Ervural, 2018). These attacks don't just take advantage of holes in our defense technology, but also in our people.

Starting in the early 2000s, the healthcare industry became a target of cyberattacks. About 78.8 million medical records were taken in a single incident in 2015, out of a total estimated loss of 113 million(Ekshmi, 2022). More attacks and data breaches using sophisticated tools and strategies over an expanding attack surface were seen in the years that followed. According to research performed by the World Economic Forum, cyber threats were a major problem in the healthcare industry during the 2009 Covid 19 outbreak. The spread of the pandemic has hastened the development of telemedicine and related digital health infrastructure. The risk of cyber mishaps has grown alongside the advancement of technology and the increasing digitalization of healthcare.

Three-quarters of UK NHS trusts were hit by the WannaCry attack in 2017. (United Kingdom). Eighty thousand hospitals were impacted, seven thousand appointments were cancelled, including several hundred surgeries, and some emergency rooms were closed. Based on their research, the National Audit Office concluded that the NHS could have avoided the WannaCry assault by following some very basic information technology protocols. The vast majority of compromised devices were running unpatched operating systems, which allowed the attackers to exploit software flaws. However, despite being the largest healthcare provider in the world and possessing formidable cyber capabilities, a little oversight led to a major loss. On May 14, 2021, a human-operated Conti ransomware attack crippled Ireland's national health institution, the Health Service Executive (HSE)(Tully et al., 2020). Several health systems were knocked offline, and the vast majority of services had to be halted when malicious activity on the health network was detected and shut down. The whole healthcare system fell down, and no one in the industry could access the internet database. This event has prompted policymakers to reconsider whether or not healthcare cybersecurity merits the same level of investment as other industries.

During the Covid 19 outbreak, the healthcare sector in Spain was the worst damaged by cyberattacks(Javed & Afaq, 2021). In 2020, there were over 50,000 recorded attacks or over 430 attacks per week for each company. The number of threats reached 626 in only the month of January 2021. There are many different types of threats, from phishing emails to ransomware. According to the research, ransomware is more common in Spain. Spain has taken emergency measures to improve its cyber defence capabilities in an effort to contain the problem(Ekshmi, 2022).

Figure 3. Reports of cybercrimes in India from 2012 to 2021

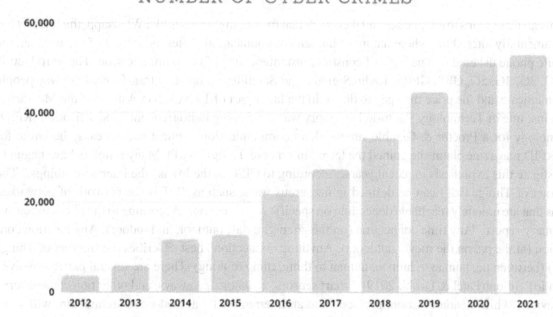

NUMBER OF CYBER CRIMES

Risks Associated With the Healthcare Sector

Numerous cyber-related challenges, ranging from virus threats to distributed denial of service attacks, plague the healthcare sector. Apart from financial damage and privacy violations, all of these threats pose particular issues to the healthcare sector(Require & Capabilities, n.d.). The following are the most commonly recognized and growing risks in the health sector:

- Data theft for monetary gain – the stealing of a person's private information for monetary advantage.
- Data theft for effect - high-profile people's health files are taken and publicly disclosed.
- Ransomware - Malware that prevents users from gaining access a computer or threatens to destroy data until a monetary demand is satisfied.

- Denial of service attack - the act of interrupting a computer or network by overloading it with excess requests for the purpose of extortion, vengeance, or protest.
- Compromise in business email - generating phoney personal correspondence for financial advantage.
- Insider cyberattack entails system interruption or data loss as a result of purposeful or inadvertent insider activities within the industry.
- Third-party suppliers - Healthcare is a large industry that hires contractors for specific activities such as cleaning. They may also be granted access to the organisational network without being aware of the associated hazard.
- Poor disposal of obsolete hardware - Even after erasing or rewriting the data from the device, the data can be recovered(Srinivas et al., 2019).

Cyber Threats on Smart Farming and Agriculture

From carrier pigeons to telephones and then to instant messaging services like Whatsapp, the Internet has fundamentally altered the whole nature of human communication. After the advent of the internet, the mobile phone ushered in a new era of constant, instantaneous global communication. The introduction of 2G, 3G, 4G, 5G, GPS, GPRS, Radio Signals, and Satellites completely transformed the way people communicate and the price they pay to do so. In the latter part of 1999, Kevin Ashton of the Massachusetts Institute of Technology's auto-id laboratory was developing radio frequency identification (RFID) technology for a Proctor & Gamble supply chain communication application. An essay he wrote for the RFID magazine claims he coined the term "Internet of Things" (IoT). Many scholars have begun to investigate this hypothesis in recent years. According to CISCO, the IoT is "the internet of things." The Internet of Things (IoT) can be defined in numerous ways, such as "IoT is the network of networked items that are uniquely reachable depending on specific set of criteria." According to the ITU's executive summary report, "Any time connection (on the go, night, day, outdoor, and indoor), Any location connection (at the pc, on the move, outdoors), Anything connection" best describes the Internet of Things (IoT) (between pc, human to human, human to thing, thing to thing). There are several parties involved in an IoT rollout(Patel & Doshi, 2019). Smart sensors, actuators, gateways, and other objects will serve as devices, while standardization, protocol, and an internationally agreed-upon architecture will serve as communication mediums. "INTERNET" and "THINGS" can easily conclude IoT into "Interconnected things," since IoT can also be characterized as a self-configuring capable infrastructure based on particular standards and protocols.

Following the internet rollout, the number of linked devices increased dramatically.

There will be 75.41 billion connected gadgets in use by 2025, according to a study. The smart capabilities of today's electronics are made possible by the wide variety of sensors embedded into them. A smoke detector detects smoke and alerts the system's brain, while a temperature sensor does the same for the environment's temperature. Through the use of intelligent actuators and microcontrollers, sensors provide smart devices the ability to hear, see, think, and carry out tasks. With sensors as their foundation, the IoT can build the infrastructure of the future. Improved sensor properties including range, detection, sensitivity, accuracy, linearity, and precision lay a solid groundwork for the Internet of Things. Sensors in the IoT are typically linked to microcontrollers or microprocessors(Naresh & Munaswamy, 2019).

Figure 4. IOT devices installed base worldwide from 2015-2025

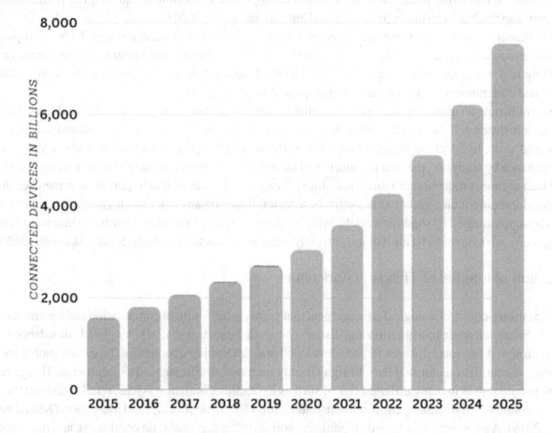

Companies in the agricultural sector and individual farmers alike are using a range of "smart farming" techniques that rely on Internet of Things (IoT) devices in pursuit of increased crop yields. An attack surface is created when sensors spread around a farm can interact with one another over the Internet. Because of this, cybercriminals have ramped up their threats against the agricultural industry, including data theft, denial of service attacks, website defacement, etc.

Safety concerns are warranted due to the rapid increase in the number of internet-connected devices, particularly in the agricultural sector, where farmers may go bankrupt from crop loss. As a result, one of the most pressing challenges facing the agricultural industry today is protecting the many sensors that make up the smart farm ecosystem. U.S. DHS has issued a paper highlighting the significance of precision agriculture (PA) and the related cybersecurity threat and possible vulnerabilities. A paradigm of information security in agriculture that emphasizes confidentiality, integrity, and availability is highlighted in this study. Several distinct types of technology contribute to "smart farming," and this article defines each of them(Barreto & Amaral, 2018).

The world faces new difficulties on a daily basis. These difficulties can also be seen in the farming and agricultural industry. In order to optimise farming processes, "smart farming" implements ICT, in particular the IoT and associated big data analytics. Smart Farming is primarily concerned with the development of digital and electronic crop monitoring in relation to environmental, soil, fertilisation, and irrigation factors. The term "smart farming" refers to the utilisation of technological advancements such as wireless connectivity, portability, adaptability, interoperability, customer and supplier partnerships, and new approaches to business management(Demestichas et al., 2020).

Intelligent networks based on cyber-physical systems are essential to smart farming (CPS). Computer and communication systems can be used to oversee, coordinate, control, and integrate a CPS's activities, enabling real-world interaction via a distributed team of agents. Sensors, actuators, control processing units, and communication devices are all examples of network agents.

Soil moisture, fertilization, and weather oscillation data, for instance, may be collected and transmitted in real time over a cellular wireless network, giving farmers instantaneous access to data and analysis on their land, crop, livestock, logistics, and machines. Because of this, the smart farm is able to enhance its performance by analyzing the data it collects and taking appropriate action based on the findings, which may lead to more production or more streamlined operations. However, it is important to remember that the development training and production of these technologies means that even high-end hardware will soon be supplemented by superior models, bringing down the price of outdated hardware that would still bring many advantages to farms that are currently without access to electricity(Sontowski et al., 2020).

Adoption of Internet of Things in Agriculture

IoT is a cutting-edge technological advancement that points to the future of computation and communication. It makes reference to a question and distant system that can design itself. As global subsidence has just returned, it has caused waves in both developed and developing economies. To ensure global food security, the farming sector will have to significantly increase its efficiency. The Internet of Things has many potential uses in many different fields, such as agriculture, human services, retail, transportation, the environment, production network administration, foundation monitoring, and many more(Khursheed et al., 2016). Agricultural uses include monitoring soil and plants, greenhouse conditions, and the supply chain from the natural pecking order. Acknowledgment and widespread adoption of IoT are contingent on IoT's underlying infrastructure being managed in a way that is both clever and useful to end users.

Machine-to-machine interface, electronic communication protocols, energy collection innovations, sensor and actuator breakthroughs, GPS devices (GPS) technology, and software all contribute directly to the development of the Internet of Things. Labeling/Geo-storing, Bio-measurements, Machine Vision, Robotics, Telepresence, Customizable Autonomy, Life Recorders, Personal Hidden Elements, and Clean Innovations are all examples of technologies that might improve the IoT. Let's examine some potential use cases for the Internet of Things (IoT) applications in farming and agriculture to get a feel for the benefits they could provide(R. K. Naresh et al., 2021).

1. Control of Water
2. Fertigation
3. Monitoring of the Health and Development of Livestock
4. Crop Communication
5. Drilling, Seeding and Spraying
6. Supply Chain Management

Types of Cyber-Attacks on Smart Farming

Several security incidents affecting the Internet of Things have been documented in recent years. The ecology of smart farming is vulnerable to similar threats. Experts believe that the architecture and protocols utilized to roll out a connected environment will have a significant impact on the susceptibility of that ecosystem to attack by malicious actors(Sontowski et al., 2020).

- Pass
- word Cracking
- Evil Twin Access Point
- Key Reinstallation Attacks
- ARP spoofing attack
- DNS spoofing attack

Figure 5. Security and privacy in smart farming
(Gupta et al., 2020)

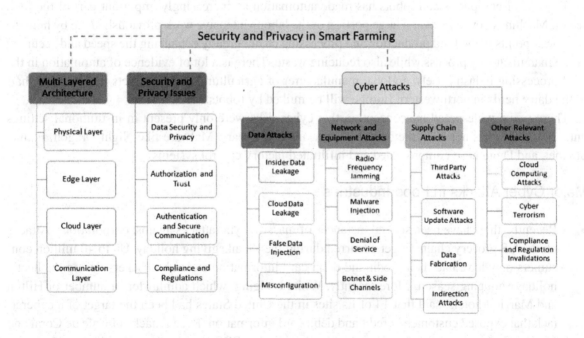

Cyber Threats on Food Industry

Since the inception of computer systems, security has been a major concern. Recent attempts by hackers to gain access to systems via novel means have revealed sensitive information. Recent trends in cyber-attacks have put the food and beverage industry at the forefront of the cybersecurity community, despite the fact that most of us do not associate these supply chains with such security threats. Based on the National Cybersecurity Institute's claim that "the Department of Homeland Security has identified the Agriculture and Food sector as one of the 16 national vital infrastructures," it is evident that these businesses face a greater risk of cyberattacks than any other industry. It's "agro-terrorism" that has to be addressed when discussing the agricultural and food sectors(Khursheed et al., 2016).

According to Forbes, agro-terrorism is "the deliberate poisoning of the food supply with the objective of frightening the populace and causing injury." There are two distinct ways in which agroterrorism might manifest itself. First, hackers can infiltrate large distribution networks and sabotage food delivery to areas that need want it. The loss of any region's food and drink supply would have disastrous consequences. As a second concern, hackers may compromise PLCs used in food irradiation, giving them the power to alter the levels of chemicals used in the process and therefore causing harm or even death to innocent people. Try to picture a world where your most beloved meals really threatened your health. Because of this, food sector cyber security is an issue that has to be addressed.

You might be wondering why the food sector, or any other manufacturing industry, needs cyber security. Why should we worry about this if manufacturing companies don't deal with credit card information or high level money and there aren't many confidential papers saved or transmitted over the internet? This is because an industry's future direction is just as vulnerable as its current stage of production to assault. In order to advance an industry as a whole, cyber security is essential for protecting the trade secrets and goodwill of individual companies within that industry(Van Der Linden et al., 2020).

The rise of computers and robots has made automation an increasingly important part of the food sector. Machines now take over a large portion of the labour-intensive work previously done by humans at various points in the food production and processing chain, greatly enhancing the speed and accuracy of the manufacturing process while also reducing waste. There is a lot of evidence of automation in the food processing industry. Lely, a global manufacturer of agricultural tools, predicts that by 2025, half of the dairy herds in northwestern Europe will be milked by robots.

There was a widespread misconception that cyber risks were only present in institutional settings until 2010. This has not been the case, however, in recent years. Malware like Night Dragon, Flame, Stuxnet, and Dugu have compromised and infiltrated factory control systems.

Major Cyber Attacks in Food Industries

- Recently, there have been several instances of massive cyberattacks against corporations. Attacks on the US grocery chain Target occurred during the Thanksgiving holiday. Up to 40 million consumers may have had their credit and debit card information stolen by hackers during the hectic holiday shopping season. More recently, White Lodging, which administers a number of Hilton and Marriott hotels, said that 14 of its sites in the United States had been the target of a cyberattack that exposed customers' credit and debit card information. Recent hacks of Cafe de Coral and Biggby Coffee show that thieves aren't simply targeting POS systems but rather looking for every opportunity to exploit(Oktaviani.J, 2018).
- Cybercriminals also targeted the global food chain Subway. In 2012, two Romanian individuals confessed to being part of a global conspiracy that compromised the credit card payment systems of over 150 different Subway franchisees, resulting in the theft of information for over 146,000 different accounts.
- The soft-serve ice cream chain Dairy Queen was also hit by cybercriminals. In 2014, a cyber-attack including third-party back-off malware infected by stolen account credentials at a third-party vendor exposed the credit card and debit card data of consumers at almost 400 Dairy Queen and

Orange Julius locations. Like many other victims of similar attacks, P.F. Chang's China Bistro had its credit card and debit card credentials for 33 of its restaurants hacked and sold on the internet in September 2013 and June 2014.

In addition to stealing consumers' private information, cybercriminals are also going after the copyrights and other intellectual property of the industry's biggest players and their most successful works of art(Khursheed et al., 2016).

PREVENTION AND RESPONSIBILITIES

It is important to have effective regulation and policy in place to protect individuals' privacy and personal data in the digital age.

One possible recommendation for improving regulation and policy around data privacy is to strengthen data protection laws and regulations. To accomplish this, laws might be drafted or revised to give people more say over their personal information and to hold businesses more accountable for the data they collect, retain, and use. The General Data Protection Regulation (GDPR) of the European Union, for instance, gives individuals the right to view, rectify, and erase any personal data that pertains to them. There are mandated breach notifications and penalties for violation imposed on businesses that store and analyze personal data.

A further suggestion may be to make data gathering and use more transparent. To achieve this goal, it may be necessary to mandate that businesses seek individuals' express consent before collecting or using their personal information, as well as to mandate that businesses produce clear and succinct privacy controls that explain how they gather and use such information. Additionally, companies could be required to disclose any third-party companies they share personal data with.

Finally, another possible recommendation is to increase awareness and education around data privacy. This could involve educating individuals on how to protect their personal data, such as by using strong passwords and avoiding public Wi-Fi networks. It could also involve educating individuals on their rights regarding their personal data, and the potential risks of sharing personal data with third-party companies.

A person must be appointed in the organization as chief information security officer (CISO) is a high-ranking executive in charge of overseeing and ensuring the project's administration and security. Assistance with and coordination of security framework setup would fall within your purview(Spremić & Šimunic, 2018).

- Ensuring and verifying the disaster recovery and business development plans. Maintaining and reviewing digital controls, methods, and attack response plans. Accept methods based on access and character.
- Having a firm grasp of the company's IT risk status and keeping that understanding up to date. Maintaining uniformity with established norms and ever-evolving regulations.
- Ensuring that all faculty members in the project have access to a streamlined internal communication system and gaining approval for the project's consistency.
- Contracting, training, and mentoring the many teams, employees, contractors, and vendors who contribute to digital security is part of this role.

- Keeping up with the ever-evolving needs of digital security and risk management to drive forward-thinking development.

To mitigate the critical impact of cyber threats on the digital economy, numerous risk management strategies have been proposed. These strategies include enhancing cybersecurity awareness and training programs, investing in advanced cybersecurity technologies, and implementing effective data governance and risk management frameworks.

Risk Mitigation Approaches

Risk Mitigation Approaches are essential for businesses to protect themselves from cyber threats in the digital economy. Here are some strategies that can be employed:

i.   *Develop a comprehensive cybersecurity policy:* Businesses should develop a cybersecurity policy that clearly outlines the roles and responsibilities of employees, and includes guidelines on how to handle sensitive information. The policy should be regularly reviewed and updated to stay relevant to the changing threat landscape.

ii. *Perform periodic security audits:* Standard security audits can assist firms in identifying system and network risks. These assessments should be conducted by experienced professionals and should cover both internal and external threats.

iii *Incorporate additional authentication methods:* With multi-factor authentication, users are required to enter two or more parts of data in order to access respective accounts, adding an additional layer of security to their login information. This can significantly reduce the risk of unauthorized access.

iv   *Educate staff members on best practises for cybersecurity:* For an organisation to foster a culture of security, employee training is essential. Employees should receive security awareness training on how to utilise business resources safely as well as how to spot and report suspicious behaviour.

v.   *Use encryption:* By encrypting sensitive data both in transit and at rest, encryption can help prevent unauthorised access to it. This may make it more difficult for fraudsters to access or intercept the data.

vi   *Network activity:* should be regularly monitored so that organisations may identify and counter any risks. To spot anomalous behaviour, this may entail putting intrusion detection systems and log management tools into place.

vii *Prepare a disaster recovery strategy:* In the case of a cyberattack, having a plan can help firms react swiftly and limit damage. The strategy should include actions for stopping the assault, regaining access to systems and data, and informing stakeholders.

Businesses can better protect themselves from cyber threats and lessen the effects of any potential breaches by putting these risk management measures into practise.

POTENTIAL POSITIVE IMPACTS OF CYBER TECHNOLOGY

Cyber technology is being employed in several ways to advance a number of sectors and society at large. Here are a few instances:

Healthcare: Healthcare is being revolutionised by cyber technology, which has improved patient care and results. For example, telemedicine allows medical experts to diagnose and treat patients from a distance, which is especially helpful for those who live in distant or underdeveloped locations. In order to offer more individualised and precise diagnoses and treatments, patient data can also be examined using machine learning algorithms.

Education: By enhancing accessibility and effectiveness, cyber technology is altering education. Students have access to online learning tools and platforms that allow them to learn at their own speed and from any location in the world. Technologies like virtual reality and augmented reality can also offer immersive and interesting learning opportunities.

Cyber technology is enhancing transportation systems by boosting productivity and minimising environmental effect. Smart traffic management systems, for instance, can enhance traffic flow and ease congestion, while autonomous and electric vehicles can cut carbon emissions while also enhancing safety.

Environment: By encouraging sustainability and lowering waste, cyber technology is assisting in addressing environmental issues. For instance, precision agriculture may decrease resource use and environmental impact while smart energy grids can optimise energy distribution and eliminate waste.

Business: By enabling more effective and efficient operations, cyber technology is revolutionising the way organisations function. For instance, data analytics can support organisations in making better decisions and enhancing performance, while automation can boost output and cut expenses.

Responsible Development and Deployment of Cyber Technologies

Understanding the possible risks and ramifications of using cyber technologies is crucial for addressing the issue of their responsible development and deployment. Integrating moral and social factors into the design and implementation process is one method to do this.

The significance of incorporating ethics and social responsibility into the creation and application of cyber technologies has received more attention in recent years. This is due to the fact that the impact of cyber attacks goes beyond only monetary loss or business interruption, but also involves the possibility of harming both specific people and society as a whole.

Organizations can think about adopting ethical frameworks and standards, like those created by the IEEE Global Initiative on Ethics of Autonomous and Intelligent Systems or the General Data Protection Regulation of the European Union, to ensure responsible development and implementation (GDPR). These frameworks offer direction on the moral and social ramifications of technology and can assist businesses in adopting more ethical procedures.

Additionally, it's critical for businesses to interact with stakeholders, such as clients, staff members, and the general public, to learn about their worries and viewpoints regarding the usage of cyber technology. This can assist organisations in identifying and addressing potential moral and societal problems as well as creating more inclusive and socially responsible solutions.

To ensure responsible development and deployment, businesses might also think about putting transparency and accountability systems in place. This can involve establishing systems for supervision and accountability as well as crystal-clear policies and processes for data management and protection. Transparent communication about the collection and use of data can also be provided.

Organizations may contribute to reduce possible dangers and make sure that the impact of these technologies on people and society is positive and useful by including social and ethical considerations into the development and deployment of cyber technologies.

It's crucial to understand that these developments also come with substantial hazards and difficulties, like cybersecurity dangers and privacy issues. In order to ensure that the advantages are increased while the hazards are decreased, responsible development and deployment of these technologies are required. This may entail taking steps to preserve user privacy, create robust cybersecurity protocols, and encourage ethical concerns during development and deployment.

CONCLUSION

The analysis of this chapter highlighted the critical impact of cyber threats on the digital economy. It showed that the emergence of big data in the ever-growing digital economy has created the necessity to secure critical organizational information. The lack of cybersecurity awareness exposes organizations to potential cyber threats, making sensitive assets vulnerable to significant risk. The health and financial industries are primary targets for malicious or criminal attacks. Remote or semi-remote working environments have made it more difficult for organizations to capture these attacks.

To tackle cybersecurity awareness challenges, personnel, management, and infrastructure capabilities were identified as thematic dimensions drawing on the dynamic capabilities framework. Moreover, risk management strategies were discussed, including proactive measures such as conducting regular cybersecurity audits, strengthening access controls, and training employees on cybersecurity best practices.

In is clear that the critical impact of cyber threats on the digital economy cannot be overstated. As such, it is crucial for organizations to be proactive in managing cyber risks and implementing cybersecurity awareness capabilities. Failure to do so not only exposes sensitive assets to significant risks but also jeopardizes the reputation and trust of the organization. Therefore, organizations must prioritize cybersecurity as a strategic imperative to remain resilient in the face of an ever-increasing threat landscape.

Rapid advances in technology have completely reshaped the food and beverage industry to the point where how those firms use that technology is crucial to their survival or failure. However, the prevalence of fraud and cyberattacks has grown alongside these technical developments. Therefore, cybersecurity is crucial to maximizing the benefits of all emerging technologies. Data breaches and threats are a severe matter for the sector, but protecting customers' private information is the first priority. Most businesses, governments, and other organizations rely heavily on internal information management (IS) and would swiftly cease to exist if the technology that supports their operational processes information technology, IT, and recently developed digital technologies were to collapse.

REFERENCES

Afaq, S. A., Husain, M. S., Bello, A., & Sadia, H. (n.d.). A Critical Analysis of Cyber Threats and Their Global Impact. In *Computational Intelligent Security in Wireless Communications* (pp. 201–220). CRC Press. doi:10.1201/9781003323426-12

Akter, S., Uddin, M. R., Sajib, S., Lee, W. J. T., Michael, K., & Hossain, M. A. (2022). Reconceptualizing cybersecurity awareness capability in the data-driven digital economy. *Annals of Operations Research*. Advance online publication. doi:10.100710479-022-04844-8 PMID:35935743

Barefoot, K., Curtis, D., & Jolliff, W. (2018). *Nicholson, Jessica R. Omohundro, R.* Defining and Measuring the Digital Economy. US Department of Commerce Bureau of Economic Analysis., https://www.tandfonline.com/doi/full/10.1081/ERC-200027380

Barreto, L., & Amaral, A. (2018). Smart Farming: Cyber Security Challenges. *9th International Conference on Intelligent Systems 2018: Theory, Research and Innovation in Applications, IS 2018 - Proceedings*, (pp. 870–876). 10.1109/IS.2018.8710531

BRIS. A. LE, & ASRI, W. EL. (2016). State of Cybersecurity & Cyber Threats in Healthcare Organizations. *Dissertation*, 2005–2013. https://www.americanbar.org/content/dam/aba/publications/books/healthcare_data_breaches.authcheckdam.pdf

Demestichas, K., Peppes, N., & Alexakis, T. (2020). Survey on security threats in agricultural iot and smart farming. *Sensors (Basel)*, *20*(22), 1–17. doi:10.339020226458 PMID:33198160

Drape, T., Magerkorth, N., Sen, A., Simpson, J., Seibel, M., Murch, R. S., & Duncan, S. E. (2021). Assessing the Role of Cyberbiosecurity in Agriculture: A Case Study. *Frontiers in Bioengineering and Biotechnology*, *9*(August), 1–9. doi:10.3389/fbioe.2021.737927 PMID:34490231

Ekshmi, A. S. (2022). Growing Concern on Healthcare Cyberattacks & Need for Cybersecurity. January. https://doi.org/ doi:10.31234/osf.io/7m4qf

Ervural, B. C., & Ervural, B. (2018). *Overview of Cyber Security in the Industry 4.0 Era.* 267–284. Springer. doi:10.1007/978-3-319-57870-5_16

Gupta, M., Abdelsalam, M., Khorsandroo, S., & Mittal, S. (2020). Security and Privacy in Smart Farming: Challenges and Opportunities. *IEEE Access : Practical Innovations, Open Solutions*, *8*, 34564–34584. doi:10.1109/ACCESS.2020.2975142

Jana, F. A. A., Kunal, S. B., & Mondal, K. (n.d.). A survey of Indian Cyber crime and law and its pre- vention approach What is the Importance of Cyber. *International Journal of Advanced Computer Technology*, 48–55.

Javed, N., & Afaq, S. A. (2021). *COVID-19 AS AN OPPORTUNITY FOR CYBERCRIMINALS. December 2022.* NIH.

Khursheed, A., Kumar, M., & Sharma, M. (2016). Security against cyber attacks in food industry. *International Journal of Control Theory and Applications*, *9*(17), 8623–8628.

Manning, L. (2019). Food defence: Refining the taxonomy of food defence threats. *Trends in Food Science & Technology*, *85*, 107–115. doi:10.1016/j.tifs.2019.01.008

Moran, A. (2020). Cyber security. *International Security Studies: Theory and Practice*, 299–312.

Naresh, M., & Munaswamy, P. (2019). *Smart Agriculture System using IoT Technology. 5*, 98–102.

Naresh, R. K., Lalit, P. K. S., Kumar, A. K., & Shivangi, M. S. C. (2021). Role of IoT Technology in Agriculture for Reshaping the Future of Farming in India: A Review. *International Journal of Current Microbiology and Applied Sciences*, *10*(2), 439–451. doi:10.20546/ijcmas.2021.1002.052

Nifakos, S., Chandramouli, K., Nikolaou, C. K., Papachristou, P., Koch, S., Panaousis, E., & Bonacina, S. (2021). Influence of human factors on cyber security within healthcare organisations: A systematic review. *Sensors (Basel)*, *21*(15), 1–25. doi:10.339021155119 PMID:34372354

Oktaviani, J. (2018). Cybersecurity and the future of agri-food industries. *Sereal Untuk*, *51*(1), 51.

Patel, C., & Doshi, N. (2019). *Security Challenges in IoT Cyber World*. Springer International Publishing., doi:10.1007/978-3-030-01560-2_8

Qaiser, S. (2020). *Cyber Crime : Rise*. Evolution and Prevention. July., doi:10.13140/RG.2.2.18533.01762

Ramadan, R. A., Aboshosha, B. W., Alshudukhi, J. S., Alzahrani, A. J., El-Sayed, A., & Dessouky, M. M. (2021). Cybersecurity and Countermeasures at the Time of Pandemic. *Journal of Advanced Transportation*, *2021*(2003). doi:10.1155/2021/6627264

Require, I. T., & Capabilities, I. (n.d.). *HEALTH CARE AND CYBER SECURITY.*

Sharma, S., & Dhote, T. (2021). Cybersecurity – Vulnerability Assessment of Attacks, Challenges and Defence Strategies in Industry 4.0. Ecosystem. *Miles IT*, *10*(2), 203–210.

Shivani, G. (2015). Cyber Security In Digital Economy. *Shivani Grover 12*(2349), 1563–1569.

Sontowski, S., Gupta, M., Laya Chukkapalli, S. S., Abdelsalam, M., Mittal, S., Joshi, A., & Sandhu, R. (2020). Cyber Attacks on Smart Farming Infrastructure. *Proceedings - 2020 IEEE 6th International Conference on Collaboration and Internet Computing, CIC 2020*, (pp. 135–143). IEEE. 10.1109/CIC50333.2020.00025

Spremić, M., & Šimunic, A. (2018). Cyber security challenges in digital economy. *Lecture Notes in Engineering and Computer Science*, *2235*, 2–7.

Srinivas, J., Das, A. K., & Kumar, N. (2019). Government regulations in cyber security: Framework, standards and recommendations. *Future Generation Computer Systems*, *92*, 178–188. doi:10.1016/j.future.2018.09.063

Teoh, C. S., & Mahmood, A. K. (2017). National cyber security strategies for digital economy. *Journal of Theoretical and Applied Information Technology*, *95*(23), 6510–6522. doi:10.1109/ICRIIS.2017.8002519

Tully, J., Selzer, J., Phillips, J. P., O'Connor, P., & Dameff, C. (2020). Healthcare Challenges in the Era of Cybersecurity. *Health Security*, *18*(3), 228–231. doi:10.1089/hs.2019.0123 PMID:32559153

Van Der Linden, D., Michalec, O. A., & Zamansky, A. (2020). Cybersecurity for Smart Farming: Socio-Cultural Context Matters. *IEEE Technology and Society Magazine*, *39*(4), 28–35. doi:10.1109/MTS.2020.3031844

WEF. (2022). The Global Risks Report 2022. 17th Edition. In *World Economic Forum.*

Chapter 6
Cyber Threats in Agriculture and the Food Industry:
An Indian Perspective

Harish Chandra Verma

https://orcid.org/0000-0002-5085-2004

ICAR-Central Institute for Subtropical Horticulture, India

Saurabh Srivastava

https://orcid.org/0000-0001-7654-0220

Integral University, India

Tasneem Ahmed

Integral University, India

Nayyar Ali Usmani

PUMA SE, Germany

ABSTRACT

A cyber threat is a harmful act meant to steal, corrupt, or undermine an organization's digital stability. At present cyber threats in agriculture and food industry is a rising concern because farming is becoming more dependent on computers and Internet access. The attacks that fall under this category include denial of service attacks, computer viruses. Growing food demand and shortage of skilled labours have necessitated for the adoption of digital agriculture. The major challenge is to prevent it from cyber threats for successful implementation. As ransomware hackers are increasingly likely to target food supply chain, the food industry is experiencing an increase in cyber-security threats, which might result in business interruptions. Due to the fragile nature of the food supply, the entire food sector needs to be protected . In this chapter, major issue on cyber threats, challenges of cyber-security, some notable cyber-attacks, and cyber-security solutions for the food/agriculture industry are discussed in detail.

DOI: 10.4018/978-1-6684-8133-2.ch006

INTRODUCTION

Globally, India is one of the major countries in the agriculture sector and agriculture is the primary source of livelihood for about 58% of India's population. Agriculture is considered the backbone of the Indian economy. It has helped the Indian economy in several ways: providing food, a source of national income, a Source of employment generation, accumulation of the National Capital, provides raw materials for industries.Similarly, according to the United Nations (UN), the world population is expected to exceed 9 billion by 2050 (Roser, 2020; Godfray et al., 2010). According to the United Nations Food and Agriculture Organization, such a rise in population necessitates an increase in food production of about 70%. Many digital devices such as smartphones, various sensors, global position systems (GPSs), robotics, and drones could be utilised to extract valuable data analysis and make effective decisions to increase food production with less human resources and intervention (Adel et al., 2022). A criminal act that destroys data, steals data, or otherwise harms digital infrastructure is considered a cyber security concern.Cybersecurity is a multidisciplinary domain consisting of cybersecurity, bio-security, and cyber-physical security (Fountas et al., 2015).

The digitalization of agriculture is an ongoing process that causes an increasing number of agricultural systems to be connected through the Internet (Adel et al., 2022). Because farming is becoming more dependent on computers and Internet connectivity, cyber security in the agriculture and food industry is a growing problem. Digital agriculture is not immune to cyber-attacks, which can range from controlling the heating and ventilation system of a greenhouse to controlling a drone used for spraying crops (Adel et al., 2022). The issue has received major research attention in recent years when the agro-technology community, the public sector, and scholars were made aware of it. Smart technology is now being used in agriculture to assist meet the rising demand for food. Farms are at a higher risk of becoming the target of cyber-attacks due to the increased automation and connection that comes with it. Agriculture keeps implementing cutting-edge smart technologies that enable expanded remote monitoring of livestock and crops.

Better internet connectivity allows for many productivity improvements and improves the farming system in other ways. However, many of these systems are mission-critical, such as milking systems in the dairy industry. Such systems must be constantly available as downtime can quickly cause harm to the livestock(Nikander et al., 2020). Many of the systems are dependent on an uninterrupted supply of electricity, water and, increasingly, network connectivity. In the past few years, the agricultural sector has realized that connecting machinery to the Internet also exposes these systems to a wide range of cyber threats (Barreto, and Amaral, 2018; Cooper, 2015; DHS, 2018; Jahn et al., 2019; Schimmelpfennig, 2016). There are numerous use cases where mission-critical systems now need an internet connection, ranging from remote monitoring and control of animal shed automation to tractor implements remotely connected to farm management software via the ISOBUS-10 data communications standard (ISO, 2015).Critical connected machinery that is required at a crucial time could be disabled by an attack on the companies that supply fertiliser and agricultural equipment. It could change the fertilisers' nutrient content (Jahn, 2019) which could seriously destroy the crops rather than nourish them. Cooper (2015) give a broad review of cybersecurity in the food and agricultural sectors. They also talk about plans, policies, and cyber-terrorism.DigAg (pronounced "Didge-Ag") has many applications. Some are crop management, automation, precision farming (Hedley, and Yule, 2009), and monitoring activities. The latter include watching over or controlling irrigation and water quality (Salam, 2019), soil(Shamal et al., 2016), weather, farm, pests, and diseases (Katta et al., 2022). The subsequent sections highlight the use of DigAg in smart irrigation(Blender et al., 2016) and intelligent machinery (Seselja, 2022), discussing some of the threats that malicious actors could exploit. By using smart irrigation, Chile has lowered the amount of water required for farming by 70% thanks to sensors buried in the soil to measure blueberry irrigation (Alvino and Marino, 2017). In India, monitoring activity has used agricultural data to forecast and prevent crop diseases, which has decreased the risk associated with crop output failure (Oerke, and Dehne, 2004). Similarly, Fruit farmers in Slovenia have used similar data-driven strategies to combat pests successfully. The Drones and Internet *of Things* (IoT) provide new technologies and innovations. Smart agriculture, smart farming, and Agriculture 4.0 are the names given to these emerging technologies and advancements used in agriculture. To help farmers benefit from advancements, smart farming incorporates a variety of technologies, tools, protocols, and computing paradigms (Zanella et al., 2020).

The use of smart farming techniques increases your likelihood of coming across previously undetected zero-day attacks. Researchers (Abdelsalam et al., 2017; Chandola et al., 2009; Wang et al., 2010; Wang et al., 2011; Azmandian et al., 2011) reported that anomaly detection is a very important solution against such attacks. Any anomalous activity that differs from the established database of typical behaviour is sought out using anomaly detection tools (Gupta et al., 2020). The event of a cyberattack on the food ecosystem that targets farms, transportation infrastructure, or food processing industrial control systems (ICSs) might rise enormously (Gupta et al., 2020). Another new technology, blockchain, promises to be a trustworthy source of information about farms, inventory, and contracts in agriculture, otherwise gathering such data is frequently quite expensive (Xiong et al., 2020;). A trustworthy method of tracking transactions between anonymous individuals is provided by blockchain technology. By implementing smart contracts, fraud and malfunctions can be rapidly identified, and issues can be notified in real-time(Xiong, et al., 2020; Haveson et al., 2017; Sylvester, 2019) . farmers produce many agricultural products. Traditional e-commerce does not want to serve small farmers because of the low transaction volume and tiny scale, which keeps these participants out of the market. With the use of blockchain technology, transaction costs can be drastically reduced and integrated into the market(Gupta et al., 2020; Karame, 2016). In this chapter, types of cyber threats, major issues, challenges, and solutions to cyber-security are discussed. Some notable Cyber-attacks in the domain of the food/agriculture industry are also discussed in detail.

DIFFERENT TYPES OF CYBER THREATS

The increasing application of smart technology and devices only elevates the risk of the agricultural industry being impacted by a cyber-attack.Several potential cyber-attack scenarios could have a significant negative impact on precision agriculture. Some of these instances of attacks that have occurred or are foreseen with a high degree of probability in the agricultural industry are as follows-

Ransomware Attack

It is a type of malicious software that infects a computer and restricts users' access to it until a ransom is paid. Ransomware was the top cyber threat in 2021, which comprised 23% of Cyber Attacks. An employee opens an email attachment and ransomware spreads across the network, encrypting data and halting production. Ransomware encryption cannot be broken, at least not currently. Many smaller businesses are unable to pay the ransom, but if you don't, your data is lost. Even after paying ransoms, data has been kept back in some recent attacks (Zanella et al., 2020; Benavides et al., 2020).

Data Integrity Attack

It is typically an intentional attack most commonly done by malware that deletes or modifies the content of a mobile device's address book. It may be human error, unintended data transfer errors, misconfigurations and security errors, malware, insider threats, and cyber-attacks(Gupta et al., 2020).

Sensor Hack

An irrigation network is breached by a cyber-threat actor, who then sends false data into a sensor network to demonstrate the continual need for watering. Since the sensor is connected to an automatic irrigation decision support system, the fields flood, seriously harming the crops(Gupta et al., 2020; Guarda et al., 2019).

IoT Attack

This attack can originate from the channels that connect IoT components. For example, A cyber threat actor modifies an Internet of Things (IoT) sensor that regulates the environment of a large chicken barn and purposely manipulates incorrect data to PLCs. The temperature and feeding conditions are severely impacted by the interference, which has an impact on animal health and productivity (Adel et al., 2022).

SOME MAJOR ISSUES RELATED TO CYBER-SECURITY IN THE FOOD/AGRICULTURE INDUSTRY

The food and agricultural sector includes a wide range of businesses that offer a wide range of goods and services. Everything from tractor auto-steer systems to crop moisture testing to automated distribution warehouses is automated and networked on large farms and ranches. Phishingis a virtual pest that aims to fraudulently obtain confidential user data, such as ID and password. Phishing usually achieves end-user from fraudulent emails or websites (Benavides et al., 2020; Guarda et al., 2019). Unlike conventional crop management techniques that rely on farmers or ground vehicles to evaluate crop health status, drone-based smart farming uses autonomous technology to perform aerial monitoring of agricultural fields to save time and money while preventing damage to crops. In this technology, a drone which monitors the field for spraying, and taking images of crop conditions is depicted in Fig. 1.

The risk of prospective cyber-attacks has traditionally been considered minimal for the agricultural sector fora long time.Cybercrime is posing a serious threat to agribusiness, as more farms and food processing facilities use new technologies to expedite operations and link with supply chain services. The number of cyber-attacks is on the rise.The agricultural and food industries, like many others, rely on just-in-time supply chains, necessitating sophisticated logistical procedures. Because supply chains affected by cyber-attacks cannot afford any downtime, it is quite likely that these companies will pay the ransom to resume operations.In addition to implementing Smart Farming and installing sensors that can track soil quality, water feed levels, and crop irrigation controls, more and more farms are expanding into new business sectors.

Figure 1. Agriculture drone sprayer
(Source: https://www.tradeindia.com/)

The major issues of cyber-security in the food and agricultural sector include a wide range of businesses as given below:

1. Food production networks and food firm business networks are at risk because cyber threat actors want to stop production, endangering the lives of people. Any large-scale food production or distribution operations that are shut down produce an untenable situation that gives cyber-criminals an unbeatable edge.
2. Restaurants and retail establishments require a dependable and accessible supplier of food supplies. Any disruption may lead to price increases or shortages that have an impact on people's daily life.
3. The world's food supply chain is fragile and is controlled by a very limited number of significant food businesses.
4. The nation's food supply chain is made up of several interdependent businesses. A halt or slowdown during harvest season, for instance, might have an impact on the entire industry as food distribution

networks and processing facilities experience the consequences of a possible ransomware attack that may have happened weeks in advance.

5. Disrupting any large-scale food distribution or production operations results in an uncomfortable situation that gives cybercriminals an unbeatable edge. Companies and authorities are aware that an immediate solution is necessary to prevent public unrest. It benefits the perpetrator because the victim must move quickly.

6. Your business' supply chain still depends in some way on network infrastructure. The systems are vulnerable to cyberattacks if they are online. Rather than if, it is a matter of when cybercriminals will target it.

7. Malicious hackers are constantly searching for new weaknesses to exploit and any chances to make money. Incorrectly setup devices that are left open to the internet can still be found and controlled by cybercriminals anywhere in the world via their IP address, posing a security risk. Any of these flaws can give an attacker quick access to a smart farming network giving the adversary the option of seizing control to carry out sabotage or encrypting your data and holding it hostage.

SOME UNUSUAL CYBER ATTACKS ON FOOD/AGRICULTURE INDUSTRY

Home Chef

Home Chef is a startup that sells culinary supplies, meal kits, and recipes to its clients. It is owned by Kroger Foods. In May 2020, security experts said that they discovered Home Chef users' usernames and passwords being sold on the dark web. The Chicago-based business said shortly after that information about an unspecified number of its customers had been compromised as a result of a security issue. The risk to users of these services comes from this type of security incident, which does not endanger the food supply(Bowcut, 2021; Zahidi, 2022).

Loaves and Fishes

Through a network of mobile "drive-through" style food distribution stations, non-profit food provider Loaves & Fishes provides wholesome goods to people and families going through temporary hardship. They revealed that private client data was stolen during the larger Blackbaud assault in August 2020. Blackbaud, a company that offers software and cloud hosting solutions, halted a ransomware attack from encrypting files but paid the demanded ransom to stop the hackers from revealing secure information about its clients, one of whom was Loaves & Fishes. Blackbaud stated that although there is no proof that the data was sold online, it is always possible (Bowcut, 2021).

JFC International

JFC International said that several of its IT systems had been impacted by a ransomware assault in March 2021. JFC is a significant wholesaler and distributor of Asian culinary items for the US and European markets. The corporation said the attacks affected the Europe Group of JFC International. Soon after informing law police, staff members, and business partners about the occurrence, they were able to restart regular operations (Xiong et al., 2020).

Harvest Sherwood Food Distributors

Data that leaked on the Happy Blog, a Tor-hidden service, in May 2020 showed that Harvest Sherwood Food Distributors had been hacked by hackers using the REvil ransomware. Critical company data was stolen by the attackers, who also threatened to make it publicly known. The ransomware known as REvil is the same one later employed against JBS Meats. Approximately 2,600 files from the food wholesaler were stolen by the attackers. Cash flow analysis, distributor information, business insurance content, and vendor data were among the stolen data. Additionally, there were scans of the driver's licences of those who were part of the Harvest Sherwood distribution network.

CASE STUDY: JBS-THE MEATPACKER

The largest beef supplier in the world, JBS, fell prey to a ransomware attack in 2021 that was launched by a Russian-based criminal organisation. The strike sent shockwaves through the entire food business by paralysing a sizable chunk of the beef supply chain (Bowcut, 2021; Duncan et al., 2019). The FBI confirmed that the REvil ransomware was used in the cyberattack. Thirteen meat plants, including JBS facilities in Colorado, Iowa, Minnesota, Pennsylvania, Nebraska, and Texas, had their operations halted as a result of the attack. This type of ransomware has been linked to GOLD SOUTHFIELD, a financially motivated group that operates a "Ransomware as a service" criminal enterprise. Utilizing exploit kits, scan-and-exploit strategies, RDP servers, and software installers with backdoors, the gang disseminates ransomware.The JBS hack set off a domino effect that quickly spread across the entire country. The imbalance between supply and demand rapidly tipped out of whack, sending wholesale meat prices skyrocketing. Because farms and ranches were unable to transport their livestock to markets, there was an excess, which lowered wholesale prices. Restaurants and wholesalers were unable to obtain packaged and processed meat. The corresponding scarcity drove consumer prices skyward.

The damaging consequences of this attack on just one link in the global food supply chain serve as a reminder of how precarious our food supply is. Restaurant owners were already hard-pressed to find reliable meat sources as the world opened up after the Coronavirus pandemic. As a result of the necessity to ensure a reliable food supply, the stakes were high. JBS decided to comply with the hacker's demand and pay the ransom. JBS settled their differences with the hackers by giving them $11 million in Bitcoin.

CHALLENGES OF CYBER SECURITY IN THE FOOD/AGRICULTURE INDUSTRY

The fact that the food supply chain typically functions so well is one of the primary reasons Americans give little thought to threats and the fragility of the system. As a result, while being one of the 16 essential infrastructure sectors identified by the Department of Homeland Security, the nation's food supply chain receives much less attention from security experts than other sectors like airport security or the power grid (Hedley, and Yule, 2009). Automation is crucial to the food and agriculture sector's ability to maintain competitive prices and efficient distribution. Because they may be isolated from the internet via dedicated or segmented networks, systems that enable automation are frequently believed to be at a lesser risk for cyber-attack.

This notion that there is a technological barrier separating automated food processing systems from the internet is a red herring. These systems are rarely totally isolated, and even when they are, the operating system and production software must always be updated. The updating procedure has the potential to introduce vulnerabilities. Attack probability rises when there is a false sense of security. Attackers do not require access to the automated systems that power food production companies to halt production, even if they were hypothetically completely cut off from the internet. As the JBS Meat ransomware assault shows, when a food supplier's business activities are shut down, its ability to continue producing food is also shut down. The food and agriculture industries have adopted digital business systems and production automation technology more quickly than they have upgraded their cyber-security operations. According to some experts, this is because the food and agriculture sector has generally escaped cyber-criminals notice up until recently when ransomware has proliferated, making any company a potential target.

Malware that sought to extract money by encrypting data was the precursor to ransomware. By encrypting the data, the attackers may prevent authorised people from accessing it and then demand a ransom to decrypt it. Targeted security research has been conducted to discover and remove these dangers as a result of the growth in ransomware attacks. Every file on a target machine must be encrypted, which takes time, and businesses can restore data from backups without paying the ransom.

Data theft and data encryption were combined in double extortion assaults, and some ransomware operators have since changed their attention to pure extortion, skipping encryption altogether. These ransomware data breaches are more efficient for cybercriminals and pose a bigger threat to cloud third-party threats since they are quicker to carry out, harder to detect, and cannot be corrected using backups. The adoption of cloud computing by businesses is growing, and this decision has significant security ramifications. Unfamiliarity with cloud security best practices, the cloud-shared security model, and other factors can make cloud environments more vulnerable to attack

While hackers are increasingly utilising exploits for new vulnerabilities to target cloud infrastructure, a new and concerning strategy is the targeting of cloud service providers. Cybercriminals can access sensitive client data and even their IT infrastructure by focusing their assaults on cloud service providers and cloud solutionsAttackers can significantly extend the scope and impact of their attacks by taking advantage of the trust relationships that exist between organisations and their service providers. Mobile malware has arisen as a rising danger as mobile devices have been more commonly utilised. Mobile malware has become more prevalent on both official and illegal app stores, disguising it as trustworthy and harmless programmes like games, lamps, and QR code scanners. When a vulnerability has been found but there isn't a workaround for the problem, it's considered a "zero-day." Corporate cybersecurity is at serious but short-term risk from zero-day vulnerabilities. However, even if a fix is released, companies don't always implement it right away. The software supply chain is one area where zero-day assaults and unpatched vulnerabilities are particularly dangerous.

CYBER-SECURITY SOLUTIONS FOR THE FOOD/AGRICULTURE INDUSTRY

As was already indicated, the food/agriculture sector may generally need to make up ground in terms of cyber-security. Many businesses in this industry can take precautions to safeguard themselves from dangers by applying some security steps shown in Fig. 2.

Figure 2. Framework of security measures for the food/agriculture industry

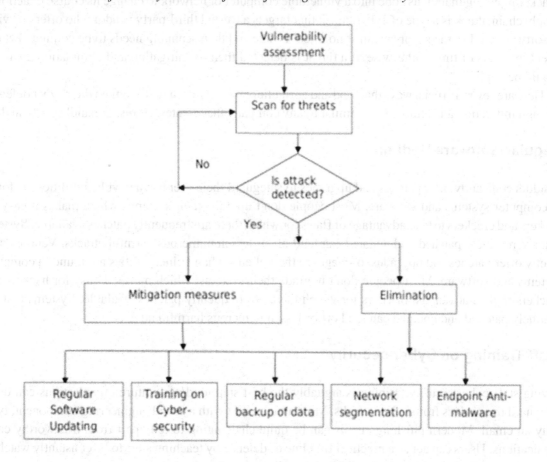

As shown in Fig.2, for applying security measures, first of all,the system should be scanned for any possible threat. Different types of cyber threats are-Malware, Denial-of-Service (DoS) Attacks, Phishing, Spoofing, Identity-Based Attacks, Code Injection Attacks, Supply Chain Attacks, etc.Malware is a program or code that is created with the intent to harm a computer, network or server. Malware is the most common type of cyber-attack. Malware contains many subsets such as ransomware, trojans, spyware, viruses, worms, keyloggers, bots, etc. Ransomware attacks are usually launched through malicious links delivered via phishing emails, but unpatched vulnerabilities and policy misconfigurations are used as well. Here attackers demand money.A Denial-of-Service (DoS) attack is a malicious, targeted attack that floods a network/ server with false requests to disrupt business operations.Phishing is a type of cyber-attack that uses email, SMS, social media, and social engineering techniques to entice a victim to share sensitive information — such as passwords or account numbers — or to download a malicious file that will install viruses on their computer.Spoofing is a technique through which a cybercriminal disguises themselves as a known or trusted source. In so doing, the adversary can engage with the target and access their systems or devices with the ultimate goal of stealing information. Identity-driven attacks are extremely hard to detect. When a valid user's credentials have been compromised and an adversary is masquerading as that user, it is often very difficult to differentiate between the user's typical behaviour and that of the hacker using traditional security measures and tools.Code injection attacks consist of an

117

attacker injecting malicious code into a vulnerable computer or network to change its course of action. A supply chain attack is a type of cyber-attack that targets a trusted third-party vendor who offers services or software vital to the supply chain. If no threat is detected then scanning needs to be continued at different intervals of time. Otherwise, if a threat is detected then its mitigation and elimination measures should be applied.

Here are several crucial ways that food and agriculture businesses may strengthen their cyber defences through mitigation and elimination, similar to any company that creates, stores, or handles critical data:

Regular Software Updating

Vendors constantly offer patches and upgrades to safeguard their clients when vulnerabilities are found in computer systems and software. Most people don't upgrade their systems, which makes it easy for hackers and crackers to take advantage of flaws for which there are frequently patches available. Systems that are routinely patched and updated can fend off or lessen numerous harmful attacks. Vendors constantly offer patches and upgrades to safeguard their clients when vulnerabilities are found in computer systems and software. Most people don't upgrade their systems, which makes it easy for hackers and crackers to take advantage of flaws for which there are frequently patches available. Systems that are routinely patched and updated can fend off or lessen numerous harmful attacks.

Staff Training on Cyber-security

Giving staff cyber-security training is arguably the best step food/agriculture organisations can do to safeguard themselves from cyber-attacks. Most attacks start with a social engineering component, typically an email. Modern phishing emails can be quite challenging to tell apart from trustworthy communications. Users can act as a practical first line of defence by teaching staff to be constantly watchful in seeing the telltale symptoms of a phishing email.

Regular Backup of Data

Ransomware in the food and agriculture sectors relies on threat actors' capacity to deploy malware that prevents firms from accessing their vital data. Attackers can restrict food manufacturers' ability to operate by preventing them from accessing their business systems. The simplest feasible mitigating method to stop ransomware thieves is to keep a recent backup. To prevent hackers from encrypting or stealing both the original files and backup copies, backup data should be separated from the original files.

Network Segmentation

Food/agriculture IT administrators can improve security by separating business networks from production networks and segmenting them into smaller segments. Because they are logically separated, a company's infrastructure can be isolated in case suspicious activity is seen in another area of the network. As was already established, malware that is introduced to a specific area of the network, such as when updating programmes, can nevertheless compromise even segmented infrastructure. However, segmenting can stop harmful malware from spreading throughout the entire organisation. The author (Zahidi,2018) audited six dairy farms in Finland, and it was found that most of the networking equipment was physically not secured and default credentials were used, which could be easily compromised.

Endpoint Anti-Malware Software

Malware is designed to harm digital systems, steal data, encrypt files, or gain unauthorised access to them. The vital nature of the food and agriculture industries means that it is the cyber threat that these firms encounter most frequently. Numerous dangerous software versions, including trojans, worms, and ransomware, are referred to as malware. Anti-malware software uses behavioural analysis, artificial intelligence, and signature detection to stop malware from being used in attacks. Anti-malware software must be deployed on all network's digital endpoints. It might be difficult to make sure that current anti-malware is correctly deployed across all devices with network access in today's BYOD (bring your device) workplaces.

DISCUSSION

The 2022 World Economic Forum survey put cyber-security failure in the top 10 risks, worsening in the COVID-19 crisis, while at the regional level; it is in the top 5 risks (Duncan et al., 2019). Most research revolves around traditional threats and mitigation, in particular hardware and Software security and cryptography (Adel et al., 2022). We discussed the cyber-threats and related open challenges, both technical and non-technical, concerning digital agriculture. Most of the farmers lacked high-speed internet access and backup internet, regular data backups. The farm networks generally had room for improvement in the design, implementation and maintenance of thefarm local network and the wider cyber-physical environment. If farmers want to improve the cyber-security of their farms, they must have to understand the importance of cyber-security. Generally, farmers give very low importance to the Internet and cyber-security in India.

Effective cybersecurity requires a variety of strategies. Frameworks for managing cyberthreats, threat intelligence, and threat-hunting procedures are all crucial elements of effective cybersecurity.Understanding the different kinds of cyber risks that can affect a specific firm is a smart place to start. By doing this, networks and systems for information technology will be secured against intruders. Additionally, the appropriate personnel, procedures, and technological frameworks will be developed to control cyber risks and overall cybersecurity.

Several embedded and linked technologies are utilised in precision agriculture to produce data that is then used to improve livestock and agricultural management. Vulnerabilities and cyber threat risks have surfaced as the usage of precision agriculture technology has expanded. An attacker could gain access to confidential information, take things, and damage equipment by using precision agricultural vulnerabilities.Applying IoT technology is an effective way to boost efficiency and address the problems that modern agriculture is facing. As a result, we are seeing the development of Precision Agriculture (PA) and Smart Farming (SF). Every person on the planet is directly impacted by the food sector. Smart and automated farming methods will be used in the food and agriculture sector in the future. Generally speaking, both smart farming and precision agriculture refers to the use of contemporary technologies like the Internet of Things (IoT), drones, robotics, and Artificial Intelligence (AI) in the control and management of farms to improve productivity and yield while lowering input, land, and labour requirements. Automated 'agro-bots' will monitor and treat, using high-tech tools designed to help maximize yields and minimize disease. Blockchain technology helps address the challenge of tracking products in the wide-reaching supply chain due to the complexity of the agri-food system. The technology thus provides solutions to issues of food quality and safety, which are highly concerned for consumers, the government, etc (Gupta et al., 2020). Blockchain's capability of tracking ownership records and tamper-resistance can be used to solve urgent issues such as food fraud, safety recalls, supply chain inefficiency and food traceability in the current food system.

CONCLUSION

For their lives and livelihoods, millions of people rely on the food and agriculture industry, just like they do on healthcare, electricity, transportation, and financial services. Farmers are using information acquired by GPS, satellite photos, internet-connected gadgets, and other technology to produce more efficiently, which is why precision agriculture is growing in popularity. Although the technology underlying these techniques allows hackers and crackers to attack farming machinery to halt food production, these techniques can increase crop yields and cut costs. The possibility of a sizable cyber-attack becomes more real as these crucial industries become more and more reliant on digital technologies for corporate operations. It is crucial to implement contemporary cyber defences to safeguard the global food supply chain. Blockchain technology is playing important role in counteracting fraud/duplicity in the food supply chain. Additionally, when developing new automation systems, cyber security must be prioritised. The entire industry must be safeguarded with the most cutting-edge and efficient instruments and regulations due to the brittle and interconnected character of the food supply because eating is the most vital thing for everyone.

REFERENCES

Abdelsalam, M., Krishnan, R., & Sandhu, R. (2017). Clustering-based IaaS cloud monitoring. *Proc. IEEE 10th Int. Conf. Cloud Comput. (CLOUD)*, (pp. 672-679). IEEE. 10.1109/CLOUD.2017.90

Alahmadi, A. N., Rehman, S. U., Alhazmi, H. S., Glynn, D. G., Shoaib, H., & Solé, P. (2022). Cyber-Security Threats and Side-Channel Attacks for Digital Agriculture. *Sensors (Basel)*, *22*(9), 3520. doi:10.339022093520 PMID:35591211

Alvino, A., & Marino, S. (2017, June). Remote sensing for irrigation of horticultural crops. *Horticulturae*, *3*(2), 40. doi:10.3390/horticulturae3020040

Azmandian, F., Moffie, M., Alshawabkeh, M., Dy, J., Aslam, J., & Kaeli, D. (2011, July). Virtual machine monitor-based lightweight intrusion detection. *Operating Systems Review*, *45*(2), 38–53. doi:10.1145/2007183.2007189

Barreto, L., & Amaral, A. (2018). Smart farming: Cyber security challenges. In *International Conference on Intelligent Systems (IS)* (pp. 870–876). IEEE. https://ieeexplore.ieee.org/abstract/document/8710531

Benavides, E., Fuertes, W., Sanchez, S., & Sanchez, M. (2020). *Classification of phishing attack solutions by employing deep learning techniques: a systematic literature review, Developments and advances in defence and security.* Springer Singapore.

Blender, T., Buchner, T., Fernandez, B., Pichlmaier, B., & Schlegel, C. Managing a mobile agricultural robot swarm for a seeding task. In *Proceedings of the IECON 2016-42nd Annual Conference of the IEEE Industrial Electronics Society*, (pp. 6879–6886). IEEE. 10.1109/IECON.2016.7793638

Bowcut, S. (2021). Cybersecurity in the food and agriculture industry. *Cybersecurity Guide, 2021.* Cybersecurity Guide. https://cybersecurityguide.org/industries/food-and-agriculture/

Chandola, V., Banerjee, A., & Kumar, V. (2009). Anomaly detection: A survey. *ACM Computing Surveys*, *41*(3), 15. doi:10.1145/1541880.1541882

Cooper, C. (2015). Cybersecurity in food and agriculture. *Protecting Our Future*, 2, 2015.

DHS. (2018). *US Department of homeland security: threats to precision agriculture.* DHS. (https://www.dhs.gov/sites/default/files/publications/2018%20AEP_Threats_to_Precision_Agriculture.pdf)

Duncan, S. E., Reinhard, R. R., Williams, C., Ramsey, F., Thomason, W., Lee, K., Dudek, N., Mostaghimi, S., Colbert, E., & Murch, R. (2019). Cyberbiosecurity: A new perspective on protecting U.S. food and agricultural system. *Frontiers in Bioengineering and Biotechnology*, *7*(Mar), 63. doi:10.3389/fbioe.2019.00063 PMID:30984752

Fountas, S., Sorensen, C. G., Tsiropoulos, Z., Cavalaris, C., Liakos, V., & Gemtos, T. (2015). Farm machinery management information system. *Computers and Electronics in Agriculture*, *110*, 131–138. doi:10.1016/j.compag.2014.11.011

Godfray, H. C. J. J., Beddington, R., Crute, I. R., Haddad, L., Lawrence, D., Muir, J. F., Pretty, J., Robinson, S., Thomas, S. M., & Toulmin, C. (2010). Food security: The challenge of feeding 9 billion people. *Science*, *327*(Jan), 812–818. doi:10.1126cience.1185383 PMID:20110467

Guarda, T., Augusto, M. F., & Lopes, I. (2019). The art of phishing. Advances in intelligent systems and computing. Springer, Cham.

Gupta, M., Abdelsalam, M., Khorsandroo, S., & Mittal, S. (2020). Security and Privacy in Smart Farming: Challenges and Opportunities. IEEE Access. IEEE.

Haveson, S., Lau, A., & Wong, V. (2017). *Protecting Farmers in Emerging Markets with Blockchain.* Cornell Tech.

Hedley, C., & Yule, I. (2009). A method for spatial prediction of daily soil water status for precise irrigation scheduling. *Agricultural Water Management*, *96*(12), 1737–1745. doi:10.1016/j.agwat.2009.07.009

Jahn, M. M. (2019). *Cyber Risk and Security Implications in Smart Agriculture and Food Systems.* Jahn Research Group. https://jahnresearchgroup.webhosting.cals.wisc.edu/wp-content/ uploads/ sites/ 223/2019/01/ Agricultural-Cyber-Risk-and-Security.pdf

Jahn, M.M., Oemichen, W.L., & Treverton, G.F. (2019). *Cyber Risk and Security Implications in Smart Agriculture and Food Systems.*

Karame, G. (2016). On the security and scalability of bitcoin's blockchain. In *Proceedings of the 2016 ACM SIGSAC Conference on Computer and Communications Security*. ACM. 10.1145/2976749.2976756

Katta, S., Ramatenki, S., & Sammeta, H. (2022). Smart irrigation and crop security in agriculture using IoT. In *AI, Edge and IoT-Based Smart Agriculture*. Academic Press. doi:10.1016/B978-0-12-823694-9.00019-0

Nikander, J., Onni, M., & Mikko, L. (2020). Requirements for cybersecurity in agricultural communication networks. *Computers and Electronics in Agriculture*, *179*, 105776. doi:10.1016/j.compag.2020.105776

Oerke, E.-C., & Dehne, H.-W. (2004). Safeguarding production—Losses in major crops and the role of crop protection. *Crop Protection (Guildford, Surrey)*, *23*(4), 275–285. doi:10.1016/j.cropro.2003.10.001

Roser, M. (2020). Future Population Growth. *Our World in Data*. https://ourworldindata.org/future-population-growth

Salam, A. (2019). A path loss model for through the soil wireless communications in digital agriculture. In *Proceedings of the 2019 IEEE International Symposium on Antennas and Propagation (IEEE APS)*. IEEE.

Schimmelpfennig, D. (2016). *Farm Profits and Adoption of Precision Agriculture; Technical Report ERR-217*. U.S. Department of Agriculture, Economic Research Services.

Seselja, E. (2021). *Cyber Attack Shuts Down Global Meat Processing Giant JBS*. ABC. https://www.abc.net.au/news/2021-05-31/cyber-attack-shuts-down-global-meat-processing-giant-jbs/100178310

Shamal, S., Alhwaimel, S. A., & Mouazen, A. M. (2016). Application of an on-line sensor to map soil packing density for site specific cultivation. *Soil & Tillage Research*, *162*, 78–86. doi:10.1016/j.still.2016.04.016

Sylvester, G. (2019). E-agriculture in Action: Blockchain for Agriculture (Opportunities and Challenges). Bangkok: International Telecommunication Union (ITU).

Wang, C., Talwar, V., Schwan, K., & Ranganathan, P. (2010). Online detection of utility cloud anomalies using metric distributions. *Proc. IEEE Netw. Oper. Manage. Symp. (NOMS)*, (pp. 96-103). IEEE.

Wang, C., Viswanathan, K., Choudur, L., Talwar, V., Satterfield, W., & Schwan, K. (2011). Statistical techniques for online anomaly detection in data centers. *Proc. 12th IFIP/IEEE Int. Symp. Integr. Netw. Manage. (IM) Workshops,* (pp. 385-392). IEEE. 10.1109/INM.2011.5990537

Xiong, H., Dalhaus, T., Wang, P., & Huang, J. (2020). Blockchain Technology for Agriculture: Applications and Rationale. *Front. Blockchain*, *3*, 7. doi:10.3389/fbloc.2020.00007

Zahidi, S. (2018). *The Global Risks Report 2022*. We Forum. https://www3.weforum.org/docs/WEFThe-GlobalRisksReport2022.pdf

Zanella, A. R. A., da Silva, E., & Albini, L. C. P. (2020). Security challenges to smart agriculture: Current state, key issues, and future directions. *Array (New York, N.Y.)*, *8*, 100048. doi:10.1016/j.array.2020.100048

Chapter 7
Security Issues in the Internet of Things for the Development of Smart Cities

Mohammad Haroon
Integral University, India

Dinesh Kumar Misra
Indian Space Research Organization, India

Mohammad Husain
Islamic University of Madinah, Saudi Arabia

Manish Madhav Tripathi
Integral University, India

Afsaruddin Khan
Dr. A.P.J. Abdul Kalam Technical University, India

ABSTRACT

A city is defined as a group of living and nonliving objects; cities generally have good systems for housing, transportation, hygiene, services, among other things. In prior years, a larger amount of the population was rural, whereas in modern times, the concept of urbanization and a mass exodus to cities has had a profound impact of sustainability on a global scale. A smart city is a concept that participates in information and communication technology with the use of various physical devices to help reduce and optimize the city's daily routine. When thinking of a smart city, one can imagine a layered architecture with infrastructure at the bottom; and connectivity accessibility in security systems in the middle; and at the top are different services that are gearted towards various consumers of the city.

DOI: 10.4018/978-1-6684-8133-2.ch007

INTRODUCTION

Some of the key security issues in the IoT for the development of smart cities are:

1. **Lack of Standardization:** IoT devices and systems are often developed by different vendors using different protocols and technologies, which makes it difficult to ensure interoperability and security across different devices and systems
2. **Week Authentication and Authorization:** Many IoT devices and systems use weak or default passwords, making them vulnerable to brute force attacks or password guessing. Additionally, some devices and systems may not have proper authentication and authorization mechanisms, allowing unauthorized access to sensitive data
3. **Data Privacy:** IoT devices collect and transmit vast amounts of data, including personal and sensitive information. Therefore, it is crucial to implement proper data encryption, data anonymization, and other measures to protect the privacy of citizens.
4. **Lack of Updates and Patches:** Many IoT devices and systems are deployed without the capability to receive updates or patches, leaving them vulnerable to known security vulnerabilities and exploits.
5. **Malware and Botnets:** IoT devices are often targeted by malware and botnets, which can be used to launch distributed denial of service (DDoS) attacks or other cyber-attacks.
6. **Physical Security:** IoT devices can be physically tampered with, leading to unauthorized access or data theft. Therefore, it is crucial to ensure physical security measures such as tamper-evident packaging and secure installation.

To mitigate these security issues, it is essential to develop and implement comprehensive security policies and frameworks for IoT devices and systems in smart cities. These policies should include guidelines for secure development, deployment, and management of IoT devices and systems, as well as regular security assessments and testing to identify vulnerabilities and risks. Additionally, public awareness and education campaigns can help citizens understand the potential security risks of IoT devices and how to protect themselves from cyber threats.

Comprehensive Security Policies and Frameworks for IoT Devices and Systems in Smart Cities

As the use of IoT devices and systems increases in smart cities, it is important to implement comprehensive security policies and frameworks to protect against potential cyber threats. Here are some key considerations for developing such policies and frameworks:

1. **Authentication and Authorization:** All IoT devices and systems should require strong authentication and authorization mechanisms to ensure that only authorized users and devices can access them.
2. **Encryption:** All data transmitted and stored by IoT devices and systems should be encrypted to prevent unauthorized access or tampering.
3. **Access Control:** Access controls should be implemented to limit the number of people who can access IoT devices and systems. Only authorized personnel should be allowed to access them.

4. **Incident Response:** A comprehensive incident response plan should be developed to quickly detect, respond to, and recover from security incidents.
5. **Patch Management:** Regular updates and patches should be applied to all IoT devices and systems to address any security vulnerabilities.
6. **Physical Security:** Physical security measures should be implemented to protect IoT devices and systems from theft or unauthorized access.
7. **Data Privacy:** Data privacy should be a top priority, and all data collected by IoT devices and systems should be protected and secured according to relevant data protection regulations.
8. **Vendor Management:** Effective vendor management is crucial to ensure that all IoT devices and systems are secure. Vendors should be required to follow security best practices and provide regular security updates.
9. **Risk Assessment:** A thorough risk assessment should be conducted to identify potential security threats and vulnerabilities.
10. **Security Testing:** Regular security testing should be conducted to identify any weaknesses in the security policies and frameworks and to ensure that they are working effectively.

Cyber Risk for the Development of Smart Cities

Smart cities rely heavily on information and communication technology (ICT) systems to operate, which makes them vulnerable to cyber risks. Cyber security threats to smart cities can take various forms, including data breaches, cyber-attacks, and ransomware.

One of the primary risks associated with smart cities is the potential for a cyber-attack on critical infrastructure systems, such as power grids, transportation systems, and emergency services. An attack on these systems could cause significant disruption and damage, potentially leading to public safety concerns.

Another risk is the collection, storage, and processing of large amounts of sensitive data in smart city systems, which could be targeted by hackers for theft or manipulation. This could lead to a breach of personal data privacy and identity theft, among other negative outcomes.

To mitigate these risks, it is essential to implement robust cybersecurity measures, including encryption, multi-factor authentication, and access controls. Additionally, regular security audits and updates should be conducted to ensure that the smart city infrastructure remains secure against emerging cyber threats.

As smart cities continue to develop and expand, it is crucial to prioritize cybersecurity as a fundamental aspect of their design and implementation. This will help to ensure that the benefits of smart city technology are realized without compromising the safety and security of its citizens.

SMART CITY VS. NORMAL CITY

A smart city is a city that uses advanced technology and data analysis to improve the quality of life for its citizens and enhance its overall sustainability. A normal city, on the other hand, refers to a traditional urban area that operates without the use of advanced technology.

The key differences between a smart city and a normal city are:

1. **Technology:** Smart cities use advanced technology such as Internet of Things (IoT) devices, sensors, and data analytics to gather and analyse information about the city's infrastructure, traffic,

and other systems. Normal cities may use some technology, but not to the same extent or level of integration.

2. **Sustainability:** Smart cities focus on sustainability, using technology to reduce energy consumption, waste production, and carbon emissions. This includes initiatives such as renewable energy sources, smart transportation, and green buildings. Normal cities may not have as much emphasis on sustainability.

3. **Citizen Engagement:** Smart cities engage citizens in decision-making through technology such as mobile apps, social media, and online platforms. Citizens can provide feedback, report issues, and participate in city planning. Normal cities may not have as much citizen engagement through technology.

4. **Efficiency:** Smart cities use technology to increase efficiency in areas such as transportation, waste management, and public services. This can save time, money, and resources. Normal cities may not have as much focus on efficiency.

A smart city is designed to be more efficient, sustainable, and responsive to citizen needs than a normal city. However, implementing smart city technology and infrastructure can be costly and complex, which is a challenge for many cities around the world.

REQUIREMENTS FOR AN IoT PLATFORM IN A SMART CITY ENVIRONMENT

Smart cities have many definitions and implementations. as I pointed out in the introduction section. From the Smart City infrastructure point of view, all the city has their own highly capable ICT network system, connected to high-speed internet. this network has various kinds of Network sensors and wired and wireless broadband connectivity. having e advanced Data Analytics mechanism that helps in the analysis of various kinds of data collected by ICT-based devices and takes the necessary actions. And also settle down the basis of the development of intelligent applications and services for the smart city (Nitti et al., 2017). Various things are required for the development of IoT systems for the smart city.

Table 1. Various IoT applications in smart city

Smart Home	Smart Parking IoT	Healthcare	Weather and Water System	Transport and Vehicular Traffic	Environmental Pollution	Surveillance System
Demond impedance	Vehicles count	tracing	Weather status	Inquiry camera condition	Greenhouse gas inquiry	CCTV
Fire detection	Departure and arrival	Identification	Water quality	Environment inquiry	Energy efficiency inquiry	Violence detection
Temperature inquiry	Environment inquiry	Data gathering	Water leakage	Travel scheduling	Renewable energy usage	Public place inquiry
Security system	Mobile ticketing	Data classification	Water level	Traffic jam reduction	Air quality inquiry	People and object tracing
Social network peripheral	Traffic congestion control	Sensing	Water contamination	Assisted driving	Noise level inquiry	Public police

SECURITY SYSTEMS

These days on the planet have more connected devices concerning the people. about 50 Billion associated devices exist on the planet .and all the devices are fully controlled and connected by high-speed wireless and wired IoT platforms. means they are controlled and accessible by the internet. Various attacks and misconfigured network attacks are also possible on IoT-based systems. for Smart City Development IoT platforms must have a strong Security System so that Intruder cannot break the IoT network and the internet. the connected system with the IoT infrastructure for it the Smart City designer has taken various security protocols and security devices, security mechanisms, and the private Internet coding so that a network attack will not be possible on IoT based smart cities (Gomez et al., 2019).

The various security requirement checked during the implantation and the life cycle of the IoT network are given below.

Datacentre security is one of the important aspects, and outside threads continue to be challenged. While at the same time in IoT networks, the workforce and device mobility become more sophisticated. The device at the edge of the network is providing network security, such as load balancers and load schedulers.it prevents outside thread attacks like DoS attacks and Denial of DoS attacks (Sandeep et al., 2018). For security purposes, all computing devices in the IoT network are password protected.

Several authors have proposed various research works to give fruitful password authentication key management, where the encrypted key is exchanged with each other. Although numerous of the first approaches were defective (Husain & Haroon, 2020), the permanent and greater forms of EKE competently shared a keyword and collective keys are increased, which can be used in secure communication, encryption, and message communications. Procedure for cryptographic key exchange, allow together to produce a strong key, in the uncertain network (Husain & Haroon, 2020).

IoT Security Challenges

in IoT-based network security is a big constraint, several authors proposed a lot of security issues. Hossain et al proposed three basic security constrain (Paganelli et al., 2014). hardware security constraints, software security constraints, and network security constraint. In hardware security constraint are, computational power and energy constrain, memory constraints, designing of various devices, and register packing of IoT devices constrain. Software constraint are security patches, and various special kinds of software required for low power-based devices. And the network constraints are connection mobility of devices, communication channel security patch, communication protocol patch, and many more.

Internet of Things (IoT) devices are becoming increasingly popular in our daily lives, from smart homes and wearable's to industrial automation and healthcare. However, with the proliferation of IoT devices comes a range of security challenges. Here are some of the main IoT security challenges:

Lack of Standardization: IoT devices come in many different shapes and sizes, and often use different protocols and communication methods, making it difficult to create a standardized security framework.

Weak Passwords: Many IoT devices come with default passwords that are easily guessable or can be found online. This makes them vulnerable to brute force attacks and hacking attempts.

Limited Computing Power: Many IoT devices have limited computing power, making it difficult to implement strong encryption or run security software.

Firmware Vulnerabilities: IoT devices often use embedded firmware, which can contain vulnerabilities that can be exploited by attackers.

Table 2. Various algorithms, protocols, and devices used in IoT systems for security systems

Name of Devices/ Protocol	Applications of Devices/Protocol
Cryptographic algorithms	Cryptographical security systems are recommended for data transmission in IoT-based systems. however cryptographic systems have some kind of problem in key exchange and data signature and message authentication.
Public-key cryptography	Public key cryptography is recommended for data transmission, node authentication, and signature verification in IoT based system
Key Management Techniques	key Administration is a significant aspect of safekeeping features in IoT-based systems. lightweight protected key diffusion is very important in IoT-based secure communication.
Routing algorithm:	general network routing protocol or not applicable on IoT-based network. the IoT-based routing fully ensures the validity of root evidence and dropping must be avoided while communication concluded wireless medium. all the routing AI algorithms IoT-based networks must prevent various kinds of attacks such as the dos, wormhole, black hole, and discriminating promotion routes.
Data classification	various kinds of data are float in an IoT network might be either efficient data or non-functional data. various kinds of data Protection schemes will define inside the IoT-based network. the degree of production requires for data is dependent on the degree of understanding of data.
Protecting device at production time:	all other interfaces of IoT-based devices should be removed during the production time. When any kind of security attack would be possible on a device. all the device's requirements have the appropriate admission control. device place showing location must have a hardened proof, casing all the shield to avoid the side-channel attack.
Operating system	Special kinds of operating systems are designed for IoT-based devices. only for components, packages, and Libraries, required for running IoT devices. during the deployment of IoT devices, library updates must be planted designer. the port protocol and services that are not used in a system that must be disabled.
Application gateway	The application gateway must authorize all collected data earlier it is getting calculated. A safe software development life cycle technique is suggested.
Network connections	The numeral of interfaces of IoT devices through which the IoT devices are connected to the different networks should be minimum. the device must be able to access through nominal port boundary and services. The protected protocol is used to access the external network by IoT devices. The receiver must validate earlier sending any sensitive data.

Physical Security: IoT devices are often deployed in public spaces or unsecured environments, making them vulnerable to physical attacks and theft.

Privacy Concerns: IoT devices collect large amounts of data, including personal and sensitive information, which can be compromised if not properly secured.

Lack of Updates: Many IoT devices do not receive regular software updates or security patches, leaving them vulnerable to newly discovered vulnerabilities and exploits.

Complexity of Ecosystems: IoT devices are often part of complex ecosystems that include multiple devices and platforms. This can make it difficult to identify and address security vulnerabilities across the entire system

Insecure Network Communication

in IoT technology, rapidly growing the IoT network, and IoT devices, the security standard is driving more and more consciousness. a lot of security software updates are also required. physically maintenance of local and global internet. That is cost-oriented and logically practical for the implementation. over air updating is generally used in IoT software updating as well as from were addition. majority of smartphones, laptops and other digital devices are used for the update of IoT devices. challenging and emerging software model is also required regularly for firmware updating. all the security vulnerability security breaches must be mitigating a real-time system. criterion is the IoT suite software, is deployed in the majority of IoT networks, and it's regularly updated to mitigate the security and privacy concerns of IoT networks. the regular competition of IoT Suite and IoT software devices helps us to one-click maintain of IoT network and it is up to date and saves. all software application allows how to fix and remove the box and allow to install new feature inside the IoT devices remotely. I need also to save time cost as well as energy. In IoT software, a lot of system software and application software are used like operating systems, embedded software android-based software like nimbus and Hadoop. Furthermost of the IoT software is constructed on data congregation, process interface, and real-time integration. IoT devices conned with the internet through a special kind of embedded software and operating system (Paganelli et al., 2014).

Data Leaks From Cloud

authorized broadcasting of data inside an organization and outside of the organization is known as a data leak. the data can be transferred through electronic media or by physical media without the consent of the data owners. it generally occurs via the web or email threads. these days some data leaks can also occur why mobile, storage devices, optical media, USB, and laptops. data outflow is also known as data shoplifting. this is an enormous problem of data safety and its damage cause to any organization. Various kinds of data leaks are possible that are within an organization data leak, and outside of an organization data leak. Most of the time data leak is the existential type unknowingly accidentally sending them to the wrong recipient address and sending a mail. An intentional leak can happen and result in the same penalty and reputation damage as they do not mitigate head legal responsibility (Misra & Zaheer, 2017).

We describe the specific characteristic of a smart city with the help of IoT devices and networks. All the services are governed by an IoT network and with the mutual consent of local government bodies like (municipal corporations, PWD, electricity departments, and many more) We then overview the web-based approach for the design of IoT services (Arasteh et al., 2016).

IoT DEVICES

For the designing of IoT networks, several kinds of hardware are deployed, like, embedded systems, microcontrollers (Arduino, Raspberry Pi), wearable devices, digital devices gadgets, sensors, low power digital gadgets, and many more. IoT hardware devices in a smart city are present with the individual of the city, and all induvial conned with the IoT devices, via the internet. Therefore, at the all-time citizen of the city are conned with high-speed internet, so all time it's a risk of security attack, therefore hardware designer is more concerned about the security issue during the designing of the devices. These devices can easily tamper. Due to the permeability of IoT devices, sometimes it's difficult to provide a software solution for security updates. IoT hardware is always under security attacks, such as DOS, and DDoS (Paganelli et al., 2014).

Table 3. Service requirement for smart city

Service	Network Type	Energy Source	Traffic Rate	Feasibility
Health structure	WI FI ethernet	All devices are battery powered	1 packet transfer every 10 minutes for every device	Easy to understand, but seismographs might be hard to integrate
Waste administration	Wifi 3G and4G	All devices are battery-powered or energy harvest	1 packet every hour for every device	Possible to realize but require smart garbage containers.
Air quality inquiry	Wifi Bluetooth	Photovoltaic panel for each device	1 packet every 30 minutes for every device	Easy to realize, a greenhouse gas sensor is required.
Noise inquiry	Ethernet	Battery-powered or energy harvest	1 packet transfer every 10 minutes for every device	The sound pattern detection system is required for noise inquiry
Traffic congestion	Bluetooth Wi-Fi ethernet	Battery-powered or energy harvest	1 packet transfer every 10 minutes for every device	The system requires the realization of air quality and noise inquiry.
Energy consumption	PLC and ethernet	Battery-powered	1 packet transfer every 10 minutes for every device	Simple to implant but require authorization for system operations
Smart parking	Ethernet	Energy harvest	On-Demand	Smart parking systems are available and easy to operable.
Smart lighting	Wifi and ethernet	Mains powered	On-demand	Does not present major difficulty but requires involvement in the present organization.
Automation and dependability of public building	Wifi and ethernet	Mains powered and battery-power	1 packet transfer every 10 minutes for remote inquiry, and 1packet for every 30 seconds for loco control	Does not present major difficulty, but requires intervention in existing infrastructure

IoT Firmware and Software

IoT technology, rapidly growing the IoT network, and IoT devices, the security standard is driving more and more consciousness. A lot of security software updates are also required. physically maintenance of local and global internet. That is cost-oriented and logically practical for the implementation. over the air updating is generally used in IoT software updating as well as from were addition. majority of smartphones, laptops and other digital devices are used for the update of IoT devices. challenging and emerging software models are also required regularly for firmware updating. all the security vulnerabilities and security breaches must be mitigating a real-time system. cinterion is the IoT suite software, that is deployed in the majority of the IoT network, and it's regularly updated to mitigate the security and privacy concerns of the IoT network. the regular competition of IoT Suite and IoT software devices helps us to one-click maintain of IoT network and it is up to date and safe. all software application allows how to fix and remove the box and allow to install new feature inside the IoT devices remotely. I need also to save time cost as well as energy. In IoT software, a lot of system software and application software are used as operating systems, embedded software android-based software like nimbus and Hadoop. Most of the IoT software is based on data gathering, process interface, and real-time integration. IoT devices conned with the internet through special kinds of embedded software and operating system (Paganelli et al., 2014).

Role of IoT in Smart City

The computing device is rapidly growing. these days the IOT devices quantity is now in billion. these devices are communicated to each other through the network internet worldwide they can be remotely monitored and controlled. in IoT devices smart sensors, and other devices are included. due to the low cost of IoT, it is very easy to monitor and manage. all the activities that were not reachable. the cost of IoT based system is significantly reduced. IoT for the normal human being is a smartphone it is very easy to move from one place to another place by carrying a Smartphone. we perform many works with the help of a smartphone, including phone calls, internet connectivity, railway reservation, electricity bill paying, and many more. with the help of a smartphone anywhere anytime computing or possible.

Pollution and Air Inquiry by IoT Systems

Siemens has developed a complete cloud-based software package, that is known as a city air management tool. This particular tool is used to capture the data related to city pollution in real-time, and forecast emissions. after the data analysis, it found 90% accuracy given by City manager tools. these software suits are fully based on the algorithm that worked with the help of an artificial neural network. City management Air Control tool is fully cloud-based software air that works on a real-time information system, and it is used to work the air quality detection by the sensor across the city and predict the value for the upcoming 3 to 5 days. Indian Communication and remote sensing satellite have many optics and sensors on board which can provide valuable data and images of smart cities on half an hourly basis to improve better control of air and air pollution in smart cities (Paganelli et al., 2014).

Traffic Administration

Traffic management is one of the biggest attributes in the development of a smart city. all smart city has their traffic management system, the traffic management system is built by intelligent devices, and sensors. Traffic management is one of the biggest attributes in the development of a smart city, it is the biggest challenge to manage and optimize traffic in a city. a lot of intelligent sensors and intelligent devices are used to send real-time updates, and data related to the traffic to the central traffic organization system. and the central traffic management system automatically examines the data and regulates the traffic light to the circulation situation within the second. traffic management system uses past data to forecast where traffic can be abstracted and where the traffic can go and everything is performed by intelligent devices (Sandeep et al., 2018). Indian "NavIC" system having a constellation of nine geosatellites onboard is providing very accurate navigation data (accuracy in position less than 10m and in time less than 10 nanoseconds) better than GPS and GLONASS systems available globally. Though the Indian "NavIC" system is providing navigation data for the Indian continent and 1500Km outer periphery other than the Indian continent. Rather to this India have the largest constellation of remote sensing satellite as well as communication satellite which services will be very useful to have a watchdog from space to manage the traffic management of smart cities with the aid of IoT systems system itself can be said a product of satellite communication which is managing huge traffic in smart cities. (Nitti et al., 2015; Paganelli et al., 2014)

Smart Parking

for the parking of a vehicle in a Smart City, smart parking systems are deployed. In smart parking a lot of intelligent sensors, and devices are used, to identify the free parking palace. a driver can easily identify where the left parking area. the sensor in the ground report is used to send the data via smartphone to the driver and with the help of this data drives easily park their vehicle. for the designing of smart parking is an authenticity today and does not necessitate complex infrastructure and a high level of investment. NavIC satellite systems and Remote sensing satellites have optics and sensors onboard which can provide the ground report and can be used to send the data via smartphone to the driver connected through a communication satellite transponder and with the help of these data drivers can easily park their vehicle. The designing of smart parking is a requirement today and does not necessitate complex infrastructure and lower cost consumption.

Smart Waste Management

smart waste collection systems are used in the smart city. Intelligent sensors and intelligent containers are used for waste collection as well as waste disposal in Smart City. when the waste container is full, it automatically container sends a notification to the truck driver, and the truck driver receives a warning notification on the smartphone. Smartphones are connected to IoT systems and IoT systems are connected via satellite systems which will provide alert messages in a fraction of milliseconds. After getting an alert message the truck driver of the container will dump the waste collected at a specified location. after that truck driver of the container. the waste management solution helps to optimize and progress the effectiveness of waste collection as well as waste disposal to reduce the operational cost as well as the better the environmental issue associated with an inefficient waste collection. With the availability of satellite images, wasteland mapping can be done in smart cities, and location updating can be shared with people in smart cities. It will help in a better way in disposing of waste and waste management systems.

IoT TECHNOLOGY

There are several technology devices are used in IoT deployment and development.

Radio Frequency Identification

it uses radio wave to capture the data from various location and also allow automatic identification of the data.

Wireless Sensor Node

The majority of an attribute in Smart City is fully dependent on sensor node, wireless sensor nodes have a small microprocessor with intelligent software. the wireless sensor node consists of devices that are used to monitor the physical or environmental conditions, as well as to monitor various kinds of things. like traffic situation, garbage collection, and the various activity done by the municipal corporation, PWD Corporation, and many more. the wireless sensor network node, with an RFID system, can track the status of various things likely location, temperature, and movement. wireless sensor node and RFID system both jointly are deployed for various purposes in smart cities.

Embedded Sensor

data, business analytics, and IoT tools, jointly transfer their information via the embedded system to the business intelligence and data analytic centers. this data is used to solve a business-related problem and provide good quality and value-added services to the customer. for this computational Intelligence, and special kind of software technologies are used, for data analysis as well as data maintenance, data retrieval, and data storage. and also send information from one node to another. big data is extensively generated by IoT technology. however, in Smart City Development big data with embedded systems and data analytics with artificial intelligence play a significant role, to capture the data analysed the data, make unstructured data to structure form. And also provide a lot of data analytic tools for knowledge engineering as well as understanding (Husain & Haroon, 2020).

IEEE 802.15.4

IEEE 802.15.4 is a wireless Technology; it is proposed to allow control applications and monitor the application of wireless personal area networks. this particular technology is useful for low-rate transfer in communication, and low energy ingesting communication. it is generic Communication Technology; it is designed for special kinds of work.

BLE

is low energy different from standard Bluetooth? all devices that provide a classic Bluetooth system can also sustain BLE system. Therefore, we can stimulate its widespread occurrence in a smartphone. the BLE is used to accumulate the data from or send the command to the neighbouring sensor and actuators. the smartphone can also be used as a gateway for interaction between sensors, actuators, and another internet for data collection. now BLE has converted foremost in the various area of adjustable tablets and other consumer electronic devices.

ITU T G.9959 (Z Wave)

Z wave technology is used for home automation purposes, and this technology is specially designed for the smart home. all the intelligent devices, sensor-based devices, that are deployed in the home automation, are coordinated and controlled by z-wave. it is an open standard that stipulates the inferior layer of the protocol wireless protocol stack.

DECT-ULE

DECT ULE is a low-energy device, it's like a wireless sensor node. This device is used to convert the data into voice and voice to data and vice versa. communication amid a gateway and sensors or actuators in a very low range like in the home, by manipulating the strong presence of DECT equipment.

NFS

NFS is a wireless technology that is used for intrinsic security propose. NFS is used to minimize the unauthorized access of the device. NFS allows different communication modes such as card immolation, reader mode, and peer-to-peer communication. the main ad identifies another unauthorized in of wire devices.

IEEE 802.11

IEEE 802.11 is a wireless LAN. It is massively used in wireless communications. It's also known as wi-fi. the wi fi is operated on very low power, and the power consumption is also very minimal.

LoRa WAN

LoRaWAN is an unrestrained band of wireless technology, this technology is going to low power WAN . LoRaWAN uses LoRa technology at physical layers, it allows for increasing the physical range of communications. Created on a star topology, A technology-centric viewpoint method collects data from up to hundreds of thousands of policies such as sensors, it offers a low infrastructure cost, at the expense of severe message rate and bit rate limitations.

Sigfox

Sigfox is an additional wireless Technology is used for long and low infrastructure coverage from my account of wireless communication. the expense of wireless communication with the help of signal of very low this technology is operated on an unlicensed frequency, wireless technology and it is skilled by the corporation that is also called Sigfox, it based on Star topology.

NB IoT

Narrowband IoT is another application of wireless technology. This technology is fully based on the licensed spectrum, and it is supporting many sensor and wireless devices. for a single base station, more devices are operated.

Power Line Communication

Power LINE Communication is fully based on wired communication media. it is subject to Interface; therefore its subject impairment is similar to those of wireless media. in power line Communication, a low bit rate of data transfer is possible. it is a licensed spectrum, and it is based on IEEE 1901.2 this is also known as ITU-T G 9903. communication, after being used in Smart home, is related to applications such as a smart grid.

Master-Slave Token Passing

It's a wired technology, it is from to BAC net family, and Devices that practice MS/TP are normally grid-powered. While the distinct constructions do not attitude the similar degree of limitations as other technologies overviewed in this Section, devices that use MS/TP are measured, and the physical layer, created on RS-485 requirement, offers a low bit rate (Husain & Haroon, 2020).

Tool/Devices Are Used in IoT System

Table 4. Various tools/ device is used in IoT system

Tool/Device	Frequency Range	Communication Range (in Meters)	Bit Rate	Organization Name
IEEE 802.15.4	868/9152/2400	10^2	20/40/250	IEEE
BLE	2400	10^2	1000	BLUETOOTH
ITU	868/915	10^2	96/40/100	ITU-T
DELT	1900	10^1	1152	ET51
NFC	1356	10^3	106/212/24	NFC FORUM
IEEE802.11	<1000	10^3	150-7800	IEEE
LoRaWAN	433/868/915	10^5	.25-.5`	LoRaWAN
SIGFOX	868/902	10^5	60/30	SIGFOX
NBIOT	SEVERAL LICENCED	10^5	60/30	3GPP
PIC	<.5	10^3	500	IEEEITU
MS/TP	BASEBAND	10^3	115.2	ANSI

SPACE APPLICATION TECHNOLOGY APPLICATION IN DEVELOPING SMART CITIES IN INDIA

Smart cities require very good urban mapping and planning for their local citizens and townships. Smart city sprawl mapping and large-scale mapping could become possible with the availability of satellite images of any smart city. Satellite-based top map updating, Digital Elevation Model (Carto-DEM), and Cadastral level mapping are other methods of planning smart cities and townships. Seiesmo-tectonic studies, Engineering, and geo-environmental studies could become possible with aid of satellite-based space technology. For such an application, India has many satellites (around 10 satellites to help the Government of India in mapping, planning, and developing smart cities. Of course, in one shot we can get very good GIS images from Remote sensing satellites of Indian indigenous satellite systems. India's new Navigation program "NavIC" launched in 2016 has paved the path very easily and has a relaxed dependency on other countries. Smart city authorities are getting valuable Navigation data and satellite images of the intended location very easy to develop the planned city.

For such intended application, India has a series of cartographic satellites delivering cartographic images which are, in turn, very useful to the smart city administrator and management system to plan the city in the best way and as per standard requirements.

With the availability of valuable data and satellite image, ensuring the Master/structure plan of the smart city become less time, labour,and cost-consuming. With this easiness and one-shot readiness of structure, the city planning department and their administrator have reduced the long-time planning aspect and in turn development time as well. With the availability of valuable data and satellite images, comprehensive development plans, and base map generation of smart cities/towns become easy with less effort, cost, and time. It also has paved the way for to the development of a National urban information system (Nitti et al., 2015).

Water resource management in smart cities is a big need of hours. Providing good drinking water and managing water resource optimally is a big challenge not only in smart cities but in other parts and cities of India. National Drinking Water Mission, Water resource information system, Reservoir capacity evaluation, and site selection could become possible with the aid of space technology. Wasteland mapping/updating, watershed development and inquiry, Land records modernization plan, and landslide zonation could become possible with the use of available space technology of country in even smart cities and another part of the country also.

Smart cities have villages, and their developments are done through village resource centres equipped with IoT systems linked through satellite technology. Each piece of information is readily available at VRC through the IoT system from where it is provided to all developmental authorities to do standard planning and development of villages that come under smart cities.IoT system of smart cities requires reliable and better communication amongst systems, and it could become possible through satellite communication (Pl refer network of communication amongst centres. (Nitti et al., 2015).

And it could become possible through satellite communication (Pl refer network of communication amongst centers (Misra & Zaheer, 2017; Paganelli et al., 2014).

Smart city communications with the aid of IoT systems can be planned to utilize space technology. Remote areas and locations can be linked up with the aid of space technology and IOT systems which in turn be useful in the standardization of smart cities. In the near future and in forthcoming days will be space technology and space technologies have touched each era of life now itself. This will be a big factor in developing smart cities. (Arasteh et al., 2016; Misra & Zaheer, 2017; Paganelli et al., 2014)

In a nutshell, it is observed that space technology is helpful in all eras of life as shown in the below figure. Smart cities require such developmental aid and tools.

CONCLUSION

This vision of a smart city is making it a leading digital city where every individual is always connected to each other, which creates a better human network. In smart cities the uses of internet of things including water and waste management systems. Some other applications would be creating intelligent sustainable buildings, and building a management which helps manage the infrastructure; the creation of smart health inquiry systems; and traffic management systems. The overall objective of the smart city is to develop a better human network, and fully utilize natural resources so that wastage should be minimized.

REFERENCES

Arasteh, H. Hosseinnezhad, V., Loia, V., Tommasetti, A., Troisi, O., Shafie-Khah, M., & Siano, P. (2016). Iot-based smart cities: A survey. In *EEEIC 2016 - International Conference on Environment and Electrical Engineering*. IEEE.

Sandeep, C. HKumar, NKumar, SKumar, P. (2018, November). Security Challenges and Issues of the IoT System. *Indian Journal of Public Health Research & Development, 9*(11).

Misra, D. & Zaheer, M. M. (2017). NavIC –An Indigeneous Developments for Self Reliant Navigation Services. ICACIE 2017, Springer transactions, CU. Ajmer.

Gomez, C., Chessa, S., Fleury, A., Roussos, G., & Preuveneers, D. (2019). Internet of Things for enabling smart environments: A technology-centric perspective. *Journal of Ambient Intelligence and Smart Environments, 11*(1), 23–43. doi:10.3233/AIS-180509

Husain, M. & Haroon, M. (2020). Enriched Information Security Framework From Various Attacks in the Iot. *International Journal of Innovative Research in Computer Science & Technology, 8*(4).

Nitti, M., Pilloni, V., Colistra, G., & Atzori, L. (2015). The virtual object as a major element of the internet of things: A survey. *IEEE Communications Surveys and Tutorials, 18*(2), 1228–1240. doi:10.1109/COMST.2015.2498304

Nitti, M., Pilloni, V., Giusto, D., & Popescu, V. (2017). IoT Architecture for a sustainable tourism application in a smart city environment. *Mobile Information Systems, 2017*, 2017. doi:10.1155/2017/9201640

Paganelli, F., Turchi, S., & Giuli, D. (2014). A web of things framework for restful applications and its experimentation in a smart city. *IEEE Systems Journal, 10*(4), 1412–1423. doi:10.1109/JSYST.2014.2354835

Talari, S., Shafie-Khah, M., Siano, P., Loia, V., Tommasetti, A., & Catalão, J. P. (2017). A review of smart cities based on the internet of things concept. *Energies, 10*(4), 421. doi:10.3390/en10040421

Zanella, A., Bui, N., Castellani, A., Vangelista, L., & Zorzi, M. (2014). Internet of things for smart cities. *IEEE Internet of Things Journal, 1*(1), 22–32. doi:10.1109/JIOT.2014.2306328

Chapter 8
Forensics Analysis of NTFS File Systems

Kumarbhai Shamjibhai Sondarva

Sardar Vallabhbhai National Institute of Technology, India

Adarsh Kumar

Sardar Vallabhbhai National Institute of Technology, India

Bhavesh N. Gohil

Sardar Vallabhbhai National Institute of Technology, India

Sankita J. Patel

Sardar Vallabhbhai National Institute of Technology, India

Sarang Rajvansh

National Forensics Sciences University, India

Ramya T. Shah

National Forensic Sciences University, India

ABSTRACT

The internet and computers are reaching everywhere, and all are getting connected through it. Users are utilizing computers to make life easier and work faster. At the same time, many attacks and instances of cybercrime have happened. Therefore, digital forensics is necessary and plays a crucial role. NTFS is one of the most popular file systems used by the Windows operating system, and this chapter provides information for forensic analysis of NTFS file system. This chapter describes digital forensics, stages of digital forensics, and types of digital forensics. NTFS is discussed in brief along with the master file table (MFT). In the same section, it also discusses the method to detect the hidden data in the boot sector, analysis of registry, prefetch, shellbags, and web browsers. They have discussed the collection of volatile and non-volatile data. It also provides the artifacts which an investigator must be seeking, along with the tools used to collect and analyze them and strategies used for investigation and analysis. Data recovery and file carving are also discussed.

DOI: 10.4018/978-1-6684-8133-2.ch008

INTRODUCTION

The science of locating, obtaining, evaluating, and presenting digital evidence that has been kept on digital electronic storage devices in order to be used as evidence in a court of law is known as 'digital forensics' (Alazab et al., 2009).

The main stages of digital forensics are mentioned below:

1. Identification of evidence
2. Preservation of evidence
3. Collection of digital evidence.
4. Examination and analysis of evidence
5. Reporting and presentation

Whenever cyber crime has taken place there is a sequence of steps to be followed in order, while investigating the crime scene. Important steps to be taken at crime scene are as follows:

1. Secure the Crime Scene.
2. Documentation of the Crime Scene.
3. Search for Digital Evidence.
4. Identification of Digital Evidence.
5. Evidence Collection in Forensically sound manner.
6. Maintain Chain of Custody during transportation of Digital Evidence.
7. Submit Digital Evidence in Forensic Science Laboratory.

An investigator has to carry to tools and equipments such as: Crime scene securing tapes, digital camera, extra batteries, video cameras, sketch pads, blank sterile storage media: Portable USB hard disks and pen drives (to store the evidence image), write-blocker device, labels, pens, permanent markers, storage containers, anti-static bags, faraday bags, Toolkit and rubber gloves.

Types of digital forensics are mentioned below:

1. Computer forensics
2. Mobile forensics
3. Network forensics
4. Email and Social media forensics
5. Database forensics

Computer memory storage is of two types: (1) Volatile storage and (2) Non-Volatile Storage. Therefore, Computer forensics can be further categorized as Volatile and Non-volatile forensics.

First of all, collect Volatile information because volatile information is lost when a system is powered off; it typically resides in system RAM. Non-volatile data is not affected by system shutdown or power outages. Hard drives are where non-volatile data is typically stored. However, it can also be found on USB storage devices, CD-ROMs, and mobile devices. Hence the first step of collecting digital evidence must be collecting volatile data. Once the volatile data has been collected, non-volatile data can be collected. Non-volatile data resides in the hard disk. A digital forensic investigator can remove the hard drive, place it in a faraday bag, and send it to the lab for further investigation.

There are different types of OS in computers, such as Windows, Linux, and Mac, that can be found on the computer under investigation. Windows OS uses NTFS (New Technology File system) file system. NTFS is an upgraded version of the previous file system that is FAT32. Let's discuss NTFS. Windows OS is one of the widely and commonly used OS.

There are many file systems developed for Windows OS, which are upgraded with time, and some are discussed here. FAT stands for File Allocation Table, and its first version was called FAT12, where 12 represent the number of bits used by the allocation table for cluster information. Then after FAT16 was built for a disk larger than 16MB, the same as the previous 16 represents the number of bits used by the allocation table for cluster information. FAT16 supports partitions up to 32GB. Similarly, there is FAT32 which improves the functionality of FAT 16. FAT32 supports partitions up to 2TB. FAT32 is also more reliable than FAT16 as it stores backup copies of some important data structures. After the FAT32, NTFS was developed to overcome the limitations of FAT32 and add some new features.

NTFS

New Technology File System (NTFS) is one of the file systems supported by Windows. It supports features such as file-level security, compression, and auditing. NTFS can also repair itself. NTFS provides data security by encrypting or decrypting data, files, or folders. By providing the feature of encryption and decryption, it has provided user integrity, and it makes the user's data safe from malicious access. NTFS makes a note of all the changes that the user has made to the file in a specific log file. Table 1 shows freshly formatted NTFS volume. Here MFT(Master File Table) is considered to be the heart of NTFS.

Table 1. Layout of a freshly formatted NTFS volume

Boot	MFT	Free Space	More Metadata	Free Space

(Russon & Fledel, 2004)

The first record of MFT describes MFT itself. The second Record stores the mirror of MFT, MFT-Mirr, which is the same as the first record. The third record stores a log file that records the changes made to each file.

In NTFS, each and everything is a file, and MFT stores information about everything, including itself. Attributes of files are written into the MFT in their allocated spaces. Table 2 shows the MFT record for small files. Small files and directories are smaller than 64-bit.

Table 2. MFT record for small file

Standard Information	File or Directory name	Security Descriptor	Data or index	Free Space

(Russon & Fledel, 2004)

Considering the FAT(File Allocation Table) file system, NTFS file access is faster. Because the FAT uses a file allocation table that stores the file name and the file location (address) of the file. And comparing that with this NTFS design, it is clear that NTFS access is faster.

Now take a look at the places where we can hide data and find tempering. In NTFS, everything is a file, and each file in the volume is represented by a record in a file called the Master File Table (MFT) (Lan-ying & Jin-wu, 2005) (Hermon et al., 2023). MFT and $Boot (Boot Sector File) list each other, and MFT lists itself (Hermon et al., 2023). As shown in Table 2, metadata is located on the disk, and the metadata of interest is $MFTMirr and $LogFile(Russon & Fledel, 2004).

If the MFT is damaged, then the volume could be recovered from the MFT Mirror, which is an exact copy of the first four records of the MFT. The LogFile is a journal of all the events waiting to be written to disk. It can be used to restore the disk state(Russon & Fledel, 2004).

In the paper NTFSDataTracker (Oh et al., 2021), they create a method that uses the transaction information stored in the $LogFile to replicate changes to the metadata within the $MFT file by file. They employ this method to keep track of all data modifications, along with the dates and times of each modification, for a particular file kept in the $LogFile. They developed a tool called NTFS Data Tracker (Oh et al., 2021).

$Boot file stores the boot record. It is stored at a fixed location, which is the first cluster of the file system. NTFS allocates 16 sectors to this file, and half of these contain non-zero bits. The other half of the $Boot can be used to hide the data. The size of the data to be hidden will also be limited.

Comparing the boot sector with the backup boot sector should be the first step in the examination of hidden data in the $Boot file. The last sector contains the backup boot sector. Let's assume that the partition contains 6,136,830 sectors. Use the subsequent commands to verify the integrity (Huebner et al., 2006).

```
$ dd if=/case1/image1 bs 512 count=1 skip=6136829 of=/case1/backupbootsector
$ dd if=/case1/image1 bs=512 count=1 of=/case1/ boot sector
$ md5sum /case1/backupbootsector
$ md5sum /case1/bootsector
```

(Huebner et al., 2006)

A file has been altered if the checksum is different. Even if they match, it's still possible that the modified boot sector was copied to its backup in order to avoid detection. To further analyze, you can use the hex editor to view the content of the boot sector. The next section gives details about the collection of volatile data.

This is an example of how to analyze the $MFT file using FTKImager. First of all, create an image of the NTFS file system using FTKImage. Now open the image in FTKImager as shown in Figure 1.

Now, open the $MFT file, and its hex will be shown in the below-given dialog box. Each $MFT entry starts with the "FILE0" signature/header. As each $MFT entry has file creation, last modified, and last accessed time here, it is shown in Figure 1. To check file creation time, go to offset 80 and select 8 bytes which represents the file creation time. The next 8 bytes represent the last modified time, and further next 8 bytes represent the last accessed file time. One can verify this time as it is also stored at offset 184, as shown in Figure 2.

Figure 1. $MFT file analysis(creation time of file)

Figure 2. $MFT file analysis (verify creation time of file)

To check the file name, go to offset 242 as shown in Figure 3, and in this case, it is $MFT as we are analyzing the $MFT file and the first entry in $MFT is of the file itself.

One can also analyze the image/disk using a simple hex editor. The author has shown how to analyze the same using a hex editor named Hxd Editor. Follow the following steps and instructions to perform the analysis.

- Open HxD as Administrator.
- Load the image or load the disk. (In case of loading the disk make sure "read only" mode is selected.

Figure 3. $MFT file analysis (file name)

- Once the file is opened it will be as shown in Figure 4. Here the first sector in NTFS is $boot and it contains the address of the $MFT and sector per cluster is at offset 0x30 and 0x08.
- In this case the value at 0x30 is 0x0C0000 and at 0x08 is 8 sectors per cluster.
- Therefore the address of $MFT in sector in decimal is
  - 0x0C0000 * 0x08 = 600000 =(6291456)decimal
- Jump to sector 6291456 as shown in Figure 5.
- First attribute can be found at 0x14-0x15 which is 0x0038
- Go to offset 0x38, value at this (0x38-0x3B) place is 0x10 which means that it is $Standard_ Information attribute.
- Value at offset 0x3C gives length of the whole attribute. In this case it is 0x60.
- To go to the next attribute add length of current attribute to current attribute offset. 0x38+0x60 = 0x98.
- Go to offset 0x98 and check the value at 0x98-0x9B, it is 0x30 which means it is $File_Name Attribute. This has been discussed earlier. Length of this attribute is at 0x9C-0x9F which is 0x68.
- Next attribute is at 0x98 + 0x68 = 0x100. Value 0x100-0x103 is 0x80 which means it is $DATA attribute. The $MFT entry that is currently under analysis is of $MFT file itself and the $MFT file's content data cannot be stored in one $MFT entry which means that it is a non-resident entry. That can also be verified at offset 0x108 where value is 0x01 which means the non-resident flag is set. Similarly, you can find the other attributes.
- To identify whether the file is fragmented or not check for the clusters that have been allocated to the $DATA non-resident attributes. The non-resident attributes are stored in cluster runs which store the starting address and the length of the run. Analyze the runs and check whether all the runs are in order and in consecutive address order, if it is then it is not fragmented else it is a fragmented file.

Figure 4. $Boot file analysis with HxD editor

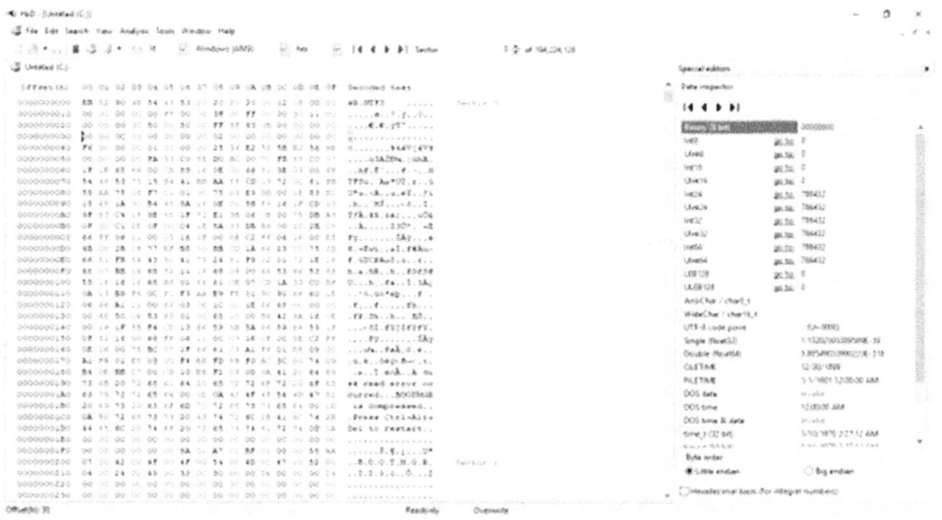

Figure 5. $MFT analysis with HxD editor

COLLECT VOLATILE DATA

Once the system is turned off, the volatile data is lost. Therefore, investigators should collect the contents of the RAM right at the beginning of the investigation to minimize the impact of further steps on the integrity of the contents of the RAM. Tools like Magnet Ram Capture, Belkasoft, Dumpit, and FTKImager can be used to collect volatile data with integrity. Investigators must be well aware that the instruments they are using to gather additional volatile information may change the memory's contents (Martínez, 2021).

Volatile information can help to analyze log files and cache and can also be useful for discovering the password (Naiqi, 2008). Volatile information also comprises information on processes, network connection, state of the system, process memory, and all other things that exist in RAM.

Note: Never turn off the internet connection or take the system out of the network, because if you do so, then you will lose the data about where it was connected and the person remotely using it.

While collecting the volatile data, the first step should be to collect the system time. The collected time information can help in the reconstruction of events. It also tells when the investigator has started the investigation. Use the below-given command.

```
$ date /t & time /t
```

Collect logged-on user's details as it has details of users who had remote access to the system along with the locally logged-on users. This is the phase where if you have turned off the connection, you will lose the critical data. You can use tools like 'PsLoggedOn' and 'net sessions' to get the logged-on user's information (Carvey, 2009). The syntax for tools is given below.

```
$ psloggedon [-] [-l] [-x] [computername | username ]
$ net sessions [computername] [/delete] [/list]
```

The file and application that are open play an important role as it might be the case that the suspect got the news about investigators and being in hurry he has left the files and application open. Collecting the list and details of the files that are open at the time of seizing it can help in the process, and you can use 'net file.' The syntax for tools is given below.

```
$ net file [ID [/close]]
```

As discussed previously, the data about the systems and network connected remotely plays a major role in the investigation as it may be the case that the suspect is remotely using the evidence computer and also the victim can be remotely connected. Collect the network information so that you can identify the other system(s) connected to the compromised system and the network. Useful information for investigation is mentioned below:

- Data content of packets.
- IDS/IPS, firewall, server, and application log.
- Session information
- Port information

A record of connections made to other systems is kept in the NetBIOS name table cache. The distant system name and IP address are stored in the NetBIOS database. The NetBIOS name table cache can be viewed using the command-line tool 'nbtstat'. The syntax for the tool is given below.

```
$ nbtstat [-A IP address] [-a Remotename] [-c] [-n] [-s] [-r] [-S] [-R] [-RR]
[interval]
```

There is another tool also called 'Netstat' which collects information about network connection and UDP and TCP connections, their state and traffic. In digital forensics, there can be more than one tool for performing the same task. There can be paid as well as free tools. In this chapter, only free tools are used so that everyone can learn. The syntax for the tool is given below.

```
$ netstat [-e] [-a] [-o] [-n] [-r] [-S] [-p <Protocol>] [interval]
```

Collect the information about the processes on the system, which plays an important part in the investigation process. An investigator should look for the below-given information.

- Full path of the image.
- Time duration for which the process was running.
- User information of the process.
- Other modules and processes that have been loaded by the current process.
- Lastly, the Memory content of the process.

Some important tools and cli used to collect the process information are Tasklist, Pslist, ListDlls, Handle, etc... . Pslist shows basic information about the already running process. ListDlls shows dlls loaded into processes. For any process running in the system, Handle displays details about the open handles. All tasks running on a local or remotely connected computer are listed in the tasklist along with their associated services and applications with process identifiers. A combination of data gathered with the help of these four tools will be more meaningful. The syntax for the tool is given below.

```
$ tasklist [/u domain\user [/p password]] [/m [ModuleName] | /svc | /v]  [/nh]
[/fi FilterName [/fi Filtername2 [/..]]] [/s computer] [/fo {TABLE|LIST|CSV}]
$ listdlls [-v | -u] [-r]  [processname|pid]
$ listdlls [-v] [-r] [-d dllname]
$ handle [[-a] [-u] | [-v] | [-c <handle> [-l] [-y]] ] [-p <processname>|<pid>>
[name]
```

The data related to the port is also important as some processes might be using a port for malicious activity or they can be the gateway through which the attack or crime has happened, therefore collect process-to-port- mapping data. Process-to-port mapping traces the port used by a process and protocol connected to the IP. A command for retrieving the port-to-process mapping is given below.

```
$ netstat -a -o -n
```

Running processes might be harmful or malicious in intent. In order to determine whether a process is malicious or suspicious, you can use tools like 'ProcessExplorer' (Malin, 2008). ProcessExlporer comes with inbuilt support for the Virus tool. To collect all the processes or to take a dump of all the processes use tools like 'ProcDump' and 'ProcessDumper' to investigate.

To determine whether a wireless access point is connected to the system and what IP address is being used, gather information from the network interface cards (NICs) of the system. You can use tools and cli like Ipconfig, PromiscDetect, and Promqry for network status detection . Ipconfig is a utility native to Windows systems that displays information about NICS and their status. The network configuration of the system's NICs is shown by the IPconfig command.

PromiscDetect checks to see if the network adapter(s) are active in promiscuous mode, which could indicate the presence of a sniffer on the system. Primary is a command line tool that detects network interfaces running in promiscuous mode.

Analyze the copied data and, for that, collect clipboard content because the clipboard is the area that stores copied data. When you utilize the copy and cut features of the Windows OS, information is kept in memory and can be viewed using the Free Clipboard Viewer. It displays the current content of the clipboard. There can be cases where you can get important phone numbers, emails, social media accounts IDs, passwords, links, credit card details, text from chat, license keys, UPI, crypto wallet details, and many more important data. All possible data shows the importance of analyzing the clipboard content.

When conducting an investigation, if there are too many command prompts, the user's typing of commands like 'ftp' or 'ping' could conceal important clues. The investigator can use the command prompt's upward-moving scroll bar to view the commands they've already entered. However, if the user had entered the 'cls' command to clean the screen, the investigator would not be able to utilise the scroll bar to view any of the commands they had entered. Instead, the investigator should utilise the 'doskey /histor' command, which shows the history of the commands entered into that prompt. Collecting the command history and analyzing it can be very helpful as it can recreate the crime scene it can, prove the attack or the victim, and can detail the scene using a timeline. Also, with the help of command history, you can identify the type of attack or how the victim was made to fall into a trap. It can be important in proving suspects guilty (Reith, 2022). It can give information about the background process. There can be a background process that is malicious and was there in the background with the intention of wiping the data when the unknown user or investigator tries to access the files and open the file, which triggers the action of shutting down or formatting the computer. Once a computer is shut down, volatile data will be lost, and when it formats data, there are chances that the digital evidence may get lost and you cannot prove the suspect guilty.

Network resources that can be accessed from a distant computer using LAN are known as shared resources. Forensic investigators should use the 'net share' command in the command prompt to retrieve data on all shared resources on the local computer. There may be the case that there was a shared file, which is executable, with a malicious user. Malicious user has no permission to access the other data except the shared one. A malicious user has write permission on a shared file so that he can write the malicious code in the shared file. To identify such scenarios, it is important to collect details of the shared resources.

These are the necessary and general volatile information that needs to be collected. With experience, one will be better at finding the right artifacts to present in the court. The next section gives details about collecting non-volatile data.

COLLECT NON-VOLATILE DATA

As an investigator, you can take out the hard disk from the CPU and can take it to the forensics lab to make an image of the hard disk. Hard disks can be 512 GB, 1TB, or 2Tb, and therefore making the image of the hard disk will take time therefore, you can take the hard disk to the lab.

First of all, create an image of a hard disk using a write blocker. And then use the image for further analysis. You can use tools like Belkasoft, FTKImager, Encase Imager, and Tableau Forensic Imager TX1.

Non-volatile data can also be found in swap files, slack space, and unallocated drive space in addition to hard drives, where it is often stored. Smart phones, USB storage devices, and CD-ROMs are other non-volatile data storage devices.

Accessing file system data and rebuilding file system events is an important part of an investigation. File systems comprise five sections as mentioned below:

- File system data: File system data gives details about the file system structure, such as file system and file system block size, number of allocated blocks, etc.
- Content data: The majority of the file system's information is present in this data. It consists of the file system's contents.
- Metadata: Metadata generally provides information about content locations, file size, and MAC timestamps. Application data:
- Application data gives information about the file system journal quota statistics.

The command "dir /o:d" should be entered into the command prompt by the investigator. They can do this to check the OS installation date and time as well as the service packs, patches, and frequently updating subdirectories (e.g., drivers, etc.).

For an investigator windows registry is one of the important places to search for evidence or clues for the evidence. The Windows registry is a central hierarchical database intended to store information that is necessary to configure the system for one or more users, applications or hardware devices (Reddy N., 2019). The data is stored in the main folder and it is further organized as a tree-like structure called hive and its subfolders are referred to as keys and subkeys.

Note: Uncheck system protected files from hidden menu.

Path for windows registry is: c:\windows\system32\config

"Ntuser.dat" is a registry file for every profile and its path is: C:\users\username

Table 3 describes 5 root keys and the value content in them.

Table 3. Root keys and their description

Root keys	Description
HKEY_CURRENT_USER (HKCU)	It contains information about the user who is logged in and the user's setting information
HKEY_LOCAL_MACHINE (HKLM)	It contains information about the computer such as hardware and software installed on it and software configurations.
HKEY_USERS (HKU)	It contains information about all the users who have logged on to the computer.
HKEY_CURRENT_CONFIG (HKCC)	It contains the information about the currently installed hardware.

To analyze the registry, export the registry files and open the exported registry file in Registry Explorer tool (https://ericzimmerman.github.io/). To export the registry files from live machine you can use FTKImage, go to File->Obtain protected files and select the path to store the exported registry files.

Now open the registry files in Registry Explore as shown in Figure 6. Now go to path HKCU(ntuser. dat)\SOFTWARE\Microsoft\Windows\Current Version\Explorer. Figure6 shows the \RecentDocs which shows most recent open documents through which an investigator can analyze the most recent document. Similarly, \RunMRU shows the most recent used run command as shown in Figure 7. And \UserAssit shows which program was executed by which user and for how many times it was executed as shown in Figure 8.

Figure 6. Registry Explorer (\RecentDocs)

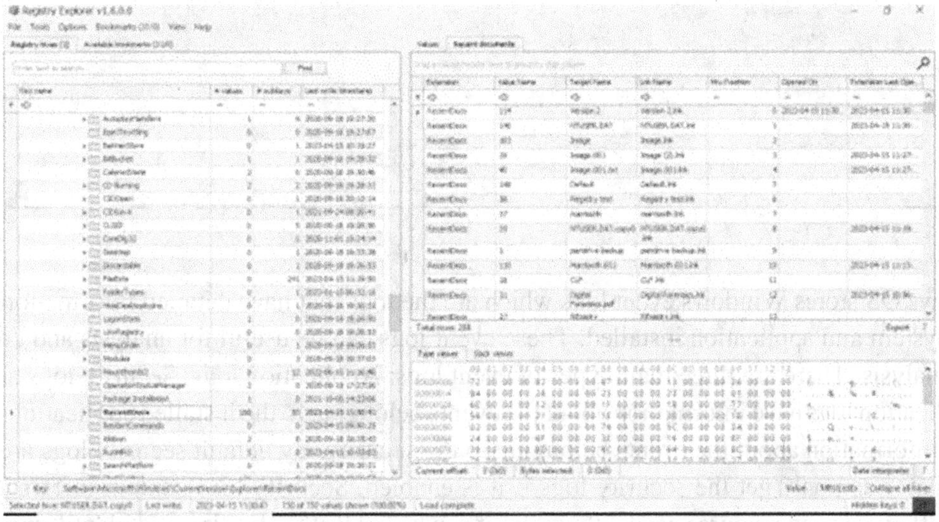

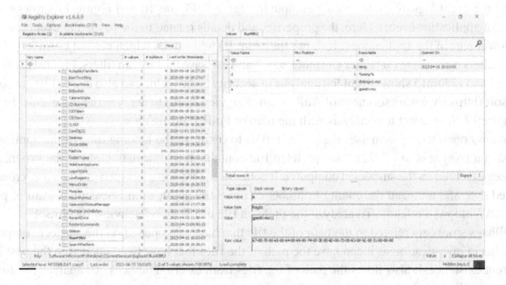

Figure 7. Registry Explorer (\RunMRU)

Figure 8. Registry Explorer (\UserAssit)

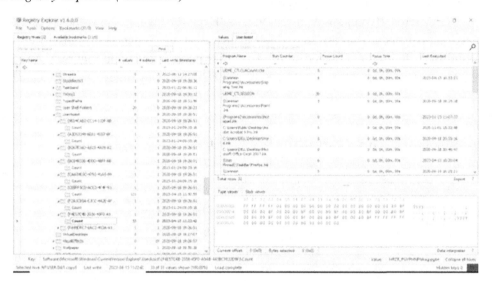

Windows OS stores Windows event logs which are the logs that have detailed information about the security, system and application installed. These event logs can be useful for analysis and creating the timeline analysis. There are three main types of event logs: Application logs, Security logs and System logs. Application logs have information about the events belonging to the installed applications. Security logs have information about the events belonging to the security. By default security logs are disabled, an investigator can only get the security logs if it is enabled. Security logs contain information about logon/logoff events and resource access therefore it can be helpful for finding and identifying unauthorized access/activities.

An investigator can use windows event viewer to analyze the event logs of current computer or they can load the event logs of the suspected computer. Figure 9, Figure 10 and Figure 11 shows event log analysis of application events. Here, the properties and details related to the particular event can be seen in the lower part of the applications. It shows the event ID which tells which kind of event it is. One can also use filters by clicking on "Filter Current Logs.." and can save the custom filters. Figure12, Figure 13, Figure 14 and Figure15 shows event log analysis of security events. One can also use FullEventLogView by Nirsoft (https://www.nirsoft.net/utils/full_event_log_view.html) to analyze the log events. Figure 16 and Figure 17 show event log analysis with the help of FullEventLogView.

Windows operating system uses the prefetch files to optimize the loading time of the application in the next run (Neyaz et al., 2022). This prefetch file contains the information about the programs that have been executed on the suspected computer. It contains the information such as filename, created and modified date and time and the count of number of times the application is executed. Path of prefetch file is: C:\Windows\Prefetch . To analyze the prefetch file use Winprefetchview by NirSoft.

Shellbags store data related to the path of the file that has been opened on the suspect computer.

It helps in investigation as it can have the path of the files that have been opened in the past but has no current existence. It also stores the path of the files from external devices. To analyze the shellbags files use Shellbag Explorer.

Figure 9. Event Viewer Application Log

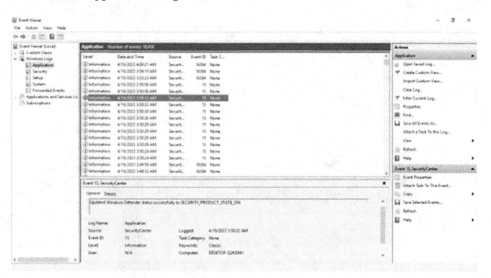

Figure 10. Event Viewer Application Log

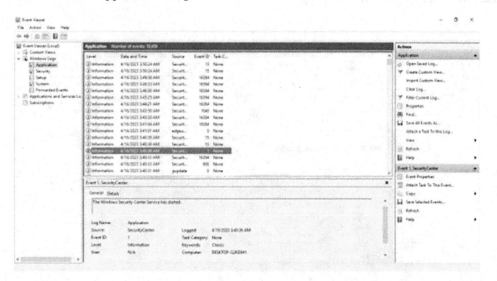

Many Microsoft applications on Windows OS use the data-storing technology known as Extensible Storage Engine (ESE). From a forensics point of view, the ESE database is important because it stores and manages main records pertaining to systems and users in Windows OS. The ESE is also referred to as JET Blue. ESE database files are denoted by the .edb extension. Some examples of ESE database files are contacts.edb, Windows.edb, and Datastore.edb.

The ESEDatabaseView tool is used to extract valuable evidence from .edb files. ESEDatabaseView shows a list of all the tables present in the opened database file, allowing the user to select the table they want to see and see every record in it. It can be useful to find evidence as many applications use this technology to store data. It parses the data and makes it readable.

Figure 11. Event Viewer Application Log

Figure 12. Event Security Application Log

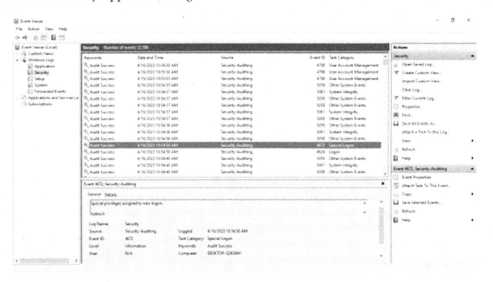

Windows OS uses an index database called Windows Search Index that allows the indexing of files and other content and enables the quicker and more accurate search of data on the system; it also stores indexed information for all content that is searched by users. Hence, it can be the place from where an investigator can find the evidence or can find the link/hint of the evidence. Windows Search Index is stored in Windows.edb file. Therefore, it can be analyzed with the help of the ESEDatabaseView tool. Windows.edb file is located in the following directory:

```
C:\ProgramData\Microsoft\Search\Data\Applications\Windows.
```

Figure 13. Event Viewer Application Log

Figure 14. Event Viewer Application Log

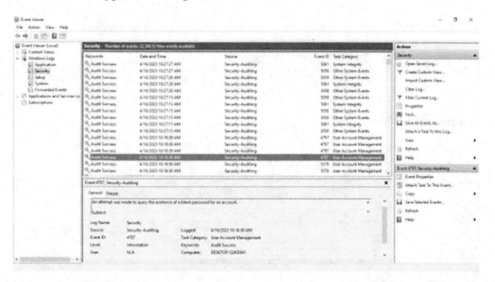

It may happen that from the information that you have gathered till now, you came to a file that was once accessed but now it is no longer on the hard disk. It was on some external media. For such scenarios, collect the data of connected external media.

Detect the devices connected to a system as it helps forensic investigators to determine if any external media has been used by the suspect to commit cybercrime. Investigators can use the DriveLetter View tool to list all the devices/drives on the system, even if they are currently not plugged in. On computers running Windows OS, DevCon, or Device Console, is a command line utility that shows comprehensive information about devices. Devices can be installed, configured, removed, enabled, or disabled using DevCon. It has features as mentioned below:

- Displays driver and device information
- Searches for devices
- Changes device settings
- Restarts the device or computer

Figure 15. Event Viewer Application Log

Figure 16. FullEventLogView

Figure 17. FullEventLogView with Filter

Slack space, also known as file slack, is the space created between the end of a file that has been stored and the end of the disc cluster as a result of the current file's size being smaller than the file that came before it on the same cluster. Slack space may contain data either from a previously deleted file or unused space by the currently allocated file. Without knowing the underlying file system, it might be possible to store data that you want to keep private in slack space. DriveSpy creates a file from every bit of slack space on a given partition. It is helpful when the suspect has some forensics knowledge he will try to overwrite the content of the evidence file. Because if it is deleted, then only the entry is removed, and the data will be there as it is, which can be further recovered. But if the data is overwritten, then it will be difficult to recover. While overwriting, there may be some slack space that will be created as a result of the size of the file used to overwrite. Hence, DriveSpy can be useful in such scenarios.

A logical portion of a disc known as a hidden partition is inaccessible to the operating system. It could have documents, folders, private information, or system backups. Tools like "Partition find & mount" and "Partition Logic" can be used. Hidden partitions are one of the commonly used places to hide data. Such partitions are inaccessible to the operating system.

A utility for managing data and partitioning hard drives is called Partition Logic. Partitions can be created, deleted, erased, formatted, defragmented, resized, copied, moved, and have their attributes changed. It can transfer full hard drives between two computers. A novel idea for recovering lost or deleted partitions is implemented by Partition Find & Mount. It finds the lost partitions and mounts them onto the system, making them accessible. It will also function if any Boot Record is lost, harmed, or rewritten, even the Master Boot Record.

Sometimes you can get information from thumbnails of the file, especially if the evidence file is a graphic file. Consider a scenario where an investigator has to prove that the suspect has a particular image file, but the file is not found on the storage device. And also, it is not recovered through any of the software. Then an investigator can analyze the thumbnail cache. If an investigator can find the thumbnail of the evidence image file, then he can prove that the image file was once on the computer and can further prove the suspect guilty. The thumbnails of graphic files such as JPEG, BMP, PNG, GIF, TIFF, etc., are stored in the following directory:

```
C:\Users\[User Profile]\AppData\Local \Microsoft\Windows\Explorer
```

The cache files are stored as thumbcache\mathunderscore ***.db, where '***' refers to the pixel dimensions. In forensics investigation, the database files that contain information such as original file-name, date and times, and EXIF data, serve as a potential source of graphical evidence. The thumbnails of deleted files also remain in the thumb cache database files and can be extracted using tools such as Thumbcache Viewer and Thumbs Viewer.

Table 4. Tools and CLI to collect or examine artifacts

Artifacts	Tools and CLI
Logged-on users	psloggedon, netsessions
Opened files	net file
Network Information	nbtstat, netstat
Process Information	TaskList, Pslist, ListDlls, Handle
Process-to-port Mapping	netstat
Check Malicious File	ProcDump, ProcessDumper
NICs Information	Ipconfig, Promqry, PromiscDetect
Clipboard content	Free Clipboard Viewer
Command History	doskey, history
Shared Resources	net share
Windows Registry	Registry Explorer
Event Logs	Windows Event Viewer, FullEventLogView
Prefetch file	Winprefetchview
Shellbags	Shellbag Explorer
Extensible Storage Engine(ESE) Windows Search Index	ESEDatabaseView
Externally Connected Devices	Device Console
Slack Space	Drive Spy
Hidden Partition	Partition Find & Mount, Partition Logic

Examine Web Browser Data

An investigator must also examine web browser content like caches, history, and cookies. From this data you can get the online activities performed like sites visited, files downloaded and most recently visited and most visited websites and this information can be of great evidentiary value.

Mozilla Firefox

Cache Location. C:\Users\<Username>\AppData\Local\Mozilla\Firefox\Profiles\XXXXXXXX.default\ cache2 (View and Restore Firefox Cache Files, 2023)

Cookies Location. C:\Users\<Username\AppData\Roaming\Mozilla\Firefox\Profiles\XXXXXXXX.
default\cookies.sqlite (View and Restore Firefox Cache Files, 2023)

History Location. C:\Users\<Username>\AppData\Roaming\Mozilla\Firefox\Profiles\XXXXXXXX.
default\places.sqlite (View and Restore Firefox Cache Files, 2023)

You can use the below-given tools to display and analyze the data:

- MZCacheView
- MZCookiesView
- MZHistoryView

Google Chrome

Cache Location. C:\Users\{user}\AppData\Local\Google\Chrome\User Data\Default\Cache (Google
Chrome History Location | Chrome History Viewer, n.d.)

History Cookies Location. C:\Users\{user}\AppData\Local\Google\chrome\User Data\Default (Google
Chrome History Location | Chrome History Viewer, n.d.)

You can use the below-given tools to display and analyze the data:

- ChromeCacheView
- ChromeCookiesView
- ChromeHistoryView

Microsoft Edge

Cache Location. C:\Users\Admin\AppData\Local\Microsoft\Windows\WebCache (Microsoft Edge
History Location | Edge History Viewer, n.d.)

Cookies Location. C:\Users\Admin\AppData\Local\Packages\Microsoft.MicrosoftEdge_xxxxxxxxxx\
AC\MicrosoftEdge\Cookies (Microsoft Edge History Location | Edge History Viewer, n.d.)

History Location. C:\Users\Admin\AppData\Local\Microsoft\Windows\History (Microsoft Edge His-
tory Location | Edge History Viewer, n.d.)

You can use the below-given tools to display and analyze the data:

- IECacheView
- EdgeCookiesView
- BrowserHistoryView

By analyzing the browser, you can detect the behavior of the user. Based on the user's search history,
you can find the patterns and can analyze the types of data, website, and shopping of the user.

RECOVERY

Data recovery is the process of retrieving deleted or inaccessible data (Pal & Memon, 2009). In order to study data recovery, one needs to study how the files are allocated in NTFS and how they are deleted, and what data is left from which you can retrieve the original file.

File Allocation in NTFS

- File information is kept in a B-Tree in NTFS; however, in contrast to the FAT, NTFS has a separate structure known as a bitmap (BMP) to indicate the allocation status of clusters. This is in contrast to the FAT, which does not have this structure.
- In the BMP file ($bitmap) that represents clusters, a value of one is assigned to each cluster if the cluster belongs to an existing file, and a value of zero is assigned to each cluster if the cluster does not belong to an existing file.
- Because it reads and interprets the BMP, NTFS is able to decide in a flash where on the disc would be the least fragmented location for a given file.
- In addition, exactly like FAT, the file cluster linkages are stored in the NTFS file system.

Deletion

- When a file is destroyed, the clusters in the BMP that are associated with it are reset to zero. When files are deleted, the real data are not removed in the same way as they are not removed when using the FAT file system.
- In contrast to the FAT, the file cluster links are not removed either; hence, if the record for the deleted file is still preserved, this indicates that the original cluster links are also still present.
- Because the whole cluster link that represents the file is still present, this makes it significantly simpler to recover the file using NTFS.
- In the $bitmap file, the clusters are merely displayed as having their storage space deallocated.

Recovery

- When the file entry is still available on an NTFS volume, it is not difficult to recover deleted files from that volume.
- This is because the file's cluster numbers should also be present, and all that needs to be done is check to see if the file's clusters have been overwritten or if they are being used by another file.
- The reason for this is that the file's cluster numbers should also be present. In the event that the file system is corrupted or the entries of the deleted file are removed, the metadata stored within the file system cannot be utilized for recovery purposes.

Now let's say the File table has been tampered with or deleted. Then also, you can recover the data. Recovering the data without using any metadata from the structure is called file carving. File carving works bit by bit. It identifies the file type with the help of Magic Bytes (Hickok at el., 2005). Magic bytes are the signature of the file, and they are stored in the head cluster. The first few bytes of the head cluster are the magic bytes of the file. For example, the magic bytes of the .jpg file type are 'FFD8'. To verify the magic bytes, open the image in the hex editor and check the bytes 'FFD8'.

Let's have a demo of how to use recovery software. Download the windows version of Photorec(CGSecurity, 2022) from https://www.cgsecurity.org/wiki/TestDisk_Download and extract the .zip file. Paste the extracted content at c:\Program Files\ as shown in Figure 19. and follow the below given steps.

1.   Open the qphotorec_win.exe (Figure 20).
2.   Select the drive you want to recover (Figure 21). The author has used his formatted 8GB pendrive (Figure 18).
3.   Select the path of the folder where you want to store the recovered data.
4.   Click on "File Formats" and select the file formats you want to recover from the drive under recovery process (Figure 22). The author has selected all the file formats.
5.   Click on "Search" and it will start recovering the files as shown in Figure 23.
6.   Once the process has been completed it will show the number of recovered files for each type of file format as shown in Figure 24.
7.   After completion of the recovery process go to the folder where the recovered data is stored. It will be stored in folders named as recup_dir.[1,2,3,...] (Figure 25). The recovered data is inside these folders.

The details mentioned till now are very useful for an investigator or the one who is learning digital forensics as it covers the forensics of the NTFS file system which is widely used by Windows OS. Adding experience to this knowledge will help find the evidence much faster.

Figure 18. Formatted pendrive of size 8GB

Figure 19. Paste extracted folder at c:\Program Files

Figure 20. Open qphotorec_win

FORENSICS ANALYSIS STRATEGY

Depending on the type of case, the investigator uses its experience to solve the case by finding the evidence. Let's consider the case where the investigator needs to find the file or to prove that the particular file has been accessed by a suspected computer. Then the investigator should search the file name through prefetch and shellbags. From there he can get the path of the evidence file if it has been opened on the suspected computer. Then analyze the path from shellbags and decide whether the evidence file accessed is in the internal or external storage. If it is in the external storage then finds the details of the external device and the device itself. If the file is on internal storage go to the file location and get the file. If the file path or file does not exist in both the cases then use the recovery tools to recover the files.

Figure 21. From the drop down select the drive to be recovered and select the directory where you want to store the recovered data.

Figure 22. Click on "File Formats" and select the file formats you want to recover and click "ok".

Figure 23. After you have selected the file formats click on "Search" and it will start recovering the file.

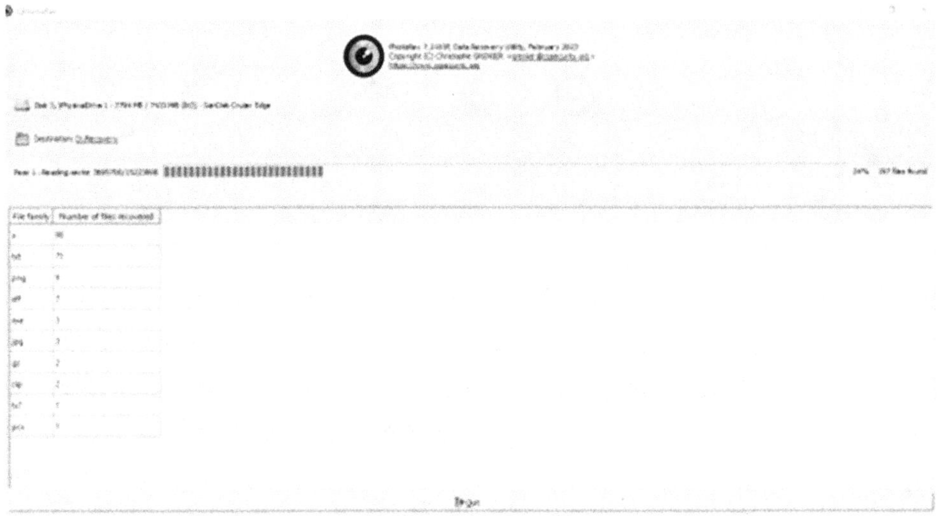

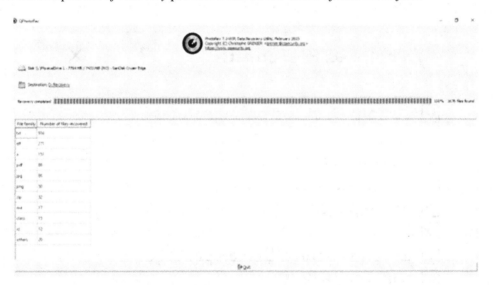

Figure 24. On completion of recovery process it shows the count of recovered files

In some cases the file extensions are changed so that it will be difficult to open the files. In such scenarios use magic bytes to find the type of the file.

In cases which involve the terrorist attack where there is a suspect machine and there is a suspicion that the data related to explosives and weapons is stored in this particular machine an investigator should search for words such as nitro, nitrates, amines, peroxides for explosives and the gun names. An investigator can use the "image to text" functionality and then search on the text as it can be the case that the names are stored in an image.

Figure 25. All the recovered data will be stored in the folder name as "recup_dir.[1,2,3,..]"

Search for passwords or important notes/information written on the wall, notes or any surface. As it will play a crucial role in investigation. The notes can also contain information about the crypto currency which can be a place for evidence.

Note: Maintain the chain of custody while investigating. Never take any step that can be used against the investigator in court of law. Always work on the image of the evidence and not on the original evidence. Take the hash of the image and evidence file into consideration.

CONCLUSION

In this chapter the author has described the whole forensics analysis process for NTFS(Windows) File system. In the beginning of the chapter they have described the Digital forensics, types of digital forensics, steps for crime scene management, tools and equipment to carry along when appearing at the crime scene and basics of FAT and NTFS. They have mentioned and discussed the artifacts that must be taken into consideration while investigating along with the tools that can be used to analyze the corresponding artifacts. They have also described the type of evidence that can be found from particular artifacts. Along with the same they have mentioned the importance of each artifact and the scenarios where it can play a crucial part. If the evidence file is missing or there are unallocated/formatted storage devices/drives then the investigators can use recovery tools and processes discussed in this chapter. They have also discussed the strategies used for forensics analysis. Future work of this chapter is using machine learning to find the evidence from the data gathered from the case description.

REFERENCES

Belkasoft. (n.d.). *Accelerate Your DFIR Investigation*. Belkasoft. https://belkasoft.com/

Alazab, M., Venkatraman, S., & Watters, P. (2009). Effective digital forensic analysis of the NTFS disk image. *Ubiquitous Computing and Communication Journal*, *4*(1), 551–558.

Alazab, M., Venkatraman, S., & Watters, P. (2009, June). Digital forensic techniques for static analysis of NTFS images. In *Proceedings of ICIT2009, Fourth International Conference on Information Technology*. IEEE Xplore.

Carrier, B. (2005). *File system forensic analysis*. Addison-Wesley Professional.

Carvey, H. (2009). *Windows forensic analysis DVD toolkit*. Syngress.

CGSecurity. (2022, November 4). *Testdisk download*. CGSecurity. https://www.cgsecurity.org/wiki/TestDisk_Download

Foxton Forensics. (n.d.). *Google chrome history location: chrome history viewer*. Foxton Forensics. https://www.foxtonforensics.com/browser-history-examiner/chrome-history-location

Hermon, R., Singh, U., & Singh, B. (2023). Ntfs: Introduction and analysis from forensics point of view. *2023 International Conference for Advancement in Technology (ICONAT)*, (pp. 1–6). IEEE. 10.1109/ICONAT57137.2023.10080271

Hickok, D. J., Lesniak, D. R., & Rowe, M. C. (2005, April). File type detection technology. In *Proceedings from the 38th Midwest Instruction and Computing Symposium*. IEEE.

Huebner, E., Bem, D., & Wee, C. K. (2006). Data hiding in the NTFS file system. *Digital investigation*, *3*(4), 211-226.

Lan-ying, W., & Jin-wu, J. (2005). Analysis of NTFS file system structure [J]. *Computer Engineering and Design*, *27*(3), 418–420.

Malin, C. H., Casey, E., & Aquilina, J. M. (2008). *Malware forensics: investigating and analyzing malicious code*. Syngress.

Martínez, M. F. (2021). Impact of Tools on the Acquisition of RAM Memory. *International Journal of Cyber Forensics and Advanced Threat Investigations*, *1*(1-3), 3–17. doi:10.46386/ijcfati.v1i1-3.12

Foxton Forensics. (n.d.). Microsoft edge history location: edge history viewer. Foxton Forensics. https://www.foxtonforensics.com/browser-history-examiner/microsoft-edge-history-location

Naiqi, L., Zhongshan, W., & Yujie, H. (2008, August). Computer forensics research and implementation based on NTFS file system. In *2008 ISECS International Colloquium on Computing, Communication, Control, and Management (Vol. 1*, pp. 519-523). IEEE. 10.1109/CCCM.2008.236

Neyaz, A., & Shashidhar, N. (2022). Windows prefetch forensics. In K. Daimi, G. Francia III, & L. H. Encinas (Eds.), *Breakthroughs in Digital Biometrics and Forensics* (pp. 191–210). Springer International Publishing., doi:10.1007/978-3-031-10706-1_9

Oh, J., Lee, S., & Hwang, H. (2021). NTFS Data Tracker: Tracking file data history based on $ LogFile. *Forensic Science International: Digital Investigation*, *39*, 301309.

Pal, A., & Memon, N. (2009). The evolution of file carving. *IEEE Signal Processing Magazine, 26*(2), 59–71. doi:10.1109/MSP.2008.931081

Reddy, N. (2019). Windows forensics. In N. Reddy (Ed.), *Practical Cyber Forensics: An Incident-Based Approach to Forensic Investigations* (pp. 29–68). Apress., doi:10.1007/978-1-4842-4460-9_2

Reith, M., Carr, C., & Gunsch, G. (2002). An examination of digital forensic models. *International Journal of digital evidence, 1*(3), 1-12.

Russon, R., & Fledel, Y. (2004). NTFS documentation. *Recuperado el, 1.*

Svensson, A. (2005). *Computer forensics applied to windows NTFS computers.* Stockholm's University, Royal Institute of Technology.

View and restore firefox cache files. (2023, February 22). EaseUS. https://www.easeus.com/file-recovery/view-and-restore-firefox-cache-temp-files.html

KEY TERMS AND DEFINITIONS

Digital Forensics: The process of identifying, collecting, preserving, examining, analyzing, and presenting digital evidence is called digital forensics.

File Carving: Recovery of data without the help of a file system or metadata provided by the file system.

File System: A method to store and retrieve data from a specific data structure and it varies with the operating system.

Magic Bytes: First few hex values that are the signature of the corresponding file type are called Magic Bytes

Non-Volatile Data: Non-volatile data exists in the memory even after power is turned off. Data stored in a hard disk is Non-volatile data.

Recovery: Retrieving deleted or inaccessible data is called recovery.

Volatile Data: Data stored in memory whose life span is until the power is off. Data stored in ram is one example, once the system is turned off all the data in ram will be lost.

Chapter 9
Workplace Cyberbullying in the Remote–Work Era:
A New Dimension of Cyberology

Nashra Javed
https://orcid.org/0000-0003-2810-6352
Integral University, India

Tasneem Ahmed
https://orcid.org/0000-0003-2702-3168
Integral University, India

Mohammad Faisal
Integral University, India

Halima Sadia
https://orcid.org/0000-0002-0476-7976
Integral University, India

Emilly Zoë Jeanne Sidaine-Daumiller
Osnabrück Universität, Germany

ABSTRACT

Information and communication technologies are being used as weapons in a combat zone created by the norm that forces individuals to work from home during this pandemic. The upsurge in workplace cyberbullying is visible in various reports. Workplace cyberbullying may appear to be a less severe form of harassment, but the shift to a more dispersed workforce has made it worse. It is the intimidation experienced by a remote or hybrid employee which results in a breakdown in communication with or mistreatment from leaders. While it makes sense to believe that because we are not at the office, occurrences of antagonism and harassment are drastically reduced, that's not the reality. Spiteful employers and demeaning coworkers might pose a virtual threat. Remote work settings are becoming toxic due to harmful, unkind workplace behavior, including derogatory language, social exclusion, and threats via phone, email, or social media. This chapter unveils a new dimension of cyberology.

DOI: 10.4018/978-1-6684-8133-2.ch009

INTRODUCTION

The pandemic left all offices closed across the globe, and personal spaces transformed into office spaces, contemplating the possible upsides of the new professional conundrum felt like a means of survival. During that time a huge tumult was there, and many people thought that workplace harassment will drop as everyone became boxes on Google Meet, Zoom, Webex, or text bubbles in a chat, and physically separated from colleagues and clients. The hidden flame quickly turns the tables and rapidly went dark. The rising incidents of bullying virtually started with the adoption of video calling during COVID-19 and it has provided fertile ground for incidents of bullying to flourish not abate. According to 2023 ZogbyAnalytics polls, there was a 57% rise in the number of employees reporting face-to-face bullying since 2017, whereas 40% reported it while working remotely(ehstoday.com, 2022).In one of the surveys conducted by the Workplace Bullying Institute (WBI), it was seen that bullying happened during virtual meets. It seems workplace bullies were cognizant of the risk of leaving a paper trail, as would be generated through email. Almost 50% respondents of in that survey admitted that they had experienced or witnessed mistreatment during virtual meetings – mistreatment that was the equivalent of being berated at a group meeting. Due to COVID-19 and the necessity for social isolation, businesses had to find new locations for their staff to work because offices were no longer safe. As a result, companies were able to conduct the majority of their operations utilizing mobile or other digital platforms, giving birth to remote working arrangements or work-from-home (WFH)(Kompella, 2022). Regardless of the nature of the task or the employees' skills, remote working was a must rather than a desire or an option for them. Home-based workers have to swiftly adjust to the situation and carry out their assigned tasks.

Around the world the prevalence of cyberbullying has already been a worry for parents before the COVID-19 pandemic, Figure 1 shows the countries that reported cyberbullying the most where India has the highest number of reported cyberbullying cases compared to other countries. The rise in workplace cyberbullying has been reported in various surveys, which represents unexplored factors that are responsible for cyberbullying in a remote work environment(Bradley, 2022; Workplace Bullying Persists despite Remote Work, *2022) during COVID-19.One of the key things that differentiate cyberbullying from traditional bullying is that the trail of evidence that can be used to report cyberbullying can be easy. The majority of employees are unaware of how to deal with workplace cyberbullying when they are working remotely(Akram et al., 2022).*

Cyberbullying is typically seen as an adolescent concern. However, because the issue has grown to include adults, particularly in recent years, the workplace is not immune to cyberbullying. Due to the COVID-19 pandemic, many businesses moved their work environments online, which increased the amount of workplace cyberbullying. Because of the use of technology and the blending of our personal and professional lives, harassment doesn't always happen during working hours and doesn't always stop when the victim leaves the office. Cyberbullying generally takes a more subtle form than traditional workplace bullying, but it may be easier for employers to investigate. When opposed to cyberbullying aimed at children, cyberbullying at work carries a higher risk since, if it is caught, the offender may face reprimands or even termination(Ali, 2022; Anasori et al., 2020). Workplace Cyberbullying and virtual harassment have been intertwined during the 2020 pandemic.

Figure 1. Countries with the most reported cyberbullying

WORKPLACE CYBERBULLYING

Workplace cyberbullying may appear to be a less severe form of harassment, but the shift to a more dispersed workforce has made this issue worse. Workplace cyberbullying is the harassment experienced by a remote or hybrid employee as a result of a breakdown in communication with or mistreatment from leaders. While workplace interpersonal conflict is ubiquitous and frequently addressed by rules and regulations, the shift to hybrid and remote work arrangements has increased the frequency and difficulty of workplace harassment incidents. The WBI poll indicated that 47% of managers were the top offenders of workplace cyberbullying. Also, compared to 33% of women, 67% of men were found to be bullies. The poll reveals that this kind of harassment happened in virtual meetings with other employees or one-on-one (50%) and over email (9%), while the other respondents said they had never been subjected to abuse because of their distant employment(Ali, 2022; Anasori et al., 2020; Kompella, 2022).

Workers may feel helpless in their abilities to express and handle such concerns since harassment frequently originates from higher-level personnel. Yet this cycle of cyberbullying and concern over consequences breeds dishonesty, mistrust, and disloyalty at work(Kowalski et al., 2018; MyDisability-Jobs, 2023).Figure 2 shows the frequency of abuse and harassment happening to males or females in the workplace. The stats clearly states that both men and women are victims of workplace cyberbullying in their routine work life. Sometimes it is quarterly or monthly, in more severe cases the victims have reported that it happens daily. The victims of cyberbullying are more hesitant to report any type of abuse or harassment to higher officials due to their professional image among their peers.

Cyberbullying can affect employees during and after working hours(Kalkan, 2019). Cyberbullying is the act of an aggressor making offensive comments or publishing offensive images against a target employee via phone messages, emails, websites, and social media posts(Kowalski et al., 2018). In most cases, the cyberbully maintains their anonymity while posting comments on social media platforms. Cyberbullying affects the workers in the workplace; it can happen on its own or in conjunction with more conventional bullying. When frequent acts of aggressive behavior characterize cyberbullying and occur between two persons with a power imbalance, which eventually impacts the employee's performance in the office, it is evident that the victim is under great stress. It is prominent that traditional face-to-face bullying at work is conceptually comparable to workplace cyberbullying. Contrary, the level of anonymity that the cyberbully has access to while engaging in bullying behavior distinguishes cyberbullying from bullying at a distant job. Anonymity has been linked to high rates of bullying because cyberbullies frequently maintain their anonymity on numerous platforms. Bullying may be seen, heard, and identified when it takes place in a remote job, though. Another difference is that in the case of a remote workplace, the bullying episodes remain within the team, as opposed to cyberbullying, which facilitates the sustenance and escalation of the bullying episodes through the numerous likes and shares available on social media platforms(Ali, 2022; Bradley, 2022; Workplace Bullying Persists despite Remote Work, *2022).*

Figure 2. Frequency of workplace cyberbullying

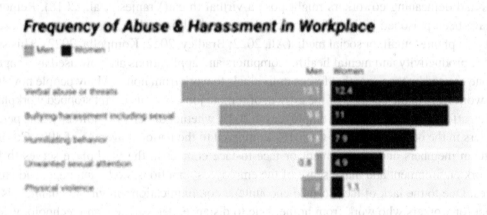

VIRTUAL HARASSMENT

Any form of workplace harassment happens when an employee abuses their position of authority over a coworker or member of the staff by using a protected feature, such as race, gender, gender preference, seniority, or socioeconomic status. The end result is what is known as a hostile work environment, which is a setting that makes one feel insecure, may be perceived as a danger to one's identity, or prevents workers from performing their duties. Whether done in person or not, threatening actions, threatening words, and menacing pictures can all constitute harassment. The degree to which remote work made it simpler for some workers to exercise influence over those who were more vulnerable shocked many. This is due to the fact that text, phone, and video communications used for remote work sometimes go unnoticed, unreported, or take place on platforms not provided by the employer. Also, knowing no one is looking might encourage wrongdoing(Lyu et al., 2022). Bystanders can be "a source of protection" in a physical office setting if they are skilled, competent, or bold enough to intervene. But, working from home deprives us of bystanders; while we're on a call at home, the coworker who could normally overhear an odd statement in the office is not present. 52% of women reported experiencing harassment or micro-aggression in the past year, according to a Deloitte survey titled Women at Work: A Global Outlook. This harassment or micro-aggression could have taken the form of comments about a person's physical appearance, communication style, race, gender preference, or status as a caretaker. These discriminatory practices were much more prevalent among L.G.B.T.Q. and women of color. Another study by the nonprofit Project Include, which works to speed up diversity and inclusion in the tech industry, found that during the pandemic, 25% of respondents reported more harassment or hostility based on their gender, 10% reported more hostility based on their race or ethnicity, and 23% reported more harassment or hostility based on their age(Czakert et al., 2021; Vranjes et al., 2015).

WORKPLACE CYBERBULLYING IN REMOTE WORK

Even if working online has been the best solution during the pandemic, bullying and harassment at work still find a way to reach an individual. While it makes sense to believe that because people are not at the office, occurrences of antagonism and harassment have drastically reduced, that's not the case. Rude employers and demeaning coworkers might pose a virtual threat(Vranjes et al., 2018). Remote work settings have been poisoned by harmful, toxic behavior, which includes abusive language, exclusion, and threats via phone, email, or social media(Ali, 2022; Bradley, 2022; Kompella, 2022). This situation affects work productivity and mental health. Computers and applications are now used as weapons in a combat zone created by the norm that forces individuals to work from home. Many people now have the chance to work from home because of the growth of remote jobs, but this hasn't stopped workplace bullying, which affected 61.5% of remote employees in 2021, whether directly or indirectly. The percentage of responders in the occupied sample was 61%, compared to the national average of 49%. Co-presence with the team members and management or face-to-face contact in the workplace serves to foster a positive work environment and make sense of the employees' emotions, body language, and embodied experiences. Due to the lack of face-to-face encounters, communication via virtual channels is unique and distinct for workers who work from home. Due to distance, dependency, and technology, all these variables combine to cause psychological stress for remote workers(Fessler, 2021; MyDisabilityJobs, 2023; Namie, 2021).

Figure 3. Experience with cyberbullying during remote work

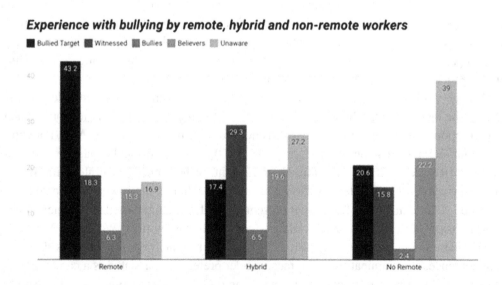

The unprecedented migration to WFH and subsequent recurrent waves of the virus have made remote employees anxious and stressed out about their jobs and performance. Figure 3 illustrates the experience with cyberbullying during remote work representing how many were bullied targeted, witnessed, bullied, believers, and unaware. In online meetings, half of those surveyed said they had been mistreated or had witnessed it (Workplace Bullying Persists despite Remote Work, 2022). *70% of online abuse took place in plain view in proximity to other users. This is analogous to receiving criticism in group meetings when offenders amplify humiliation by performing in front of the target's coworkers. Instead of taking place at a conference table, it takes place in real-time on computer (or Smartphone or tablet) displays, with the technology emphasizing facial expressions. Email abuse took place on a much lesser scale. Perhaps the worry of creating a paper trail stopped some bullies from bullying. Bullying occurs most frequently in group meetings and video conferences when people are working remotely, and the victim is often made to feel inferior or mistreated. 15% of the harassment occurs in personal encounters between the perpetrator and the victim. Group emails, when the bully is disparaged in the presence of other students, account for 6% of bullying, whereas individual emails account for 3%(Namie, 2021). Figure 4 shows the places where cyberbullying happened during remote work.*

Figure 4. Workplace cyberbullying platforms when working remotely

COVID-19 caused a lot of suffering. In our 2021 poll, 25% of participants said that it exacerbated harmful bullying. Some survey results imply that organizations are aware of the fact that as the quantity of work done remotely increases the chance of abusive behavior will also likely increase. It is expected. Employers cannot claim that they were unaware of the growth in workplace violence. They should take action to stop it from happening and fix it once it does.Bullies tend to be males more often than women, and male bullies appear to like attacking men (58%) over other women (42%). Bullies who identified as female were less "equitable" in choosing their targets. In 65% of cases, women bullied other women(Loh & Snyman, 2020; MyDisabilityJobs, 2023; Namie, 2021). Figure 5 represents the gender-wise perpetratorsand victim percentage.

The most recent survey conducted in 2021 found that, on average, 30% of employees experience or have experienced direct workplace bullying. However the survey defined those "affected" by bullying as having either direct or indirect experiences with it; for example, those who observe another employee being harassed are considered indirect victims of bullying. In the workplace, 30% experience abuse, 49% experience cyberbullying, and 66% are aware that bullying takes place. Because it might be upsetting to observe a coworker being humiliated and intimidated, the study discovered that emotional injuries incurred by witnesses of workplace bullying were comparable in intensity to those sustained by individuals who were directly abused. The number of people impacted by workplace bullying might rise to 49% as a result of this(Czakert et al., 2021; Namie, 2021). The challenges related to workplace cyberbullying during remote work have been listed in the next section of the chapter. Organizations must make proper cyberbullying control procedures and policies to prevent and monitor any activity going on in the workplace environment either physically or virtually.

Figure 5. Workplace cyberbullying platforms when working remotely

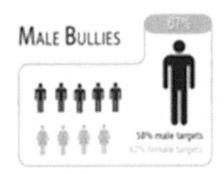 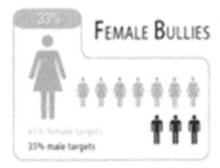

CHALLENGES DURING WORK FROM HOME

The challenges that correspond to workplace cyberbullying during the work-from-home are discussed below:

Social Exclusion

Cliques are emerging in the workplace that didn't before COVID-19. Between those who are physically on-site along with those working remotely, allies are being formed. It is normal to experience a lack of communication, a selective distribution of information, and a sensation of isolation. Bullying at work has been an issue for a while, and remote employees had issues before the epidemic. According to a 2017 Harvard Business Review research, 52% of the 1153 remote employees surveyed said they were being left out of critical decisions and felt harassed, treated poorly, and ganged up on by coworkers. According to Canada's Policy on the Prevention and Settlement of Harassment, harassment is any unlawful behavior that is objectionable to another individual in the workplace or at any event(Ramdeo& Singh, 2022).

Platform of Misconduct

In remote work environments, there is an increase in virtual misbehavior. Workplaces frequently become less formal and professionalism may suffer when work and personal life overlap. Add stress, job insecurity, and COVID weariness, and you have the perfect environment for undesirable behavior. As a result, we are hearing more reports of prejudice, discrimination, and online harassment among remote teams. According to reports, the following workplace issues are most frequently brought up by remote teams: (a) Derogatory language; (b) intimidation via messaging apps and text messages on personal phones; (c) racial and gender harassment; (d) exclusion from meetings and bullying over video calls; and (e) inappropriate remarks made over the phone, via text message, or via e-mail that denigrates others(Scisco, 2019).

Virtual Criticism

Some of the concerns are rehashed from before COVID forced everyone home, while others have a fresh vibe, according to her. "There is a perception that office gossip is now happening in the chat rooms on all the online platforms," Employee side chats during online meetings are a regular complaint; either accidentally via technical difficulties or deliberately by the aggressor or by others, these comments and insults are disclosed. Also, it's simple to misinterpret the context of emails and certain other types of information. "Work stress and disappointments seem to be causing shorter, more caustic communications," Reportedly, a lot of shouty caps are being used in emails(York, n.d.).

Meetings Dominators

Also, because technology prevents natural dialogue, workers believe they are more likely to be forgotten during meetings. Meetings are frequently dominated by those who talk quickly and loudly, leaving others feeling disrespectful or completely ignored(Tiamboonprasert&Charoensukmongkol, 2020). The meeting dominators always have competition among their peers to compete and outperform at the workplace, even if it's happening in a virtual environment.

Favouritism

There are reportedly rising conflicts among employees for issues like who is "allowed" to work from home and who is viewed as an "essential worker" at a particular firm. In the comfort of your home, "the phrases favouritism and bogus charges of 'getting paid while doing nothing' are used regularly."(Anasori et al., 2020).

HANDLING WORKPLACE CYBERBULLYING

Digital communication is expanding quickly, and platforms like Teams, WhatsApp, and Slack provide helpful alternatives for workers to communicate and cooperate while working from home. However, as home working has increased, our workplaces have grown less formal and the lines between our personal and professional lives have blurred. Particularly when these applications have traditionally been used primarily for social contact, communication gaps are now easy to resolve(ehstoday.com, 2022). Unwelcome remarks about a worker's looks, demeanor, physical surroundings, productivity, or political beliefs are a few typical instances of incivility and harassment. The fact that businesses are so badly equipped to deal with remote workplace harassment may be the most damning aspect of the problem(Nayak et al., 2021). The majority of companies still lack standards and procedures on what is acceptable and human resource departments have not yet caught up with how virtual forms of misbehavior and harassment behave. Employees find it challenging to know what to do when they feel uncomfortable, and employers find it challenging to hold employees accountable, when there are no rules about how to act or communicate on Slack, Zoom, email, or any other remote platform. Before the pandemic, reporting compliance was a problem, but now that virtual platforms are our main method of communication, it is much more difficult. But there are undoubtedly things that businesses can do(York, n.d.). A strong remote harassment policy should first include a thorough explanation of what workplace harassment is and entails. The next step is creating the channels an employee may use to report, as well as a clear process to follow if a complaint is received. Even if the reporting employee has not maintained receipts for obvious reasons, retention regulations for business emails and text messages on corporate phones provide you an opportunity to go back and gather proof(Zhang et al., 2022).The mental health of workers is a major concern in the workplace cyberbullying environment whether it happens remotely or face-to-face(Ikeda et al., 2022). Table 1 shows the workplace mental health strategies that can be followed by any organization to create a mentally healthy workplace.

Table 1. Workplace cyberbullying mental well-being guide

Workplace mental health strategy	Examples of broad actions implemented in the workplace
Manage and Design work to minimize harm	Meet safety standards to lower risks of mental and physical injury and allow employees to govern their work schedules and participate in decision-making.
Promoting protective factors to maximize resilience	Create an environment where work can be done anywhere, at any time, and in any way. Give employees the chance to participate in choices that affect the business as a whole.Ensure senior staff engage in mental health promotion and develop a positive team/organizational climate and a psychosocial safety climate. Provide professional development opportunities. Provide resource groups to support workers in career management. Provide leadership training, including workplace mental health education. Ensure policies and processes are in place to maximize organizational justice.
Enhancing personal resilience for the employees	Encourage regular physical exercise in the workplace; provide stress management and resilience training that makes use of evidence-based techniques; provide stress management and resilience training for people who work in high-risk occupations; and provide mentorship and coaching.
Promote and facilitate early help-seeking to the workers	Consider performing wellness checks. Provide stress management training. Verify that any Employee Assistance Program and workplace counselling programs are in place. Consider the role of peer support programs. Ensure that workplace trauma response policies are supported by research and do not rely solely on routine psychological debriefing.
Supporting workers' recover from mental illness	Provide training courses for managers and leaders on how to aid employees' healing. Provide support to workers returning to work and those having work-focused exposure treatment.
Increasing awareness of mental illness and reducing stigma	Conduct regular mental health awareness training and programs. Promote mental health-related events and make information and resources available. Incorporate mental health education into employee induction and people development programs.

*Since many workers won't report, management should adopt preventive measures as well. Currently, employers need to be especially race-aware, checking in with each employee personally and paying close attention to what employees of color might require(*Workplace Bullying Persists Despite Remote Work*, 2022). It's critical to acknowledge racial trauma openly rather than pretending it doesn't have an impact on the workplace and to promote employees' self-care and time off(Kalyar et al., 2020; Madden & Loh, 2020). Employers have a responsibility to take reasonable precautions to safeguard employees against bullying and harassment while they are on the job. Employers cannot afford to take any action as more and more people who have experienced bullying and harassment are speaking out about it* *publicly(Sadia et al., 2022).The efficacy of bullying and harassment rules should be routinely assessed, and any adjustments should be communicated to personnel (hrexecutive.com, 2021; Kurter, n.d.). The following are some suggestions for preventing issues from arising:*

- Provide examples of what your bullying and harassment policy considers to be unacceptable or threatening behavior, including instances from work events and third-party harassment by clients, vendors, and consultants.
- Review your Information Technology (IT) policy to include digital communications and give examples of what is unacceptable.
- To ensure that managers are aware of their responsibilities in dealing with all sorts of improper behavior, it is advisable to train them on good digital communication in the workplace.
- Give staff members a way to voice concerns before things get out of hand so they feel empowered to speak out when they believe boundaries have been breached.
- Be ready to take disciplinary action if a bullying complaint is confirmed from any employee.

CONCLUSION

Even though there is still much to learn and spread about this issue, more and more individuals are becoming aware of workplace bullying and taking action to stop it. Even while we still have a ways to go, things are changing. It is crucial to be aware of the many types of bullying since being able to see it will enable you to combat it. The ability to respond effectively to this circumstance is equally essential. Understand the processes and business regulations about this issue to make a prompt aid request when bullying happens. The majority of policies require reporting to managers and the Human Resources department. The fact that some industries could be more vulnerable to workplace bullying than others is also crucial to recognize.

REFERENCES

Akram, Z., Khan, A. G., Akram, U., Ahmad, S., & Song, L. J. (2022). A contemporary view of interpersonal aggression and cyberbullying through ICT: Multilevel insights from LMX differentiation. *Internet Research*, *32*(5), 1700–1724. doi:10.1108/INTR-11-2020-0659

Ali, A. (2022, September 19). The Rise Of Cyberbullying—How To Address Harassment In The Remote Workforce. *Allwork.Space*. https://allwork.space/2022/09/the-rise-of-cyberbullying-how-to-address-harassment-in-the-remote-workforce

Anasori, E., Bayighomog, S. W., & Tanova, C. (2020). Workplace bullying, psychological distress, resilience, mindfulness, and emotional exhaustion. *Service Industries Journal*, *40*(1–2), 65–89. doi:10.1080/02642069.2019.1589456

Bradley, L. (2022, October 17). *Tackling workplace bullying in the remote era*. Employee Management Ltd. https://employeemanagement.co.uk/tackling-workplace-bullying-in-the-remote-era/

Czakert, J. P., Reif, J., Glazer, S., & Berger, R. (2021). Adaptation and Psychometric Cross-Cultural Validation of a Workplace Cyberbullying Questionnaire in Spain and Germany. *Cyberpsychology, Behavior, and Social Networking*, 24(12), 831–838. doi:10.1089/cyber.2020.0856 PMID:34152860

Sparkman, D. (2022, September 26). *Don't Allow Bullying to Become the New Normal*. Zogby Analytics. https://zogbyanalytics.com/soundbites/1177-don-t-allow-bullying-to-become-the-new-normal

Fessler, L. (2021, June 8). Workplace Harassment in the Age of Remote Work. *The New York Times*. https://www.nytimes.com/2021/06/08/us/workplace-harassment-remote-work.html

Shutan, B. (2021, December 20). *Workplace bullying: A 'wildly out of control' epidemic*. Zogby Analytics. https://zogbyanalytics.com/soundbites/1063-workplace-bullying-a-wildly-out-of-control-epidemic

Ikeda, T., Hori, D., Sasaki, H., Komase, Y., Doki, S., Takahashi, T., Oi, Y., Ikeda, Y., Arai, Y., Muroi, K., Ishitsuka, M., Matsuura, A., Go, W., Matsuzaki, I., & Sasahara, S. (2022). Prevalence, characteristics, and psychological outcomes of workplace cyberbullying during the COVID-19 pandemic in Japan: A cross-sectional online survey. *BMC Public Health*, 22(1), 1087. doi:10.118612889-022-13481-6 PMID:35642023

Kalkan, A. (2019). *The Level Of Exposure To Cyber Bullying For Employees In Workplace*. EP. doi:10.15405/epsbs.2019.01.02.3

Kalyar, M. N., Saeed, M., Usta, A., & Shafique, I. (2020). Workplace cyberbullying and creativity: Examining the roles of psychological distress and psychological capital. *Management Research Review*, 44(4), 607–624. doi:10.1108/MRR-03-2020-0130

Kompella, S. (2022). Persisting Menace: A Case-Based Study of Remote Workplace Bullying in India. *International Journal of Bullying Prevention : an Official Publication of the International Bullying Prevention Association*, 1–17. doi:10.100742380-022-00152-8 PMID:36570782

Kowalski, R. M., Toth, A., & Morgan, M. (2018). Bullying and cyberbullying in adulthood and the workplace. *The Journal of Social Psychology*, 158(1), 64–81. doi:10.1080/00224545.2017.1302402 PMID:28402201

Kurter, H. L. (n.d.). CEOs, Here Are 3 Ways You Can Prevent Bullying In The Remote Workplace. *Forbes*. https://www.forbes.com/sites/heidilynnekurter/2021/10/29/leaders-here-are-3-ways-you-can-prevent-bullying-in-the-remote-workplace/

Loh, J., & Snyman, R. (2020). The tangled web: Consequences of workplace cyberbullying in adult male and female employees. *Gender in Management*, 35(6), 567–584. doi:10.1108/GM-12-2019-0242

Lyu, M., Sun, B., & Zhang, Z. (2022). Linking online voice to workplace cyberbullying: Roles of job strain and moral efficacy. *Kybernetes*. doi:10.1108/K-03-2021-0246

Madden, C., & Loh, J. (2020). Workplace cyberbullying and bystander helping behaviour. *International Journal of Human Resource Management*, 31(19), 2434–2458. doi:10.1080/09585192.2018.1449130

MyDisabilityJobs. (2023, March 31). Workplace Bullying Statistics Research & Facts I Updated 2023. *MyDisabilityJobs.Com*. https://mydisabilityjobs.com/statistics/workplace-bullying/

Namie, G. (2021, February 24). 2021 WBI U.S. Workplace Bullying Survey. *Workplace Bullying Institute*. https://workplacebullying.org/2021-wbi-survey/

Nayak, S., Budhwar, P., Pereira, V., & Malik, A. (2021). Exploring the dark-side of E-HRM: A study of social networking sites and deviant workplace behavior. *International Journal of Manpower*, *43*(1), 89–115. doi:10.1108/IJM-03-2021-0125

Ramdeo, S., & Singh, R. (2022). Cyberbullying in the Workplace. In *Research Anthology on Combating Cyber-Aggression and Online Negativity* (pp. 1116–1128). IGI Global. doi:10.4018/978-1-6684-5594-4.ch056

Sadia, H., Yadav, S., & Faisal, M. (2022). Mapping Cyberbullying and Workplace Cyberbullying: A Road Towards Understanding Research Gaps in the Indian Context. In Research Anthology on Combating Cyber-Aggression and Online Negativity (pp. 640–668). IGI Global. doi:10.4018/978-1-6684-5594-4.ch035

Scisco, J. L. (2019). Cyberbullying in the Workplace: A Review of the Research. In *Cyberbullying in Schools, Workplaces, and Romantic Relationships*. Routledge. doi:10.4324/9781315110554-6

Tiamboonprasert, W., & Charoensukmongkol, P. (2020). Effect of Ethical Leadership on Workplace Cyberbullying Exposure and Organizational Commitment. *The Journal of Behavioral Science*, *15*(3), 3.

Vranjes, I., Baillien, E., Vandebosch, H., & De Witte, H. (2018). *Understanding Workplace Cyberbullying: More than just an old problem in a new guise*. Lirias. https://lirias.kuleuven.be/1990170

Vranjes, I., Baillien, E., Vandebosch, H., Erreygers, S., & De Witte, H. (2015, January 1). *The dark side of working online: The rise of workplace cyberbullying*. WAOP Conference, Amsterdam, The Netherlands. https://lirias.kuleuven.be/1678547

Workplace Bullying Persists despite Remote Work. (2022, October 5). Noggin. https://www.noggin.io/blog/workplace-bullying-persists-despite-remote-work

York, J. (n.d.). *How workplace bullying went remote*. BBC. https://www.bbc.com/worklife/article/20220819-how-workplace-bullying-went-remote

Zhang, S., Leidner, D., Cao, X., & Liu, N. (2022). Workplace cyberbullying: A criminological and routine activity perspective. *Journal of Information Technology*, *37*(1), 51–79. doi:10.1177/02683962211027888

Chapter 10
The Rise of Deepfake Technology:
Issues, Challenges, and Countermeasures

Mohd Akbar
Integral University, India

Mohd Suaib
Integral University, India

Mohd Shahid Hussain
College of Applied Sciences, University of Technology and Applied Sciences, Oman

ABSTRACT

Deepfake technology is an emerging technology prevailing in today's digital world. It is used to create fake videos by exploiting some of the artificial intelligence (AI) based techniques and deep learning methodology. The facial expressions and motion effects are primarily used to train and manipulate the seed frame of someone to generate the desired morphed video frames that mimic as if they are real. Deepfake technology is used to make a highly realistic fake video that can be widely used to spread the wrong information or fake news by regarding any celebrity or political leader which is not created by them. Due to the high impact of social media, these fake videos can reach millions of views within an hour and create a negative impact on our society. This chapter includes the crucial points on methodology, approach, and counter applications pertinent to deep-fake technology highlighting the issues, challenges, and counter measures to be adopted. Through observations and analysis, the chapter will conclude with profound findings and establishes the future directions of this technology.

DOI: 10.4018/978-1-6684-8133-2.ch010

INTRODUCTION

Online social media is an eccentric media and can be considered as an immense organization which keeps the entire world associated and involved mentally and psychologically for all 27x7 time. It's an economic and efficient medium of correspondence connecting people across the world.

The main ingredient in deepfakes is machine learning, which has made it possible to produce deepfakes much faster at a lower cost. To make a deepfake video of someone, a creator would first train a neural network on many hours of real video footage of the person to give it a realistic "understanding" of what he or she looks like from many angles and under different lighting (Hsu, C.-C., & Lin, C.-W., 2017). Then they'd combine the trained network with computer-graphics techniques to superimpose a copy of the person onto a different actor. While the addition of AI makes the process faster than it ever would have been before, it still takes time for this process to yield a believable composite that places a person into an entirely fictional situation. The creator must also manually tweak many of the trained program's parameters to avoid telltale blips and artifacts in the image. The process is hardly straightforward. Many people assume that a class of deep-learning algorithms called generative adversarial networks (GANs) will be the main engine of deepfakes development in the future (Yang et al. 2019). GAN- generated faces are near-impossible to tell from real faces. The first audit of the deepfake landscape devoted an entire section to GANs, suggesting they will make it possible for anyone to create sophisticated deepfakes. "Many deepfake videos these days are generated by face image synthesis algorithms in which GANs play a very prominent role," (Cao et al. (2019) (Koopman, Rodriguez, & Geradts, 2018).

GANs are hard to work with and require a huge amount of training data. It takes the models longer to generate the images than it would with other techniques and most important GAN models are good for synthesizing images, but not for making videos (Yang et al. 2019). They have a hard time preserving temporal consistency, or keeping the same image aligned from one frame to the next.The best-known audio "deepfakes" also don't use GANs. When Canadian AI company Dessa (now owned by Square) used the talk show host Joe Rogan's voice to utter sentences he never said, GANs were not involved. In fact, the lion's share of today's deepfakes are made using a constellation of AI and non-AI algorithms (Chesney & Citron, 2019).

Deepfake technology can seamlessly stitch anyone in the world into a video or photo they never actually participated in. Such capabilities have existed for decades—that's how the late actor Paul Walker was resurrected for Fast & Furious 7. But it used to take entire studios full of experts a year to create these effects. Now, deepfake technologies can synthesize images and videos much more quickly and accurately. There's a lot of confusion around the term "deepfake," however, computer vision and computer graphics researchers have been defining a fine boundaries between these two as distinct one. It has become a catchall to describe everything from state-of-the-art videos generated by AI to any image that seems potentially fraudulent (Kanozia et al., 2021).

Web-based media has a huge impact on our lives and society today. Web-based media is currently the ideal medium for communicating your viewpoints. Additionally, online media now offers a way to share what's happening in the world around you. People who live in the other location are aware of what is happening there thanks to this online social media. Additionally, people learn about other cultures' ways of living. However, certain evil elements use online media to disseminate their erroneous ideas, which have an impact on both our lives and society. With its cruel effects on society, social media's darker side is now clearly visible. For example, Deep-Fake is widely spread on social media (Hussain, S., et al., 2021). If the "Deep-Fake" isn't handled with a reasonable amount of prudence, it's anything but a forest fire.

Additionally, this fake news could irritate certain people, and occasionally it might even spark riots in the city or among the populace. Therefore, in the present, it is crucial to identify Deep-Fake by separating the true from fake information that is being shared on social media networks. It presents a significant difficulty to address this issue. The system should be trained using machine learning techniques so that it can identify the Deep-Fake through image analysis and take well-defined remedial action to avert a disastrous reciprocal effect on society (Badrinarayanan, V., Kendall, A., & Cipolla, R., 2017).

The Impact of Social Media

Today, social media is a world unto itself where everyone may freely express their opinions and speak out in public on any topic. Social networking has made it feasible for people to reconnect with old school pals and relive their memories with them in ways that weren't before conceivable. It has dissolved national boundaries and drawn even remote people closer together.

Through social networking, you can make new friends and learn about different cultures, religions, and lifestyles. People can now communicate with one another through social media about news that has yet to be reported by a newspaper or television program. Social media has provided a tool for battling the injustice done to us so that we can communicate the society and let the world know what wrong is happening with us.

What is Deep-Fake?

Deepfake is a new kind of technology that creates tampered videos by using artificial intelligence (AI) and deep learning technology by learning the facial expression and motion effect of the target object in the video of a person Jafar, M. T., et al. (2020). Deepfake technology is used to make a highly realistic fake video that can be widely used to spread the wrong information or fake news by regarding any celebrity or political leader which is not created by them (Botha, J., & Pieterse, H., 2020). Due to the high impact of social media, these fake videos can reach millions of views within an hour and create a negative impact on our society. The results suggest that deepfakes are a threat to our celebrities, political system, religious beliefs, and business, they can be controlled by rules and regulations, strict corporate policy and awareness, education, and training to the common internet users. The expression "Deep-Fake" have constantly been utilized as a pejorative term in news-casting now days (Botha, J., & Pieterse, H., 2020).

Use of Deepfakes

Deepfakes were primarily utilized in online forums to create fake celebrity erotica when they first became popular in 2017 (Gandhi, A., & Jain, S., 2020). According to a poll conducted by the company Sensity, 96 percent of all publicly posted deepfakes were sexual even in 2019. People who work in the entertainment sector are frequently the targets of deepfakes (those whose faces are replaced in deepfakes). As per the forensics analysis of deepfake images, the distribution of the 49,081 deepfakes were reported to have been circulated and have adversely affected the lives of common people as of Jan 2020 (Guarnera, L., et al. 2020). People frequently create viral films that replace actors from movies with other actors. However, others would argue that Deepfake is already being used in Hollywood movies since a long, nevertheless its usage has got increased many folds in its finest form. Regarding the effectiveness of the de-aging technique utilized in the movie "The Irishman," Netflix came under a lot of fire. In response, a de-aging deepfake was used on the movie, with astonishing results. Perhaps it won't be long until these tools are directly used in Hollywood productions. Deepfakes have not been employed in major blockbusters, but there are reports of smaller studios experimenting with these kind of technologies.

Figure 1. Today's social media platforms

Deep-Fake Generation and Social Media

As we are all aware, every coin has two sides, one good and the other and social media is no exception to this rule. Some people aim to confuse people by spreading Deep-Fake on social media. Because of this, people's feelings are wounded, and occasionally this leads to riots in the community. The growth of Deep-Fake in social media must be stopped because it costs the nation and its citizens both lives and property (Guarnera, L., et al. (2020).

DETECTING A DEEP-FAKE

It is stated that every crime a criminal commit leaves some sort of mark. Similar to this, when someone writes Deep-Fake, he or she undoubtedly commits some error, and it is thanked to this error that we can determine that the news is false Swathi, P., & Sk, S. (2021). There are six key methods for determining if news or information is accurate or not:-

1. Analytical Mindset
2. Investigation of Source of News
3. Analyze the Video Frames
4. Look at the Morphing Evidence
5. Try not to take Video Frames at Face Value
6. Investigate That it "appears Right"

Need of Deep-Fake Detection

People increasingly use social media to promote Deep-Fake and attempt to discredit others. Unsavory individuals have started utilizing inappropriate images or manipulated movies to agitate members of all religions and social groups. These Deep-Fake could cause riots and the loss of life as well as property (Hussain, S., et al., 2021). Deep-Fake must be identified and halted as soon as possible because it hurts people's sentiments and cannot be made up for. (Vurimi Veera, et al., 2022).

Many people agree that the use of online media contributes to people feeling anxious and disappointed. It is also becoming a factor in children's slow mental development. Excessive use of online media interferes with sleep. Online media has greatly increased adolescent's "Dread of Missing Out" (FOMO), which has various other negative effects including cyber-bullying, photo tainting, and so on (Younus, M. A., & Hasan, T. M.. 2020).

Because of this, it is now crucial to identify Deep-Fakes by separating the information that is being spread on social media networks into the true and the false. It presents a significant difficulty to address this issue. In order for the system to be able to spot the Deep-Fake through analysis and take well-defined corrective measures to avert a disastrous reciprocal effect in society, a workable solution to this challenge would be to train the system using machine learning techniques (Westerlund, M., 2019).

The figure 2 illustrates the fake news statistics of U.S. Election stories. In this we can easily see the how fast fake news contents are getting spread which is challenging and posing threat to the society.

MACHINE LEARNING AND AI APPROACHES FOR DEEP-FAKE DETECTION

Machine learning, which is part of our field of computer science, is the finest tool for resolving the Deep-Fake issue. By using this strategy, we can create a tool that will enable systems to identify Deepfake as soon as they are posted on social media. Once the Deep-Fake is located, we can stop it from propagating on social media and stop its adverse effects on society in turn.

Figure 2. Report on fake news
Source: statica.com

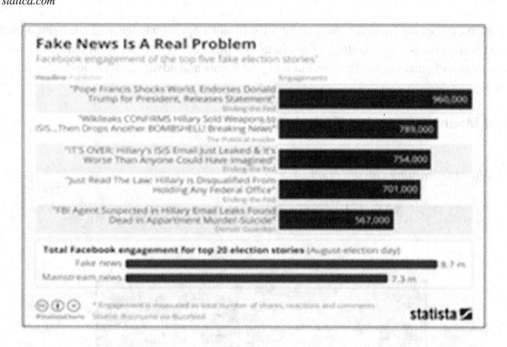

Figure 3. ML Model for detecting deep-fake media content

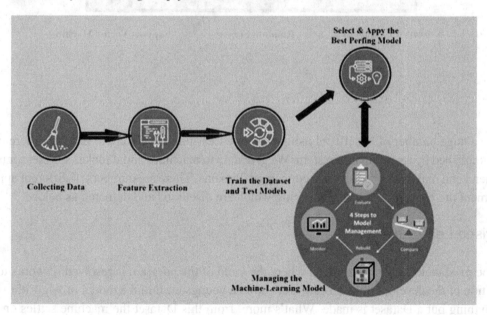

Machine Learning

ML is a form of learning in which the machine itself picks up knowledge without being specifically trained to do so. This is a unique type of artificial intelligence (AI) application that gives the system the ability to automatically learn from recent and past events and advance to a high degree of precision and accuracy.

Types of Machine Learning Techniques

Figure 4. Machine learning classification

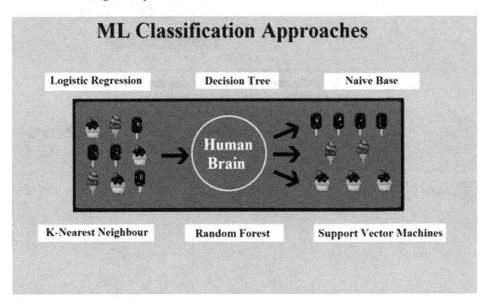

There are a huge number of benefits of using Machine Learning in our day-to-day life where our work gets accomplished by an automated system. We give data to machines and it makes simpler for us to use, comprehend and make wise decisions in concerned domains. There are numbers of different approaches to implement the concept of machine learning which are discussed and depicted as below.

Supervised Learning

This is the most well-known piece of AI where the yield of the program is resolved. It works totally on the direction of the developer like an educator shows a youngster. Initial a model of Algorithm is set up in it's anything but a Dataset is made. What's more, from this Dataset the machine settles on forecast or takes Decision. For instance, we have made a program in which it is said that Mohan is 5 years of age, Sohan is 10 years of age, and Ramesh is 15 years of age. So assuming we ask this machine who is 15 years of age, the machine will promptly tell that it is 15 years of age dependent on its dataset. Along these lines, the yield is precise.

Unsupervised Learning

In this Algorithm of ML, Dataset isn't completely named so the yield isn't completely affirmed. The fundamental utilization of this computation is to take out covered data from the given primary piece of dataset. In Unsupervised Learning, the actual machine continues to look for new examples and connections from the information. Furthermore, it continues to make changes in its dataset. In this, almost no data is given to get familiar with the machine and it's anything but a great deal from a similar information.

Reinforcement Learning

These Algorithms are totally different and they are being utilized the most in the present trend-setting innovation. These are Self Dependent Algorithms in a manner that is equipped for taking totally various kinds of choice themselves. Such projects commit numerous errors and continue to improve their projects with their missteps and experience. Support Learning is very perplexing, which can likewise adjust the product made when required. An illustration of this can be visualized as Auto Driving Cars which consistently goes to the new region and consistently sees and comprehends various things.

Classification of ML Algorithms

There are numerous algorithms to solve complex problems based on machine learning phenomena. Though the applicability of a particular ML algorithm is subject to the type & nature of the problem as well as the constraint and application domain, in general, there are some robust ML approaches that are well accepted and applied in the majority of ML-based problems. To detect Deep-Fake on the basis of those 6 criteria as mentioned earlier below mentioned approaches are worth adopting to give high precision results in Deep-Fake analysis.

Linear Regression

Linear Regression alludes to the connection between two factors and substances. For instance, X and Y are two factors, if as you increase in the worth of X, the worth of Y will continue expanding. So we can tell this sort of connection through Linear Regression. Direct Regression will give us the best fit line which will be telling the connection among X and Y.

So how about we attempt to comprehend it as per maths –

As per Figure (C), we realize that a straight line has the condition $Y = mX + B$. Where X and Y are two pivot, m is an incline and B, Y is the block where the line will cross the Y hub.

Slant (M) -: According to the figure (D), we can characterize the incline by the accompanying recipe -

$M = $ (change in Y)/(change in X)

Being founded on the probabilistic model and Bayes theorem, Naive Bayes classifier works under regulated learning.The specific highlights which is portrayed in a class that are not identified with the another highlights.

How Linear Regression Work in Supervised Learning?

Let us try to understand this through an example, suppose we want to build our house, we have to buy a place for it and we have to find out what will be the cost of land in the next year or the coming years, then some old years data for that. collect,

Table 1. Year-wise deep-fake count

Deep-Fake Articles	Year
100000	2014
150000	2015
200000	2016
250000	2017

Now we will plot (draw) this data on a graph, then it will appear as per some picture (A).

Now we will draw a line inside this graph which will pass through the maximum data point, then it will appear as per picture (B). Even if we do not have data in continuous manner, we can still predict an approximate price, suppose the data we have is showing some pictures on the graph as per (E). So it must be coming in your mind that we cannot cover these data points by a single line. So we will draw such a line which is touching the maximum data point, and its distance from the data point which it is not touching, should be the minimum.

Figure 5. Linear regression

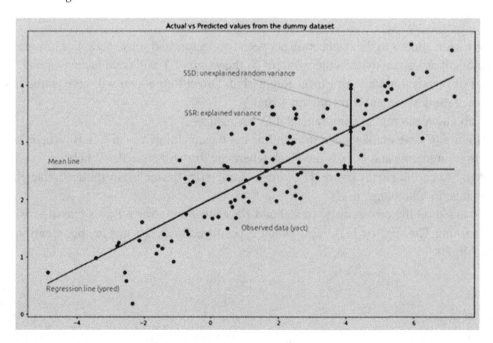

Logistic Regression

It is also used to implement supervised machine learning. The output of Logistic Regression is always a binary value (0 or 1, True / False, Yes / No), indicating the probability that an event will not occur. Inside this, the output of the dependent variable always only content a binary value. For this reason it is also called logic regression. For example, whether there will be a match tomorrow or not? Will it rain tomorrow or not? etc.

Figure 6. Linear regressions vs. logistic regression

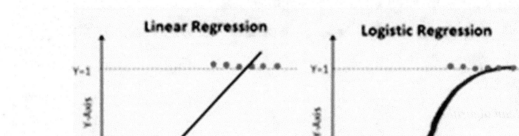

Decision Tree

Decision Tree is a popular machine learning algorithm that is being used to classify problems within supervised learning. It can be used in both Regression and Classification. It classifies the input data within a particular class. While preparing the Decision Tree model, it is trained in such a way that whenever it is given any unknown input data, it can find out which class it belongs to. For example, take an insurance company and suppose that company has to sell its insurance policies, then with the help of decision tree, they can find out how many people can buy insurance if according to their age through decision tree. If they are classified, we may have following illustration in fig 3.6.

K-Means

Is unsupervised machine learning algorithm that is used to solve the problem of clustering. Within this, the data sets are classified inside the clusters. Here cluster means the same type of data group, which keep the same type of information by containing it. Here the number of the cluster is represented by k. The K-Means algorithms picks up some points inside the cluster, those points are called cetroids.

Figure 7. Decision tree

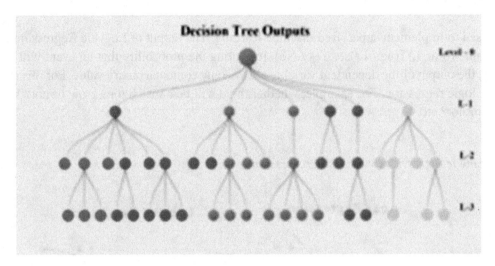

Figure 8. K-Mean algorithm

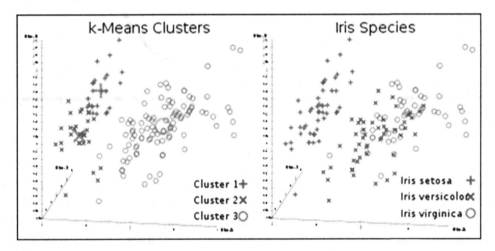

Random Forest

Random forest tree is an algorithm of machine learning and it is an advanced form of decision tree. There are different decision trees in the random forest tree algorithm and all these trees generate different results. Then the prediction of the results of all these decision trees is combined to form a new decision tree. And the prediction result from that is the final one.

Generative Adversarial Networks (Gans)

While these videos imply deepfakes may be valuable for the entertainment business, the majority of them have just served as quick demonstrations, and no significant Hollywood production has yet to utilise deepfakes. However, others would argue that Deepfakes should already be used in Hollywood.

Figure 9. Random forest algorithm

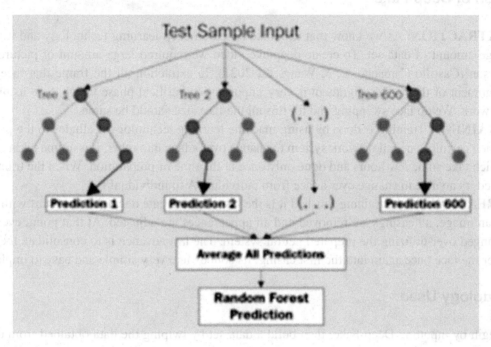

Regarding the effectiveness of the de-aging technique utilised in the movie "The Irishman," Netflix came under a lot of fire. In response, a de-aging deepfake was used on the movie, with astonishing results. Perhaps it won't be long until these tools are directly used in Hollywood productions. Deepfakes have not been employed in major blockbusters, but there are reports of smaller studios experimenting with them. The discriminator model is tricked about half the time, indicating that the generator model is producing believable examples, when the two models are trained together in an adversarial, zero-sum game (Goodfellow, I., et al., 2014). With their capacity to produce realistic examples across a variety of problem domains, most notably in image-to-image translation tasks like translating photos of summer to winter or day to night, and in producing photorealistic images of objects, scenes, and people that even humans cannot tell are fake, GANs are an exciting and rapidly evolving field.

CREATION AND SOLUTION TO DEEP-FAKE

Zhang, W., Zhao, C., & Li, Y. (2020) describe, the creation of deepfake, at times, adopts Feature Extraction Technique to create or expose Face-Swap Images using deep learning which results in well refined deepfake matter mimicking the original. But in the simplest way, the deepfake creation is merely involved with three steps- a) Extraction, b) Training, c) Creation. Whereas the viable solution to detect Deep-Fake lies in the effort of developing a mechanism by use of machine learning techniques so that any Deep-Fake can be detected at the first scan and precautionary measures can be initiated so that its ripple effect can be stopped and societal harm could be minimized. It involves formulating an algorithm using deep learning approaches to find out, whether the video is genuine or not and whether or not the matter is fake (Ismail, A., et al. (2021)..

Creation of Deep-Fake

- **EXTRACTION:** As we know that deepfake based on deep learning technology and it required large amount of data set. To create deepfake video we required large amount of picture of that person (Castillo Camacho, I., & Wang, K., 2021). In extraction all the frame that face and do alignment of them. The alignment is very important and critical phase which done using neural network. We do face swapping and for this all the face size should be same.
- **TRAINING:** Training is done by using machine learning technology it alludes to the procedure which permits a neural network system to change over a face into other. It is a time taking process which take some few hours and done only once at the time of preparation. When the training finished it can able to change over a face from individual A to individual B.
- **CREATION:** As the training finished it is the last step to create deepfake. It is start with a video or an image, all casings are removed and all appearances are adjusted. At that point, everyone is changed over-utilizing the prepared neural system. The last advance is to consolidate the change over the face once again into the first casing. Its sounds like very simple and easy to implement.

Methodology Used

We'll begin by inputting Deep-Fake, then build a data set by twiping the data obtained from that particular news and then scraping the web data. In the subsequent phase, the cleansing of the dataset will be done to remove any grammarless data from it. Further, a more meaning full dataset will be created and then feature selection of each data will be done by selecting the attributes like, source, date & time. After that, we'll prepare for testing dataset to generate a test dataset.

Figure 10. Process diagram

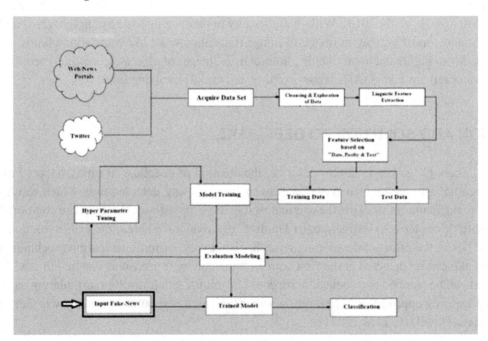

In the next step a model will be created in which the **"news_source", "news_date", "news_loca-tion"** and **"news_time-stamp"** will be recorded. Further, the input news from that model shall be ana-lyzedbased on the above parameters. If we get matching news related to the features of the news pushed from Faithful Sources, then we generate & assign a quantitative score to it. If the score lies between **1** to **3** then it will be Deep-Fake, and if the score ranges between **3** to **20** then it may be true news and if the news exceeds **20** then the news is true. The flow of the proposed solution can be briefed as follow –

Taking Dataset for Machine Learning

Two types of datasets have been taken, one dataset which collects the true news and the other which collects the Deep-Fake. These data sets of news will be used to train the machine. The figures below illustrate the data sets depicting the difference between Deep-Fake and a True news

Figure 11. True news dataset

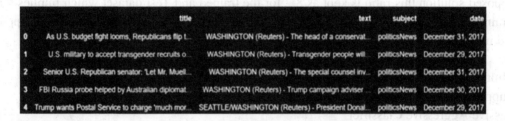

Figure 12. Deep-fake dataset

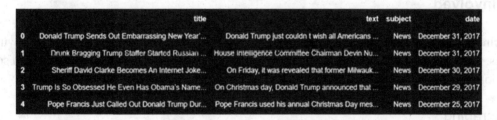

Use of Dictionary

A dictionary is prepared which stores some features of each news like title of news, date of news, time of news source of news. And on this basis then we verify every news from current news which we get from twipy and web scraping and we give score 1 to the news which is true. And we provide 0 to the news which is wrong.

Here the news has been divided on the basis of its title, text, date, time, source, so that we can know exactly what type of news is. Here we are including the news of 8 sectors, which includes **National, Politics, International Politics, Sports, Entertainment, Science**.

Table 2. Dictionary

Title	String
Text	String
Subject	String
Date	Date
Time	Time
Location	String
Source	URL

Classification of Datasets

In this, a classification Technique is used to divide the dataset into two parts. While dividing the dataset, it is important to keep in mind that the Trained and Test datasets are divided in the correct ratio. In this proposed solution this ratio is kept as 8:2 for the trained and Test dataset which implies that 80% is the trained dataset and 20% is the test dataset. Classification gets below-mentioned ML approaches involved in the process.

(i)   MultiNomial Naïve Bayes
(ii)   Support Vector Machine
(iii)   Passive Aggressive Classifier
(iv)   Count Vectorizer

Tools Involved

To acquire news-based information to major sources have been considered here such as Twitter and Websites. For collecting datasets from these sources two major tools are used in the proposed solution. These tools are-

Web Scraping

Web scraping alludes to the extraction of information from a site. It's a technique through which one can fetch the data from a particular website such as URLs of the sites, HTML code, text, images, tables used in the websites, and find out what works the site basically. This gives a great insight about a website to a major extent. For web scraping, some settings need to be made in the browser itself, through which these information could be fetched.

Tweepy

Tweepy is an open source Python bundle that gives you a helpful method to get to the Twitter API with Python. Tweepy incorporates a bunch of classes and strategies that address Twitter's models and API endpoints, and it straightforwardly handles different execution subtleties. Practically all the usefulness given by Twitter API can be utilized through Tweepy. The only constraint, as of versio 3.7.0, is that Direct Messages don't work as expected because of some new changes in the Twitter API.

Proposed Algorithm

Using the tools "**Web Scraping &Tweepy**" and ML techniques- "**SVM, Naive Bayes & NLP**" an effective algorithm is developed that produces the intended results with fair degree of accuracy and precision. The algorithm is termed as "**Fake-Check Algorithm**" and it goes like-

Fake-Check Algorithm:

1. Read the query news in q
2. Split the query in words w[] array
3. Scraping the data using w[] from news sites and store it dataset[]
4. Read the tweets using w[] from tweeter and store it int tweets[]
5. Clean the data and create a single dataset

```
Td[] = dataset[]+tweets[]
```

6. Extract the features of each row

```
for Kx in td[]
if  Kx.date = q.date
ifKx.text in q.text
collect I p[]=Kx.text
```

7. Trained the dataset p[] and create the model m[x][y]
8. Test the query in the basis of Naive Bayes and get classifier score

```
3. If   score= 0 then
Print news in fake
elseif   score>0 and scrore<=10
Print news semi true
else
print news is true
```

(End of Algorithm)

IMPLEMENTATION& OUTPUT

The implementation of the proposed algorithm produces the below results which are then compared with other existing techniques for Deep-Fake analysis using machine learning.

Figure 13. Working model of algorithm

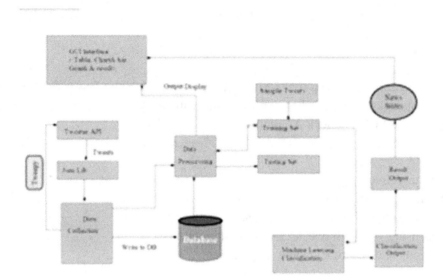

Figure 14. Entering to check whether the news is fake or not

From this graph, we get to know how many active users of which social media are in the virtual and this also shows that how many people from the real world are exchanging their views in this virtual world. And from this graph we get to know that today most users in the virtual world are from Facebook. And it has also been seen that most of the Deep-Fake is spread through Facebook and WhatsApp. In the above graph, the X-axis represents the subject and the Y-axis represents the no of Deep-Fake.

Figure 15. Getting data from web scraping and from Tweepy

Figure 16. We get the result news is fake or not

Through this graph, we can see that most of the Deep-Fake based on religion is posted. And people associated with other no pay politics spread Deep-Fake for their personal interest. This also lets us know that my tool works properly, quick these two subjects cause more related problems.

Figure 17. Active users of social media sites

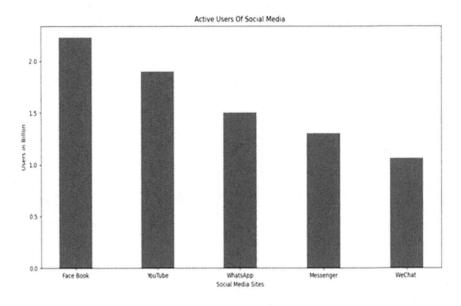

Figure 18. Subject wise deep-fake analysis

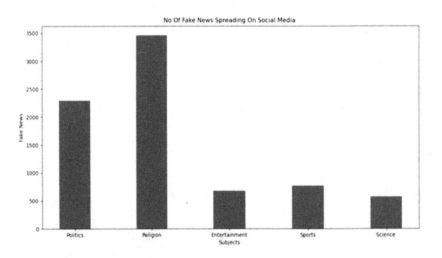

Table 3. Subject wise deep-fake analysis

Subject	Politics	Religion	Entertainment	Sports	Science
Deep-Fake Counts	2288	3456	634	743	562

RESULTS AND DISCUSSIONS

No result is confirmed until we compare our result with the result of some other research paper. That's why in this section we will fabricate our data with the results of different algorithms, so that we will know that our result is correct and how much is wrong. We will fabricate our obtained result with Different Machine Learning Algorithm written Logistic Regression, Decision Tree, and our Naive Bayse+SVM.

Analysis on the Basis of Politics Related Deep-Fake

In this graph, we are trying to find out which algorithm is working correctly through different algorithms on 1000 politics based news dataset. In this graph we can see that our algorithm is working best

Figure 19. Analysis on the basis of politics related deep-fake

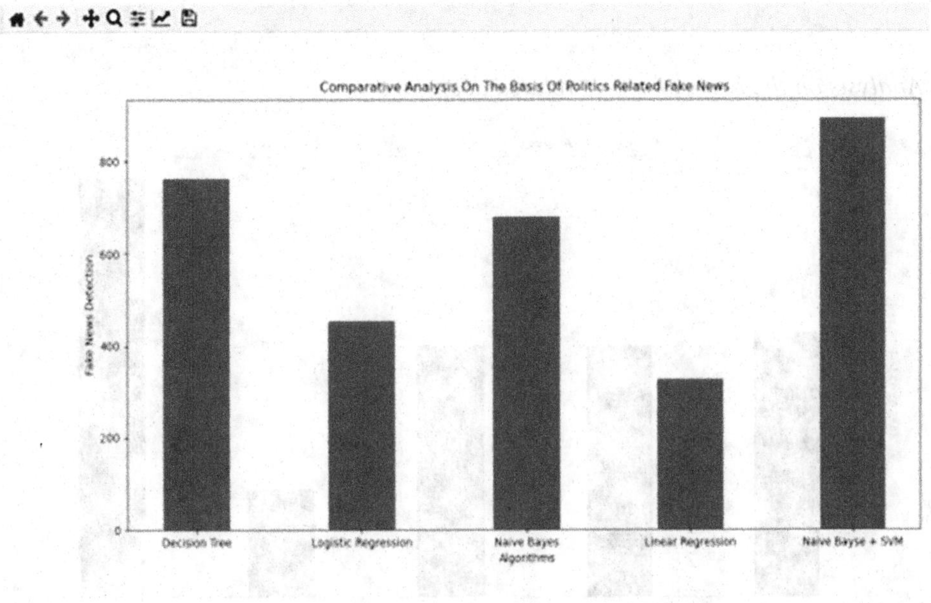

Analysis on the Basis of Religion Related Deep-Fake

In this graph, we are trying to find out which algorithm is working correctly through different algorithms on 1000 religion based news dataset. In this graph we can see that our algorithm is working best.

Analysis on the Basis of Sports Related Deep-Fake

In this diagram, we are attempting to discover which calculation is working accurately through various calculations on 1000 Sports based news dataset. In this diagram we can see that our calculation is working best.

Figure 20. Analysis on the basis of religion related deep-fake

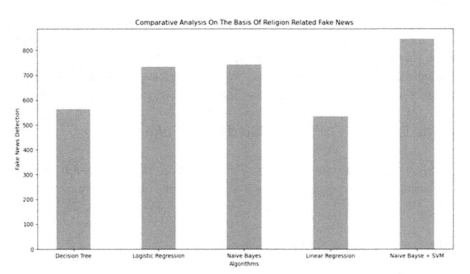

Figure 21. Analysis on the basis of sports related deep-fake

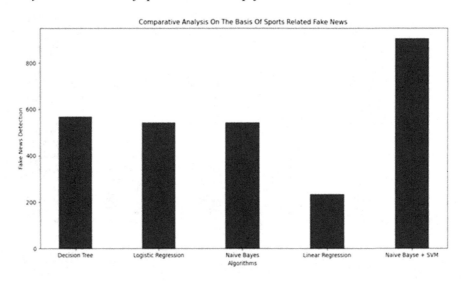

Analysis on the Basis of Religion and Politics Dataset

On the basis of all these analysis, it is concluded that if analysis is performed over **5000** news dataset, then the proposed algorithm works far better and gives outstanding results. The accuracy of the result comes around **89%**.

Figure 22. Analysis on the basis of religion and politics dataset

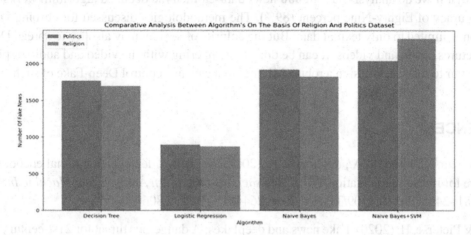

CONCLUSION

Deepfake is a genuine impending threat to public trust in the digital age. The dilemma of whether or not to believe what we see in the digital world is a major one for the upcoming day Nguyen, T. T., et al. (2019).. Deepfake pornography is frequently used to extort the press, politicians, and social activists. Additionally, it is used to rig elections, posing a severe threat to democracy (Lyu, S. (2020). To prevent this damage from happening, we must create a system that can quickly determine whether a video is genuine or not. People should be able to recognize any deeply phoney videos that have gone viral online and verify their legitimacy. There are many technologies available for deepfake detection, including Recurrent Neural Networks (Güera, D., & Delp, E. J. 2018). Optical Flow Based CNN, Analysis of Convolutional Traces, and many more, but these technologies have limitations in that they are time-consuming and difficult to use in comparison to the ease with which deepfake videos can be created online (Jafar, M. T., et al., 2020).

While detecting the deepfake video using image-frame analysis, the average Laplacian value of a video frame can be used to determine whether or not a video is deep-faked (Trinh, L., et al., 2021). The likelihood of the video being legitimate is higher if the difference between the average value and the other frame is more than the average value, which is extremely changeable. This methodology aids in the first detection of video authenticity so that the detection of deepfakes should be quick. To this process, more parameters might be added to boost the accuracy of the results. In order to make the deepfake analysis process accessible to the general public, we also develop an internet portal for it where users can upload a suspect video and receive the analysis' findings. So far the aspects of social media are discussed, it can be concluded that every coin has two sides, head & tail or good & bad. It depends, on what we choose. Exactly the same thing is also with social media platforms and in today's time some people are misusing it more. Some wrong people are doing great harm to society by posting Deep-Fake. The critical issues and methodologies to detect Deep-Fake as discussed in this chapter can prove to be very helpful in curbing Deep-Fake. If it is implemented on the social media platform, then any Deep-Fake can be stopped before it reaches among the masses and do harm to the society. People can also use it to verify any news that they have seen on any social media platform, so that they can take the right decision with respect to the authenticity and gravity of the news. On the basis of all these analysis, it is concluded that if we do analysis out of **5000** news dataset, then the deduced algorithm works far better with an accuracy of Eighty-Nine percent (**89%**). The methodologies discussed for curbing Deep-Fake propagation is limited to only textual data. But the culprits of society may also try to spread Deep-Fake through pictures, audio and videos. It can be done by tampering with the video and audio or picture. So it would be fair to foresee & design a robust ML tool that can also control Deep-Fake of such categories.

REFERENCES

Badrinarayanan, V., Kendall, A., & Cipolla, R. (2017). Segnet: A deep convolutional encoder-decoder architecture for image segmentation. *IEEE Transactions on Pattern Analysis and Machine Intelligence, 39*(12), 2481–2495. doi:10.1109/TPAMI.2016.2644615 PMID:28060704

Botha, J., & Pieterse, H. (2020). Fake news and deepfakes: A dangerous threat for 21st-century information security. In *ICCWS 2020 15th International Conference on Cyber Warfare and Security.* Academic Conferences and publishing limited.

Cao, J., Hu, Y., Yu, B., He, R., & Sun, Z. (2019). 3D aided duet GANs for multi-view face image synthesis. *IEEE Transactions on Information Forensics and Security, 14*(8), 2028–2042. doi:10.1109/TIFS.2019.2891116

Castillo Camacho, I., & Wang, K. (2021). A Comprehensive Review of Deep-Learning-Based Methods for Image Forensics. *Journal of Imaging, 7*(4), 69. doi:10.3390/jimaging7040069 PMID:34460519

Chesney, B., & Citron, D. (2019). Deepfakes: A looming challenge for privacy, democracy, and national security. *California Law Review, 107*, 1753.

Gandhi, A., & Jain, S. (2020). Adversarial perturbations fool deepfake detectors. In *2020 International Joint Conference on Neural Networks (IJCNN).* IEEE. 10.1109/IJCNN48605.2020.9207034

Goodfellow, I. (2014). Generative adversarial nets. *Advances in Neural Information Processing Systems, 27*.

Guarnera, L. (2020). Preliminary forensics analysis of deepfake images. In *2020 AEIT International Annual Conference (AEIT).* IEEE. 10.23919/AEIT50178.2020.9241108

Güera, D., & Delp, E. J. (2018). Deepfake video detection using recurrent neural networks. In *2018 15th IEEE International Conference on Advanced Video and Signal Based Surveillance (AVSS).* IEEE. 10.1109/AVSS.2018.8639163

Hasan, H. R., & Salah, K. (2019). Combating deepfake videos using blockchain and smart contracts. *IEEE Access : Practical Innovations, Open Solutions, 7*, 41596–41606. doi:10.1109/ACCESS.2019.2905689

Hsu, C.-C., & Lin, C.-W. (2017). Unsupervised convolutional neural networks for large-scale image clustering. In *2017 IEEE International Conference on Image Processing (ICIP).* IEEE. 10.1109/ICIP.2017.8296309

Hussain, S. (2021). Adversarial deepfakes: Evaluating vulnerability of deepfake detectors to adversarial examples. In *Proceedings of the IEEE/CVF Winter Conference on Applications of Computer Vision.* IEEE. 10.1109/WACV48630.2021.00339

Ismail, A. (2021). A New Deep Learning-Based Methodology for Video Deepfake Detection Using XGBoost. *Sensors (Basel)*, *21*(16). Advance online publication. doi:10.339021165413 PMID:34450855

Jafar, M. T. (2020). Forensics and analysis of deepfake videos. In *2020 11th International Conference on Information and Communication Systems (ICICS)*. IEEE. 10.1109/ICICS49469.2020.239493

Kanozia, R. (2021). A study on fake news subject matter, presentation elements, tools of detection, and social media platforms in India. *Asian Journal for Public Opinion Research*, *9*(1), 48–82.

Koopman, M., Rodriguez, A. M., & Geradts, Z. (2018). Detection of deepfake video manipulation. In *The 20th Irish Machine Vision and Image Processing Conference (IMVIP)*. IEEE.

Li, C.-T., & Li, Y. (2011). Color-decoupled photo response non-uniformity for digital image forensics. *IEEE Transactions on Circuits and Systems for Video Technology*, *22*(2), 260–271. doi:10.1109/TCSVT.2011.2160750

Lukas, J., Fridrich, J., & Goljan, M. (2006). Digital camera identification from sensor pattern noise. *IEEE Transactions on Information Forensics and Security*, *1*(2), 205–214. doi:10.1109/TIFS.2006.873602

Lyu, S. (2020). Deepfake detection: Current challenges and next steps. In *2020 IEEE International Conference on Multimedia & Expo Workshops (ICMEW)*. IEEE. 10.1109/ICMEW46912.2020.9105991

Nguyen, T. T. (2019). Deep learning for deepfakes creation and detection: A survey. arXiv preprint arXiv:1909.11573.

Swathi, P., & Sk, S. (2021). DeepFake Creation and Detection: A Survey. In *2021 Third International Conference on Inventive Research in Computing Applications (ICIRCA)*. IEEE.

Trinh, L. (2021). Interpretable and trustworthy deepfake detection via dynamic prototypes. In *Proceedings of the IEEE/CVF Winter Conference on Applications of Computer Vision*. IEEE. 10.1109/WACV48630.2021.00202

Veera, V. (2022). Deepfake Detection in Digital Media Forensics. *Global Transitions Proceedings*.

Westerlund, M. (2019). The emergence of deepfake technology: A review. *Technology Innovation Management Review*, *9*(11), 39–52. doi:10.22215/timreview/1282

Yang, W., Hui, C., Chen, Z., Xue, J.-H., & Liao, Q. (2019). FV-GAN: Finger vein representation using generative adversarial networks. *IEEE Transactions on Information Forensics and Security*, *14*(9), 2512–2524. doi:10.1109/TIFS.2019.2902819

Chapter 11
An Extensive Study and Review on Dark Web Threats and Detection Techniques

Wasim Khan

Koneru Lakshmaiah Education Foundation, India

Mohammad Ishrat

Koneru Lakshmaiah Education Foundation, India

Mohd Haleem

Era University, India

Ahmad Neyaz Khan

Integral University, India

Mohammad Kamrul Hasan

Universiti Kebangsaan Malaysia, Malaysia

Nafees Akhter Farooqui

Babu Banarsi Das University, India

ABSTRACT

The Dark Web is a difficult and anonymous network used by cybercriminals, terrorists, and state-sponsored agents to carry out their illicit goals. Dark web cybercrime is very similar to offline crime. However, the vastness of the Dark Web, its unpredictable ecology, and the anonymity it provides are all obstacles that must be overcome in order to track down criminals. To reach the dark web, which is not indexed by search engines, you must use the anonymous Tor browser. The anonymity and covert nature of the network make it ideal for criminal activity and the launch of carefully orchestrated, malicious assaults. Online criminal activity is rampant and getting more intense, according to specialists in cyber security. This chapter has provided a thorough analysis of the various attacks and attack strategies utilized on the dark web. In addition, the authors examine the strengths and weaknesses of the various methods currently in use for threat detection, and how they apply to anonymity networks such as Tor, I2P, and Freenet.

DOI: 10.4018/978-1-6684-8133-2.ch011

INTRODUCTION

There is an unprecedented quantity of digital data in the world wide web (WWW), a complicated system. Search engines like Google and Yahoo are used for reaching the common Internet that is used every day. Large portions of the Internet, however, are not indexed and are concealed from common search engines (Weimann, 2016a). The Deep Web, which accounts for about 96 percent of the World Wide Web, is this hidden area of the Internet. The DarkWeb, also known as the Dark Net, is a section of the Deep Web that is primarily used for illegal purposes (Anjum et al., 2021). According to a survey by the University of Surrey, there was roughly $1.5 trillion in revenue generated by cybercrimes in 2018 (Saleem et al., 2022), and these crimes are expected to grow in frequency and aggression over time(Attaallah et al., 2022; Husain, 2019, 2020; M. Z. Khan, Husain, et al., 2020; W. Khan & Haroon, 2022b; Sahu et al., 2020).

The TOR network, which allows users to secretly and anonymously share information via peer-to-peer connections rather than a centralised computer server, is the most well-known tool on the Dark Web (Masinde & Graffi, 2020). The U.S. Naval Research Laboratory created this service in 2002 with the goal of allowing users to access blocked content, get around censorship, and protect the privacy of confidential communications (Watson, 2012). Due to the TOR network's anonymous nature, it is very difficult to monitor the Dark Web. Due to its untraceable and challenging to close down infrastructure, criminals use the Onion Router (TOR) to access the Dark Web (Gehl, 2016). The intense strain placed on security organisations and law enforcement to track and monitor activity on the Dark Web is one of the reasons for this.

The majority of dark web sites are secured, which aids in protecting user anonymity and making their actions difficult to track. Overlay networks are the basis for anonymity tools that allow users to interact globally without disclosing their identities or locations (Vasserman et al., 2009). Researchers have applied overlay methods to a wide range of problems, including anonymous communication and polling; communication censorship; private information retrieval; taxonomy; traffic analysis; and more. Anonymizer.com and gotrusted.com are just two examples of the many businesses and individuals who supply privacy services; others include the open-source Tor Network, FreeNet, Subgraph Operating System, and the Invisible Internet Project (I2P) (Zhang & Zou, 2020) (Marcella, 2021; Quasim et al., 2023). Onion sites, also known as secret services, are a type of website found on the dark web that can only be accessed by using a special browser. Tor's wide adoption can be attributed to the anonymity it affords users, making them less of a target for oppressive governments (Gallagher et al., 2017; Husain & Khan, 2019; M. Z. Khan, Mishra, et al., 2020; M. Z. Khan, Shoaib, et al., 2020).

Criminals typically set up a relay point in the TOR to hide their Dark Web activities from authorities. Because of this, when authorities use TOR to identify a criminal act, they can only pinpoint the location of the last TOR departure relay (Kaur & Randhawa, 2020). Experts have created a wide range of techniques for keeping tabs on the Dark Web and uncovering criminal activity. U.S. Defense Advanced Research Projects Agency's (DARPA) Memex Project is one of the most effective data mining tools on the Dark Web (Ehney & Shorter, 2016a) (Afaq et al., 2023). A study that details how to proactively monitor the hidden areas of the Internet maps the hidden services directory, discusses monitoring social media sites, tracks consumer data, employs semantic analysis and profiles markets. Law enforcement agencies have used social media, IP addresses, user activity tracking, and Bitcoin account surveillance to track down offenders (AlShahrani, 2021; Godawatte et al., 2019a; Sahu et al., 2021). The purpose of this survey is to take a look at how the dark web is doing right now in terms of its popularity and development. We have discussed the dark web anonymity with vulnerabilities, and the different cyberattacks that can compromise that anonymity. The effectiveness and limitations of threat intelligence methods in detecting attacks and developing suitable countermeasures have also been reviewed.

Particularly, this initiative seeks answers to the following questions: How and to what extent do the privacy networks Tor, I2P, and Freenet offer their users? How significant is the dark web for cybercriminal operations and activities? iii) What threat intelligence methods are currently available for detecting cybercriminal activities, and how should we classify them? This paper is valuable because it gives a comprehensive overview of the dark web in a single, easy-to-read document. There hasn't been a paper like this before that covers the fundamentals of the hidden web. Since there was a void in the literature, it seemed like a good idea to fill it in with this article. This study lays the groundwork for creating a prototype that can identify cyberthreats and respond appropriately.

A systematic evaluation of the scientific literature is useful for several reasons, not the least of which is that it can help researchers pinpoint the problems that need answering in their field. The purpose of a systematic literature review (SLR) is to locate systematically studied works in a certain field. Authors have done studies to analyse the Dark Web, but a systematic literature review on the assessment of the Dark Web in the context of risks has not been properly explored, prompting us to provide this survey.

The remainder of the paper is organized as follows. Section 2 presents the different dark web threats. Section 3 discusses various cybercrime detection techniques that use different technologies. Research challenges are presented in section 4. Finally, the paper is concluded in along with some future research trends in Section 5.

DARKWEB THREATS

Based on our analysis of the articles we chose; we have identified seven main criminal threats posed by the Dark Web. Below is a summary of potential criminal acts:

Human Trafficking and Sex Trafficking

With the rise of online communities, chat rooms, and the anonymity provided by the Deep Web, human and sex exploitation have become increasingly common forms of organised crime (Chertoff, 2017). It's widely acknowledged that human trafficking is a major problem in terms of human rights. The UN Office on Drugs and Crime (Hodge, 2014) estimates that about 2.5 million people are currently victims of contemporary slavery. Victims are compelled into lives of begging, sex work, child soldiers, industrial and household labour, and other forms of commercial exploitation. Human traffickers use a variety of methods, including extortion, promises, and contracts, to lure potential captives into their networks.

Because the networks used by traffickers are constantly changing, they are able to evade the detection, censorship, and tracking systems used by the government and antihuman trafficking organisations (Prylinski, 2020). Human trafficking of a covert or underground variety presents significant detection challenges. An estimated 40.3% of the global workforce is involved in some form of modern slavery, with 24.9 million victims of forced labour and 15.4 million victims of coerced marriage in 2016, according to the International Labour Organization (ILO). This means that there are 5.4% as many modern-day slaves as there are people in the globe. One out of every four victims are a modern-day prisoner, which is a deeply troubling statistic. Out of the 24.9 million people who were victims of forced labour, approximately 16 million were enslaved to perform work in the home, in the building industry, or in agriculture; 4.8 million people were victims of sexual slavery; and the remaining 4 million were victims of forced labour. There is a 99 percent and 58 percent exploitation of women and girls in the commercial sex business and other sectors, respectively (Monzini, 2005).

Darknet's anonymity-preserving algorithms actually aid human traffickers and shield users from authorities. Darknet is proven to aid illegal activities by providing them with non-standard protocols, anonymous IP allocations, peer-to-peer content sharing platforms, and untraceable financial transactions, as shown by multiple studies and documents. Bitcoin and other cryptocurrencies make it simple to pay for illegal services offered on the Darknet. These criminally advantageous aspects of the Dark Web give bad guys an upper hand.

Pornography

Women in situations of human trafficking or sex trafficking are the most common victims of the pornography business (McCabe, 2017). Fear of death is used by traffickers to coerce victims into signing agreements with males for the creation of pornography. The sex trafficker secretly films their victims without their knowledge and then sells the footage to the highest bidder in the pornographic market. Video and photographs taken by traffickers are also frequently posted on their websites (Nichols, 2016). The DarkWeb hosts a large number of pornographic websites. DarkWeb, social media, and online forums are used by the pornographic business in the same way that human and sex traffickers do to hide the identities of their victims before kidnapping them (Baker, 2016). The pictures and videos of prostitution found on the Internet often depict highly graphic acts of violence and new types of criminal behaviour (DeKeseredy & Corsianos, 2015). Prostitution has evolved alongside the rise of social media. Effective surveillance of prostitution activity is incredibly challenging from an investigative standpoint, as it requires interviewing victims, witnesses, and tracking behaviour.

Al Mutawa et al. (Al Mutawa et al., 2015) conducted study into P2P child pornography transmission using a combination of forensic technical capabilities and a BEA investigative system. Evidence from 15 separate cases collected from the Dubai Police Department of Electronic Evidence has been analysed using a BEA analytical approach. Case-specific photographs and other electronic files including logs, contact lists, emails, and history documents are included in the data set. The researchers have used a deductive method, looking into each individual case.

Assassins and Marketing

Criminals advertise their killing abilities on the dark web. Advertisements for offenders were posted on the websites MailOnline, White Wolves, and C'thuthlu for a total of $10,000 USD in the US and £12,000 GBP in Europe. It costs between $40,000 and $15,000,000 to employ a police officer or a high-ranking politician. Most users access the Deep Web via hidden wikis or deep search engines, which provide access to hundreds of onion sites (Weimann, 2016b).

Under "Commercial Services," researchers compiled a catalogue of 13 illegal onion sites. Some of the most sought-after resources included the Sheep Market forum, the Silk Road forum, and the Black-Market Reloaded website. From 2011 to 2013, the Silk Road was the most prominent illegal Deep Web market for drug sales and discussions among those who shared a commitment to free markets, restricted government, and individual liberties. In spite of its short lifespan (less than three years), the initial Silk Road website had a profound effect on the world. Since Silk Road was a Tor hidden site, its users could communicate in complete secrecy. In addition, bitcoin was the only accepted form of payment for purchases made on Silk Road (Böhme et al., 2015). To purchase goods and services from Tor's secret services, Bitcoin is the most popular method of payment. Even though Bitcoin activities can be tracked, it is difficult to deanonymize them (Al Jawaheri et al., 2020).

Drug Transactions

The Deep Web typically hosts two distinct kinds of drug marketplaces. The markets that sell only one sort of drug, like heroin, are an example of this. This type is very common because of the high quality of the product knowledge and the vendor-customer connection it provides. The second kind of drug market is a general store where customers can purchase a wide variety of illegal goods, including drugs, weapons, pornographic materials, stolen jewellery, counterfeit money, and cigarettes. The most typical products are those used in the production of drugs, such as equipment used to make drugs and chemicals used in this process (Harviainen et al., 2020). Since users of the Deep Web can remain anonymous while making purchases, a digital narcotic black market has emerged. Due to the lack of need for direct human interaction, the Dark Web has become a popular venue for the purchase and sale of illegal substances. Examples of Dark Web drug markets include Silk Road, where sellers raked in over a billion dollars and mailed their wares using DHL or drop delivery (Rügemer, 2019; Wolak et al., 2019).

Mr. Nice Guy was another anonymous online market place where users could buy and sell drugs like marijuana and cocaine as well as other illicit and legal products. In comparison to the average website, this one has superior security and registration processes (Aldridge & Decary-Hétu, 2016).

Child Abuse

A growing number of young people today communicate with one another using anonymous social media and messaging apps like Omegle and Ask.fm (Livingstone et al., 2017). Some paedophiles exploit the accessibility of these programmes to engage with minors. Pedophiles and other sexually violent offenders make extensive use of the Dark Web to exchange child pornographic images and videos. To store pornographic material aimed at minors, Freedom Hosting utilised 550 servers located across Europe (Dilipraj, 2014).

The FBI's operation pacifier resulted in the apprehension of hundreds of paedophiles in the United States and abroad, involving two million users, twenty-three thousand sexually (Wittes et al., 2016)explicit images, and nine thousand sexually explicit video files (Boghosian, 2021). The suicide of Canadian teen Amanda Todd, 15, drew widespread attention to the issue of child abuse in cyberspace. In the YouTube video she posted just weeks before she took her own life in 2012, she explained how she had been blackmailed into revealing her genitals via a webcam, harassed, and struck. It's become increasingly common for children as young as 13 to be exploited sexually online through webcam prostitution, in which the victim merely trades live sexual pictures through VoIP programmes. VoIP apps are being used to create and sell live images of child abuse via their video streaming features (Suthar & Rughani, 2020).

According to a 2011 report, 95% of TOR-accessible child pornographic content was hosted by the freedom hosting company. Before it was shut down in 2013 (Liggett et al., 2020), the site housed several hundred child pornographic websites with thousands of users. The second iteration of Freedom Hosting was discovered in 2017 by hackers who had previously breached the first. According to the hackers, more than half of Freedom Hosting's content is linked to child pornography, and the data are dumped, but they can identify the users of these sites (Shakarian et al., 2016).

Terrorism

There is a significant threat to national security posed by terrorism and extremist organizations operating in the Deep Web. Terrorist organizations like al-Qaeda/ISIS and ISIL, ISIS, have used the Dark Web's anonymity characteristics to spread propaganda and further their own nefarious ends (Alemian, 2019; Greene, 2015). In order to fundraise, spread propaganda, and communicate amongst themselves during shifts in leadership, the Islamic State of Iraq and Syria (ISIS) has turned to the dark web. According to Defense One's technology editor, there's evidence that ISIS and affiliated organisations aren't just using the Dark Web to spread propaganda and recruit new members; they're also interested in the platform for other reasons. Terror group ISIS accepts Bitcoins as payment for services on the underground market. The U.S. military keeps an eye on the DarkWeb in an effort to track ISIS, but so far neither law enforcement nor the military have discovered an effective method to do so without violating users' privacy (Ehney & Shorter, 2016b).

ISIS broadcasts and records executions of captives live on the Dark Web as a tool of terrorism. They post brief videos of their heinous deeds to the Dark Web, where they can be widely disseminated. They also use the dark web to enlist new members among their global army (Everton & Cunningham, 2015). ISIS has been using the Dark Web as a means of evading hackers and protecting its members' names. Using Dark Web sites and other internet platforms, they disseminated information about the November 2015 attacks in Paris. Al-Hayat Media Center, ISIS's official media outlet, announced their new Dark Web site on an ISIS-affiliated forum, complete with a URL and instructions. Telegram, an encrypted messaging app for smartphones and Windows, was used to send the communication over the TOR network. The Telegram team was far too modest to give a reward for anyone who cracked their encryption (Weimann, 2016c).

DarkNet Currency Exchange

Users of the Dark Web marketplace can maintain their anonymity when transacting with Bit Coin, a form of crypto money. Many marketplaces on the Dark Web only take bitcoin. The Silk Road illegal market was able to generate over $1.2 billion in illicit profits (Ormsby, 2019). Bitcoin's legitimacy as a currency has been debated, but it has been backed as a means to facilitate and hide money trafficking (Albrecht et al., 2019).

There are three stages involved in the money-laundering procedure. The Financial Crimes Enforcement Network of the United States Treasury provides a definition for each of these. The process involves introducing the illicit funds into the legitimate financial system, hiding them within other transactions, and incorporating them into the system as a whole (Naheem, 2016). Forensic research performed by Elliptic was used to determine which bitcoins in the transaction data between 2013 and 2016 came from illegal sources (Irwin & Turner, 2018). Since the Bitcoin blockchain stores all transactions openly, it can be easily analysed, but scammers still use the tried-and-true escrow system (Ali, 2023).

DARKWEB THREAT DETECTION METHODS

The dark web is home to a thriving criminal subculture. A close eye from law enforcement and security product and service suppliers is also necessary to keep up with the ever-evolving nature of threats. Companies that specialise in antivirus and other forms of security have traditionally protected their customers from malware by using signatures drawn from previously discovered examples of the same type of attack. But there is a change towards protection that is more proactive. In order to better handle security, data collection and analysis are integral parts of threat intelligence. For the purposes of monitoring and detecting threats, we can broadly classify threat detection methods into five categories. These five categories, which include forums, online markets, websites, traffic monitoring, and honeypots, are applicable in any setting.

We used a standard method to summarize the framework for detection. The procedure for analysing building frameworks is shown in Figure 1.

- Data Gathering explains where the information came from, how much of it was collected, and whether or not it can be used with the models. Many different kinds of data are used by researchers and companies alike. Data scraped from online sources has been used in numerous studies, while onion sites and Tor traffic have also been used.

Figure 1. Framework for threat detection

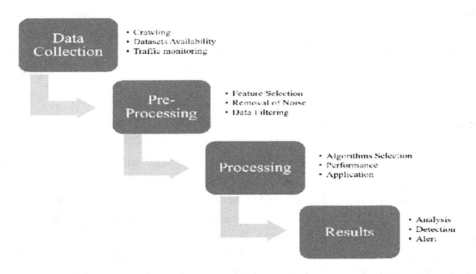

- Pre-processing of data is a vital step in any data handling workflow. Important characteristics are chosen, filtered, extracted, and replicated or noise is reduced. This is the standard procedure in a large number of investigations, and it is followed by providing the model with the necessary inputs.

- Data processing is a crucial part of any model because it includes running tests on training and test data, applying data classifications like clustering and labelling, and implementing algorithms like machine learning (ML).
- The outcomes, which can change based on the model that is put into place, are the end goal of developing the framework. Alerts, reports, graphs, email messages, and maltego are all possible examples.

Dark Web Forums Monitoring

Improved security can be achieved through the identification of dark web communities where criminal and illegal activities are discussed. In this part, we've attempted to present several methods for protecting the anonymity and privacy of the Tor network that have been developed by experts in cyber security. Marin routinely notifies authorities of a status-based key hacker proof of identity problem in order to legitimise the findings. Three primary methods, content analysis, social network analysis, and analysis based on seniority, were modified in their rewrite to better identify the most influential hackers operating in the dark web. The training and testing of the model are performed using an optimization metaheuristic. Machine learning algorithms are compared for their effectiveness. Models trained on a single hacker forum are generalised by cross-validating the findings through the other two forums. This means that 87.5% of the time (or more), Genetic Algorithms provide the finest results (Marin et al., 2018).

By using a machine learning (ML) model called Support Vector Machine (SVM), Deliu was able to automatically recognise posts made on hacker sites and then classify them into groups with the help of latent Dirichlet allocation. (LDA). Nulled.IO is a famous hacker forum where members frequently download copies of leaked data to use in experiments. Data from the discussion was cleaned up by removing low-frequency words from the corpus, for example. The SVM was trained using a subset of over a million messages from hacker forums, and the rest were analysed for security-related content. The aforementioned one million tweets were filtered by the trained SVM to remove irrelevant content. About 90% of potentially dangerous tweets were detected using SVM (Deliu et al., 2018).

Using a post association analysis, Yang et al. (Yang, Yang, et al., 2019)were able to visualize a forum system on the dark web by graphically displaying the relationships between various forum posts and posters. It was designed to accommodate a large number of separate communities, each with its own data. Latent states gathered from various time sequences during experimental work can be identified using Beta Process (BP-HMM). The next step is to combine the BP-HMM information.

To assess the connections between underground discussion groups, Alnabulsi and Islam (Alnabulsi & Islam, 2018) suggested a methodology. Data from three underground online communities is imported into an M.S. Excel le, and the VSM is then used for data mining to determine the topic distribution across the boards. At last, they use Weka 3.9 to sort the information into eight categories of illegal behaviour, and they create a VSM diagram to see how the various platforms are related to one another.

Sarkar (Alsamhi et al., 2019) created a system for foreseeing attacks at any given moment t in the future. Over the course of a year, they analysed 53 dark web forums with a supervised learning model, feeding it features gleaned from those forums in order to anticipate an attack at a time index t equal to 1 day in the future. Two separate intrusions were discovered during the investigation.

Marketplace's Surveillance

Blackhat users and law enforcement agencies around the globe have taken an interest in the deep web, darknet, and marketplaces (Godawatte et al., 2019b). Dark web marketplaces and monitoring operation software can be analysed quantitatively and statistically. The following describes some investigation into the monitoring of underground markets on the web. Dong developed a system for monitoring dark web marketplaces using text mining methods to identify cyber threats. Information is gathered, alerts are given, the information is processed by an algorithm and a data processing unit, and finally the terms are verified. Information analysis web sites are infiltrated using a shaky framework at the data collection stage. Information from the market, such as hacking, security, and cyberthreats, can be folded into a more manageable structure with the help of a tailored parse. To perform stemming and reduce the text matrix size, Porter Stemmer is used. The classification algorithm employed is a Multi-Layer Perceptron. Items are sorted into categories using text mining methods, and this process falls under the hacking heading. AlienVault OTX is used to confirm the legitimacy of potential dangers and determine if they are fresh or already known. Following the completion of the verification process, an error is produced (Dong et al., 2018).

Using threat intelligence and information about vulnerable systems, Nunes et al. (Nunes et al., 2018) developed a system that concurrently makes a decision and provides supporting evidence for that decision. This study analyzes the discussion-based platform, vendor, and product hypotheses, as well as the at-risk factor. The final technique is a combination of DeLP and classifiers learned computationally. This system combines traditional methods for representing and reasoning on information with those based on machine learning. The authors compiled conversations from over two hundred underground communities and markets to assess the threat intelligence firm's offering. Compared to traditional methods, the precision of the designs improved by 15%-57% while memory was preserved.

Dark Websites Monitoring

In 2019, Alkhatib and Basheer (AlKhatib & Basheer, 2019) used the Python library Scrapy1, also called Darky, to conduct an experiment. This repository collects black market data and processes it to catalogue a wide variety of items according to their respective categories. In terms of website updates, crawling is an approach that can only be used on one page at a time. Ferry et al. (Ferry et al., 2019) used a standard monitoring strategy to conduct their dark web scan. The writers kept track of dark web resources and ordered them in logical groups. The native Linux tool, Alyze, is what they used to acquire onion domains. Semantic analysis and keyword frequency counts are both performed using an API service. Based on their intended use, websites are divided into one of six groups.

In 2019, a Hadoop-based framework was created to identify the distinctiveness of dark network perpetrators' systems through using HDFS as a database and web crawler archive for collected Tor data (Yang, Yu, et al., 2019). The author has addressed the dangers of the dark web by analysing intelligence data using Hadoop. Personal trait extraction is a vital part of threat intelligence. Specifically, Wang et al. (Wang et al., 2018) proposed a three-stage process—block filtering, attribute candidate generation, and attribute candidate verification—to collect individual characteristics. This novel technique, block filtration, is based on the quantization approach and it is responsible for generating the candidate attributes that are then verified by the binary classifier. Information about the top K darknet organizations, nations, email domains, and people is a huge step towards identifying the most powerful criminals on the dark web, and it can be gleaned by extracting and analysing attributes information from the darknet.

Honeypot Deployment

Cybercriminals frequently target the network server in their attacks in an effort to infiltrate the system or disseminate malicious software throughout the network. Another effective method to keep tabs on criminal activity in the TOR network is to monitor network traffic (Fan et al., 2017). Several studies (Catakoglu et al., 2017; Koniaris et al., 2014) have suggested using honeypots in this context to identify illegal activity in network traffic and cyberattacks.

Techniques known as "honeypots" have been used to identify ransomware. Illegal access can be discovered using this method, as honeypot fools the attackers by posing as a decoy computer. By identifying compromised secure socket connections, attacks such as DoS, SSH port monitoring, SSH brute-force, phishing, and others can be avoided. To identify SSH with malicious behaviour, a detection model based on machine learning and honeypots was put into place (Sadasivam et al., 2018).

Malign Traffic Detection

Kumar et al. (Joshi & Dinesha, 2020) suggest a technique for threat detection based on the continuous monitoring of dark web traffic with the aid of a machine learning classifier. The proposed architecture includes means of producing and collecting traffic, features extraction, dataset processing, and classification design. The top research network software, SURFnet, was used to gather darknet traffic. The data was collected by keeping an eye on traffic with a dark web sensor. However, frequent traffic was also gathered via a variety of apps such as Facebook, Twitter, YouTube, etc. Using Microsoft Azure ML for both pre-processing and training, a machine learning model was created after 76 features were extracted from the produced traffic data. Both malicious and benign traffic can be identified with a precision of up to 99% using the suggested framework.

Social Media

Together, the Deep Web and social media platforms can be used to uncover illegal activity on the Dark Web. Social media platforms like Twitter, YouTube, and Facebook are used to track down criminals (Surette, 2015). RSA reports that criminals frequently use Facebook, WhatsApp, Telegram, Instagram, and other similar services to buy and sell personal data such as credit card details.

Cybercriminals use these methods because spreading malware through them is relatively easy. These platforms typically feature more adverts, social buttons, and plug-ins than a standard website would. Malware can be easily spread to a larger audience because to the hundreds to thousands of people who are connected on these sites. Cybercriminals earn roughly $3.25 billion annually by exploiting popular social networks, according to the findings of a global six-month study done last year by a criminology expert from the University of Surrey in the UK (W. Khan et al., 2022; Lindsey, 2019; Rasool & Khan, 2015).

On the bright side, law enforcement agencies are finding new methods to use social media to investigate and solve crimes. Insights into criminal activity can be gleaned from the vast number of social media users through both passive and active means (W. Khan, 2021; W. Khan & Haroon, 2022a; Kundra et al., 2022; Tarık, n.d.). Florida burglar Raderius Glenn Collins was apprehended after uploading a seven-minute video on Facebook bragging about a $500,000 jewellery heist that received 3,000 views; Derek Medina, 33, was given a life sentence for the second-degree killing of his wife with the assistance of social media. The perpetrator uploaded a photo of his murdered wife to Facebook and wrote about the crime; first-degree murder charges were brought against Maxwell Marion Morton after he shared a Snap Chat photo of a classmate who had been shot in the face; and police in Cincinnati made 71 arrests following a nine-month investigation that relied on social media to identify key gang members.

DARPA

The Défense Advanced Research Projects Agency (DARPA) found that there are multiple commercially accessible resources for law enforcement to use in their hunt for criminals who are accessing the Dark Web. The FBI has previously made use of the Metasploit Decloaking Engine in its exploration of the Dark Web. In order to locate offenders, especially human traffickers, operating in the Deep Web, law enforcement in the United States employs the Metasploit Decloaking Engine and Memex systems, which perform an intelligent indexing of Deep websites (Challenge, 2019).

DARPA (Defense Advanced Research Projects Agency) has developed a set of tools known as Memex (Ehney & Shorter, 2016c) to aid law enforcement in their hunt for criminals operating on the DarkWeb. These resources were created in tandem with academic institutions and are mainly written in the Python programming language. After two years of investigation, the Drug Enforcement Administration (DEA) closed its case in 2012 regarding the Farmer's Market, a Dark Web-based marketplace that sold drugs to more than 3,000 customers in dozens of nations and all 50 states in the United States. According to a press statement issued by the DEA, the operation relied on the TOR anonymity network. Thanks to TOR's distributed network of relays, users' real IP addresses were never revealed, even when conducting financial operations or sending emails across the globe.

Bit Coin Flow

You can make purchases on the Dark Web with synthetic currency known as bit coins. Authorities track criminals by following the movement of bitcoins on the Dark Web. Law enforcement agencies can track criminal behavior by examining the circulation of digital currencies like bitcoin. The Silk Road server (Lane, 2013) is one example of an effective effort to track down criminals operating in the Deep Web. The FBI traced the server's IP address to an Icelandic data center by monitoring the movement of bitcoin transactions there. Although Silk Road was run on the anonymous TOR network, the site was eventually discovered due to a configuration error on the login screen that revealed the server's IP addresses and location (Greenemeier, 2015). Darkode, an underground site where thieves meet every day to swap information and plan fresh heists, has also been successfully hacked by the FBI. The massive child-pornography site Welcome to Video Dark Web, which went up in June 2015, was shut down in March 2018 (ElBahrawy et al., 2020).

Jong Woo Son, the site's operator, was arrested and turned over to U.S. authorities after a joint investigation by the National Crime Agency of the United Kingdom and the Republic of Korea. Apart from hacking or encrypted correspondence, tracing bitcoin transactions has enabled this takedown. Each user's account had its own bitcoin wallet address, and the site used to collect payments in bitcoin from all users. Users from all over the globe who used bitcoin to buy and sell files on the site were tracked by IRS-CI. A second success was tracking down the site's manager. Agents from IRS-CI deanonymized bitcoin transactions based on blockchain analysis, leading to the discovery of hundreds of global predators (Erb, 2019).

RESEARCH CHALLENGES

After surveying the existing literature, a number of impediments to further study in this field have become apparent. Detailed below are:

- What is the relationship between the rise of the cryptocurrency market and the rate at which dark web crimes are increasing?
- How consistent are the present hidden services on the dark web, if at all?
- In order to monitor and anticipate potential threats in online communities and marketplaces, how can we implement artificial intelligence as an automatic reaction tool?
- What role can successful attacks on Tor play in compromising the anonymity of its users?
- To what extent does the traceback attack work against the I2P system?
- When using anonymizing proxies like Tor, I2P, Freenet, etc., how effective are denial-of-service attacks?
- The technical nature of the Dark Web makes it difficult to create crawlers that collect and evaluate the necessary data. Researchers should also think about effective preventative measures because the methodologies and instruments they use are potentially exposed to disclosure and cyberattacks.

CONCLUSION AND FUTURE SCOPE

To be more specific, this paper details the threats posed by the Dark Web, the technical and forensic difficulties posed by its anonymous network structures, and the methods, algorithms, tools, and strategies used to track down criminals and their activities on the Dark Web. Criminals on the Dark Web are getting smarter about how to avoid detection. Therefore, difficulties have increased. Crossing international borders is one of the most difficult jobs for law enforcement and security agencies. Due to the vastness of the Dark Web, more efficient methods are required to mitigate its risks. In order to catch criminals using cutting-edge techniques, it is necessary to track the covert market and the transactions taking place there. Dark Web crime detection is complicated by the network's lack of a database, its decentralized nature, and its many layers. Due to the volatile nature of the Dark Web environment, wherein defunct sites are replaced by new ones daily, forensic law enforcement agencies need access to robust digital evidence in order to successfully apprehend and quantify criminals.

Cyber intelligence methods have been compared with respect to their theoretical and practical consequences. The dangers, methods of detection, and knowledge gaps associated with the dark web were all addressed in this report. Current threat intelligence techniques, their success in detecting attacks, the number of attacks identified, their shortcomings, and the aspects that need improvement have all been outlined. We also identify open areas for future investigation.

A lot of work remains to be done to aid future study, such as exposing criminal activity on the dark web and determining the relative crime ratio of reported and real-time crimes, and learning how the growth of the dark web is related to the growth of the cryptocurrency market. Researchers also need to think about how to use AI to spot and stop threats in real time across vast data sets. Current solutions are restricted to a single type of monitoring and can only manage a small amount of data. A prototype that can simultaneously monitor forums, markets, websites, and traffic to gather insight into cybercriminals is needed by law enforcement, researchers, and Whitehat hackers in order to make the dark web anonymous and less vulnerable for everyone. It is important to compare traffic attacks across different anonymity methods, and further study is needed to determine whether or not Denial of Service attacks are successful on Tor, I2P, and Freenet.

REFERENCES

Afaq, S. A., Husain, M. S., Bello, A., & Sadia, H. (2023). A Critical Analysis of Cyber Threats and Their Global Impact. In *Computational Intelligent Security in Wireless Communications* (pp. 201–220). CRC Press.

Al Jawaheri, H., Al Sabah, M., Boshmaf, Y., & Erbad, A. (2020). Deanonymizing Tor hidden service users through Bitcoin transactions analysis. *Computers & Security*, *89*, 101684. doi:10.1016/j.cose.2019.101684

Al Mutawa, N., Bryce, J., Franqueira, V. N. L., & Marrington, A. (2015). Behavioural evidence analysis applied to digital forensics: an empirical analysis of child pornography cases using P2P networks. *2015 10th International Conference on Availability, Reliability and Security*, (pp. 293–302). IEEE.

Albrecht, C., Duffin, K. M., Hawkins, S., & Morales Rocha, V. M. (2019). The use of cryptocurrencies in the money laundering process. *Journal of Money Laundering Control*, *22*(2), 210–216. doi:10.1108/JMLC-12-2017-0074

Aldridge, J., & Decary-Hétu, D. (2016). Cryptomarkets and the future of illicit drug markets. *The Internet and Drug Markets*, 23–32.

Alemian, T. I. (2019). *Terrorists' Propaganda and the Use of Media: Case Study of the Islamic State of Iraq and Syria*. US Army Command and General Staff College Fort Leavenworth United States.

Ali, A. (2023). *Decentralised Escrow Protocol that Facilitates Secure Transactions between Trustless Parties*. Social Science Research Network.

AlKhatib, B., & Basheer, R. (2019). Crawling the Dark Web: A Conceptual Perspective, Challenges and Implementation. *J. Digit. Inf. Manag.*, *17*(2), 51. doi:10.6025/jdim/2019/17/2/51-60

Alnabulsi, H., & Islam, R. (2018). Identification of illegal forum activities inside the dark net. *2018 International Conference on Machine Learning and Data Engineering (ICMLDE)*, (pp. 22–29). IEEE. 10.1109/iCMLDE.2018.00015

Alsamhi, S. H., Ma, O., Ansari, M. S., & Almalki, F. A. (2019). Survey on collaborative smart drones and internet of things for improving smartness of smart cities. *IEEE Access : Practical Innovations, Open Solutions*, *7*, 128125–128152. doi:10.1109/ACCESS.2019.2934998

AlShahrani, B. M. M. (2021). Classification of cyber-attack using Adaboost regression classifier and securing the network. [TURCOMAT]. *Turkish Journal of Computer and Mathematics Education*, *12*(10), 1215–1223.

Anjum, A., Kaur, D., Kondapalli, S., Hussain, M. A., Begum, A. U., Hassen, S. M., Boush, A., Sharafeldin, M., Benjeed, A. O. S., & Osman Abdalraheem, D. (2021). A Mysterious and Darkside of The Darknet: A Qualitative Study. *Webology, 18*(4).

Attaallah, A., Alsuhabi, H., Shukla, S., Kumar, R., Gupta, B. K., & Khan, R. A. (2022). Analyzing the Big Data Security Through a Unified Decision-Making Approach. *Intelligent Automation & Soft Computing, 32*(2).

Baker, D. (2016). *Online sex slaves: The internet's powerful role in sex trafficking*. CORE.

Boghosian, H. (2021). *"I Have Nothing to Hide": And 20 Other Myths About Surveillance and Privacy*. Beacon Press.

Böhme, R., Christin, N., Edelman, B., & Moore, T. (2015). Bitcoin: Economics, technology, and governance. *The Journal of Economic Perspectives*, *29*(2), 213–238. doi:10.1257/jep.29.2.213

Catakoglu, O., Balduzzi, M., & Balzarotti, D. (2017). Attacks landscape in the dark side of the web. *Proceedings of the Symposium on Applied Computing*, (pp. 1739–1746). 10.1145/3019612.3019796

Challenge, D. R. (2019). *Defense Advanced Research Projects Agency*.

Chertoff, M. (2017). A public policy perspective of the Dark Web. *Journal of Cyber Policy*, *2*(1), 26–38. doi:10.1080/23738871.2017.1298643

DeKeseredy, W., & Corsianos, M. (2015). *Violence against women in pornography*. Routledge. doi:10.4324/9781315652559

Deliu, I., Leichter, C., & Franke, K. (2018). Collecting cyber threat intelligence from hacker forums via a two-stage, hybrid process using support vector machines and latent dirichlet allocation. *2018 IEEE International Conference on Big Data (Big Data)*, (pp. 5008–5013). IEEE. 10.1109/BigData.2018.8622469

Dilipraj, E. (2014). Terror in the Deep and Dark Web. *Air Power Journal*, *9*(3), 121–140.

Dong, F., Yuan, S., Ou, H., & Liu, L. (2018). New cyber threat discovery from darknet marketplaces. *2018 IEEE Conference on Big Data and Analytics (ICBDA)*, (pp. 62–67). IEEE. 10.1109/ICBDAA.2018.8629658

Ehney, R., & Shorter, J. D. (2016a). DEEP WEB, DARK WEB, INVISIBLE WEB AND THE POST ISIS WORLD. *Issues in Information Systems*, *17*(4).

ElBahrawy, A., Alessandretti, L., Rusnac, L., Goldsmith, D., Teytelboym, A., & Baronchelli, A. (2020). Collective dynamics of dark web marketplaces. *Scientific Reports*, *10*(1), 1–8. doi:10.103841598-020-74416-y PMID:33139743

Erb, K. P. (2019). IRS followed bitcoin transactions, resulting in takedown of the largest child exploitation site on the Web. *Forbes*.

Everton, S. F., & Cunningham, D. (2015). Dark network resilience in a hostile environment: Optimizing centralization and density. *Criminology, Crim. Just. L & Soc'y, 16*, 1.

Fan, W., Du, Z., Fernández, D., & Villagra, V. A. (2017). Enabling an anatomic view to investigate honeypot systems: A survey. *IEEE Systems Journal*, *12*(4), 3906–3919. doi:10.1109/JSYST.2017.2762161

Ferry, N., Hackenheimer, T., Herrmann, F., & Tourette, A. (2019). Methodology of dark web monitoring. *2019 11th International Conference on Electronics, Computers and Artificial Intelligence (ECAI)*, 1–7.

Gallagher, K., Patil, S., & Memon, N. (2017). New me: Understanding expert and non-expert perceptions and usage of the Tor anonymity network. *Thirteenth Symposium on Usable Privacy and Security (SOUPS 2017)*, (pp. 385–398). IEEE.

Gehl, R. W. (2016). Power/freedom on the dark web: A digital ethnography of the Dark Web Social Network. *New Media & Society*, *18*(7), 1219–1235. doi:10.1177/1461444814554900

Godawatte, K., Raza, M., Murtaza, M., & Saeed, A. (2019a). Dark web along with the dark web marketing and surveillance. *2019 20th International Conference on Parallel and Distributed Computing, Applications and Technologies (PDCAT)*, 483–485.

Godawatte, K., Raza, M., Murtaza, M., & Saeed, A. (2019b). Dark web along with the dark web marketing and surveillance. *2019 20th International Conference on Parallel and Distributed Computing, Applications and Technologies (PDCAT)*, 483–485.

Greene, K. J. (2015). *ISIS: Trends in terrorist media and propaganda*.

Greenemeier, L. (2015). Human traffickers caught on hidden internet. *Scientific American*, 8.

Harviainen, J. T., Haasio, A., & Hämäläinen, L. (2020). Drug traders on a local dark web marketplace. *Proceedings of the 23rd International Conference on Academic Mindtrek*, (pp. 20–26). ACM. 10.1145/3377290.3377293

Hodge, D. R. (2014). Assisting victims of human trafficking: Strategies to facilitate identification, exit from trafficking, and the restoration of wellness. *Social Work*, *59*(2), 111–118. doi:10.1093wwu002 PMID:24855860

Husain, M. S. (2019). Social media Analytics to predict depression level in the users. In *Early Detection of Neurological Disorders Using Machine Learning Systems* (pp. 199–215). IGI Global. doi:10.4018/978-1-5225-8567-1.ch011

Husain, M. S. (2020). Nature inspired approach for intrusion detection systems. *Design and Analysis of Security Protocol for Communication*, 171–182.

Husain, M. S., & Khan, M. Z. (2019). *Critical Concepts, Standards, and Techniques in Cyber Forensics*. IGI Global.

Irwin, A. S. M., & Turner, A. B. (2018). Illicit Bitcoin transactions: challenges in getting to the who, what, when and where. *Journal of Money Laundering Control*.

Joshi, P. S., & Dinesha, H. A. (2020). Survey on identification of malicious activities by monitoring darknet access. *2020 Third International Conference on Smart Systems and Inventive Technology (ICSSIT)*, (pp. 346–350). IEEE. 10.1109/ICSSIT48917.2020.9214121

Kaur, S., & Randhawa, S. (2020). Dark web: A web of crimes. *Wireless Personal Communications*, *112*(4), 2131–2158. doi:10.100711277-020-07143-2

Khan, M. Z., Husain, M. S., & Shoaib, M. (2020). Introduction to email, web, and message forensics. In *Critical concepts, standards, and techniques in cyber forensics* (pp. 174–186). IGI Global. doi:10.4018/978-1-7998-1558-7.ch010

Khan, M. Z., Mishra, A., & Khan, M. H. (2020). Cyber Forensics Evolution and Its Goals. In Critical Concepts, Standards, and Techniques in Cyber Forensics (pp. 16–30). IGI Global. doi:10.4018/978-1-7998-1558-7.ch002

Khan, M. Z., Shoaib, M., & Ahmad, F. (2020). Cyber Forensic Lab Setup and Its Requirement. In Critical Concepts, Standards, and Techniques in Cyber Forensics (pp. 103–115). IGI Global. doi:10.4018/978-1-7998-1558-7.ch007

Khan, W. (2021). An exhaustive review on state-of-the-art techniques for anomaly detection on attributed networks. [TURCOMAT]. *Turkish Journal of Computer and Mathematics Education, 12*(10), 6707–6722.

Khan, W., & Haroon, M. (2022a). An efficient framework for anomaly detection in attributed social networks. *International Journal of Information Technology : an Official Journal of Bharati Vidyapeeth's Institute of Computer Applications and Management, 14*(6), 3069–3076. doi:10.100741870-022-01044-2

Khan, W., & Haroon, M. (2022b). An unsupervised deep learning ensemble model for anomaly detection in static attributed social networks. *International Journal of Cognitive Computing in Engineering, 3*, 153–160. doi:10.1016/j.ijcce.2022.08.002

Khan, W., Haroon, M., Khan, A. N., Hasan, M. K., Khan, A., Mokhtar, U. A., & Islam, S. (2022). DVAEGMM: Dual Variational Autoencoder With Gaussian Mixture Model for Anomaly Detection on Attributed Networks. *IEEE Access : Practical Innovations, Open Solutions, 10*, 91160–91176. doi:10.1109/ACCESS.2022.3201332

Koniaris, I., Papadimitriou, G., Nicopolitidis, P., & Obaidat, M. (2014). Honeypots deployment for the analysis and visualization of malware activity and malicious connections. *2014 IEEE International Conference on Communications (ICC)*, (pp. 1819–1824). IEEE. 10.1109/ICC.2014.6883587

Kundra, H., Khan, W., Malik, M., Rane, K. P., Neware, R., & Jain, V. (2022). Quantum-inspired firefly algorithm integrated with cuckoo search for optimal path planning. *International Journal of Modern Physics C, 33*(02), 2250018. doi:10.1142/S0129183122500188

Lane, J. (2013). Bitcoin, silk road, and the need for a new approach to virtual currency regulation. *Charleston L. Rev., 8*, 511.

Liggett, R., Lee, J. R., Roddy, A. L., & Wallin, M. A. (2020). The dark web as a platform for crime: An exploration of illicit drug, firearm, CSAM, and cybercrime markets. The Palgrave Handbook of International Cybercrime and Cyberdeviance, 91–116.

Lindsey, N. (2019). *Cyber criminals have turned social media cyber crime into a $3 billion business.* CPO Magazine.

Livingstone, S., Davidson, J., Bryce, J., Batool, S., Haughton, C., & Nandi, A. (2017). *Children's online activities, risks and safety: a literature review by the UKCCIS evidence group.* LSE.

Marcella, A. J. (2021). *Cyber Forensics: Examining Emerging and Hybrid Technologies*. CRC Press. doi:10.1201/9781003057888

Marin, E., Shakarian, J., & Shakarian, P. (2018). Mining key-hackers on darkweb forums. *2018 1st International Conference on Data Intelligence and Security (ICDIS)*, (pp. 73–80). IEEE.

Masinde, N., & Graffi, K. (2020). Peer-to-peer-based social networks: A comprehensive survey. *SN Computer Science*, *1*(5), 299. doi:10.100742979-020-00315-8

McCabe, K. A. (2017). Common forms: sex trafficking. In *Human Trafficking* (pp. 122–137). Routledge. doi:10.4324/9781315679990-6

Monzini, P. (2005). *Sex traffic: Prostitution, crime and exploitation*. Zed Books.

Naheem, M. A. (2016). Money laundering: A primer for banking staff. *International Journal of Disclosure and Governance*, *13*(2), 135–156. doi:10.1057/jdg.2015.10

Nichols, A. J. (2016). *Sex trafficking in the United States: Theory, research, policy, and practice*. Columbia University Press. doi:10.7312/nich17262

Nunes, E., Shakarian, P., & Simari, G. I. (2018). At-risk system identification via analysis of discussions on the darkweb. *2018 APWG Symposium on Electronic Crime Research (ECrime)*, (pp. 1–12). IEEE. 10.1109/ECRIME.2018.8376211

Ormsby, E. (2019). Dealer's chance: The dark web, bitcoin and the fall of silk road. *Griffith REVIEW*, *64*, 184–194.

Prylinski, K. M. (2020). Tech Trafficking: How the internet has transformed sex trafficking. *J. High Tech. L.*, *20*, 338.

Quasim, M. T., Al Hawi, A. N., & Meraj, M. (2023). *System Penetration: Concepts, Attack Methods, and Defense Strategies*. EasyChair.

Rasool, M., & Khan, W. (2015). Big data: Study in structured and unstructured data. [IJTIR]. *HCTL Open International Journal of Technology Innovations and Research*, *14*, 1–6.

Rügemer, W. (2019). *The Capitalists of the 21st Century: An Easy-to-Understand Outline on the Rise of the New Financial Players*. tredition.

Sadasivam, G. K., Hota, C., & Anand, B. (2018). Detection of severe SSH attacks using honeypot servers and machine learning techniques. *Software Networking*, *2018*(1), 79–100. doi:10.13052/jsn2445-9739.2017.005

Sahu, K., Alzahrani, F. A., Srivastava, R. K., & Kumar, R. (2020). Hesitant fuzzy sets based symmetrical model of decision-making for estimating the durability of web application. *Symmetry*, *12*(11), 1770. doi:10.3390ym12111770

Sahu, K., Alzahrani, F. A., Srivastava, R. K., & Kumar, R. (2021). Evaluating the impact of prediction techniques: Software reliability perspective. *Computers, Materials & Continua*, *67*(2), 1471–1488. doi:10.32604/cmc.2021.014868

Saleem, J., Islam, R., & Kabir, M. A. (2022). The anonymity of the dark web: A survey. *IEEE Access : Practical Innovations, Open Solutions, 10*, 33628–33660. doi:10.1109/ACCESS.2022.3161547

Shakarian, J., Gunn, A. T., & Shakarian, P. (2016). Exploring malicious hacker forums. *Cyber Deception: Building the Scientific Foundation*, 259–282.

Surette, R. (2015). Performance crime and justice. *Current Issues in Criminal Justice, 27*(2), 195–216. doi:10.1080/10345329.2015.12036041

Suthar, D., & Rughani, P. H. (2020). A Comprehensive Study of VoIP Security. *2020 2nd International Conference on Advances in Computing, Communication Control and Networking (ICACCCN)*, 812–817.

Tarık, A. K. (n.d.). Law Enforcement And Technological Facilities In Changing Agenda Of The Public Safety And Security. *Güvenlik Bilimleri Dergisi*, 21–32.

Vasserman, E., Jansen, R., Tyra, J., Hopper, N., & Kim, Y. (2009). Membership-concealing overlay networks. *Proceedings of the 16th ACM Conference on Computer and Communications Security*, (pp. 390–399). ACM.

Wang, M., Wang, X., Shi, J., Tan, Q., Gao, Y., Chen, M., & Jiang, X. (2018). Who are in the darknet? Measurement and analysis of darknet person attributes. *2018 IEEE Third International Conference on Data Science in Cyberspace (DSC)*, (pp. 948–955). IEEE. 10.1109/DSC.2018.00151

Watson, K. D. (2012). The tor network: A global inquiry into the legal status of anonymity networks. *Wash. U. Global Stud. L. Rev., 11*, 715.

Weimann, G. (2016a). Going dark: Terrorism on the dark web. *Studies in Conflict and Terrorism, 39*(3), 195–206. doi:10.1080/1057610X.2015.1119546

Weimann, G. (2016c). Terrorist migration to the dark web. *Perspectives on Terrorism, 10*(3), 40–44.

Wittes, B., Poplin, C., Jurecic, Q., & Spera, C. (2016). *Sextortion: Cybersecurity, teenagers, and remote sexual assault*. Center for Technology at Brookings.

Wolak, M., Lysionok, A., Kosturek, B., Wiśniewski, J., Wawryszuk, B., Kawa, A., Davidson, R., Maćkowiak, M., Starzyk, M., & Kulikowska-Wielgus, A. (2019). *Technological revolution. Directions in the development of the transport-forwarding-logistics (TFL) sector*.

Yang, Y., Yang, L., Yang, M., Yu, H., Zhu, G., Chen, Z., & Chen, L. (2019). Dark web forum correlation analysis research. *2019 IEEE 8th Joint International Information Technology and Artificial Intelligence Conference (ITAIC)*, (pp. 1216–1220). IEEE.

Yang, Y., Yu, H., Yang, L., Yang, M., Chen, L., Zhu, G., & Wen, L. (2019). Hadoop-based dark web threat intelligence analysis framework. *2019 IEEE 3rd Advanced Information Management, Communicates, Electronic and Automation Control Conference (IMCEC)*, (pp. 1088–1091). IEEE.

Zhang, H., & Zou, F. (2020). A survey of the dark web and dark market research. *2020 IEEE 6th International Conference on Computer and Communications (ICCC)*, (pp. 1694–1705). IEEE.

Chapter 12
Recent Advances in Cyber Security Laws and Practices in India:
Implementation and Awareness

Neyha Malik
Integral University, India

Firoz Husain
Integral University, India

Anis Ali
Prince Sattam Bin Abdulaziz University, Saudi Arabia

Yasir Arafat Elahi
Integral University, India

ABSTRACT

The growth of the internet and proliferation of applications, products, and services has given rise to cyber threats which require far more stringent security measures than ever before. Some common types of cybercrimes are job fraud, phishing, baiting, vishing, smishing, credit and debit card fraud, child pornography, cyberbullying, etc. Cyber laws need constant upgrading and refinement to keep pace with the increasing technology. In India, various statutes and initiatives have been launched to ensure its cyber security such as Information Technology Act, 2000 (IT Act), Indian Penal Code, 1860 (IPC), National Cybersecurity Framework (NCFS), financial assistance, Cyber Crime Prevention against Women & Children (CCPWC), Indian Cyber Crime Coordination Centre (I4C), National Cyber Crime Reporting Portal, Citizen Financial Cyber Fraud Reporting and Management System, Indian Computer Emergency Response Team (CERT-In), and Ministry of Electronics & Information Technology (MeitY).

DOI: 10.4018/978-1-6684-8133-2.ch012

INTRODUCTION

The mission of this chapter is to give knowledge of and bring awareness for Cyber Laws. With the unprecedented growth of internet and its applications, products & services on this dynamic domain, citizens are now empowered and their lives transformed. However with the growth of internet, cyber threats have also emerged due to this cyber revolution which requires far stringent security measures than ever before. Past two decades have witnessed a giant leap in Cyber Revolution around the world and subsequently cyberattacks have increased exponentially. Furthermore before the outbreak of Covid pandemic, where there were only about 35% of the global workforce had been into remote working setup, since the pandemic event, the usage of internet and requirement of cloud for storing and transferring confidential information has increased manifold. Cyber attackers, hackers, and scammers have used this opportunity to their advantage. According to Aaysha (2020), data privacy and security has three parameters namely confidentiality, integrity and availability. Alnahari & Quasim, (2021) envisioned that every country now strives for Smart cities comprising IoT devices at vehicles; cameras at streets, residential apartments, offices; health care facilities and even the military regarding enhancing security. However, this technological arrangement is associated with significant security and privacy risks because they generate tons of government and private data, making them a lucrative target for exploitation by malicious attackers. Currently, most IoT device implementations utilize the Client-Server access model which poses a significant risk of user data utilization for nefarious purposes behind the central server. The recent development of technology leads to several security threats and breaches. Those security challenges are related to confidentiality, privacy, integrity and availability. To withstand these cyber-attacks, network resources are needed to be optimized (Al Shahrani, 2021). According to Khan, Husain, & Shoaib, (2020) one of the most popular and commonly used means of online communication, E-mail communication is also on target. The year 1978 was the year when the first computer-related crime took place in the form of alteration or deletion of data. To achieve accuracy, an intensive investigation environment, equipment and labs are needed to forensically examine a variety of digital devices (Khan, Shoaib, & Ahmad, 2020). According to Ahmad, F., & Khan, M. Z. (2019), "advancing technologies, especially computer technologies, have necessitated the creation of a comprehensive investigation and collection methodology for digital and online evidence." Marcella, A. J. (Ed.). (2022) examines "how cyber forensics can be applied to identifying, collecting, and examining evidential data from emerging and hybrid technologies, while taking steps to proactively manage the influence and impact, as well as the policy and governance aspects of these technologies and their effect on business operations". On the other hand, an advanced approach known as Data Mining Approach using Machine Learning Techniques, wherein data scientists and researchers have put considerable efforts to use the advanced technologies such as Wireless Sensor Networks (WSN) and Internet of Things (IoT) in order cultivate the fruits of healthy environment (Mishra, et al, 2022). Quasim & Al Hawi, (2022) have advocated Penetration testing as an integral part of a comprehensive security program. "Pen tests are conducted by ethical hackers to mimic the strategies and actions of the attacker". Tripathi, Haroon, Khan, & Husain, (2022) In today's modern medical field, medical technology has been enhanced and digitized to help patients and medical professionals. Apart from diagnosis, this medical data can also be used to predict future disease in patients and advise accordingly.

This chapter includes the overview of the concepts of cybercrime, evolution of cyber threats, its impact on economy and society, international cyber laws for prevention, Indian cyber laws, recent advances and amendments, government initiatives to create awareness to curb cybercrime. This writing is ideal for government officials, policymakers, industry professionals, researchers, practitioners, instructors, students, academicians and scholars.

CYBER CRIME

Cyber World which is also known as Virtual world is the world created by digital and network technology. It provides assorted transactional communication benefits and e-commerce facilities. However it has given rise to a new terminology known as Cybercrime. The 10th United Nations Congress on the Prevention of Crime and Treatment of Offenders defined "Cybercrime as any illegal behavior done by the means of electronic operations that targets the security of computer systems and the data processed in the narrow sense where as in the broader sense as any illegal behavior, illegal possession or distributing information committed by means of a computer operating system or network" (Chhabra, Gunjan & Chhabra, Kanika, 2014). Cybercrime can be against any person, property or government (Patel, Ravikumar S. Patel & Kathiriya, Dr.Dhaval, 2013).

Cybercrime can be defined as any illegal activity, the end result of which are achieved using the unauthorized access of computer or computer network. In other words, criminal activity committed with the aid of computer or computer network qualify as cybercrime. Recent years have seen a growing concern about new cybercrime terminologies such as cyber war, cyber espionage, cyber security, cyber conflict, cyber intrusion etc. Crimes related to cyberspace can be broadly divided into the heads of Finance, Identity, Privacy and Child. Over the past decade, there has been an explosion in cybercrime and this has become an approximate $1.5T industry. Cyberattacks like SolarWinds program (2020), REvil collective (2021), zero-day threat (2021), May ransomware attack (2022), Slack attack, teapotuberhacker and A mid-September hack (2022) have made their presence felt in the recent years and near future is threatened by bigger and more sophisticated machine-learning and AI tools based cyber security breaches. Somewhere indeed they are staying one step ahead of cybersecurity agencies in this ongoing cyber challenge. Among many cyber threats, Ransomware is considered to be one of the biggest cyber security threats in 2022 across the globe.

The debate in the United Nations about Cyber Space Governance based on the Cyber intrusion between US and China, two theories came into light regarding Cyber Space Governance viz. Sovereignty based model of Cyber governance as advocated by Russia and China and the other one is having the contrasting vision advocated by US, UK and their allies.

The academic findings of the study of Kristen E. Eichensehr addresses the state-to-state governance of cyber issues. The term Cyber Space is as wide and generic as the high seas, outer space and Antarctica and it should command the global governance. The above mentioned domains follow the following norms:

a). multilateral governance b). governance by treaty c). some level of demilitarization

Likewise Cyber space should follow the above norms with modifications viz.

a). multi stakeholder governance
b). governance through norms
c). regulated militarization

CYBER CRIMINAL OR CYBER TERRORIST

Cyber Criminals are the people who "devious ways to part people and organizations from their data and dollars" (arcticwolf.com). The factor that differentiates a simple crime from a cybercrime is that cybercrime is directed at a computer or other digital devices and ICT technologies are used to commit such crime (John Sammons & Michael Cross, 2017). Not all hackers can be considered as cybercriminals. Many of them are simple computer enthusiasts who take pleasure in gaining access to computer network with the objective of either defacing a Web site for personal or political motives or simply to gain acclaim among their peers. Cybercriminal are talented programmers who tries to steal money using debit card or credit card information, hacks bank accounts or personal information whereas a Cyber terrorist tries to cause destruction, disruption or commit cyber espionage (to steal secrets) particularly on critical infrastructure. Greengard (2010) identified a range of cyber-attack methods that can be deployed by cyber terrorists, including "vandalism, spreading propaganda, gathering classified data, using distributed denial-of-service attacks to shut down systems, destroying equipment, attacking critical infrastructure, and planting malicious software." Cyber terrorism can be considered as the identical twin or a distant cousin of Cyber-crime. The intention of any cybercriminal is to make money or steel information however in order to evade capture and prosecution, they would not want anyone to know what they were doing. On the other hand cyber terrorist have a different agenda of maximum public impact using softer targets that are less likely to be secure.

TYPES OF CYBER CRIMES

There is a long list of cybercrimes, and it keeps evolving and adding with the advent of new technology every day. The regular variety of cybercrimes include hacking, phishing, distribution of malware, electronic theft, DDOS attack and ransomware attacks. Some common types of cybercrimes are as follows:

Baiting: to lure people into checking out tampered devices left in public areas

Scareware: giving false alarms and scaring users so that they buy infected software

Impersonation or Identity Theft: When a hacker fraudulently uses electronic signature, password, or any other unique identifier of another person, it is called Impersonation or Identity Theft. The hacker steals and resales corporate and personal data for money.

Cryptojacking: When computing resources (electricity, hardware and other mining resources) are hijacked by the hackers to mine cryptocurrency without payment. Cryptojacking is also known as malicious cryptomining.

Ransomware Attacks: It is a type of malware that prevents a person or organizations from accessing his/her computer or the data stored on it. This malware also affects the computer where it may become locked or its data might get stolen, deleted or encrypted for malicious intentions.

Email Fraud or Email Scam: Using the email of an individual, the hacker do intentional deception related to either making money or to damage another individual reputation.

Child Pornography or Child Sexually Abusive Material (CSAM): It includes any material wherein the child being exploited or abused may be seen. It contains sexual images of child in any form. Section 67(B) in the Information Technology Act has provision in which the publication or transmission of material depicting children in sexually explicit activities in an electronic form is punishable.

Cyberbullying: It is a type of bullying conducted through the use of digital technology. When a hacker harasses or bullies someone using electronic devices such as computers, laptops, mobile phones etc. It involves the use of social media, messaging platforms, gaming platforms and mobile devices etc. Cyberbullying also involves any type of repeated behaviour which is intended to scare, anger or shame the targeted person.

Cyberstalking: It is the online methodical, persistent and deliberate harassing and/or stalking of another person using the means of internet and related ICT technologies such as texts, emails, social media posts, and other forms.

Cyber grooming: It is a type of cyber bullying which involves building relationship through luring, teasing, or even putting pressure on any teenager with the intention to perform a sexual act.

Online sextortion: It is a type of cyber bullying when the cybercriminal threatens any individual to publish his/her sensitive and private material on internet in order to get a sexual image, sexual favour, or money from the victim.

Phishing: In this type of cyber fraud, malicious links are sent through emails. The email may appear to be from a legitimate source but it contains a malicious attachment that is designed to steal personal information from the user such as their ID number, PIN, Credit/Debit card number, its expiration date, CVV, etc. and then selling the information on the dark net for extracting money.

Vishing: This is a type of fraud committed through the means of mobile phones. In vishing personal confidential information from victims is stolen using their phone. Cybercriminals pose themselves as the polite callers and pretend that they are from any government organization, tax department, police department, or victim's bank using sophisticated social engineering tactics. The victim under the legal pressure reveals their private information and give access to their personal accounts details.

Smishing: In this type of cyber fraud, text messages purporting to be from reputable companies are sent in order to induce individuals to reveal their personal information such as passwords or debit/credit card numbers. Smishing is the amalgamation of SMS and fraud that is why it may be understood as the fraud that uses text messages (SMS) via mobile phones to trick its victims into visiting a fraudulent website, calling a fake phone number, or downloading malicious software.

Credit card and debit card fraud: In credit card (or debit card) fraud, unauthorized purchases or withdrawals from another person's card are made to gain access to their financial accounts. In this type of fraudulent activity, the unscrupulous hacker gains access to the cardholder's debit/credit number, or their personal identification number (PIN). It is one of the most frequent and common type of cybercrime.

Online job fraud: These are the type of fraudulent schemes which misleads job seeking people into better jobs in India or abroad with higher wages/salaries in return for hefty commissions and later on not giving any jobs. Reserve Bank of India (RBI) has advised and issued directives to people not to fall prey to job scams.

CYBER ATTACKS: DATA

In 2021 alone the Ransomware attacks as reported by various agencies were targeted on all sorts of industries such as energy, technical, academic, technological, energy, government, academic, transport, healthcare, finance etc. There is a long list of public and private companies all over the world that fell prey to these cyber-attacks.

The renowned organizations that got attacked by Ransomware Attacks in 2021 are as follows to name a few: Kaseya, Salvation Army, Grupo Fleury, City of Liege, Lucky Star Casino, MRWD, RBA, Judson ISD, Humber River Hospital, Invenergy, Sol Oriens, Edward Don, Skinners' schools, LineStar, iConstituent, St. Clair County, UF Health, Steamship Authority, ParkMobile, Sierra College, Betenbough, Waikato Hospitals, AXA, Ireland HSE, Yamabiko, City of Tulsa, Volue Technology, Scripps Health, Swiss Cloud, Presque Isle PD, Whistler, Aspire, Merseyrail, UnitingCare, VTA, Gyrodata, Hoya, The Dixie Group, NBU, University of Portsmouth, Owner Federal Group, Bakker Logistiek, Durham, City of Lawrence, Haverhill School, NCI Technological University, Home Hardware Stores, Applus, Coral Glades High School, Boggi Milano, MIDC, University of California, University of Maryland, Nine Network, Sierra Wireless, CMAT, CSET, South & City College, Buffalo Public Schools, Molson Coors, Oloron-Sainte-Marie, Qualys, Standley Systems, Flagstar, Cochise Eye & Laser, Prism HR, Staring College, Yuba County, Jones Day Law Firm, Discount, CPCC, Dax-Côte d'Argent HC, Ness DE, ReMax Kelowna, Foxtons Group, DSC Logistics, TWU, Palfinger, WestRock, CHwapi, City of Angers, Wentworth, Dassault Falcon Jet, AKVA, OmniTRAX, Northern Territory Govt, Hackney Council, Amey, Apex Laboratory, UKRI (informationisbeautiful.net).

The organizations that faced Data Breaches in 2021 alone are as follows: Cathay Pacific Airways, Aadhaar, Apollo, Dropbox, Uber, Facebook, Adobe, Houzz, Google+, Instagram, China Software Developer Network, Chile Ministry Of Education, ShareThis, YouNow, HauteLook, Animoto, EyeEm, 8fit, Whitepages, Ixigo, Fotolog, 500px, GovPayNow.com, Armor Games, BookMate, Blank Media Games, CoffeeMeetsBagel, Stronghold Kingdoms, Roll20, Toyota, Vårdguiden, Blur, WiFi Finder, Unknown, Ge.tt, Artsy, Petflow, DataCamp, Coinmama, Yahoo, Spambot, Yahoo, Facebook, Friend Finder Network, Marriott International, OxyData, River City Media, Twitter, Indian citizens, Microsoft, Chinese, resume leak, Court Ventures, Deep Root Analytics, MySpace, Dubsmash, Massive American business hack, MyFitnessPal, Ebay, Equifax, Canva, Heartland, Nametests, LinkedIn, Pakistani mobile operators, VK, Capital One, Quora, Firebase, TK / TJ Maxx, AOL, Anthem, JP Morgan Chase, Securus Technologies, Wawa, BriansClub, db8151dd, MGM Hotels, EasyJet, Dutch Government, Israeli government, Marriott Hotels, Buchbinder Car Rentals, DoorDash, UCLA Health, Virgin Media, Tesco Clubcard, Zoom, Nintendo, US Marshals Service, Mount Olympus, Boots Advantage Card, MyHeritage, Dailymotion, Sony PSN, US Military, Target, Tumblr, UbiSoft, Home Depot, Philippines' Commission on Elections, Living Social, Evernote, Turkish citizenship database, Chtrbox, LocalBlox, Malaysian telcos & MVNOs, Newegg, Last.fm, Weebly, Fling, Tianya, Cardsystems Solutions Inc., Panerabread, AshleyMadison.com, Steam, SKY Brasil, Yahoo, RockYou!, Al.type, Facebook, Suprema, TicketFly, US Dept of Vet Affairs, Mail. Ru, UK Revenue & Customs, Sony Online Entertainment, Zappos, Yahoo Japan, US Office of Personnel Management (2nd Breach), Quest Diagnostics, Korea Credit Bureau, AOL, Auction.co.kr, Disqus, Zomato, T-Mobile, Deutsche Telecom, Telegram, Experian / T-mobile, Texas voter records, Careem, Blizzard, Nexon Korea Corp, Kromtech, Apple, Mossack Fonseca, GS Caltex, Premera, Dixons Carphone, Interpark, Twitch, Sony Pictures, Chinese gaming sites, Lynda.com, Greek government, LinkedIn, eHarmony, Last.fmm Gamigo, Minecraft, ClixSense, Office of the Texas Attorney General, Saks and Lord & Taylor, Amazon, Clinton campaign, Gmail, CheckFree Corporation, Tricare, SnapChat, Community Health Systems, BNY Mellon Shareowner Services, Sutter Medical Foundation, Desjardins Group, Hannaford Brothers Supermarket Chain, US Office of Personnel Management, UPS, European Central Bank, Advocate Medical Group, Nintendo, ssndob.ms, KDDI, Norwegian Tax Authorities, Adult Friend Finder, Citigroup, Hong Kong Registration & Electoral Office, Banner Health, South Carolina State Dept. of Revenue, State of Texas, Sanrio, Educational Credit Management Corp, Helse Sør-Øst

RHF, Grindr, Cellebrite, Swedish Transport Agency, Viacom, Three Iranian banks, Epsilon, Driving Standards Agency, HSBC Turkey, JP Morgan Chase, Cense AI, Countrywide Financial Corp, Drizly, Zhenhua, CarPhone Warehouse, AOL, Betfair, World Check, University of Utah Hospitals & Clinics, University of Miami, T-Mobile, Linux Ubuntu forums, Ubuntu, Vodafone, Bell, Health Net – IBM, New York State Electric & Gas, Snapchat, Imgur, New York City Health & Hospitals Corp., UK Ministry of Defence, TIO Networks, Nemours Foundation, Monster.com, SingHealth, KM.ru & Nival, National Security Agency, Global Payments, Gawker.com, Health Net, RBS Worldpay, GEDmatch, MBM Company, Sega, Washington Post, AvMed, Inc., Staples, Carefirst, Neiman Marcus, Blue Cross Blue Shield of Tennessee, Waterly, Drupal, D&B, Altegrity.

The enormous list above poses a great danger on the credibility of the organizations and the reasons recorded for these breaches are poor security, lost device, corrupted email address or online information, hacking of SSN/personal details, credit card information, leaking of health & other personal records etc. The Indian government with the help of National Critical Information Infrastructure Protection Centre (NCIIPC) has identified four 'Critical Sectors' that needs to be prepared in terms of cybersecurity:

a.   Energy & Power;
b.   Finance, Insurance, and Banking
c.   Telecommunications;
d.   Transportation
e.   Administration;
f.   Public and Strategic Enterprises

The major reasons for numerous cyber-attacks lies in the loopholes in the software and hardware of the information and communication devices. Among these loopholes, one is the Internet of Things (IoT) which is a term used to describe how millions of devices from all around the world connect to the internet to store, transmit and receive data. Hackers use the internet connectivity as a gateway to access such data. Outdated software (also called Mishandling Patches) is also one of the most common sources of cyberattack. An example of data breach due to Mishandling Patches was the WannaCry Ransomware Attack of 2017 which affected more than 200,000 computers across 150 countries where cyber attackers were able to exploit outdated Microsoft Windows software to gain access to users' data. In the recent Volkswagen and Audi cyber exposures, negligent data handling had put millions of consumers' sensitive information in the hands of hackers. Cloud services are among the most vulnerable sources to a variety of cyberattacks, including account takeover and Denial of Service (DoS) attacks which prevent individuals and businesses from accessing their own data.

CYBERSECURITY

In order to tackle the above cyber threats and attacks, Cybersecurity has emerged to be a field dedicated to securing sensitive information and systems through which such information is processed, transmitted or stored. Cybersecurity can be defined as the collection of technologies, processes, and practices that are intended to prevent networks, devices, programs and data from being attacked, damaged or accessed by unauthorized persons. Alternatively, cyber security may also be referred to as Information Technology Security. Sensitive information includes information pertaining to national security, health or finance.

Figure 1. World's biggest data breaches and hacks
(Source: informatioisbeautiful.net)

Cyberspace is an extremely difficult territory to deal with grey activities such as Dark Net and which is grueling to bring under the governance of law and order. Cyber laws need constant up-gradation and refinement to keep pace with the increasing technology. Cyber stakeholder viz. individuals, banks, shopping websites, lawmakers, internet providers and other intercessors should ensure that they stay within the confines of cyber laws. Open networks such as Internet where commercial activities, business transactions and government services are realized, has led to the fast development of new cyber threats and information security breach issues which are utilized by cyber criminals. This increased complexity of the communication and networking infrastructure require stringent laws for cybersecurity.

"Due to the data protection laws aimed at modernizing the global regulatory framework, the legal domain of any country has to face many infrastructural challenges at a rapid pace. This makes it essential to study and discuss strategies, policies and laws that can regulate and monitor cyber activities and modify laws that should be implemented in order to protect cyber users" (Handbook of Research on Cyber Law, Data Protection, and Privacy. (2022). United States: IGI Global).

Cyberspace law covers a wide range of topics including aspects of contract law, privacy laws, and intellectual property laws. There are many different laws governing cybersecurity, largely depending on each country's territorial extent. The punishments for the same also vary according to the offence committed, ranging from fines to imprisonment. The Computer Fraud and Abuse Act (CFAA) of United States cybersecurity (1986) was the first cyber law that was ever to be enacted for computer related offences. It prohibited unauthorized access to federal computers and the illegal use of digital information.

CYBER CRIME SCENERIO IN INDIA

Governments in almost all the countries have constituted Cyber Laws and different cyber security tools have been developed to fight against these types of threats. A comprehensive and coordinated effort is needed to strengthen the mechanism to deal with cybercrimes. Cyber Laws around the globe need to be updated to incorporate the latest legal and technological developments and to address the challenges of cyber threats posed by the rapid development of technology. This situation will continue to increase as the country like India starts developing smart cities and rolling out 5G network among other initiatives in the near future.

It has been reported that cybercrime in India increased by 11.8% in the year 2020, which accounted for reporting around only 50,000 cases. Cybercrime is one of the tidiest crimes to solve due to many challenges faced such as underreporting, the jurisdictional complication of cybercrime committed, the lack of public unawareness and the high cost of investigation. It also involves usage of high-tech technology and the requirement for the involvement of experts into the matter making it more sophisticated. There are a number competent laws in India to adjudicate cybercrime however the jurisdictional issues pose a major hindrance in solving cyber cases. Due to the low awareness level and even lower accessibility to cyber tools, the rate of conviction in cybercrime cases is still low. According to an Economic Times analysis of cybercrime, India is losing nearly R. 1.25 lakh crore per annum to cyber-attacks overall (2021).

Figure 2. Highest number of cybercrimes in India in 2021
(Source: National Crime Records Bureau, India)

In India, cybercrime is governed by the Information Technology Act (IT Act) (2000), specific sections of Indian Penal Code (IPC) (1860), National Cybersecurity Framework (NCFS) and Information Technology Rules (IT Rules). On the auspicious occasion of Indian Independence Day on August 15, 2022, Prime Minister Narendra Modi announced that a new National Cyber Security Strategy (NCSS) will be implemented to ensure a safe, secure, trusted, resilient and vibrant cyberspace for India because its dependence on cyberspace will increase multi-fold in the near future. National Cyber Security Strategy (NCSS) will focus on building a lot of indigenous capabilities, central apex body, legislative framework and cyber security incidence and response teams at the central and state levels that will ensure decentralized remedy of the cyber-attacks in an effective and efficient manner.

Data is the heart of all algorithm that drives the modern digital economy. Finance, gaming, E-commerce and our day-to-day online errands are unsustainable in the absence of this significant voluminous digital personal information. However the basic risk of digital surveillance is the erosion of autonomy and falling in the hands of ruthless hackers.

Total Cyber Crime reported between Q1 (Jan, Feb and March) and Q2 (April, May and June) of 2021 was nearly 74.32% which was also the time of the second wave of Covid19. It was almost a year since people have encountered cyber activities and started to learn to mitigate the dangers associated with it. Even till the Q3 (July, Aug and Sept), this danger loomed approx. at 47.22%.

However in the last quarter (Q4: Oct, Nov and Dec), it was reported at its least point of 9.19%

Table 1. Comparative analysis of total cybercrime reported

Comparative analysis of total cybercrime reported			
Qtrs	**Complaints Reported**	**Q/Q change (%)**	**QoQ change (%)**
Q1 2021	55740		
Q2 2021	97167	74.32	
Q3 2021	143049	47.22	
Q4 2021	156197	9.19	
Q1 2022	206153	31.98	269.85
Q2 2022	237658	15.28	144.59

Source: CYBER PRAVAHA, Indian Cyber Crime

Figure 3. Comparative analysis of total cybercrime reported

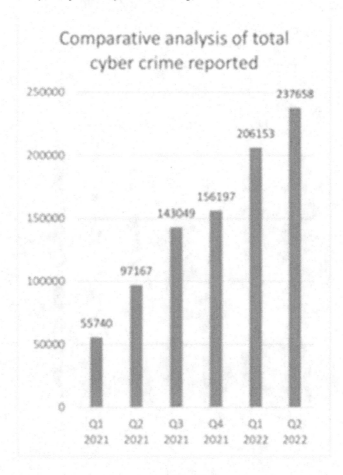

(Q/Q: Quarter to Quarter; QoQ: Quarter on Quarter)

An upward trend could be seen in the online financial fraud of **UPI fraud complaints** as India was going steadily fast towards online wallet payments.

Table 2. UPI fraud complaint

Qtrs	UPI Fraud Complaints	Q/Q change (%)	QoQ change (%)
Q1 2021	9037		
Q2 2021	18864	108.74	
Q3 2021	39570	109.76	
Q4 2021	50806	28.40	
Q1 2022	62350	22.72	589.94
Q2 2022	84145	34.96	346.06

(Source: CYBER PRAVAHA, Indian Cyber Crime)

Figure 4. UPI fraud complaints

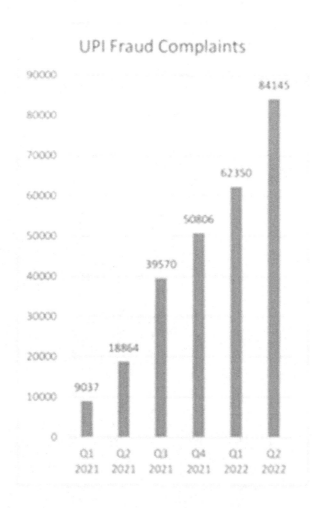

(Q/Q: Quarter to Quarter; QòQ: Quarter on Quarter)

A downward trend in **<u>Debit/Credit Card frauds</u>** shows that people are aware and educated now regarding the online financial usage. MeitY supplements the initiatives of the Law Enforcement Agencies (LEAs) through various schemes and advisories for capacity building in cyber frauds.

(Q/Q: Quarter to Quarter; QoQ: Quarter on Quarter)

Figure 5. Debit/credit card/SIM swap fraud

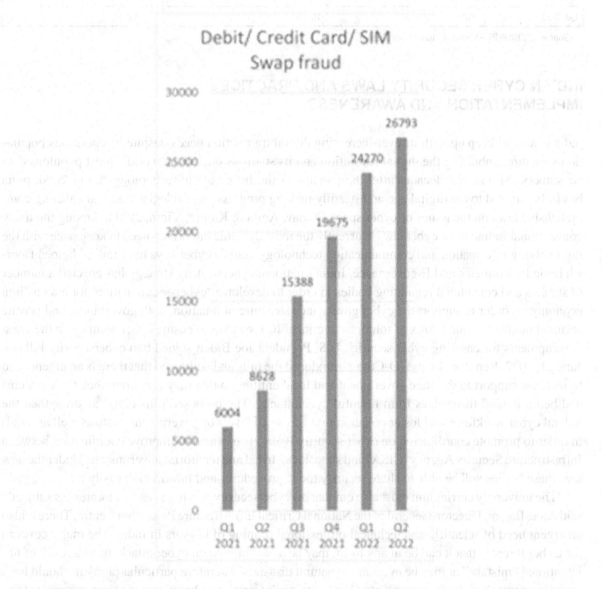

Table 3. Debit/Credit card/ SIM swap fraud

Qtrs	Debit/ Credit Card/ SIM Swap fraud	Q/Q change (%)	QoQ change (%)
Q1 2021	6004		
Q2 2021	8628	43.70	
Q3 2021	15388	78.35	
Q4 2021	19675	27.86	
Q1 2022	24270	23.35	304.23
Q2 2022	26793	10.40	210.54

(Source: CYBER PRAVAHA, Indian Cyber Crime)

INDIAN CYBER SECURITY LAWS AND PRACTICES: IMPLEMENTATION AND AWARENESS

India is able to keep up with its ever-increasing digital transaction needs despite its enormous population structure embracing the digital revolution and its status as one of the world's most populous data consumers. Almost two decades after the passage of the Information Technology Act in 2000, India has fully adapted to the digital age and steadily making progress toward legislating and enacting comprehensive laws on the issues of cyber space (Yadav, Anita & Kumar, Vipin, 2021). Among the many conventional Indian laws, cyber law is currently the most dynamic law which need to keep pace with the fast evolving information and communication technology. India's cyber laws have indeed helped flourish basic E-commerce and E-governance. India's national cybersecurity strategy has enacted a number of statutes and constituted regulating bodies in order to develop a 'cyber-secure nation' for a $5 trillion economy. In order to support the cyber governance structure of a nation, both government and private sector should find suitable mix of solutions in critical ICT systems to ensure cyber security. In the latest developments for ensuring cyber security, U.S. President Joe Biden signed two cybersecurity bills on June 21, 2022. Rep. Joe Neguse (D-Colo.) introduced the bills and addressed that there is an urgent need to increase support to the state government and local entities so that they can strengthen their systems and better defend themselves from harmful cyberattacks. The proposed bills aims 'to strengthen the federal cyber workforce and foster collaboration across all levels of government (state as well as local) in order to promote coordination on cyber security issues. It is aimed to improve coordination between Infrastructure Security Agency (CISA) and state, local, tribal and territorial governments. Under the new law, these bodies will be able to share security tools, procedures and information easily'.

"The university curriculum must also emphasize cybersecurity as a high-decibel awareness subject", said Ajeet Bajpai, Director-General of the National Critical Infrastructure Protection Centre. There is also an urgent need of scientific and technical professional training of lawyers in India. The major concern for Cyber threat is that it can be in any form, may be as an intentional cyber-attack, or as a result of unintentional "mistake" or may be even due to natural disasters. Therefore particular problem should have specific approach in the framework of cyber laws. It is interesting to know that the term cybercrime has not been defined in any statute or rulebook. It is in fact a slang for anything that is related to computers, internet, virtual reality or information technology.

<u>**Information Technology Act (IT Act) 2000**</u> is the first cyber law approved by the Indian Parliament to provide for a statutory remedy for cybercrimes was the. IT Act's scope has now been broadened to include all the latest communication devices. It is applicable to the entire legal framework of India and directs entire investigation process for adjudicating cybercrimes. Its scope has now been broadened to include all the latest communication devices. The first cyber law of India is IT Act 2000 which provided provisions to deal with cybercrimes but related to only E-commerce. The jurisdiction in the context of the internet under it was unclear. Also the issue of territorial jurisdiction was not satisfactorily addressed in the initial IT Act (2000). In the year 2008, IT Act (amendment) 2008 was passed where it outlined the definition and punishment of Cybercrime and consequently the territorial jurisdiction of cyber law was also extended.

<u>**Indian Penal Code (IPC) 1860**</u> is the official criminal code of India and the law enforcement agencies can use various sections of IPC to provide legal remedy to the cyber aggrieved, such as the sections 292, 354C, 354D, 379, 420, 463, 465, 468, 471 etc. IPC has several sections that can be applied by law enforcement agencies to deal with cybercrime, if the sections under IT Act are not sufficient to cover specific cybercrimes. Below such some relevant IPC sections are discussed.

Section 292: This section of IPC includes crimes involving sale of obscene materials. It also addresses sexually explicit acts or exploitation of children in published form or transmitted electronically. The punishment is upto 5 years imprisonment and upto Rs. 5000 fine.

Section 354C: This section of IPC includes crimes involving taking or publishing pictures of private parts of any woman or watching a woman's sexual actions (voyeurism) without her consent. Though section 66E of IT Act and section 292 of IPC are broad enough to include offences of an equivalent nature. The punishment for first-time offenders is upto 3 years imprisonment and for second-time offenders is upto 7 years imprisonment along with fine in both cases.

Section 354D: This section of IPC includes crimes involving all types of stalking. Cyberstalking is the tracking of a woman using internet and electronic means without her consent. The punishment for first-time offenders is upto 3 years imprisonment and for second-time offenders is upto 5 years imprisonment along with fine in both cases.

Section 379: This section of IPC includes crimes involving stolen data, stolen electronic devices or computers. The punishment for such theft can be up to three years and fine.

Section 420: This section of IPC includes crimes involving cheating and dishonesty. The punishment is 7 years imprisonment and fine. The cyber feature of this section includes cyber frauds such as creating fake websites, password theft etc.

Section 463: This section of IPC includes crime involving electronically preparing false documents or records, email spoofing. The punishment is 7 years imprisonment and fine and fine.

Section 465: This section of IPC includes crime involving forgery. The punishment is ranging upto 2 years imprisonment and fine.

Section 468: This section of IPC includes crime involving fraud committed with the intention of cheating. The punishment is 7 years imprisonment and fine.

IT, ACT, and IPC: Overlapping Provisions

Indian cyber security laws are a half-empty arsenal to fight cybercrimes. It is important to note that cyber criminals use IPC provisions as an easy avenue to escape the cyber offences. The term "Cyber" should not be the sufficient reason for the differential treatment of an offence. Such as a theft is theft, may it be of physical property or digital property.

Furthermore there has been an overlapping of the provisions of IT Act and IPC for cybercrime. Certain offences are bailable and/or compoundable and/or cognizable under IT Act but not under IPC and vice versa. As highlighted in an article by Vinod Joseph and Deeya Ray (10 February 2020, Mondaq) "Hacking and Data Theft: Sections 43 and 66 of the IT Act penalize a number of activities ranging from hacking into a computer network, data theft, introducing and spreading viruses through computer networks, damaging computers or computer networks or computer programmes, disrupting any computer or computer system or computer network, denying an authorized person access to a computer or computer network, damaging or destroying information residing in a computer etc. The maximum punishment for the above offences is imprisonment of up to 3 (three) years or a fine or Rs. 5,00,000 (Rupees five lac) or both if the conduct involves hacking or data theft, offences under sections 43 and 66 of the IT Act are bailable and compoundable, whereas offences under Section 378 of the IPC (intending to take dishonestly any movable property out of the possession of any person without that person's consent) are not bailable and offences under Section 425 of the IPC (Mischief) are not compoundable.

Additionally, if the offence was the receipt of stolen property, the offence under section 66B of the IT Act was bailable while the offence under Section 411 of the IPC was not.

In the same manner, in respect of the offence of identity theft and cheating by impersonation, the offences are compoundable and bailable under sections 66C and 66D of the IT Act, whereas the offences under Sections 463, 465, and 468 of the IPC are not compoundable and the offences under sections 468 and 420 of the IPC are not bailable."

Indian Computer Emergency Response Team (CERT-In) is the nodal agency in India to deal with cyber security threats. CERT-In is an office within the <u>Ministry of Electronics and Information Technology</u> of the Government of India operational since January, 2004 by the Government of India under Information Technology Act, 2000 under Section-70B, under the Ministry of Communications and Information Technology to help strengthen security-related defense of the Indian Internet domain. (CERT-In) issues directives and advisories regarding latest cyber threats and vulnerabilities related to information security practices, procedure, response, reporting and prevention of cyber incidents. A number of advisories have been issued by the CERT-In till date for all types of individual as well as corporate internet users. CERT-In helps in the collection, analysis and dissemination of cyber incidents data, issues forecasts and alerts for cyber security issues, coordinates cyber incident response activities of related agencies and provides emergency measures for handling cybercrime incidents in order to minimize cybercrime and create awareness on safe usage of digital technology.

Ministry of Electronics & Information Technology (MeitY): Another executive agency of Government of India for cyber governance is the **Ministry of Electronics & Information Technology (MeitY)** which was carved out of the Ministry of Communications and Information Technology on 19 July 2016 as a standalone ministerial agency responsible for IT policy, strategy and development of the electronics industry to generate cyber security awareness. (Wiki). MeitY conducts programs, prints books, broadcasts videos and develops online materials to be disseminated through portals like www.infosecawareness.in and www.csk.gov.in for internet users especially parents and children relating to cyber security. It covers two Acts: Information Technology Act 2000, Right to Information Act as well as MeitY Business Rules. The objectives set out by MeitY are as follows (https://www.meity.gov.in/):

Table 4. IT ACT V/S IPC (Com: Compoundable, Bail: Bailable, Cog: Cognizable)

IT Act	Offence	Sentence	IPC	Offence	Sentence
43 (h) read with Sec 66 (Com, Bail)	Hacking and Data theft	3 yrs jail, Rs 50 lakh fine	378, 379 & 424 (Non-Bail, Comp)	Theft of movable property; (424) conceal or remove property, also applies to data theft	3 yrs jail (378), 2 yrs jail (424); and fine
65 (Com, Bail)	Tampering	3 yrs jail, Rs 1 lakh fine	408 & 409 (Non-Com, Non-Bail)	Breach of Trust (by Clerk, 408)	7 yrs jail and fine (408); 10 yrs jail (409)
66-B (Com, Bail)	Receipt of Stolen Property	3 yrs jail and Rs 1 lakh fine	411 (Non-Bail)	Receipt of Stolen Property	3 yrs jail and any amount of fine
66-C & D (Com, Bail)	Identity theft or Impersonation; Impersonation by Computer (66-D)	3 yrs jail and Rs 1 lakh fine	419 (Com)	Cheating by Impersonation	3 yrs jail and fine
66-E (Com, Bail)	Violation of Privacy	3 yrs jail, Rs 2 lakh fine (Both gender)	425 & 426 (Com, Non-Cog)	Mischief	3 months jail and fine
66-F (Com, Bail)	Cyber Terrorism				
67 (Non-Bail)	Online Child pornography or child sexually abusive material (CSAM)	3 yrs jail (5 to 7 yrs for extended term) and a fine of Rs. 5 lakh upto 10 lakh	292, 294 and 509 (Comp, Bail)	Obscenity in offline form (justice only for women); Insulting women (509)	2 yr jail upto 5 yrs and/or fine of Rs 2000 upto Rs 5000
69A	Government can choose to take down content from the Internet				
Offences under IPC like Sec 420 (Cheating), 463, 465 & 468 (Forgery), 469 (Harming Reputation) are Non-Bail, Non-Com, Non-Cog and have 7 yrs jail and fine					

- e-Government: Providing e-infrastructure for delivery of e-services
- e-Industry: Promotion of electronics hardware manufacturing and IT-ITeS industry
- e-Innovation / R&D: Implementation of R&D Framework - Enabling creation of Innovation/ R&D Infrastructure in emerging areas of ICT&E/Establishment of mechanism for R&D translation
- e-Learning: Providing support for development of e-Skills and Knowledge network
- e-Security: Securing India's cyber space
- e-Inclusion: Promoting the use of ICT for more inclusive growth
- Internet Governance: Enhancing India's role in Global Platforms of Internet Governance.

Indian government has also constituted various non-judicial bodies, agencies and infrastructure for the efficient and effective prevention, detection, investigation and prosecution of cybercrime. In July 2013, Indian government published National Cyber Security Policy (NCSP), however it proved to be only providing the guidelines for the standard operating procedure.

National Cybersecurity Framework (NCFS) approved by National Institute of Standards and Technology (NIST) in conjunction with ISO/IEC 27001 that is the world's most credible global certification body for information security management systems (ISMS) and their requirements (iso.org). These standards keeps IT security, cybersecurity and privacy protection safe. This framework includes guidelines, standards, directives, and best practices for ensuring cybersecurity in the organizations, companies as well as across the entire supply chain.

Indian Cyber Crime Coordination Centre (I4C): I4C under the Ministry of Home Affairs provides a robust coordinated framework and eco-system to handle cybercrime through various centre, units, teams, portals and laboratories so as to empower all States and Union Territories (UTs) as well as the Law Enforcement Agencies (LEAs). These bodies have been constituted at key regions of India under the I4C in order to solve the issues of jurisdictional complexity in the vast landscape of India.

Figure 6. I4C framework
Source: Cyber Pravah Newsletter of I4C

Among the various components of I4C as mentioned above, the most important and widely accessible to general public is the **National Cyber Crime Reporting Portal** launched by the Indian Government under the IP address (www.cybercrime.gov.in) to enable the general public to report incidents related to all types of cybercrimes, especially the cybercrimes against women and children. This portal is an initiative of the Government of India to help facilitate the complainants/ victims to online report about cybercrime with a special focus on cybercrimes against women and children, the vulnerable section of the society. A toll-free helpline number 1930 has also been operationalized for lodging on-call complaints and online assistance is provided in lodging online cyber complaints. Complaints reported on this portal are dealt by Law Enforcement Agencies (LEAs) for prompt action. Another wing of National Cyber Crime Reporting Portal is the Citizen Financial Cyber Fraud Reporting and Management System launched on 01 April, 2021, integrates Law Enforcement Agencies (LEAs), banks and financial Intermediaries for immediate reporting of financial frauds. It has got the active support and cooperation from the Reserve Bank of India (RBI), all major banks in India, Payment Banks, Wallets and Online Merchants to help stop siphoning off fund by the cyber fraudsters.

The IT (Information Technology) Rules, 2021

The Central Government of India along with MeitY (Ministry of Electronics and Information Technology) and MIB (Ministry of Information and Broadcasting) have developed the Information Technology Rules, 2021. The major highlights of these rules/guidelines are:

- **The Information Technology (Guidelines for Intermediaries and Digital Media Ethics Code) Rules, 2021:** These rules govern the role of social media intermediaries to prevent the transmission of harmful content on internet and observe due diligence while discharging their duties. An 'intermediary' has been defined in Section 2(w) of the Act as "any person who on behalf of another person receives, stores or transmits that record or provides any service with respect to that record and includes telecom service providers, web-housing service providers, search engines, online payment sites, online auction sites, online market places and cyber cafes".
- **The Information Technology (Reasonable Security Practices and Procedures and Sensitive Personal Data or Information) Rules, 2011:** Organizations holding individuals' sensitive personal information must maintain certain specified security standards.
- **The Information Technology (Guidelines for Cyber Cafe) Rules, 2011:** Cybercafés must register and maintain records of users' identities and their internet usage.
- **The Information Technology (Electronic Service Delivery) Rules, 2011:** These rules govern the delivery of certain services, such as applications, certificates, and licenses, by electronic means.
- **Information Technology (The Indian Computer Emergency Response Team and Manner of Performing Functions and Duties) Rules, 2013 (the CERT-In Rules):** A 24-hour cybersecurity incident response helpdesk must be operational at all times to report cybersecurity incidents by the individuals, organisations and companies.

Besides the law enacted and governing bodies constituted, Indian authorities frequently releases guidelines that highlight best practices for securing applications, infrastructure and compliance crimes in a comprehensive and coordinated manner. Some of these recent initiatives are:

Cyber Surakshit Bharat: In order to create a robust cybersecurity ecosystem in India, Ministry of Electronics and Information Technology (MeitY) has launched National E-Government Division (NeGD) sponsored a Cyber Surakshit Bharat initiative which aligns the government's vision for a 'Digital India' with the cyber secure infrastructure.

Cyber Swachhta Kendra (Botnet Cleaning and Malware Analysis Centre): Section 70B of the IT Act, 2000 authorizes CERT-In to operate and install these centres under the Ministry of Electronics and Information Technology (MeitY) which detects botnet infections and enables end-users to clean their systems and secure their systems so as to prevent future infections thereby creating secure cyberspace for Indian users.

CISO: A skilled information security leader known as a Chief Information Security Officer (CISO) is required in all government agencies who can timely identify, report and document any cyber security threat. These officers also assist and train other non-technical individuals for an added support system.

Website Audit: Government of India has appointed approximately 90 security auditing organizations to audit information security, online applications and websites amid the increasing number of malicious attacks such as government website hacking, email phishing, and data theft.

Drills & Training: cybersecurity mock drills assess and prepare system administrators and CISOs for cyber-attacks. Finance, telecommunications, power and defense, among other major industries have benefitted from such initiatives of CERT-In according to MeitY. Furthermore, around 265 organizations from several states and sectors have organized and conducted regular training programs and workshops since October 2019, about 19 training sessions have already taken place with more than 515 public as well as private participants.

Other than that individuals and businesses around the world are taking up cybersecurity courses on their own initiatives to keep themselves away cyber mishaps.

Ministry of Home Affairs (MHA) provides financial assistance to all the States & UTs under the Cyber Crime Prevention against Women & Children (CCPWC) scheme for training, hiring of cyber experts and junior cyber consultants; for setting up of cyber forensic-cum-training laboratories and improving cyber forensic facilities; issuance of alerts and advisories for spreading awareness about cybercrimes in offline and online format so as to reach the majority of masses; and capacity building of law enforcement agencies (LEA) such as judicial officers, personnel and prosecutors.

Reserve Bank of India (RBI), CERT-In and Digital India jointly carry out a cyber security awareness campaign called 'Beware and Be Aware of Financial Frauds' through Digital India Platform.

CONCLUSION

Internet has become an integral part of our daily life. It has unprecedentedly transformed the way we play games, do shopping, share information, communicate and engage with friends & family. In this digital environment, there has been a phenomenal increase in use of softwares, financial transactions, e-commerce platforms, information dissemination, and online stock trading and so has cybercrimes where computer is either used target or/and tool to commit unlawful activities. Interestingly Cybercrime is a multi-billion dollar problem which has led to a multi-dimensional impact on all the areas of an economy. It is interestingly very easy to commit but very difficult to detect. Due to the fast advancement of information and communication technology, the list of cybercrime is long and updating such as from unauthorized access, denial of service attacks and hacking to Trojan attacks, virus and worm attacks, cyber vandalism, cyber violence, cyber rape and cyber terrorism. Therefore this malice needs immediate cyber law enforcement (in the form of legislatures, regulations and governance). In fact many countries have declared data protection a fundamental right.

The aim of this chapter has been to create awareness for cyber threats that technology pose at personal, societal, business and governmental levels. Subsequently to bring awareness for cyber laws among students, research scholars, working professionals, policy makers, technical community and interested individuals. The proper formation of critical infrastructure, rigorous framework, significant budget and most importantly the establishment of seamless public-private partnerships is the key for cyber security. It is important to regularly assess the implementation of cyber laws and initiatives in the field of healthcare, ecommerce, agriculture, banking and digital currency among others that will help create a more secure cyberspace.

Table 5. Summary table related to latest development of work

Summary Table Related to Latest Development of Work
Indian Penal Code (IPC) 1860
Information Technology Act (IT Act) 2000
Indian Computer Emergency Response Team (CERT-In) (2004)
Ministry of Electronics & Information Technology (MeitY) (2016)
National Cybersecurity Framework (NCFS)
Indian Cyber Crime Coordination Centre (I4C)
National Cyber Crime Reporting Portal
the Citizen Financial Cyber Fraud Reporting and Management System (2021)
The IT (Information Technology) Rules, 2021
The Information Technology (Guidelines for Intermediaries and Digital Media Ethics Code) Rules, 2021
The Information Technology (Reasonable Security Practices and Procedures and Sensitive Personal Data or Information) Rules, 2011
The Information Technology (Guidelines for Cyber Cafe) Rules, 2011
The Information Technology (Electronic Service Delivery) Rules, 2011
Information Technology (The Indian Computer Emergency Response Team and Manner of Performing Functions and Duties) Rules, 2013 (the CERT-In Rules)
Cyber Surakshit Bharat
Cyber Swachhta Kendra (Botnet Cleaning and Malware Analysis Centre)
Cyber Crime Prevention against Women & Children (CCPWC) scheme

ACKNOWLEDGMENT

This study is supported via funding from Prince Sattam Bin Abdulaziz University project number (PSAU/2023/R/1444).

REFERENCES

Aaysha, F. (2020). *An Effective Data Privacy Model for Cloud Environment*. OneTrust.

Alnahari, W., & Quasim, M. T. (2021, July). Privacy concerns, IoT devices and attacks in smart cities. In *2021 International Congress of Advanced Technology and Engineering (ICOTEN)* (pp. 1-5). IEEE. 10.1109/ICOTEN52080.2021.9493559

AlShahrani, B. M. M. (2021). Classification of cyber-attack using Adaboost regression classifier and securing the network. [TURCOMAT]. *Turkish Journal of Computer and Mathematics Education, 12*(10), 1215–1223.

ChhabraG.ChhabraK. (2014). A Study on Emerging Issue on Cyber Law. doi:10.13140/RG.2.1.3007.8568

Eichensehr, K. (2014-15). E., The Cyber-Law of Nations, 103. *Geological Journal, 317*. https://heinonline.org/HOL/LandingPage?handle=hein.journals/glj103&div=13&id=&page=

Greengard, S. (2010, December). The New Face of War. [ACM.]. *Communications of the ACM, 53*(12), 20–22. doi:10.1145/1859204.1859212

Dewani, N., Khan, Z., Agarwal, A., Sharma, M., & Khan, S. (2022). *Handbook of Research on Cyber Law, Data Protection, and Privacy*. IGI Global.

Khan, M. Z., Husain, M. S., & Shoaib, M. (2020). *Introduction to email, web, and message forensics. Critical Concepts, Standards, and Techniques in Cyber Forensics*. IGI Global.

Marcella, A. J. (Ed.). (2022). *Cyber Forensics: Examining Emerging and Hybrid Technologies*. CRC Press.

Mishra, A., Khan, M. H., Khan, W., Khan, M. Z., & Srivastava, N. K. (2022). A Comparative Study on Data Mining Approach Using Machine Learning Techniques: Prediction Perspective. *Pervasive Healthcare: A Compendium of Critical Factors for Success*, 153-165.

Office of Joe Neguse. (2022, May 17). *Neguse, Peters state and local government cybersecurity bill heads to president's desk for signature*. Office of Jow Neguse. https://neguse.house.gov/media/press-releases/neguse-peters-state-and-local-government-cybersecurity-bill-heads-to-presidents-desk-for-signature

Patel, R. S. & Kathiriya, D. (2013). Evolution of Cybercrimes in India. *International Journal of Emerging Trends & Technology in Computer Science, 2*(4).

Quasim, M. T., & Al Hawi, A. N. (2022). *Mechanisms of System Penetration: Concepts, Attack Methods, and Defense Strategies (No. 9197)*. EasyChair.

Sammons, J., & Cross, M. (2017). *Cybercrime, The Basics of Cyber Safety*. Syngress. https://www.sciencedirect.com/science/article/pii/B978012416650900005X, doi:10.1016/B978-0-12-416650-9.00005-X

Shinder, L., & Cross, M. (2008). *The Evolution of Cybercrime, Scene of the Cybercrime* (2nd ed.). Syngress. https://www.sciencedirect.com/science/article/pii/B9781597492768000029, doi:10.1016/B978-1-59749-276-8.00002-9

Tripathi, M. M., Haroon, M., Khan, Z., & Husain, M. S. (2022). Security in Digital Healthcare System. *Pervasive Healthcare: A Compendium of Critical Factors for Success*, 217-231.

Yadav, A., & Kumar, V. (2021). A Study on Legislative Responses of Data Protection in India. *Ignited Minds Journals, 18*(7), 272 – 278. doi: (https://ignited.in/I/a/306067) doi:10.29070/JASRAE

Compilation of References

Aaysha, F. (2020). *An Effective Data Privacy Model for Cloud Environment*. OneTrust.

Abdelsalam, M., Krishnan, R., & Sandhu, R. (2017). Clustering-based IaaS cloud monitoring. *Proc. IEEE 10th Int. Conf. Cloud Comput. (CLOUD)*, (pp. 672-679). IEEE. 10.1109/CLOUD.2017.90

Adu, E., Mills, A., & Todorova, N. (2021). Factors influencing individuals' personal health information privacy concerns. A study in Ghana. *Information Technology for Development*, 27(2), 208–234. doi:10.1080/02681102.2020.1806018

Afaq, S. A., Husain, M. S., Bello, A., & Sadia, H. (n.d.). A Critical Analysis of Cyber Threats and Their Global Impact. In *Computational Intelligent Security in Wireless Communications* (pp. 201–220). CRC Press. doi:10.1201/9781003323426-12

Ahmad, F., & Khan, M. Z. (2020). Forensic Case Studies. In Critical Concepts, Standards, and Techniques in Cyber Forensics (pp. 248-264). IGI Global. doi:10.4018/978-1-7998-1558-7.ch015

Ahmed, A. (2015). Sharing is Caring: Online Self-disclosure, Offline Social Support, and Social Network Site Usage in the UAE. *Contemporary Review of the Middle East*, 2(3), 192–219. doi:10.1177/2347798915601574

Akram, Z., Khan, A. G., Akram, U., Ahmad, S., & Song, L. J. (2022). A contemporary view of interpersonal aggression and cyberbullying through ICT: Multilevel insights from LMX differentiation. *Internet Research*, 32(5), 1700–1724. doi:10.1108/INTR-11-2020-0659

Akter, S., Uddin, M. R., Sajib, S., Lee, W. J. T., Michael, K., & Hossain, M. A. (2022). Reconceptualizing cybersecurity awareness capability in the data-driven digital economy. *Annals of Operations Research*. Advance online publication. doi:10.100710479-022-04844-8 PMID:35935743

Al Jawaheri, H., Al Sabah, M., Boshmaf, Y., & Erbad, A. (2020). Deanonymizing Tor hidden service users through Bitcoin transactions analysis. *Computers & Security*, 89, 101684. doi:10.1016/j.cose.2019.101684

Al Mutawa, N., Bryce, J., Franqueira, V. N. L., & Marrington, A. (2015). Behavioural evidence analysis applied to digital forensics: an empirical analysis of child pornography cases using P2P networks. *2015 10th International Conference on Availability, Reliability and Security*, (pp. 293–302). IEEE.

Alahmadi, A. N., Rehman, S. U., Alhazmi, H. S., Glynn, D. G., Shoaib, H., & Solé, P. (2022). Cyber-Security Threats and Side-Channel Attacks for Digital Agriculture. *Sensors (Basel)*, 22(9), 3520. doi:10.339022093520 PMID:35591211

Alazab, M., Venkatraman, S., & Watters, P. (2009, June). Digital forensic techniques for static analysis of NTFS images. In *Proceedings of ICIT2009, Fourth International Conference on Information Technology*. IEEE Xplore.

Alazab, M., Venkatraman, S., & Watters, P. (2009). Effective digital forensic analysis of the NTFS disk image. *Ubiquitous Computing and Communication Journal*, 4(1), 551–558.

Albrecht, C., Duffin, K. M., Hawkins, S., & Morales Rocha, V. M. (2019). The use of cryptocurrencies in the money laundering process. *Journal of Money Laundering Control*, *22*(2), 210–216. doi:10.1108/JMLC-12-2017-0074

Aldridge, J., & Decary-Hétu, D. (2016). Cryptomarkets and the future of illicit drug markets. *The Internet and Drug Markets*, 23–32.

Alemany, J., Del Val, E., & García-Fornes, A. (2021). Who should I grant access to my post? Identifying the most suitable privacy decisions on online social networks. *Internet Research*, *31*(4), 1290–1317. doi:10.1108/INTR-03-2020-0128

Alemian, T. I. (2019). *Terrorists' Propaganda and the Use of Media: Case Study of the Islamic State of Iraq and Syria*. US Army Command and General Staff College Fort Leavenworth United States.

Ali, A. (2022, September 19). The Rise Of Cyberbullying—How To Address Harassment In The Remote Workforce. *Allwork.Space*. https://allwork.space/2022/09/the-rise-of-cyberbullying-how-to-address-harassment-in-the-remote-workforce

Ali, A. (2023). *Decentralised Escrow Protocol that Facilitates Secure Transactions between Trustless Parties*. Social Science Research Network.

Alkhalil, Z., Hewage, C., Nawaf, L., & Khan, I. (2021). Phishing Attacks: A Recent Comprehensive Study and a New Anatomy. *Frontiers of Computer Science*, *3*, 563060. doi:10.3389/fcomp.2021.563060

AlKhatib, B., & Basheer, R. (2019). Crawling the Dark Web: A Conceptual Perspective, Challenges and Implementation. *J. Digit. Inf. Manag.*, *17*(2), 51. doi:10.6025/jdim/2019/17/2/51-60

Alkis, A., & Kose, T. (2022). Privacy concerns in consumer E-commerce activities and response to social media advertising: Empirical evidence from Europe. *Computers in Human Behavior*, *137*, 107412. doi:10.1016/j.chb.2022.107412

Alnabulsi, H., & Islam, R. (2018). Identification of illegal forum activities inside the dark net. *2018 International Conference on Machine Learning and Data Engineering (ICMLDE)*, (pp. 22–29). IEEE. 10.1109/iCMLDE.2018.00015

Alnahari, W., & Quasim, M. T. (2021, July). Privacy concerns, IoT devices and attacks in smart cities. In *2021 International Congress of Advanced Technology and Engineering (ICOTEN)* (pp. 1-5). IEEE. 10.1109/ICOTEN52080.2021.9493559

Alouffi, B., Hasnain, M., Alharbi, A., Alosaimi, W., Alyami, H., & Ayaz, M. (2021). *A Systematic Literature Review on Cloud Computing Security: Threats and Mitigation Strategies* (Vol. 9). IEEE Access., doi:10.1109/ACCESS.2021.3073203

Alsamhi, S. H., Ma, O., Ansari, M. S., & Almalki, F. A. (2019). Survey on collaborative smart drones and internet of things for improving smartness of smart cities. *IEEE Access : Practical Innovations, Open Solutions*, *7*, 128125–128152. doi:10.1109/ACCESS.2019.2934998

AlShahrani, B. M. M. (2021). Classification of cyber-attack using Adaboost regression classifier and securing the network. [TURCOMAT]. *Turkish Journal of Computer and Mathematics Education*, *12*(10), 1215–1223.

Alvino, A., & Marino, S. (2017, June). Remote sensing for irrigation of horticultural crops. *Horticulturae*, *3*(2), 40. doi:10.3390/horticulturae3020040

Alwaheidi, M. K. S., & Islam, S. (2022). Data-Driven Threat Analysis for Ensuring Security in Cloud Enabled Systems. *Sensors (Basel)*, *22*(15), 5726. doi:10.339022155726 PMID:35957281

Amon, M., Necaise, A., Kartvelishvili, N., Williams, A., Solihin, Y., & Kapadia, A. (2023). Modeling User Characteristics Associated with Interdependent Privacy Perceptions on Social Media. *ACM Transactions on Computer-Human Interaction*, *30*(3), 1–15. doi:10.1145/3577014

Ampong, G., Mensah, A., Adu, A., Addae, J., Omoregie, O., & Ofori, K. (2018). Examining Self-Disclosure on Social Networking Sites: A Flow Theory and Privacy Perspective. *Behavioral Sciences (Basel, Switzerland)*, *8*(6), 58–66. doi:10.3390/bs8060058 PMID:29882801

Anasori, E., Bayighomog, S. W., & Tanova, C. (2020). Workplace bullying, psychological distress, resilience, mindfulness, and emotional exhaustion. *Service Industries Journal*, *40*(1–2), 65–89. doi:10.1080/02642069.2019.1589456

Anjum, A., Kaur, D., Kondapalli, S., Hussain, M. A., Begum, A. U., Hassen, S. M., Boush, A., Sharafeldin, M., Benjeed, A. O. S., & Osman Abdalraheem, D. (2021). A Mysterious and Darkside of The Darknet: A Qualitative Study. *Webology, 18*(4).

Arasteh, H. Hosseinnezhad, V., Loia, V., Tommasetti, A., Troisi, O., Shafie-Khah, M., & Siano, P. (2016). Iot-based smart cities: A survey. In *EEEIC 2016 - International Conference on Environment and Electrical Engineering*. IEEE.

Ardagna, D. (2015). Cloud and Multi-cloud Computing: Current Challenges and Future Applications. *IEEE/ACM 7th International Workshop on Principles of Engineering Service-Oriented and Cloud Systems*, pp. 1-2. 10.1109/PESOS.2015.8

Arica, R., Cobanoglu, C., Cakir, O., Corbaci, A., Hsu, M., & Della Corte, V. (2022). Travel experience sharing on social media: Effects of the importance attached to content sharing and what factors inhibit and facilitate it. *International Journal of Contemporary Hospitality Management*, *34*(4), 1566–1586. doi:10.1108/IJCHM-01-2021-0046

Arpaci, I. (2020). What drives students' online self-disclosure behaviour on social media? A hybrid SEM and artificial intelligence approach. *International Journal of Mobile Communications*, *18*(2), 229–241. doi:10.1504/IJMC.2020.105847

Attaallah, A., Alsuhabi, H., Shukla, S., Kumar, R., Gupta, B. K., & Khan, R. A. (2022). Analyzing the Big Data Security Through a Unified Decision-Making Approach. *Intelligent Automation & Soft Computing, 32*(2).

Azmandian, F., Moffie, M., Alshawabkeh, M., Dy, J., Aslam, J., & Kaeli, D. (2011, July). Virtual machine monitor-based lightweight intrusion detection. *Operating Systems Review*, *45*(2), 38–53. doi:10.1145/2007183.2007189

Badrinarayanan, V., Kendall, A., & Cipolla, R. (2017). Segnet: A deep convolutional encoder-decoder architecture for image segmentation. *IEEE Transactions on Pattern Analysis and Machine Intelligence*, *39*(12), 2481–2495. doi:10.1109/TPAMI.2016.2644615 PMID:28060704

Baker, D. (2016). *Online sex slaves: The internet's powerful role in sex trafficking*. CORE.

Bandara, R., Fernando, M., & Akter, S. (2020). Explicating the privacy paradox: A qualitative inquiry of online shopping consumers. *Journal of Retailing and Consumer Services*, *52*(1), 101947. doi:10.1016/j.jretconser.2019.101947

Barefoot, K., Curtis, D., & Jolliff, W. (2018). *Nicholson, Jessica R. Omohundro, R*. Defining and Measuring the Digital Economy. US Department of Commerce Bureau of Economic Analysis., https://www.tandfonline.com/doi/full/10.1081/ERC-200027380

Barreto, L., & Amaral, A. (2018). Smart farming: Cyber security challenges. In *2018 International Conference on Intelligent Systems (IS)*, (pp. 870–876). IEEE. 10.1109/IS.2018.8710531

Barreto, L., & Amaral, A. (2018). Smart farming: Cyber security challenges. In *International Conference on Intelligent Systems (IS)* (pp. 870–876). IEEE. https://ieeexplore.ieee.org/abstract/document/8710531

Baruh, L., Secinti, E., & Cemalcilar, Z. (2017). Online Privacy Concerns and Privacy Management: A Meta-Analytical Review. *Journal of Communication*, *67*(1), 26–53. doi:10.1111/jcom.12276

Belkasoft. (n.d.). *Accelerate Your DFIR Investigation*. Belkasoft. https://belkasoft.com/

Benavides, E., Fuertes, W., Sanchez, S., & Sanchez, M. (2020). *Classification of phishing attack solutions by employing deep learning techniques: a systematic literature review, Developments and advances in defence and security*. Springer Singapore.

Bendovschi, A. (2015). Cyber-Attacks – Trends, Patterns and Security Countermeasures. *Procedia Economics and Finance*, *28*, 24–31. doi:10.1016/S2212-5671(15)01077-1

Blackhart, G., Hernandez, D., Wilson, E., & Hance, M. (2021). The Impact of Rejection Sensitivity on Self-Disclosure Within the Context of Online Dating. *Cyberpsychology, Behavior, and Social Networking*, *24*(10), 690–694. Advance online publication. doi:10.1089/cyber.2020.0257 PMID:33606556

Blender, T., Buchner, T., Fernandez, B., Pichlmaier, B., & Schlegel, C. Managing a mobile agricultural robot swarm for a seeding task. In *Proceedings of the IECON 2016-42nd Annual Conference of the IEEE Industrial Electronics Society*, (pp. 6879–6886). IEEE. 10.1109/IECON.2016.7793638

Boghosian, H. (2021). *"I Have Nothing to Hide": And 20 Other Myths About Surveillance and Privacy*. Beacon Press.

Böhme, R., Christin, N., Edelman, B., & Moore, T. (2015). Bitcoin: Economics, technology, and governance. *The Journal of Economic Perspectives*, *29*(2), 213–238. doi:10.1257/jep.29.2.213

Botha, J., & Pieterse, H. (2020). Fake news and deepfakes: A dangerous threat for 21st-century information security. In *ICCWS 2020 15th International Conference on Cyber Warfare and Security*. Academic Conferences and publishing limited.

Bowcut, S. (2021). Cybersecurity in the food and agriculture industry. *Cybersecurity Guide, 2021*. Cybersecurity Guide. https://cybersecurityguide.org/industries/food-and-agriculture/

Bradley, L. (2022, October 17). *Tackling workplace bullying in the remote era*. Employee Management Ltd. https://employeemanagement.co.uk/tackling-workplace-bullying-in-the-remote-era/

BRIS. A. LE, & ASRI, W. EL. (2016). State of Cybersecurity & Cyber Threats in Healthcare Organizations. *Dissertation*, 2005–2013. https://www.americanbar.org/content/dam/aba/publications/books/healthcare_data_breaches.authcheckdam.pdf

Brown, A. (2020). "Should I Stay or Should I Leave?": Exploring (Dis)continued Facebook Use After the Cambridge Analytica Scandal. *Social Media + Society*, *6*(1), 2056305120913884. doi:10.1177/2056305120913884

Butterfield, A., & Ngondi, G. E. (Eds.). (21 January 2016). spoofing. Oxford Reference. Oxford University Press. . doi:10.1093/acref/9780199688975.001.0001

Cain, J., & Imre, I. (2022). Everybody wants some: Collection and control of personal information, privacy concerns, and social media use. *New Media & Society*, *24*(12), 2705–2724. doi:10.1177/14614448211000327

Cao, J., Hu, Y., Yu, B., He, R., & Sun, Z. (2019). 3D aided duet GANs for multi-view face image synthesis. *IEEE Transactions on Information Forensics and Security*, *14*(8), 2028–2042. doi:10.1109/TIFS.2019.2891116

Carrier, B. (2005). *File system forensic analysis*. Addison-Wesley Professional.

Carvey, H. (2009). *Windows forensic analysis DVD toolkit*. Syngress.

Castillo Camacho, I., & Wang, K. (2021). A Comprehensive Review of Deep-Learning-Based Methods for Image Forensics. *Journal of Imaging*, *7*(4), 69. doi:10.3390/jimaging7040069 PMID:34460519

Catakoglu, O., Balduzzi, M., & Balzarotti, D. (2017). Attacks landscape in the dark side of the web. *Proceedings of the Symposium on Applied Computing*, (pp. 1739–1746). 10.1145/3019612.3019796

Cerruto, F., Cirillo, S., Desiato, D., Gambardella, S., & Polese, G. (2022). Social network data analysis to highlight privacy threats in sharing data. *Journal of Big Data*, *9*(1), 19. doi:10.118640537-022-00566-7

CGSecurity. (2022, November 4). *Testdisk download*. CGSecurity. https://www.cgsecurity.org/wiki/TestDisk_Download

Challenge, D. R. (2019). *Defense Advanced Research Projects Agency*.

Chandola, V., Banerjee, A., & Kumar, V. (2009). Anomaly detection: A survey. *ACM Computing Surveys*, *41*(3), 15. doi:10.1145/1541880.1541882

Chan, T. (2021). Does Self-Disclosure on Social Networking Sites Enhance Well-Being? The Role of Social Anxiety, Online Disinhibition, and Psychological Stress. In Z. W. Y. Lee, T. K. H. Chan, & C. M. K. Cheung (Eds.), *Information Technology in Organisations and Societies: Multidisciplinary Perspectives from AI to Technostress* (pp. 175–202). Emerald Publishing Limited. doi:10.1108/978-1-83909-812-320211007

Chertoff, M. (2017). A public policy perspective of the Dark Web. *Journal of Cyber Policy*, *2*(1), 26–38. doi:10.1080/23738871.2017.1298643

Chesney, B., & Citron, D. (2019). Deepfakes: A looming challenge for privacy, democracy, and national security. *California Law Review*, *107*, 1753.

ChhabraG.ChhabraK. (2014). A Study on Emerging Issue on Cyber Law. doi:10.13140/RG.2.1.3007.8568

Chitturi, A. K., & Swarnalatha, P. (2020). *Exploration of Various Cloud Security Challenges and Threats. Soft Computing for Problem Solving*. Springer., doi:10.1007/978-981-15-0184-5_76

Choi, S. (2023). Privacy Literacy on Social Media: Its Predictors and Outcomes. *International Journal of Human-Computer Interaction*, *39*(1), 217–232. doi:10.1080/10447318.2022.2041892

Cloud Security Alliance. (2017). *Security Guidance for Critical Areas of Focus in Cloud Computing v4.0*. Cloud Security Alliance. https://cloudsecurityalliance.org/artifacts/security-guidance-v4/

Cooper, C. (2015). Cybersecurity in food and agriculture. *Protecting Our Future*, *2*, 2015.

Cottrill, C., Jacobs, N., Markovic, M., & Edwards, P. (2020). Sensing the City: Designing for Privacy and Trust in the Internet of Things. *Sustainable Cities and Society*, *63*(1), 102453. doi:10.1016/j.scs.2020.102453

Cupp, O. S., Walker, D. E. II, & Hillison, J. (2004). Agroterrorism in the us: Key security challenge for the 21st century. *Biosecurity and Bioterrorism*, *2*(2), 97–105. doi:10.1089/153871304323146397 PMID:15225403

Cybersecurity in Food Industry. (n.d.). *Just Food*. https://www.just-food.com/cybersecurity-in-food-industry/

Czakert, J. P., Reif, J., Glazer, S., & Berger, R. (2021). Adaptation and Psychometric Cross-Cultural Validation of a Workplace Cyberbullying Questionnaire in Spain and Germany. *Cyberpsychology, Behavior, and Social Networking*, *24*(12), 831–838. doi:10.1089/cyber.2020.0856 PMID:34152860

Daradkeh, M. (2021). Analyzing Sentiments and Diffusion Characteristics of COVID-19 Vaccine Misinformation Topics in Social Media: A Data Analytics Framework. *International Journal of Business Analytics*, *9*(3), 55–88. doi:10.4018/IJBAN.292056

Data, M. (2018). The defense against arp spoofing attack using semistatic arp cache table. In *2018 International Conference on Sustainable Information Engineering and Technology (SIET)*, (pp. 206–210). 10.1109/SIET.2018.8693155

DeKeseredy, W., & Corsianos, M. (2015). *Violence against women in pornography*. Routledge. doi:10.4324/9781315652559

Deliu, I., Leichter, C., & Franke, K. (2018). Collecting cyber threat intelligence from hacker forums via a two-stage, hybrid process using support vector machines and latent dirichlet allocation. *2018 IEEE International Conference on Big Data (Big Data)*, (pp. 5008–5013). IEEE. 10.1109/BigData.2018.8622469

Demestichas, K., Peppes, N., & Alexakis, T. (2020). Survey on security threats in agricultural iot and smart farming. *Sensors (Basel)*, *20*(22), 1–17. doi:10.339020226458 PMID:33198160

Dewani, N., Khan, Z., Agarwal, A., Sharma, M., & Khan, S. (2022). *Handbook of Research on Cyber Law, Data Protection, and Privacy*. IGI Global.

Dhir, A., Talwar, S., Kaur, P., Budhiraja, S., & Islam, N. (2021). The dark side of social media: Stalking, online self-disclosure and problematic sleep. *International Journal of Consumer Studies*. doi:10.1111/ijcs.12659

DHS. (2018). *US Department of homeland security: threats to precision agriculture*. DHS. (https://www.dhs.gov/sites/default/files/publications/2018%20AEP_Threats_to_Precision_Agriculture.pdf)

Dienlin, T., & Trepte, S. (2015). Is the privacy paradox a relic of the past? An in-depth analysis of privacy attitudes and privacy behaviors. *European Journal of Social Psychology*, *45*(3), 285–297. doi:10.1002/ejsp.2049

Dilipraj, E. (2014). Terror in the Deep and Dark Web. *Air Power Journal*, *9*(3), 121–140.

Dong, F., Yuan, S., Ou, H., & Liu, L. (2018). New cyber threat discovery from darknet marketplaces. *2018 IEEE Conference on Big Data and Analytics (ICBDA)*, (pp. 62–67). IEEE. 10.1109/ICBDAA.2018.8629658

Drape, T., Magerkorth, N., Sen, A., Simpson, J., Seibel, M., Murch, R. S., & Duncan, S. E. (2021). Assessing the Role of Cyberbiosecurity in Agriculture: A Case Study. *Frontiers in Bioengineering and Biotechnology*, *9*(August), 1–9. doi:10.3389/fbioe.2021.737927 PMID:34490231

Dubey, K., Shams, M. Y., Sharma, S. C., Alarifi, A., Amoon, M., & Nasr, A. A. (2019). A Management System for Servicing Multi-Organizations on Community Cloud Model in Secure Cloud Environment. *IEEE Access : Practical Innovations, Open Solutions*, *7*, 159535–159546. doi:10.1109/ACCESS.2019.2950110

Duncan, S. E., Reinhard, R. R., Williams, C., Ramsey, F., Thomason, W., Lee, K., Dudek, N., Mostaghimi, S., Colbert, E., & Murch, R. (2019). Cyberbiosecurity: A new perspective on protecting U.S. food and agricultural system. *Frontiers in Bioengineering and Biotechnology*, *7*(Mar), 63. doi:10.3389/fbioe.2019.00063 PMID:30984752

Ehney, R., & Shorter, J. D. (2016a). DEEP WEB, DARK WEB, INVISIBLE WEB AND THE POST ISIS WORLD. *Issues in Information Systems*, *17*(4).

Eichensehr, K. (2014-15). E., The Cyber-Law of Nations, 103. *Geological Journal*, *317*. https://heinonline.org/HOL/LandingPage?handle=hein.journals/glj103&div=13&id=&page=

Ekshmi, A. S. (2022). Growing Concern on Healthcare Cyberattacks & Need for Cybersecurity. January. https://doi.org/ doi:10.31234/osf.io/7m4qf

ElBahrawy, A., Alessandretti, L., Rusnac, L., Goldsmith, D., Teytelboym, A., & Baronchelli, A. (2020). Collective dynamics of dark web marketplaces. *Scientific Reports*, *10*(1), 1–8. doi:10.103841598-020-74416-y PMID:33139743

Eldad, E. (2005). *Reversing: secrets of reverseengineering*. John Wiley & Sons.

Erb, K. P. (2019). IRS followed bitcoin transactions, resulting in takedown of the largest child exploitation site on the Web. *Forbes*.

Ervural, B. C., & Ervural, B. (2018). *Overview of Cyber Security in the Industry 4.0 Era*. 267–284. Springer. doi:10.1007/978-3-319-57870-5_16

Everton, S. F., & Cunningham, D. (2015). Dark network resilience in a hostile environment: Optimizing centralization and density. *Criminology, Crim. Just. L & Soc'y, 16*, 1.

Faith, B. (2022). *Take Steps Now to Protect Your Company from a Cybersecurity Attack*. Global Food Safety Resource. https://globalfoodsafetyresource.com/take-steps-now-protect-company-cybersecurity-attack/

Fan, W., Du, Z., Fernández, D., & Villagra, V. A. (2017). Enabling an anatomic view to investigate honeypot systems: A survey. *IEEE Systems Journal, 12*(4), 3906–3919. doi:10.1109/JSYST.2017.2762161

Ferry, N., Hackenheimer, T., Herrmann, F., & Tourette, A. (2019). Methodology of dark web monitoring. *2019 11th International Conference on Electronics, Computers and Artificial Intelligence (ECAI)*, 1–7.

Fessler, L. (2021, June 8). Workplace Harassment in the Age of Remote Work. *The New York Times*. https://www.nytimes.com/2021/06/08/us/workplace-harassment-remote-work.html

Fife, L., Kraus, A., & Lewis, B. (2021). *Cloud Concepts, Architecture, and Design. The Official (ISC)2 CCSP CBK Reference*. Wiley., doi:10.1002/9781119603399.ch1

Fornell, C., & Larcker, D. (1981). Evaluating structural equation models with unobservable and measurement error. *JMR, Journal of Marketing Research, 18*(1), 39–50. doi:10.1177/002224378101800104

Fountas, S., Sorensen, C. G., Tsiropoulos, Z., Cavalaris, C., Liakos, V., & Gemtos, T. (2015). Farm machinery management information system. *Computers and Electronics in Agriculture, 110*, 131–138. doi:10.1016/j.compag.2014.11.011

Foxton Forensics. (n.d.). *Google chrome history location: chrome history viewer*. Foxton Forensics. https://www.foxtonforensics.com/browser-history-examiner/chrome-history-location

Foxton Forensics. (n.d.). Microsoft edge history location: edge history viewer. Foxton Forensics. https://www.foxtonforensics.com/browser-history-examiner/microsoft-edge-history-location

Gallagher, S. (2014). Photos of an NSA "upgrade" factory show Cisco router getting implant. *Ars Technica*.

Gallagher, K., Patil, S., & Memon, N. (2017). New me: Understanding expert and non-expert perceptions and usage of the Tor anonymity network. *Thirteenth Symposium on Usable Privacy and Security (SOUPS 2017)*, (pp. 385–398). IEEE.

Gandhi, A., & Jain, S. (2020). Adversarial perturbations fool deepfake detectors. In *2020 International Joint Conference on Neural Networks (IJCNN)*. IEEE. 10.1109/IJCNN48605.2020.9207034

Gautam, B. P., Wasaki, K., Batajoo, A., Shrestha, S., & Kazuhiko, S. (2016). Multi-master replication of enhanced learning assistant system in iot cluster. In *IEEE 30th International Conference on Advanced Information Networking and Applications (AINA)*, (pp. 1006–1012). IEEE. 10.1109/AINA.2016.110

Gayathri, S., & Gowri, S. (2023). Securing medical image privacy in cloud using deep learning network. *Journal of Cloud Computing (Heidelberg, Germany), 12*(1), 40. doi:10.118613677-023-00422-w

Gehl, R. W. (2016). Power/freedom on the dark web: A digital ethnography of the Dark Web Social Network. *New Media & Society, 18*(7), 1219–1235. doi:10.1177/1461444814554900

Ghadge, A., Weib, M., Caldwell, N. D., & Wilding, R. (2020). Managing cyber risk in supply chains: A review and research agenda. *Supply Chain Management, 25*(2), 223–240. doi:10.1108/SCM-10-2018-0357

Gioia, F., & Boursier, V. (2021). Young adults' attitudes toward online self-disclosure and social connection as predictors of a preference for online social interactions: The mediating effect of relational closeness. *Atlantic Journal of Communication*, 1–17. doi:10.1080/15456870.2021.1952205

Godawatte, K., Raza, M., Murtaza, M., & Saeed, A. (2019a). Dark web along with the dark web marketing and surveillance. *2019 20th International Conference on Parallel and Distributed Computing, Applications and Technologies (PDCAT)*, 483–485.

Godawatte, K., Raza, M., Murtaza, M., & Saeed, A. (2019b). Dark web along with the dark web marketing and surveillance. *2019 20th International Conference on Parallel and Distributed Computing, Applications and Technologies (PDCAT)*, 483–485.

Godfray, H. C. J. J., Beddington, R., Crute, I. R., Haddad, L., Lawrence, D., Muir, J. F., Pretty, J., Robinson, S., Thomas, S. M., & Toulmin, C. (2010). Food security: The challenge of feeding 9 billion people. *Science*, *327*(Jan), 812–818. doi:10.1126cience.1185383 PMID:20110467

Gomez, C., Chessa, S., Fleury, A., Roussos, G., & Preuveneers, D. (2019). Internet of Things for enabling smart environments: A technology-centric perspective. *Journal of Ambient Intelligence and Smart Environments*, *11*(1), 23–43. doi:10.3233/AIS-180509

Goodfellow, I. (2014). Generative adversarial nets. *Advances in Neural Information Processing Systems*, 27.

GOsafeonline. (12 November 2014). Distributed Denial of Service Attack. CSA. https://www.csa.gov.sg/gosafeonline/go-safe-for-business/smes/distributed-denial-of-service-attack#:~:text=A%20DDoS%20attack%20is%20a,sending%20it%20specially%20crafted%20requests

Graf, B., & Antoni, C. (2021). The relationship between information characteristics and information overload at the workplace - a meta-analysis. *European Journal of Work and Organizational Psychology*, *30*(1), 143–158. doi:10.1080/1359432X.2020.1813111

Greene, K. J. (2015). *ISIS: Trends in terrorist media and propaganda.*

Greenemeier, L. (2015). Human traffickers caught on hidden internet. *Scientific American*, 8.

Greengard, S. (2010, December). The New Face of War. [ACM.]. *Communications of the ACM*, *53*(12), 20–22. doi:10.1145/1859204.1859212

Gruzd, A., & Hernández-García, Á. (2018). Privacy Concerns and Self-Disclosure in Private and Public Uses of Social Media. *Cyberpsychology, Behavior, and Social Networking*, *21*(7), 418–428. doi:10.1089/cyber.2017.0709 PMID:29995525

Guarda, T., Augusto, M. F., & Lopes, I. (2019). The art of phishing. Advances in intelligent systems and computing. Springer, Cham.

Guarnera, L. (2020). Preliminary forensics analysis of deepfake images. In *2020 AEIT International Annual Conference (AEIT)*. IEEE. 10.23919/AEIT50178.2020.9241108

Güera, D., & Delp, E. J. (2018). Deepfake video detection using recurrent neural networks. In *2018 15th IEEE International Conference on Advanced Video and Signal Based Surveillance (AVSS)*. IEEE. 10.1109/AVSS.2018.8639163

Guo, M., Wang, G., Hata, H., & Babar, M. A. (2021). Revenue maximizing markets for zero-day exploits. *Autonomous Agents and Multi-Agent Systems*, *35*(2), 36. arXiv:2006.14184. . doi:10.1007/s10458-021-09522-w

Guo, Y., Wang, X., & Wang, C. (2021). Impact of privacy policy content on perceived effectiveness of privacy policy: the role of vulnerability, benevolence and privacy concern. *Journal of Enterprise Information Management*. doi:10.1108/JEIM-12-2020-0481

Gupta, M., Abdelsalam, M., Khorsandroo, S., & Mittal, S. (2020). Security and Privacy in Smart Farming: Challenges and Opportunities. IEEE Access. IEEE.

Gupta, A., & Dhami, A. (2015). Measuring the impact of security, trust and privacy in information sharing: A study on social networking sites. *Journal of Direct, Data and Digital Marketing Practice*, *17*(1), 43–53. doi:10.1057/dddmp.2015.32

Gupta, M., Abdelsalam, M., Khorsandroo, S., & Mittal, S. (2020). Security and Privacy in Smart Farming: Challenges and Opportunities. *IEEE Access: Practical Innovations, Open Solutions*, *8*, 34564–34584. doi:10.1109/ACCESS.2020.2975142

Hair, J., Hult, G., Ringle, C., & Sarstedt, M. (2017). *A Primer on Partial Least Squares Structural Equation Modeling (PLS-SEM)* (2nd ed.). Sage.

Hair, J., Risher, J., Sarstedt, M., & Ringle, C. (2019). When to use and how to report the results of PLS-SEM. *European Business Review*, *31*(1), 2–24. doi:10.1108/EBR-11-2018-0203

Harviainen, J. T., Haasio, A., & Hämäläinen, L. (2020). Drug traders on a local dark web marketplace. *Proceedings of the 23rd International Conference on Academic Mindtrek*, (pp. 20–26). ACM. 10.1145/3377290.3377293

Hasan, H. R., & Salah, K. (2019). Combating deepfake videos using blockchain and smart contracts. *IEEE Access: Practical Innovations, Open Solutions*, *7*, 41596–41606. doi:10.1109/ACCESS.2019.2905689

Haveson, S., Lau, A., & Wong, V. (2017). *Protecting Farmers in Emerging Markets with Blockchain*. Cornell Tech.

Hedley, C., & Yule, I. (2009). A method for spatial prediction of daily soil water status for precise irrigation scheduling. *Agricultural Water Management*, *96*(12), 1737–1745. doi:10.1016/j.agwat.2009.07.009

Hermon, R., Singh, U., & Singh, B. (2023). Ntfs: Introduction and analysis from forensics point of view. *2023 International Conference for Advancement in Technology (ICONAT)*, (pp. 1–6). IEEE. 10.1109/ICONAT57137.2023.10080271

Hickok, D. J., Lesniak, D. R., & Rowe, M. C. (2005, April). File type detection technology. In *Proceedings from the 38th Midwest Instruction and Computing Symposium*. IEEE.

Hodge, D. R. (2014). Assisting victims of human trafficking: Strategies to facilitate identification, exit from trafficking, and the restoration of wellness. *Social Work*, *59*(2), 111–118. doi:10.1093wwu002 PMID:24855860

Hogan, M., Liu, F., Sokol, A., & Jin, T. (2011). *NIST-SP 500-291, NIST Cloud Computing Standards Roadmap. Special Publication (NIST SP)*. National Institute of Standards and Technology. https://tsapps.nist.gov/publication/get_pdf.cfm?pub_id=909024 doi:10.6028/NIST.SP.500-291v1

Hong, Y., Hu, J., & Zhao, Y. (2023). Would you go invisible on social media? An empirical study on the antecedents of users' lurking behavior. *Technological Forecasting and Social Change*, *187*, 122237. doi:10.1016/j.techfore.2022.122237

Hsu, C.-C., & Lin, C.-W. (2017). Unsupervised convolutional neural networks for large-scale image clustering. In *2017 IEEE International Conference on Image Processing (ICIP)*. IEEE. 10.1109/ICIP.2017.8296309

https://en.wikipedia.org/wiki/Cyberattack

Huebner, E., Bem, D., & Wee, C. K. (2006). Data hiding in the NTFS file system. *Digital investigation, 3*(4), 211-226.

Husain, M. & Haroon, M. (2020). Enriched Information Security Framework From Various Attacks in the Iot. *International Journal of Innovative Research in Computer Science & Technology, 8*(4).

Husain, M. S. (2020). Nature inspired approach for intrusion detection systems. *Design and Analysis of Security Protocol for Communication*, 171–182.

Husain, M. S. (2019). Social media Analytics to predict depression level in the users. In *Early Detection of Neurological Disorders Using Machine Learning Systems* (pp. 199–215). IGI Global. doi:10.4018/978-1-5225-8567-1.ch011

Husain, M. S., & Khan, M. Z. (Eds.). (2019). *Critical Concepts, Standards, and Techniques in Cyber Forensics*. IGI Global.

Hussain, M. A., Jin, H., Hussien, Z. A., Abduljabbar, Z. A., Abbdal, S. H., & Ibrahim, A. (2016). Dns protection against spoofing and poisoning attacks. In *2016 3rd International Conference on Information Science and Control Engineering (ICISCE),* (pp. 1308–1312). IEEE. 10.1109/ICISCE.2016.279

Hussain, S. (2021). Adversarial deepfakes: Evaluating vulnerability of deepfake detectors to adversarial examples. In *Proceedings of the IEEE/CVF Winter Conference on Applications of Computer Vision.* IEEE. 10.1109/WACV48630.2021.00339

Ikeda, T., Hori, D., Sasaki, H., Komase, Y., Doki, S., Takahashi, T., Oi, Y., Ikeda, Y., Arai, Y., Muroi, K., Ishitsuka, M., Matsuura, A., Go, W., Matsuzaki, I., & Sasahara, S. (2022). Prevalence, characteristics, and psychological outcomes of workplace cyberbullying during the COVID-19 pandemic in Japan: A cross-sectional online survey. *BMC Public Health,* *22*(1), 1087. doi:10.118612889-022-13481-6 PMID:35642023

Ireland, L. (2020). Predicting Online Target Hardening Behaviors: An Extension of Routine Activity Theory for Privacy-Enhancing Technologies and Techniques. *Deviant Behavior,* 1–17. doi:10.1080/01639625.2020.1760418

Irwin, A. S. M., & Turner, A. B. (2018). Illicit Bitcoin transactions: challenges in getting to the who, what, when and where. *Journal of Money Laundering Control.*

Ismail, A. (2021). A New Deep Learning-Based Methodology for Video Deepfake Detection Using XGBoost. *Sensors (Basel),* *21*(16). Advance online publication. doi:10.339021165413 PMID:34450855

Jafar, M. T. (2020). Forensics and analysis of deepfake videos. In *2020 11th International Conference on Information and Communication Systems (ICICS).* IEEE. 10.1109/ICICS49469.2020.239493

Jahn, M. M. (2019). *Cyber Risk and Security Implications in Smart Agriculture and Food Systems.* Jahn Research Group. https://jahnresearchgroup.webhosting.cals.wisc.edu/wp-content/ uploads/ sites/ 223/2019/01/ Agricultural-Cyber-Risk-and-Security.pdf

Jahn, M.M., Oemichen, W.L., & Treverton, G.F. (2019). *Cyber Risk and Security Implications in Smart Agriculture and Food Systems.*

Jana, F. A. A., Kunal, S. B., & Mondal, K. (n.d.). A survey of Indian Cyber crime and law and its pre- vention approach What is the Importance of Cyber. *International Journal of Advanced Computer Technology,* 48–55.

Javed, N., & Afaq, S. A. (2021). *COVID-19 AS AN OPPORTUNITY FOR CYBERCRIMINALS. December 2022.* NIH.

Johnson, C., Badger, M., Waltermire, D., Snyder, J., & Skorupka, C. (2016). *Guide to Cyber Threat Information Sharing. Special Publication (NIST SP).* National Institute of Standards and Technology. doi:10.6028/NIST.SP.800-150

Joshi, P. S., & Dinesha, H. A. (2020). Survey on identification of malicious activities by monitoring darknet access. *2020 Third International Conference on Smart Systems and Inventive Technology (ICSSIT),* (pp. 346–350). IEEE. 10.1109/ICSSIT48917.2020.9214121

Kahanwal, B., & Singh, T. P. (2012). The Distributed Computing Paradigms: P2P, Grid, Cluster, Cloud, and Jungle. *International Journal of Latest Research in Science and Technology,* *1*(2), 183–187. doi:10.48550/arXiv.1311.3070

Kalkan, A. (2019). *The Level Of Exposure To Cyber Bullying For Employees In Workplace.* EP. doi:10.15405/epsbs.2019.01.02.3

Kalyar, M. N., Saeed, M., Usta, A., & Shafique, I. (2020). Workplace cyberbullying and creativity: Examining the roles of psychological distress and psychological capital. *Management Research Review,* *44*(4), 607–624. doi:10.1108/MRR-03-2020-0130

Kanozia, R. (2021). A study on fake news subject matter, presentation elements, tools of detection, and social media platforms in India. *Asian Journal for Public Opinion Research*, *9*(1), 48–82.

Karame, G. (2016). On the security and scalability of bitcoin's blockchain. In *Proceedings of the 2016 ACM SIGSAC Conference on Computer and Communications Security*. ACM. 10.1145/2976749.2976756

Katta, S., Ramatenki, S., & Sammeta, H. (2022). Smart irrigation and crop security in agriculture using IoT. In *AI, Edge and IoT-Based Smart Agriculture*. Academic Press. doi:10.1016/B978-0-12-823694-9.00019-0

Kaur, S., & Randhawa, S. (2020). Dark web: A web of crimes. *Wireless Personal Communications*, *112*(4), 2131–2158. doi:10.100711277-020-07143-2

Khan, M. Z., Mishra, A., & Khan, M. H. (2020). Cyber Forensics Evolution and Its Goals. In Critical Concepts, Standards, and Techniques in Cyber Forensics (pp. 16-30). IGI Global. doi:10.4018/978-1-7998-1558-7.ch002

Khan, M. Z., Shoaib, M., & Ahmad, F. (2020). Cyber Forensic Lab Setup and Its Requirement. In Critical Concepts, Standards, and Techniques in Cyber Forensics (pp. 103-115). IGI Global. doi:10.4018/978-1-7998-1558-7.ch007

Khan, M. Z., Husain, M. S., & Shoaib, M. (2020). *Introduction to email, web, and message forensics. Critical Concepts, Standards, and Techniques in Cyber Forensics*. IGI Global.

Khan, M. Z., Husain, M. S., & Shoaib, M. (2020). Introduction to email, web, and message forensics. In *Critical concepts, standards, and techniques in cyber forensics* (pp. 174–186). IGI Global. doi:10.4018/978-1-7998-1558-7.ch010

Khan, N., Ikram, N., Murtaza, H., & Asadi, M. (2023). Social media users and cybersecurity awareness: Predicting self-disclosure using a hybrid artificial intelligence approach. *Kybernetes*, *52*(1), 401–421. doi:10.1108/K-05-2021-0377

Khan, W. (2021). An exhaustive review on state-of-the-art techniques for anomaly detection on attributed networks. [TURCOMAT]. *Turkish Journal of Computer and Mathematics Education*, *12*(10), 6707–6722.

Khan, W., & Haroon, M. (2022a). An efficient framework for anomaly detection in attributed social networks. *International Journal of Information Technology : an Official Journal of Bharati Vidyapeeth's Institute of Computer Applications and Management*, *14*(6), 3069–3076. doi:10.100741870-022-01044-2

Khan, W., & Haroon, M. (2022b). An unsupervised deep learning ensemble model for anomaly detection in static attributed social networks. *International Journal of Cognitive Computing in Engineering*, *3*, 153–160. doi:10.1016/j.ijcce.2022.08.002

Khan, W., Haroon, M., Khan, A. N., Hasan, M. K., Khan, A., Mokhtar, U. A., & Islam, S. (2022). DVAEGMM: Dual Variational Autoencoder With Gaussian Mixture Model for Anomaly Detection on Attributed Networks. *IEEE Access : Practical Innovations, Open Solutions*, *10*, 91160–91176. doi:10.1109/ACCESS.2022.3201332

Khursheed, A., Kumar, M., & Sharma, M. (2016). Security against cyber attacks in food industry. *International Journal of Control Theory and Applications*, *9*(17), 8623–8628.

Kianpour, M., Kowalski, S., & Øverby, H. (2021). Systematically Understanding Cybersecurity Economics: A Survey. *Sustainability (Basel)*, *13*(24), 13677. doi:10.3390u132413677

Kim, Y., Nan, D., & Kim, J. (2021). Exploration of the Relationships Among Narcissism, Life Satisfaction, and Loneliness of Instagram Users and the High- and Low-Level Features of Their Photographs. *Frontiers in Psychology*, *12*(1), 707074–707074. doi:10.3389/fpsyg.2021.707074 PMID:34512463

Klostermann, J., Meißner, M., Max, A., & Decker, R. (2023). Presentation of celebrities' private life through visual social media. *Journal of Business Research*, *156*, 113524. doi:10.1016/j.jbusres.2022.113524

Kompella, S. (2022). Persisting Menace: A Case-Based Study of Remote Workplace Bullying in India. *International Journal of Bullying Prevention : an Official Publication of the International Bullying Prevention Association*, 1–17. doi:10.100742380-022-00152-8 PMID:36570782

Koniaris, I., Papadimitriou, G., Nicopolitidis, P., & Obaidat, M. (2014). Honeypots deployment for the analysis and visualization of malware activity and malicious connections. *2014 IEEE International Conference on Communications (ICC)*, (pp. 1819–1824). IEEE. 10.1109/ICC.2014.6883587

Koopman, M., Rodriguez, A. M., & Geradts, Z. (2018). Detection of deepfake video manipulation. In *The 20th Irish Machine Vision and Image Processing Conference (IMVIP)*. IEEE.

Kowalski, R. M., Toth, A., & Morgan, M. (2018). Bullying and cyberbullying in adulthood and the workplace. *The Journal of Social Psychology*, *158*(1), 64–81. doi:10.1080/00224545.2017.1302402 PMID:28402201

Kumar, A., & Paul, P. (2016). *Security analysis and implementation of a simple method for prevention and detection against evil twin attack in ieee 802.11 wireless lan. In 2016 international conference on computational techniques in information and communication technologies*. ICCTICT.

Kundra, H., Khan, W., Malik, M., Rane, K. P., Neware, R., & Jain, V. (2022). Quantum-inspired firefly algorithm integrated with cuckoo search for optimal path planning. *International Journal of Modern Physics C*, *33*(02), 2250018. doi:10.1142/S0129183122500188

Kurter, H. L. (n.d.). CEOs, Here Are 3 Ways You Can Prevent Bullying In The Remote Workplace. *Forbes*. https://www.forbes.com/sites/heidilynnekurter/2021/10/29/leaders-here-are-3-ways-you-can-prevent-bullying-in-the-remote-workplace/

Lane, J. (2013). Bitcoin, silk road, and the need for a new approach to virtual currency regulation. *Charleston L. Rev.*, *8*, 511.

Lane, J., Ramirez, F., & Patton, D. (2023). Defending against social media: Structural disadvantages of social media in criminal court for public defenders and defendants of low socioeconomic status. *Information Communication and Society*, 1–16. doi:10.1080/1369118X.2023.2166795

Lan-ying, W., & Jin-wu, J. (2005). Analysis of NTFS file system structure [J]. *Computer Engineering and Design*, *27*(3), 418–420.

Lee, Y., Hsiao, C., Weng, J., & Chen, Y.-H. (2021). The impacts of relational capital on self-disclosure in virtual communities. *Information Technology & People*, *34*(1), 228–249. doi:10.1108/ITP-11-2018-0541

Li, J., Zhao H., Hussain S., Ming J., & J., W. (2021). The Dark Side of Personalization Recommendation in Short-Form Video Applications: An Integrated Model from Information Perspective Diversity, Divergence, Dialogue. iConference 2021., vol In K. Toeppe, H. Yan, & S. Chu (Eds.), *Lecture Notes in Computer Science*. Springer, Cham.

Liang, H., Shen, F., & Fu, K. (2017). Privacy protection and self-disclosure across societies: A study of global Twitter users. *New Media & Society*, *19*(9), 1476–1497. doi:10.1177/1461444816642210

Li, C.-T., & Li, Y. (2011). Color-decoupled photo response non-uniformity for digital image forensics. *IEEE Transactions on Circuits and Systems for Video Technology*, *22*(2), 260–271. doi:10.1109/TCSVT.2011.2160750

Liggett, R., Lee, J. R., Roddy, A. L., & Wallin, M. A. (2020). The dark web as a platform for crime: An exploration of illicit drug, firearm, CSAM, and cybercrime markets. The Palgrave Handbook of International Cybercrime and Cyberdeviance, 91–116.

Li, K., Cheng, L., & Teng, C. (2020). Voluntary sharing and mandatory provision: Private information disclosure on social networking sites. *Information Processing & Management, 57*(1), 102128. doi:10.1016/j.ipm.2019.102128

Li, K., Lin, Z., & Wang, X. (2015). An empirical analysis of users' privacy disclosure behaviors on social network sites. *Information & Management, 52*(7), 882–891. doi:10.1016/j.im.2015.07.006

Lin, T. C. W. (2016). Financial Weapons of War. *Wikipedia.* https://en.wikipedia.org/wiki/Cyberattack#cite_ref-ssrn. com_3-0

Lin, C., Chou, E., & Huang, H. (2021). They support, so we talk: The effects of other users on self-disclosure on social networking sites. *Information Technology & People, 34*(3), 1039–1064. doi:10.1108/ITP-10-2018-0463

Lindsey, N. (2019). *Cyber criminals have turned social media cyber crime into a $3 billion business.* CPO Magazine.

Lipovsky, R., Cermak, M., Svorencik, S., & Kubovic, O. (n.d.). KR00K - CVE-2019-15126. *We Live Security.* https:// www.welivesecurity.com/wpcontent/uploads/2020/02/ESET Kr00k.pdf. [Online].

Livingstone, S., Davidson, J., Bryce, J., Batool, S., Haughton, C., & Nandi, A. (2017). *Children's online activities, risks and safety: a literature review by the UKCCIS evidence group.* LSE.

Li, Y., Guo, Y., & Chen, L. (2021). Predicting Social Support Exchanging among Male Homosexuals Who are HIV-Positive in Social Media Context: The Role of Online Self-Disclosure. *Journal of Homosexuality,* 1–17. doi:10.1080/0 0918369.2021.1935623 PMID:34110274

Loh, J., & Snyman, R. (2020). The tangled web: Consequences of workplace cyberbullying in adult male and female employees. *Gender in Management, 35*(6), 567–584. doi:10.1108/GM-12-2019-0242

Lukas, J., Fridrich, J., & Goljan, M. (2006). Digital camera identification from sensor pattern noise. *IEEE Transactions on Information Forensics and Security, 1*(2), 205–214. doi:10.1109/TIFS.2006.873602

Lyngdoh, T., El-Manstrly, D., & Jeesha, K. (2023). Social isolation and social anxiety as drivers of generation Z's willingness to share personal information on social media. *Psychology and Marketing, 40*(1), 5–26. doi:10.1002/mar.21744

Lyu, M., Sun, B., & Zhang, Z. (2022). Linking online voice to workplace cyberbullying: Roles of job strain and moral efficacy. *Kybernetes.* doi:10.1108/K-03-2021-0246

Lyu, S. (2020). Deepfake detection: Current challenges and next steps. In *2020 IEEE International Conference on Multimedia & Expo Workshops (ICMEW).* IEEE. 10.1109/ICMEW46912.2020.9105991

Madden, C., & Loh, J. (2020). Workplace cyberbullying and bystander helping behaviour. *International Journal of Human Resource Management, 31*(19), 2434–2458. doi:10.1080/09585192.2018.1449130

Malin, C. H., Casey, E., & Aquilina, J. M. (2008). *Malware forensics: investigating and analyzing malicious code.* Syngress.

Manning, L. (2019). Food defence: Refining the taxonomy of food defence threats. *Trends in Food Science & Technology, 85,* 107–115. doi:10.1016/j.tifs.2019.01.008

Marcel, S., Nixon, M., & Li, S. (2014). *Handbook of Biometric Anti-Spoofing: Trusted Biometrics under Spoofing Attacks. Advances in Computer Vision and Pattern Recognition.* London: Springer. . doi:10.1007/978-1-4471-6524-8

Marcella, A. J. (Ed.). (2021). *Cyber Forensics: Examining Emerging and Hybrid Technologies.* CRC Press. doi:10.1201/9781003057888

Marin, E., Shakarian, J., & Shakarian, P. (2018). Mining key-hackers on darkweb forums. *2018 1st International Conference on Data Intelligence and Security (ICDIS),* (pp. 73–80). IEEE.

Marinescu, D. C. (2013). *Cloud Computing Theory and Practice*. Elsevier.

Martínez, M. F. (2021). Impact of Tools on the Acquisition of RAM Memory. *International Journal of Cyber Forensics and Advanced Threat Investigations*, *1*(1-3), 3–17. doi:10.46386/ijcfati.v1i1-3.12

Masinde, N., & Graffi, K. (2020). Peer-to-peer-based social networks: A comprehensive survey. *SN Computer Science*, *1*(5), 299. doi:10.100742979-020-00315-8

Masinde, N., Khitman, L., Dlikman, I., & Graffi, K. (2020). Systematic Evaluation of LibreSocial—A Peer-to-Peer Framework for Online Social Networks. *Future Internet*, *12*(9), 140. doi:10.3390/fi12090140

Masur, P. (2021). Understanding the effects of conceptual and analytical choices on 'finding' the privacy paradox: A specification curve analysis of large-scale survey data. *Information Communication and Society*, 1–19. doi:10.1080/13 69118X.2021.1963460

Matthes, J., Koban, K., Neureiter, A., & Stevic, A. (2021). Longitudinal Relationships Among Fear of COVID-19, Smartphone Online Self-Disclosure, Happiness, and Psychological Well-being: Survey Study. *Journal of Medical Internet Research*, *23*(9), e28700. doi:10.2196/28700 PMID:34519657

McCabe, K. A. (2017). Common forms: sex trafficking. In *Human Trafficking* (pp. 122–137). Routledge. doi:10.4324/9781315679990-6

McCarthy, S., Rowan, W., Mahony, C., & Vergne, A. (2023). The dark side of digitalization and social media platform governance: a citizen engagement study. *Internet Research*. doi:10.1108/INTR-03-2022-0142

Mell, P., & Grance, T. (2011). *The NIST Definition of Cloud Computing. Special Publication (NIST SP)*. National Institute of Standards and Technology. doi:10.6028/NIST.SP.800-145

Millman, R. (2017). *New polymorphic malware evades three-quarters of AV scanners*. SC Magazine UK.

Mishra, A., Khan, M. H., Khan, W., Khan, M. Z., & Srivastava, N. K. (2022). A Comparative Study on Data Mining Approach Using Machine Learning Techniques: Prediction Perspective. *Pervasive Healthcare: A Compendium of Critical Factors for Success*, 153-165.

Misra, D. & Zaheer, M. M. (2017). NavIC –An Indigenous Developments for Self Reliant Navigation Services. ICACIE 2017, Springer transactions, CU. Ajmer.

Monzini, P. (2005). *Sex traffic: Prostitution, crime and exploitation*. Zed Books.

Moran, A. (2020). Cyber security. *International Security Studies: Theory and Practice*, 299–312.

Mutimukwe, C., Kolkowska, E., & Grönlund, Å. (2020). Information privacy in e-service: Effect of organizational privacy assurances on individual privacy concerns, perceptions, trust and self-disclosure behavior. *Government Information Quarterly*, *37*(1), 101413. doi:10.1016/j.giq.2019.101413

MyDisabilityJobs. (2023, March 31). Workplace Bullying Statistics Research & Facts | Updated 2023. *MyDisabilityJobs. Com*. https://mydisabilityjobs.com/statistics/workplace-bullying/

Nabity-Grover, T., Cheung, C., & Bennett Thatcher, J. (2023). How COVID-19 stole Christmas: How the pandemic shifted the calculus around social media Self-Disclosures. *Journal of Business Research*, *154*, 113310. doi:10.1016/j. jbusres.2022.113310 PMID:36188113

Naheem, M. A. (2016). Money laundering: A primer for banking staff. *International Journal of Disclosure and Governance*, *13*(2), 135–156. doi:10.1057/jdg.2015.10

Naiqi, L., Zhongshan, W., & Yujie, H. (2008, August). Computer forensics research and implementation based on NTFS file system. In *2008 ISECS International Colloquium on Computing, Communication, Control, and Management* (*Vol. 1*, pp. 519-523). IEEE. 10.1109/CCCM.2008.236

Namie, G. (2021, February 24). 2021 WBI U.S. Workplace Bullying Survey. *Workplace Bullying Institute*. https://workplacebullying.org/2021-wbi-survey/

Naresh, M., & Munaswamy, P. (2019). *Smart Agriculture System using IoT Technology. 5*, 98–102.

Naresh, R. K., Lalit, P. K. S., Kumar, A. K., & Shivangi, M. S. C. (2021). Role of IoT Technology in Agriculture for Reshaping the Future of Farming in India: A Review. *International Journal of Current Microbiology and Applied Sciences, 10*(2), 439–451. doi:10.20546/ijcmas.2021.1002.052

Nayak, S., Budhwar, P., Pereira, V., & Malik, A. (2021). Exploring the dark-side of E-HRM: A study of social networking sites and deviant workplace behavior. *International Journal of Manpower, 43*(1), 89–115. doi:10.1108/IJM-03-2021-0125

Nemec Zlatolas, L., Welzer, T., Heričko, M., & Hölbl, M. (2015). Privacy antecedents for SNS self-disclosure: The case of Facebook. *Computers in Human Behavior, 45*(1), 158–167. doi:10.1016/j.chb.2014.12.012

Neyaz, A., & Shashidhar, N. (2022). Windows prefetch forensics. In K. Daimi, G. Francia III, & L. H. Encinas (Eds.), *Breakthroughs in Digital Biometrics and Forensics* (pp. 191–210). Springer International Publishing., doi:10.1007/978-3-031-10706-1_9

Nguyen, T. T. (2019). Deep learning for deepfakes creation and detection: A survey. arXiv preprint arXiv:1909.11573.

Nichols, A. J. (2016). *Sex trafficking in the United States: Theory, research, policy, and practice.* Columbia University Press. doi:10.7312/nich17262

Nifakos, S., Chandramouli, K., Nikolaou, C. K., Papachristou, P., Koch, S., Panaousis, E., & Bonacina, S. (2021). Influence of human factors on cyber security within healthcare organisations: A systematic review. *Sensors (Basel), 21*(15), 1–25. doi:10.339021155119 PMID:34372354

Nikander, J., Onni, M., & Mikko, L. (2020). Requirements for cybersecurity in agricultural communication networks. *Computers and Electronics in Agriculture, 179*, 105776. doi:10.1016/j.compag.2020.105776

Nitti, M., Pilloni, V., Colistra, G., & Atzori, L. (2015). The virtual object as a major element of the internet of things: A survey. *IEEE Communications Surveys and Tutorials, 18*(2), 1228–1240. doi:10.1109/COMST.2015.2498304

Nitti, M., Pilloni, V., Giusto, D., & Popescu, V. (2017). IoT Architecture for a sustainable tourism application in a smart city environment. *Mobile Information Systems, 2017*, 2017. doi:10.1155/2017/9201640

Nunes, E., Shakarian, P., & Simari, G. I. (2018). At-risk system identification via analysis of discussions on the darkweb. *2018 APWG Symposium on Electronic Crime Research (ECrime)*, (pp. 1–12). IEEE. 10.1109/ECRIME.2018.8376211

Oerke, E.-C., & Dehne, H.-W. (2004). Safeguarding production—Losses in major crops and the role of crop protection. *Crop Protection (Guildford, Surrey), 23*(4), 275–285. doi:10.1016/j.cropro.2003.10.001

Office of Joe Neguse. (2022, May 17). *Neguse, Peters state and local government cybersecurity bill heads to president's desk for signature.* Office of Jow Neguse. https://neguse.house.gov/media/press-releases/neguse-peters-state-and-local-government-cybersecurity-bill-heads-to-presidents-desk-for-signature

Oh, J., Lee, S., & Hwang, H. (2021). NTFS Data Tracker: Tracking file data history based on $ LogFile. *Forensic Science International: Digital Investigation, 39*, 301309.

Oktaviani, J. (2018). Cybersecurity and the future of agri-food industries. *Sereal Untuk, 51*(1), 51.

Omrani, N., & Soulié, N. (2020). Privacy Experience, Privacy Perception, Political Ideology and Online Privacy Concern: The Case of Data Collection in Europe. [Privacy Experience, Privacy Perception, Political Ideology and Online Privacy Concern: The Case of Data Collection in Europe]. *Revue d'Economie Industrielle, 172*(4), 217–255. doi:10.4000/rei.9706

Ormsby, E. (2019). Dealer's chance: The dark web, bitcoin and the fall of silk road. *Griffith REVIEW, 64*, 184–194.

Otta, S. P., Panda, S., Gupta, M., & Hota, C. (2023). A Systematic Survey of Multi-Factor Authentication for Cloud Infrastructure. *Future Internet, 15*(4), 146. doi:10.3390/fi15040146

Paganelli, F., Turchi, S., & Giuli, D. (2014). A web of things framework for restful applications and its experimentation in a smart city. *IEEE Systems Journal, 10*(4), 1412–1423. doi:10.1109/JSYST.2014.2354835

Pal, A., & Memon, N. (2009). The evolution of file carving. *IEEE Signal Processing Magazine, 26*(2), 59–71. doi:10.1109/MSP.2008.931081

Patel, R. S. & Kathiriya, D. (2013). Evolution of Cybercrimes in India. *International Journal of Emerging Trends & Technology in Computer Science, 2*(4).

Patel, C., & Doshi, N. (2019). *Security Challenges in IoT Cyber World*. Springer International Publishing., doi:10.1007/978-3-030-01560-2_8

Perazzo, P., Vallati, C., Varano, D., Anastasi, G., & Dini, G. (2018). Implementation of a wormhole attack against a rpl network: Challenges and effects. In *2018 14th Annual Conference on Wireless On-demand Network Systems and Services (WONS)*, (pp. 95– 102). IEEE.

Pimple, N., Salunke, T., Pawar, U., & Sangoi, J. (2020).Wireless security — an approach towards secured wi-fi connectivity. In *2020 6th International Conference on Advanced Computing and Communication Systems (ICACCS)*, (pp. 872–876). IEEE.

Pizzi, G., & Scarpi, D. (2020). Privacy threats with retail technologies: A consumer perspective. *Journal of Retailing and Consumer Services, 56*(1), 102160. doi:10.1016/j.jretconser.2020.102160

Prylinski, K. M. (2020). Tech Trafficking: How the internet has transformed sex trafficking. *J. High Tech. L., 20*, 338.

Qaiser, S. (2020). *Cyber Crime : Rise*. Evolution and Prevention. July., doi:10.13140/RG.2.2.18533.01762

Quasim, M. T., & Al Hawi, A. N. (2022). *Mechanisms of System Penetration: Concepts, Attack Methods, and Defense Strategies (No. 9197)*. EasyChair.

Quasim, M. T., Al Hawi, A. N., & Meraj, M. (2023). *System Penetration: Concepts, Attack Methods, and Defense Strategies*. EasyChair.

Ramadan, R. A., Aboshosha, B. W., Alshudukhi, J. S., Alzahrani, A. J., El-Sayed, A., & Dessouky, M. M. (2021). Cybersecurity and Countermeasures at the Time of Pandemic. *Journal of Advanced Transportation, 2021*(2003). doi:10.1155/2021/6627264

Ramdeo, S., & Singh, R. (2022). Cyberbullying in the Workplace. In *Research Anthology on Combating Cyber-Aggression and Online Negativity* (pp. 1116–1128). IGI Global. doi:10.4018/978-1-6684-5594-4.ch056

Rasool, M., & Khan, W. (2015). Big data: Study in structured and unstructured data. [IJTIR]. *HCTL Open International Journal of Technology Innovations and Research, 14*, 1–6.

Reddy, N. (2019). Windows forensics. In N. Reddy (Ed.), *Practical Cyber Forensics: An Incident-Based Approach to Forensic Investigations* (pp. 29–68). Apress., doi:10.1007/978-1-4842-4460-9_2

Reith, M., Carr, C., & Gunsch, G. (2002). An examination of digital forensic models. *International Journal of digital evidence, 1*(3), 1-12.

Require, I. T., & Capabilities, I. (n.d.). *HEALTH CARE AND CYBER SECURITY.*

Richards, N., & Solove, D. (2010). Prosser's Privacy Law: A Mixed Legacy. *California Law Review, 98*(6), 1887–1924.

Roser, M. (2020). Future Population Growth. *Our World in Data.* https://ourworldindata.org/future-population-growth

Rügemer, W. (2019). *The Capitalists of the 21st Century: An Easy-to-Understand Outline on the Rise of the New Financial Players.* tredition.

Russon, R., & Fledel, Y. (2004). NTFS documentation. *Recuperado el, 1.*

Sadasivam, G. K., Hota, C., & Anand, B. (2018). Detection of severe SSH attacks using honeypot servers and machine learning techniques. *Software Networking, 2018*(1), 79–100. doi:10.13052/jsn2445-9739.2017.005

Sadia, H., Yadav, S., & Faisal, M. (2022). Mapping Cyberbullying and Workplace Cyberbullying: A Road Towards Understanding Research Gaps in the Indian Context. In Research Anthology on Combating Cyber-Aggression and Online Negativity (pp. 640–668). IGI Global. doi:10.4018/978-1-6684-5594-4.ch035

Safkhani, M., & Bagheri, N. (2017). Passive secret disclosure attack on an ultralightweight authentication protocol for internet of things. *The Journal of Supercomputing, 73*(8), 3579–3585. doi:10.100711227-017-1959-0

Sahu, K., Alzahrani, F. A., Srivastava, R. K., & Kumar, R. (2020). Hesitant fuzzy sets based symmetrical model of decision-making for estimating the durability of web application. *Symmetry, 12*(11), 1770. doi:10.3390ym12111770

Sahu, K., Alzahrani, F. A., Srivastava, R. K., & Kumar, R. (2021). Evaluating the impact of prediction techniques: Software reliability perspective. *Computers, Materials & Continua, 67*(2), 1471–1488. doi:10.32604/cmc.2021.014868

Salam, A. (2019). A path loss model for through the soil wireless communications in digital agriculture. In *Proceedings of the 2019 IEEE International Symposium on Antennas and Propagation (IEEE APS).* IEEE.

Salas-Zárate, M., & Colombo-Mendoza, L. (2012). Cloud Computing: A Review of Paas, Iaas, Saas Services and Providers. *Lámpsakos, 7*(7), 47–57. doi:10.21501/21454086.844

Saleem, J., Islam, R., & Kabir, M. A. (2022). The anonymity of the dark web: A survey. *IEEE Access : Practical Innovations, Open Solutions, 10*, 33628–33660. doi:10.1109/ACCESS.2022.3161547

Sammons, J., & Cross, M. (2017). *Cybercrime, The Basics of Cyber Safety.* Syngress. https://www.sciencedirect.com/science/article/pii/B978012416650900005X, doi:10.1016/B978-0-12-416650-9.00005-X

Sandeep, C. HKumar, NKumar, SKumar, P. (2018, November). Security Challenges and Issues of the IoT System. *Indian Journal of Public Health Research & Development, 9*(11).

Satter, R. (2017). What makes a cyberattack? Experts lobby to restrict the term. *Wikipedia.* https://en.wikipedia.org/wiki/Cyberattack#cite_ref-4)

Schatz, D., Bashroush, R., & Wall, J. (2017). Towards a More Representative Definition of Cyber Security. *Journal of Digital Forensics, Security and Law, 12* (2).

Schimmelpfennig, D. (2016). *Farm Profits and Adoption of Precision Agriculture; Technical Report ERR-217.* U.S. Department of Agriculture, Economic Research Services.

Schwartz-Chassidim, H., Oshrat, A., Tamir, M., Ron, H., & Eran, T. (2020). Selectivity in posting on social networks: The role of privacy concerns, social capital, and technical literacy. *Heliyon*, *6*(2), e03298. doi:10.1016/j.heliyon.2020.e03298 PMID:32055733

Scisco, J. L. (2019). Cyberbullying in the Workplace: A Review of the Research. In *Cyberbullying in Schools, Workplaces, and Romantic Relationships*. Routledge. doi:10.4324/9781315110554-6

Sergio, A. (2013). "Social Engineering" (PDF). upc.edu. Archived (PDF) from the original on 3 December 2013. Retrieved 5 January 2023.

Seselja, E. (2021). *Cyber Attack Shuts Down Global Meat Processing Giant JBS*. ABC. https://www.abc.net.au/news/2021-05-31/cyber-attack-shuts-down-global-meat-processing-giant-jbs/100178310

Shakarian, J., Gunn, A. T., & Shakarian, P. (2016). Exploring malicious hacker forums. *Cyber Deception: Building the Scientific Foundation*, 259–282.

Shamal, S., Alhwaimel, S. A., & Mouazen, A. M. (2016). Application of an on-line sensor to map soil packing density for site specific cultivation. *Soil & Tillage Research*, *162*, 78–86. doi:10.1016/j.still.2016.04.016

Sharif, A., Soroya, S., Ahmad, S., & Mahmood, K. (2021). Antecedents of Self-Disclosure on Social Networking Sites (SNSs): A Study of Facebook Users. *Sustainability (Basel)*, *13*(3), 1220. doi:10.3390u13031220

Sharma, S., & Dhote, T. (2021). Cybersecurity – Vulnerability Assessment of Attacks, Challenges and Defence Strategies in Industry 4.0. Ecosystem. *Miles IT*, *10*(2), 203–210.

Sheng, N., Yang, C., Han, L., & Jou, M. (2023). Too much overload and concerns: Antecedents of social media fatigue and the mediating role of emotional exhaustion. *Computers in Human Behavior*, *139*, 107500. doi:10.1016/j.chb.2022.107500

Shinder, L., & Cross, M. (2008). *The Evolution of Cybercrime, Scene of the Cybercrime* (2nd ed.). Syngress. https://www.sciencedirect.com/science/article/pii/B9781597492768000029, doi:10.1016/B978-1-59749-276-8.00002-9

Shivani, G. (2015). Cyber Security In Digital Economy. *Shivani Grover 12*(2349), 1563–1569.

Shutan, B. (2021, December 20). *Workplace bullying: A 'wildly out of control' epidemic*. Zogby Analytics. https://zogbyanalytics.com/soundbites/1063-workplace-bullying-a-wildly-out-of-control-epidemic

Sindermann, C., Schmitt, H., Kargl, F., Herbert, C., & Montag, C. (2021). Online Privacy Literacy and Online Privacy Behavior – The Role of Crystallized Intelligence and Personality. *International Journal of Human-Computer Interaction*, *37*(15), 1455–1466. doi:10.1080/10447318.2021.1894799

Smith, H., Dinev, T., & Xu, H. (2011). Information Privacy Research: An Interdisciplinary Review. *Management Information Systems Quarterly*, *35*(4), 989–1015. doi:10.2307/41409970

Sontowski, S. (2020). Cyber Attacks on Smart Farming Infrastructure. *2020 IEEE 6th International Conference on Collaboration and Internet Computing (CIC)*, (pp. 135-143). IEEE. 10.1109/CIC50333.2020.00025

Sontowski, S., Gupta, M., Chukkapalli, S. S. L., Abdelsalam, M., Mittal, S., Joshik, A., & Sandhu, R. (2020). Cyber Attacks on Smart Farming Infrastructure. *Profs and Hu*. https://profsandhu.com/confrnc/misconf/smart-farm-cic-20.pdf

Sparkman, D. (2022, September 26). *Don't Allow Bullying to Become the New Normal*. Zogby Analytics. https://zogby-analytics.com/soundbites/1177-don-t-allow-bullying-to-become-the-new-normal

Spence, P., Lin, X., Lachlan, K., & Hutter, E. (2020). Listen up, I've done this before: The impact of self-disclosure on source credibility and risk message responses. *Progress in Disaster Science*, *7*, 100108. doi:10.1016/j.pdisas.2020.100108

Spiliotopoulos, T., & Oakley, I. (2021). Altruistic and selfish communication on social media: The moderating effects of tie strength and interpersonal trust. *Behaviour & Information Technology*, 40(3), 320–336. doi:10.1080/014492 9X.2019.1688392

Spremić, M., & Šimunic, A. (2018). Cyber security challenges in digital economy. *Lecture Notes in Engineering and Computer Science*, 2235, 2–7.

Srinivas, J., Das, A. K., & Kumar, N. (2019). Government regulations in cyber security: Framework, standards and recommendations. *Future Generation Computer Systems*, 92, 178–188. doi:10.1016/j.future.2018.09.063

Steve, C. (2022). Cyber threats are a real threat to modern agriculture's expanding digital infrastructure. *AgWeb*. https://www.agweb.com/news/business/technology/cyber-threats-are-real-threat-modern-agricultures-expanding-digital

Stevens, T. (2018). "Global Cybersecurity: New Directions in Theory and Methods" (PDF). *Politics and Governance*, 6(2), 1–4. doi:10.17645/pag.v6i2.1569

Subramanian, N., & Jeyaraj, A. (2018). Recent security challenges in cloud computing. *Computers & Electrical Engineering*, 7(1), 28–42. doi:10.1016/j.compeleceng.2018.06.006

Sukianto, A. (2022), UpGuard, Third-Party Risk Management, 10 Ways to Reduce Cybersecurity Risk for Your Organization. *Upguard*. https://www.upguard.com/blog/reduce-cybersecurity-risk

Surette, R. (2015). Performance crime and justice. *Current Issues in Criminal Justice*, 27(2), 195–216. doi:10.1080/10 345329.2015.12036041

Suthar, D., & Rughani, P. H. (2020). A Comprehensive Study of VoIP Security. *2020 2nd International Conference on Advances in Computing, Communication Control and Networking (ICACCCN)*, 812–817.

Svensson, A. (2005). *Computer forensics applied to windows NTFS computers*. Stockholm's University, Royal Institute of Technology.

Swathi, P., & Sk, S. (2021). DeepFake Creation and Detection: A Survey. In *2021 Third International Conference on Inventive Research in Computing Applications (ICIRCA)*. IEEE.

Sylvester, G. (2019). E-agriculture in Action: Blockchain for Agriculture (Opportunities and Challenges). Bangkok: International Telecommunication Union (ITU).

Taddei, S., & Contena, B. (2013). Privacy, trust and control: Which relationships with online self-disclosure? *Computers in Human Behavior*, 29(3), 821–826. doi:10.1016/j.chb.2012.11.022

Talari, S., Shafie-Khah, M., Siano, P., Loia, V., Tommasetti, A., & Catalão, J. P. (2017). A review of smart cities based on the internet of things concept. *Energies*, 10(4), 421. doi:10.3390/en10040421

Tang, Y., & Ning, X. (2023). Understanding user misrepresentation behavior on social apps: The perspective of privacy calculus theory. *Decision Support Systems*, 165, 113881. doi:10.1016/j.dss.2022.113881

Tarık, A. K. (n.d.). Law Enforcement And Technological Facilities In Changing Agenda Of The Public Safety And Security. *Güvenlik Bilimleri Dergisi*, 21–32.

Technopedia. (n.d.). *What is Spoofing?* Techopedia.

Teoh, C. S., & Mahmood, A. K. (2017). National cyber security strategies for digital economy. *Journal of Theoretical and Applied Information Technology*, 95(23), 6510–6522. doi:10.1109/ICRIIS.2017.8002519

Thompson, N., & Brindley, J. (2021). Who are you talking about? Contrasting determinants of online disclosure about self or others. *Information Technology & People, 34*(3), 999–1017. doi:10.1108/ITP-04-2019-0197

Tiamboonprasert, W., & Charoensukmongkol, P. (2020). Effect of Ethical Leadership on Workplace Cyberbullying Exposure and Organizational Commitment. *The Journal of Behavioral Science, 15*(3), 3.

Toader, D., Boca, G., Toader, R., Măcelaru, M., Toader, C., Ighian, D., & Rădulescu, A. (2020). The Effect of Social Presence and Chatbot Errors on Trust. *Sustainability (Basel), 12*(1), 256. doi:10.3390u12010256

Trepte, S., Teutsch, D., Masur, P., Eicher, C., Fischer, M., Hennhöfer, A., & Lind, F. (2015). Do People Know About Privacy and Data Protection Strategies? Towards the "Online Privacy Literacy Scale" (OPLIS). In: Gutwirth S., Leenes R., de Hert P. (eds) Reforming European Data Protection Law. Law, Governance and Technology Series, vol 20. Springer, Dordrecht. . In. doi:10.1007/978-94-017-9385-8_1

Trinh, L. (2021). Interpretable and trustworthy deepfake detection via dynamic prototypes. In *Proceedings of the IEEE/ CVF Winter Conference on Applications of Computer Vision*. IEEE. 10.1109/WACV48630.2021.00202

Tripathi, M. M., Haroon, M., Khan, Z., & Husain, M. S. (2022). Security in Digital Healthcare System. *Pervasive Healthcare: A Compendium of Critical Factors for Success*, 217-231.

Tripathi, M. M., Haroon, M., Khan, Z., & Husain, M. S. (2022). *Security in Digital Healthcare System. Pervasive Healthcare: A Compendium of Critical Factors for Success*, 217-231. Research Gate.

Tully, J., Selzer, J., Phillips, J. P., O'Connor, P., & Dameff, C. (2020). Healthcare Challenges in the Era of Cybersecurity. *Health Security, 18*(3), 228–231. doi:10.1089/hs.2019.0123 PMID:32559153

Van Der Linden, D., Michalec, O. A., & Zamansky, A. (2020). Cybersecurity for Smart Farming: Socio-Cultural Context Matters. *IEEE Technology and Society Magazine, 39*(4), 28–35. doi:10.1109/MTS.2020.3031844

van der Schyff, K., & Flowerday, S. (2023). The mediating role of perceived risks and benefits when self-disclosing: A study of social media trust and FoMO. *Computers & Security, 126*, 103071. doi:10.1016/j.cose.2022.103071

Vanhoef, M., & Piessens, F. (2017). Key reinstallation attacks: Forcing nonce reuse in wpa2. In *Proceedings of the 2017 ACM SIGSAC Conference on Computer and Communications Security*, (pp. 1313–1328). ACM. 10.1145/3133956.3134027

Varnali, K., & Toker, A. (2015). Self-Disclosure on Social Networking Sites. *Social Behavior and Personality, 43*(1), 1–13. doi:10.2224bp.2015.43.1.1

Vasserman, E., Jansen, R., Tyra, J., Hopper, N., & Kim, Y. (2009). Membership-concealing overlay networks. *Proceedings of the 16th ACM Conference on Computer and Communications Security*, (pp. 390–399). ACM.

Veera, V. (2022). Deepfake Detection in Digital Media Forensics. *Global Transitions Proceedings*.

Venkatesh, V., Hoehle, H., Aloysius, J., & Nikkhah, H. (2021). Being at the cutting edge of online shopping: Role of recommendations and discounts on privacy perceptions. *Computers in Human Behavior, 121*(1), 106785. doi:10.1016/j.chb.2021.106785

View and restore firefox cache files. (2023, February 22). EaseUS. https://www.easeus.com/file-recovery/view-and-restore-firefox-cache-temp-files.html

Vranjes, I., Baillien, E., Vandebosch, H., & De Witte, H. (2018). *Understanding Workplace Cyberbullying: More than just an old problem in a new guise*. Lirias. https://lirias.kuleuven.be/1990170

Vranjes, I., Baillien, E., Vandebosch, H., Erreygers, S., & De Witte, H. (2015, January 1). *The dark side of working online: The rise of workplace cyberbullying*. WAOP Conference, Amsterdam, The Netherlands. https://lirias.kuleuven.be/1678547

Wallgren, L., Raza, S., & Voigt, T. (2013). Routing attacks and countermeasures in the rpl-based internet of things. *International Journal of Distributed Sensor Networks*, *9*(8), 794326. doi:10.1155/2013/794326

Wang, C., Viswanathan, K., Choudur, L., Talwar, V., Satterfield, W., & Schwan, K. (2011). Statistical techniques for online anomaly detection in data centers. *Proc. 12th IFIP/IEEE Int. Symp. Integr. Netw. Manage. (IM) Workshops,* (pp. 385-392). IEEE. 10.1109/INM.2011.5990537

Wang, M., Wang, X., Shi, J., Tan, Q., Gao, Y., Chen, M., & Jiang, X. (2018). Who are in the darknet? Measurement and analysis of darknet person attributes. *2018 IEEE Third International Conference on Data Science in Cyberspace (DSC)*, (pp. 948–955). IEEE. 10.1109/DSC.2018.00151

Wang, C., Talwar, V., Schwan, K., & Ranganathan, P. (2010). Online detection of utility cloud anomalies using metric distributions. *Proc. IEEE Netw. Oper. Manage. Symp. (NOMS)*, (pp. 96-103). IEEE.

Watson, K. D. (2012). The tor network: A global inquiry into the legal status of anonymity networks. *Wash. U. Global Stud. L. Rev.*, *11*, 715.

Webroot. (2018). *Multi-Vector Attacks Demand Multi-Vector Protection.* MSSP Alert.

WEF. (2022). The Global Risks Report 2022. 17th Edition. In *World Economic Forum.*

Wei, L., Gong, J., Xu, J., Eeza Zainal Abidin, N., & Destiny Apuke, O. (2023). Do social media literacy skills help in combating fake news spread? Modelling the moderating role of social media literacy skills in the relationship between rational choice factors and fake news sharing behaviour. *Telematics and Informatics*, *76*, 101910. doi:10.1016/j.tele.2022.101910

Weimann, G. (2016a). Going dark: Terrorism on the dark web. *Studies in Conflict and Terrorism*, *39*(3), 195–206. doi:10.1080/1057610X.2015.1119546

Weimann, G. (2016c). Terrorist migration to the dark web. *Perspectives on Terrorism*, *10*(3), 40–44.

Westerlund, M. (2019). The emergence of deepfake technology: A review. *Technology Innovation Management Review*, *9*(11), 39–52. doi:10.22215/timreview/1282

Wittes, B., Poplin, C., Jurecic, Q., & Spera, C. (2016). *Sextortion: Cybersecurity, teenagers, and remote sexual assault.* Center for Technology at Brookings.

Woehl, R. (2022). *Cyber Security Threats to the Food Industry: Consider the Cloud.* Global Food Safety Resource. https://globalfoodsafetyresource.com/cyber-security-threats-food-industry-consider-cloud/)

Wolak, M., Lysionok, A., Kosturek, B., Wiśniewski, J., Wawryszuk, B., Kawa, A., Davidson, R., Maćkowiak, M., Starzyk, M., & Kulikowska-Wielgus, A. (2019). *Technological revolution. Directions in the development of the transport-forwarding-logistics (TFL) sector.*

Workplace Bullying Persists despite Remote Work. (2022, October 5). Noggin. https://www.noggin.io/blog/workplace-bullying-persists-despite-remote-work

Xiao, L., Lu, Q., & Guo, F. (2020). Mobile Personalized Recommendation Model based on Privacy Concerns and Context Analysis for the Sustainable Development of M-commerce. *Sustainability (Basel)*, *12*(7), 3036. doi:10.3390u12073036

Xie, W., & Kang, C. (2015). See you, see me: Teenagers' self-disclosure and regret of posting on social network site. *Computers in Human Behavior*, *52*(1), 398–407. doi:10.1016/j.chb.2015.05.059

Xiong, H., Dalhaus, T., Wang, P., & Huang, J. (2020). Blockchain Technology for Agriculture: Applications and Rationale. *Front. Blockchain*, *3*, 7. doi:10.3389/fbloc.2020.00007

Yadav, A., & Kumar, V. (2021). A Study on Legislative Responses of Data Protection in India. *Ignited Minds Journals, 18*(7), 272 – 278. doi: (https://ignited.in/I/a/306067) doi:10.29070/JASRAE

Yang, Y., Yang, L., Yang, M., Yu, H., Zhu, G., Chen, Z., & Chen, L. (2019). Dark web forum correlation analysis research. *2019 IEEE 8th Joint International Information Technology and Artificial Intelligence Conference (ITAIC)*, (pp. 1216–1220). IEEE.

Yang, Y., Yu, H., Yang, L., Yang, M., Chen, L., Zhu, G., & Wen, L. (2019). Hadoop-based dark web threat intelligence analysis framework. *2019 IEEE 3rd Advanced Information Management, Communicates, Electronic and Automation Control Conference (IMCEC)*, (pp. 1088–1091). IEEE.

Yang, W., Hui, C., Chen, Z., Xue, J.-H., & Liao, Q. (2019). FV-GAN: Finger vein representation using generative adversarial networks. *IEEE Transactions on Information Forensics and Security, 14*(9), 2512–2524. doi:10.1109/TIFS.2019.2902819

Yesmin, T., Agasti, S., Pandit, J. K., & Mondal, B. (2023). Cyber Security and Its Prediction with Cloud Data Computing and IoT. In J. Choudrie, P. Mahalle, T. Perumal, & A. Joshi (Eds.), *ICT with Intelligent Applications. Smart Innovation, Systems and Technologies* (Vol. 311). Springer. doi:10.1007/978-981-19-3571-8_6

Yi, Y., Zhu, N., He, J., Jurcut, A., Ma, X., & Luo, Y. (2023). A privacy-dependent condition-based privacy-preserving information sharing scheme in online social networks. *Computer Communications, 200*, 149–160. doi:10.1016/j.comcom.2023.01.010

York, J. (n.d.). *How workplace bullying went remote*. BBC. https://www.bbc.com/worklife/article/20220819-how-workplace-bullying-went-remote

Zahidi, S. (2018). *The Global Risks Report 2022*. We Forum. https://www3.weforum.org/docs/ WEFTheGlobalRisksReport2022.pdf

Zanella, A. R. A., da Silva, E., & Albini, L. C. P. (2020). Security challenges to smart agriculture: Current state, key issues, and future directions. *Array (New York, N.Y.), 8*, 100048. doi:10.1016/j.array.2020.100048

Zanella, A., Bui, N., Castellani, A., Vangelista, L., & Zorzi, M. (2014). Internet of things for smart cities. *IEEE Internet of Things Journal, 1*(1), 22–32. doi:10.1109/JIOT.2014.2306328

Zhang, H., & Zou, F. (2020). A survey of the dark web and dark market research. *2020 IEEE 6th International Conference on Computer and Communications (ICCC)*, (pp. 1694–1705). IEEE.

Zhang, K., Liang, X., Lu, R., & Shen, X. (2014). Sybil attacks and their defenses in the internet of things. *IEEE Internet of Things Journal, 1*(5), 372–383. doi:10.1109/JIOT.2014.2344013

Zhang, S., Leidner, D., Cao, X., & Liu, N. (2022). Workplace cyberbullying: A criminological and routine activity perspective. *Journal of Information Technology, 37*(1), 51–79. doi:10.1177/02683962211027888

Zhen, L., Nan, Y., & Pham, B. (2021). College students coping with COVID-19: Stress-buffering effects of self-disclosure on social media and parental support. *Communication Research Reports, 38*(1), 23–31. doi:10.1080/08824096.2020.1870445

Zhou, S., & Liu, Y. (2023). Effects of Perceived Privacy Risk and Disclosure Benefits on the Online Privacy Protection Behaviors among Chinese Teens. *Sustainability (Basel), 15*(2), 1657. doi:10.3390u15021657

Zulfahmi, M., Elsandi, A., Apriliansyah, A., Anggreainy, M., Iskandar, K., & Karim, S. (2023). Privacy protection strategies on social media. *Procedia Computer Science, 216*, 471–478. doi:10.1016/j.procs.2022.12.159

About the Contributors

Mohd Shahid Husain is a research professional and faculty member with more than 14 years of teaching & research experience. He is currently working as Assistant Professor in College of Applied Sciences, Ministry of Higher Education, Oman. He has done his M.Tech. in Information Technology (spl: Intelligent System) from the Indian Institute of Information Technology, Allahabad (), India. He has done his PhD in Computer Science & Engineering from Integral University, Lucknow (), India. His area of interest are Artificial Intelligence, Information Retrieval, Natural Language Processing, Data Mining, Web mining, Sentiment Analysis and Computer Networks & Security. He has published 4 books, 12 book chapters & more than 30 research papers. He is contributing his knowledge and experience as member of Editorial Board/Advisory committee and TPC in various international Journals/Conferences of repute. He is active member of different professional bodies including ACM, IEEE young professionals, IEEE-TCII, ISTE, CSTA, IACSIT. Dr. Mohd qualified UGC-NET (National Eligibility Test) in June 2014 and GATE (Graduate Aptitude Test in Engineering) in 2008.

Mohammad Faisal is having more than 15 years of experience teaching Under Graduate and Post Graduate courses of Computer Application. Currently working as Head, department of Computer Application and Chief Warden, Integral University Hostel. his area of expertise is in Requirement Engineering, Distributed System, Operating System. He is editor of International Journal of Electronics and Computer Science Engineering (IJECSE). International Journal of Advances in Engineering Science and Technology (IJAEST). IJAEEE, IJEECS, IJTEL, IJITCS, IJAET, IJACSIT, IJCCIE, IJMCSA, IJRIET.

Halima Sadia is working as an Assistant Professor in the Department of Computer Science & Engineering at Integral University, Lucknow. She has 14 years of teaching and research experience. She is pursuing her Ph.D. in Computer Science & Engineering from Abdul Kalam Technical University, Lucknow, India. Her research interests include Software Engineering, Cyber Security, Artificial Intelligence, Machine Learning, Blockchain, and DBMS. She has published research articles in Scopus indexed Journals, National and International Conferences. She has authored a book Titled "Requirement Risk Management: A Practioner's Approach" published by Lambert Academic Publication, Germany, ISBN: 978-3-659-15494-2. She is contributing her knowledge and experience as a member of the Editorial Board/Advisory committee and TPC in International Journals/Conferences of repute. She is an active member of different professional bodies including ISTE, IAENG, UACEE, CSTA, ISOC-USA, EASST, HPC-Houston.

Tasneem Ahmed (Member, IEEE) received his PhD degree in 2016 in Image Processing from the Indian Institute of Technology Roorkee, India. Currently, he is working as an Associate Professor in the Department of Computer Application, at Integral University Lucknow, India. His research interests include digital image processing and computer vision, optical and microwave satellite image processing, image classification, data fusion, time series analysis, and SAR data analysis for land cover classification. He has published 02 edited books, 15 Journal articles, and 27 Conference papers at various National and International Conferences/Seminars. Dr. Tasneem is an active member of various professional societies like IEEE, IEEE Young Professionals, IEEE Computer Society, IAENG UACEE, and IFERP.

* * *

Syed Adnan Afaq is a research scholar, Department of Computer Application, Integral University Lucknow India.

Mohd Akbar, having 12 years of teaching & Research experience in the field of Computer Science & Engineering, owns 1 patent, authored many book chapters and published several research publications in international journals of high repute. He is an Asst. Professor at Integral University, Lucknow(India). Thrust Area: Ad-hock Networks, A.I., Mobile Computing, Cryptography & Network Security, Data Structure and C Programming. Contact: +91-9335558865

Anis Ali is working at PRINCE SATTAM BIN ABDULAZIZ UNIVERSITY, AL KHARJ, SAUDI ARABIA as an Assistant Professor in the management department, college of Business Administration. He has an enriched and relevant academic experience of more than 15 years in the higher education sector. He has published numerous papers in national and international Journals of high repute indexed in Scopus and WoS databases.

Mohammad Chaudhary is currently working as a professor in Dept of CSE, integral University Lucknow. He published more than 20 research article in SCI and Scopus Listed journal.

Mohammad Daradkeh is an Associate Professor of Business Analytics and Data Science at the College of Engineering & IT, University of Dubai. Prior to joining the University of Dubai, Dr. Daradkeh worked at Yarmouk University in Jordan and Lincoln University in New Zealand. His research interests are mainly in the areas of Business Intelligence, Data Analytics, and Innovation Management. He has published numerous research papers with reputed publishers such as Elsevier, Springer, Emerald MDPI and IGI. He has presented research papers at various international conferences. He is also a member of the editorial board of several reputed journals.

Yasir Arafat Elahi is currently working in Integral University, Lucknow as Assistant Professor. He has an enriched and relevant national as well as international academic experience of more than 10 years in higher education sector. He has published numerous papers in various journals of high repute. He has also successfully assisted UG and PG scholars in their projects as well as supervised PhD scholars as research guide.

Nafees Akhter Farooqui has a Ph.D. (Computer Science), from DIT University, Dehradun, Uttarakhand, India. He received his master's degree in computer application from Integral University, Lucknow, India in 2010, and a graduation degree in Statistics from Aligarh Muslim University, Aligarh, Uttar Pradesh, India in 2005. He has 13 years of teaching experience and presently working as Assistant Professor in the School of Computer Applications, BBD University, Lucknow, UP, India. His research interests include Artificial Intelligence, Machine Learning, Deep Learning, Computer Vision, Pattern Recognition, Natural Language Processing and Data Mining. He has published approx. 25 papers in International Journals and Conference proceedings including Web of Science and Scopus indexed Journals. He also published various book chapters in Scopus indexed Journals. He has published two books for National Publishers etc. He has been a member of International Association of Engineers (IAENG) since 2017, ACM since 2011. He guided various projects of UG and PG level Students. He received awards from various professional bodies.

Bhavesh Gohil is an Assistant Professor with the Department of Computer Science and Engineering, Sardar Vallabhbhai National Institute of Technology(SVNIT), Surat. He received a Ph.D. degree from the same institute and his research interests include Security and performance issues in Distributed/Cloud/Fog/Edge/Mobile system/computing.

Mohd Haleem completed a BSc (Hons.) in Statistics from AMU, MCA from HBTI, Kanpur, M.Tech. (CSE) from Integral University, Lucknow, Uttar Pradesh, and a PhD (CS) from Integra University, Lucknow, Uttar Pradesh, India. Having more than 12 years of teaching experience. Currently working as an Associate Professor in the department of computer science at Era University, Lucknow, India. Published more than 10 research papers in reputed international journals and conferences. Member of various professional societies. The research area is requirement engineering, requirement uncertainty data science.

Mohammad Kamrul Hasan is currently working as a Senior Lecturer, in the Network and Communication Technology research cluster, Center for Cyber Security, Universiti Kebangsaan Malaysia (UKM). He completed Doctor of Philosophy (Ph.D.) degree in Electrical and Communication Engineering from the faculty of Engineering, International Islamic University, Malaysia in 2016. Recently he was selected top 2% scientist worldwide by Stanford University USA, and Elsevier BV. He is specialized research elements pertaining to cutting-edge information-centric networks; Computer networks, Data communication and security, Mobile Network and Privacy Protection, Cyber-physical systems, Industrial IoT, Transparent AI, and Electric Vehicles Networks. He has published more than 170 indexed papers in ranked journals and conference proceedings. Dr. Kamrul is a Senior Member of the Institute of Electrical and Electronics Engineers, Member of Institution of Engineering and Technology, and the member of Internet Society. Dr. Kamrul is a certified professional technologist (P.Tech /Ts.), Malaysia. He also served the IEEE student branch as chair from 2014 to 2016. He has actively participated in many events/workshops/trainings for the IEEE and IEEE humanity programs in Malaysia. He works as the editorial member in many prestigious high-impact journals Such as IEEE, IET, Elsevier, Frontier and MDPI, and general chair, co-chair, and speaker for conferences and workshops for the shake of society and academy knowledge building and sharing and learning. He has been contributing and working as a volunteer for underprivileged children for the welfare of society.

Mohammad Husain is holding Ph.D. Degree in Computer Science & Engineering, 2008. He did his Master of Technology in Computer Science, and Bachelor of Engineering in Computer Science and Engineering,1990. He has about 33 Years of Professional experience in the field of IT & Academics. Currently, he is working with the Islamic University of Madinah, Kingdom of Saudi Arabia in the Faculty of Computer and Information Systems. He also has industrial exposure and experience in Software Design and Development. He has published about 159 papers in different National/International Journals/ proceedings. Dr. Husain has guided 14 Ph.D. and 11 M.Tech. Students. He has authored a book on the Principles of Programming Languages and contributed number of book chapters. He has given many lectures on the Gyan Vani Channel of IGNOU on All India Radio, Lucknow, India. He is also an active member of various International Journals, Committees, and Societies.

Firoz Husain has PhD in Finance and UGC-NET-JRF qualified. Currently he is working in Integral University, Lucknow as Assistant Professor. He has an enriched and relevant academic experience of more than 10 years in higher education sector. He has published numerous papers in national and international Journals of high repute such as Scopus. He has assisted UG and PG scholars in their projects as well as supervised PhD scholars with enriched research guidance.

Mohammad Shahid Husain is a Research professional and Faculty member with more than 14 years of teaching & research experience. Husain's focus has been on Sentiment Analysis, Information Retrieval, Natural Language Processing, Soft Computing, Computer Networks & Security, Software Engineering, and Data Mining.

Nashra Javed is currently pursuing PhD in Machine Learning from Integral University, Lucknow, India. She is graduated in Masters of Computer Application in the year 2013 and has been working since July 2014 as an Assistant Professor in the Department of Computer Application, Integral University, Lucknow. Her research interest span in Cyberbullying, Big Data Analytics, Data Science, Machine Learning, IoT and Blockchain.

Ahmad Khan (Member, IEEE) received the B.Sc. (Hons.) and master's degrees in computer applications from Aligarh Muslim University, India, in 2009 and 2012, respectively, and the Ph.D. degree from the School of Computer Science and Engineering, University of Electronic Science and Technology of China, Chengdu, China. He is currently an Assistant Professor with Integral University, India. His research interests include information security, machine learning, and reversible data hiding in the encrypted domain.

Wasim Khan received the Ph.D. Degree in CSE from Integral University, Lucknow. He received B.Tech.(IT) and M.Tech(CSE) degree from A. P. J. Abdul Kalam University, Lucknow, Uttar Pradesh, India. He is currently working with KL University as an Assistant Professor. He has over 15 years of teaching experience. His current research interests include machine learning, deep learning, social network analysis, anomaly detection, and network intrusion detection.

Neyha Malik has PhD in Human Resource Management and UGC-NET qualified. Currently she is working in Integral University, Lucknow as Assistant Professor. She has an enriched and relevant academic experience of more than 10 years in higher education sector. She has published numerous papers in national and international Journals of high repute. She has assisted UG and PG scholars in their projects as well as supervised PhD scholars with her enriched research guidance.

Sami Ouali is an assistant professor in the University of Technology and Applied Sciences Oman - Ibri Campus in Oman. He obtained his PhD in Computer Science from ENSI, Manouba University, Tunisia. He is a member of the RIADI labs, Manouba, Tunisia. His research interests is related to the areas of software engineering, software product line, artificial intelligence, and cloud computing. He was an international trainer with IBM for Cognos BI.

Sankita J. Patel received her Ph.D. from Sardar Vallabhbhai National Institute of Technology (SVNIT), Surat. She is presently an Assistant Professor with the Department of Computer Science and Engineering at SVNIT, Surat. Her research interests include applied research in Information Security and Privacy in various domains like Internet of Things, Cyber-Physical Systems, Online Social Networks, Data Analytics, Cloud Computing, Big Data, etc. She has co-authored several papers in refereed journals and conference proceedings.

Sarang Rajvansh is an Assistant Professor in the field of Digital Forensics.

Mohammad Samiuddin has 20+ years of teaching experience. Currently working in University of Technology and applied sciences, Oman.

Ramya Shah is working as a Assistant Professor in the Cyber Security and Digital Forensics Division of National Forensic Sciences University. He has also worked as an Scientific Intern at Forensic Science Laboratory for more than a year and helped solving many cases related to State and National Crimes. Besides teaching, he has also conducted many training programs for law enforcement agencies and he has also been a part of various consultancy projects related to digital forensics and Security pen-testing.

Kumarbhai Sondarva is a Mtech student at the Department of Computer Science and Engineering, Sardar Vallabhbhai National Institute of Technology(SVNIT), Surat.

Saurabh Srivastava received a Master of Computer Application (MCA) from Dr. A.P.J. Abdul Kalam Technical University Lucknow in 2015, and now pursuing a PhD from Integral University Lucknow. He has 7 years of experience in research including Computer Vision & Image Processing, Satellite Image Interpretation and Analysis, Land Cover Mapping, Time Series Analysis, Requirement Engineering, Multi-Agent Systems, etc.

Mohammad Suaib is currently working as Associate Professor in the Department of Computer Science and Engineering. Integral University Lucknow.

Kainat Akhtar Usmani is working as Assistant Professor in Department of Commerce and Business Management at Integral University, Lucknow, India. Her area of specialization is Human Resource. She has completed her Ph. D. in Management. She has One book and many papers to her credit. She has attended several Conferences, Seminar & FDPs at reputed institutions. She has total of over 13 year of experience in corporate, research and academic sector. She has been guiding students of BBA & MBA for project reports and dissertations from past three years.

Saman Uzma is CEO & Founder of Cubeight Solutions Sydney Australia.

Harish Verma is working as Scientist-SG(Computer Ap[plication) at ICAR-CISH, Lucknow. Areas of interest are: Digital Image Processing(DIP), AI & Machine Learning, Satellite image classification & change detection, Android app development.

Gausiya Yasmeen is a research Scholar, Department of Computer Application.

Index

A

Agriculture 62-63, 69-71, 73-74, 82, 85-86, 98-100, 102, 105, 107, 109-122, 204, 239
Antecedent-Privacy Concern-Outcome (APCO) model 38-39
anti-malware 2, 109, 119
attacks 1, 3, 11-15, 17, 19, 24-27, 30-31, 34-36, 40, 64-70, 72-75, 79-85, 87, 89-92, 94, 96-97, 99, 101-103, 105-109, 111-112, 114, 116-120, 124, 127-129, 137-138, 202, 204, 207, 209, 211, 213-215, 218, 223-226, 238, 240

B

best practices 1, 3, 16-17, 40, 106, 116, 125, 236-237

C

CERT-In 220, 234, 237-238
cloud computing 1-21, 116
cloud environment 1, 7, 14, 20, 240
Cyber Laws 88, 220-221, 227, 232, 239
cyber threats 1-3, 9, 11-12, 18-19, 27, 62-65, 67-68, 74, 76, 79, 81, 85-87, 89, 91-96, 98, 101, 104, 106-107, 109-111, 117, 124-125, 210, 214, 220-222, 226-227, 234, 239
Cyberattacks 29-31, 40, 73, 75, 87-88, 90-91, 94-97, 102, 106-107, 114, 203, 211, 213, 220-222, 226, 232
Cyberbullying 166-177, 220, 224
Cybercrime 23, 29, 40, 64, 66, 86, 91, 112, 138, 153, 202, 204, 217, 221-224, 228-229, 232-238, 240
Cybersecurity 18-19, 29, 31-32, 39-43, 58, 67, 75-81, 83-85, 87-88, 90, 92-97, 99, 101, 104, 106-108, 110, 116, 119, 121-122, 125, 202, 219-220, 222, 226-228, 232, 236-238, 240
Cyberspace 87-88, 96, 206, 219-220, 222, 227-228, 238-239

D

DarkWeb 202-205, 207-208, 212, 218
data breaches 1-2, 12-14, 16, 19, 40, 68, 76, 78, 81, 90-92, 96, 106, 116, 125, 225, 227
Deepfake Video 178-179, 190, 199-201
denial of service (DoS) 13-14, 17, 27, 71, 109, 226
Digital Forensic Investigation 138
Digital Forensics 84, 138-139, 146, 159, 163, 165, 214
Digitalization 35, 59, 62-63, 90-91, 95-96, 110
Disclosure Behavior 38

F

Fake News 61, 178, 180, 182-183, 200-201
File Carving 138, 158, 165
File System 138, 140-141, 148, 155, 158-159, 163-165
File System Forensics 138
Food 62-63, 68-70, 73-75, 82-83, 85-86, 89-91, 100-102, 106-107, 109-121
food industry 62-63, 68-69, 73, 83, 85, 91, 101, 107, 109-110
FreeNet 202-204, 213-214

H

hackers 22, 24, 28, 33, 35, 65-66, 70, 73-75, 77-80, 87, 89, 92, 94, 101-102, 109, 114-116, 118, 120, 125, 206-207, 209, 214, 221, 223, 226, 228
Healthcare 29, 62-63, 73, 75-76, 81-82, 85-86, 90-92, 94-98, 105, 107-108, 120, 127, 224, 239-240

I

I2P 202-204, 213-214
IPC 220, 228, 233-235

L

Law Enforcement 75, 203, 207-208, 210-214, 219, 231, 233, 236-239
legitimate websites 22

M

Machine Learning Model 178, 211
Magic Bytes 158-159, 162, 165
malware 1-2, 12-15, 17-19, 22, 24, 31, 33, 65-66, 69, 73-74, 77, 84, 88, 97, 102, 112, 116-119, 124, 164, 208, 211, 217, 223, 238
Master File Table 138, 140-141
MeitY 220, 231, 234, 237-238
Mental Health 166, 170, 174
Morphing 178, 182

N

National Cyber Crime Reporting Portal 220, 237
Non-Volatile Data 138-140, 147-148, 165
NTFS 140-141, 143, 158-159, 163-165

O

Onion Router 202-203
OWASP Top 10 Threats 22

P

Pandemic 59, 73, 96, 108, 115, 166-167, 170, 173, 176, 221
Phishing 12-13, 15, 30-31, 65, 73, 77, 79, 81-82, 90-91, 97, 112, 117-118, 121, 211, 220, 223-224, 238
Privacy cost 38-39, 46-47, 51-52, 54
Privacy Policies 38-41, 44-47, 50-51, 53-55
Public Safety 40, 123, 125, 219
Public Transport Facility 123

R

ransomware 1, 15, 19, 29, 69-70, 73-75, 79, 87, 90-92, 96-97, 109, 111, 114-119, 125, 211, 220, 222-226
Recovery 9, 11, 16, 30, 41, 80, 91, 103-104, 138, 158-160, 162-163, 165
Remote Work 166-172, 174, 176-177
risks 3, 14, 17, 19, 22, 26, 39, 46, 61, 63, 68, 76, 79, 81-82, 86, 88-91, 93, 95, 97, 102-106, 108, 119, 122, 124-125, 204, 213, 217, 221

S

Security 1-5, 7, 9-37, 40-41, 44, 54, 58, 61-70, 72-73, 75-96, 99-104, 106-108, 110, 112, 114-125, 127-130, 134, 137, 140, 150, 152, 200-203, 206-210, 213-216, 218-222, 226-228, 232-240
sensitive data 1-2, 9, 13-17, 19, 22, 30, 32, 35, 41, 66, 73, 77, 91, 93, 95, 104, 124-125
Smart Parking Space 123
Social Exclusion 166, 172
Social Media 31, 38-45, 47-61, 77, 88, 117, 126, 139, 147, 166, 168-170, 178-182, 194, 196, 199, 201, 203, 205-206, 211-212, 216-217, 224, 237
Social Network 38-39, 44, 46, 56-58, 61, 209, 216
Street Lighting System 123

T

the Information Technology Act 87, 223, 228, 232
threats 1-3, 9, 11-20, 22, 24-27, 31, 35, 39-40, 43, 57, 59, 62-65, 67-68, 72, 74, 76, 79-82, 85-99, 101, 104, 106-107, 110-112, 115-117, 119-121, 124-125, 166, 170, 202, 204, 208, 210, 213-214, 220-222, 226-227, 234, 239
Tor 75, 202-214, 216, 219

U

Utilities 31

V

Video Frame Comparison 178
Virtual Harassment 166-167, 169
Volatile Data 139, 141, 144-145, 147, 165
vulnerability 12, 18-19, 22, 27-28, 33-34, 36-37, 57, 65-67, 70, 72-73, 80, 108, 116, 129, 200

W

Web Application Vulnerabilities 22, 35-36
web servers 22, 26
Work-From-Home 167, 172
Workplace Cyberbullying 166-174, 176-177
WWW 25, 35-36, 83-85, 107, 113, 121-122, 150, 159, 164-165, 176-177, 202-203, 234, 237, 240

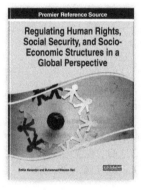

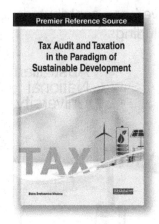

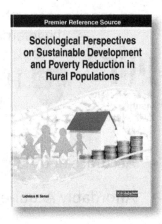

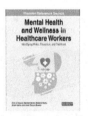

Printed in the United States
by Baker & Taylor Publisher Services